SITCOMS

THE 101 GREATEST TV COMEDIES OF ALL TIME

KEN BLOOM & FRANK VLASTNIK

FOREWORD BY JOHN LITHGOW

BLACK DOG
& LEVENTHAL
PUBLISHERS
NEW YORK

Copyright © 2007 by Ken Bloom and Frank Vlastnik

Permission to reproduce photographs is outlined on page 336, which constitutes an extension of this copyright page.
All rights reserved. No part of this book, either text or illustration, may be used or reproduced in any form without prior written
permission from the publisher.

ISBN-13: 978-1-57912-752-7

Library of Congress Cataloging-in-Publication Data

Bloom, Ken, 1949-
Sitcoms: the 101 greatest TV comedies of all time / Ken Bloom and Frank Vlastnik; foreword by John Lithgow.
p. cm.
Includes index.
ISBN 978-1-57912-752-7
1. Television comedies—United States. I. Vlastnik, Frank. II. Title.
PN1992.8.C66B56 2007
791.45'617--dc22
2007023974

Book design: Scott Citron Design
Design associate: Lu Ann Graffeo Blonkowski, 64 Second Design

Manufactured in China

Published by
Black Dog & Leventhal Publishers, Inc.
151 West 19th Street, New York, New York 10011

Distributed by
Workman Publishing Company
225 Varick Street, New York, New York 10014

g f e d c b a

Acknowledgments

As in our previous book, *Broadway Musicals: The 101 Greatest Shows of All Time*, the photographs are integral to telling the story. We have endeavored to use rarely or never-before seen photos, eschewing the same tired illustrations that have been used for decades. The majority of the photos came from Photofest, where Howard and Ron Mandelbaum gave generously of their time and energy. Jan Grenci of the Library of Congress, Prints and Photographs Division, went beyond the call of duty, helping us to locate and identify rare photos from the Library's vast collection. Manoah Bowman, a good friend both professionally and personally, lent photos from his impressive archive. Thanks also to Alison Rigney at the magnificent Everett Collection, Matt Tunia for his generosity, and our friend and colleague, Peter Filichia.

Thanks also to Peter Barros and Tim Benell, Teddy Blankowski, Chris Boneau and Adrian Bryan-Brown of Boneau/Bryan Brown, Deb Brody, Michael Cassara, Marc Cherry, Richard Hester, Aaron Mark, Robert McGarrity, Mort Milder, Frank Pisco, Cory Plowman, Bill Rudman, Beverly Sanders, Dick Scanlan, Christopher Scott, Dana Trombley, Katherine Furman, True Sims, Marie Mundaca, Iris Bass, Liz Driesbach, and Tom Wilson.

Our editor, Laura Ross, used her experience, love of sitcoms, enthusiasm, and sense of humor to guide us through the world of three-camera setups, laugh tracks, and syndication. Publisher J.P. Leventhal encouraged this effort with his usual sage advice. Our designer, Scott Citron, created a marvelous template and he and LuAnn Graffeo of 64 Second Design made the pages clear, concise, and exciting.

Friends who shared their love and encyclopedic knowledge of sitcoms, giving suggestions and proofreading the final draft, include Mary and John Armon, Ken Kantor, Barry Kleinbort, Andy Kreiss, Peter Michael Marino, Rob Moore, Joey Murphy, Robert Sixsmith, and David Standish.

Top: A heartfelt thanks to all of our *Friends*, many of whom we've known since they had mullets and their old noses.

Left: And to anyone we may have forgotten to thank, please accept our apology for the oversight and don't go all Jan Brady on us.

CONTENTS

Foreword

How does it happen? How does a brainstorm become a cultural phenomenon? How does success strike a TV series with the randomness of Cupid's arrow?

The history of each classic show is a variation on the same old story. Someone has a bright idea. Someone else loves the idea. The idea becomes a pitch, the pitch becomes a script, the script becomes a pilot. A cast comes on board, a writing staff, a show-runner, a director, a crew. A network schedules it, announces it, premieres it.

A lot of people love the show and a lot of people hate it. But bit by bit, the lovers outnumber the haters. The sturdy little show grows into a blockbuster, then a phenomenon. Its stars become household names, their faces more famous than Senators'. For most of those actors, nothing they do in the years after their sitcom success will ever touch the glamour, notoriety, and fun of that time. I know whereof I speak. For six seasons I played High Commander Dick Solomon on NBC-TV's *3rd Rock from the Sun* (alphabetically, show number 96 in this book). Before *3rd Rock* I had been a steadily employed actor with more than my share of accolades—but this was different. The success of the show put me and my fellow aliens on magazine covers, sent us to Super Bowls and All-Star Games, and gave us our first rides on company jets. And—even more important—the show gave us the chance to make millions of people laugh.

All of this resulted from a moment, a few years before, when someone suddenly had a bright idea: "Aliens on a field trip!"

I recall one moment when it dawned on me just how far the reach of *3rd Rock* had extended. My wife and I were traveling in Ireland and in a tiny village, a couple of red-headed Irish kids stopped abruptly when one of them recognized me from the show.

"Sir," he asked, a little shyly. "Would you do the salute?"

The alien salute. In a late episode from that first season, I had impulsively improvised a farewell salute to my fellow aliens. Until that time, I had only executed this dopey gesture once. But in that Irish barnyard, I suddenly realized that I had become identified with "the alien salute" forever—all over the world.

John Lithgow as Dick Solomon on NBC's hit, *3rd Rock from the Sun*. We like to think our book is good, but it's obviously not The Good Book.

All of the shows that follow have at least one of those instantly recognizable little comedic tics. They form a common language that connects everyone who grew up with television. Leaf through the pages of this book and memories flood in. Moments, years, decades of our lives are in some sense defined by the antics of these TV clowns.

Classic sitcoms tend to burn hot for awhile, then be taken for granted, entering a period of stability, reliability. Like all living things, they eventually enter old age. The cute kids become rangy young adults, hackneyed new characters are introduced, episodes begin to steal from earlier episodes, jokes become tired and predictable. There is often a spike in interest when it's time for the final good-bye. Then a hit series enters its comfortable retirement, i.e., years of syndication.

Except for a very few mighty warhorses (*The Honeymooners*, *I Love Lucy*, and *M*A*S*H* among them), even syndication ends. Great shows are half-forgotten. Then along comes a book like this one to remind us of those sparkling moments when all the elements came together, a classic sitcom was born, and all of us laughed.

—John Lithgow

Introduction

Carroll O'Connor as Archie Bunker, perhaps the single most groundbreaking character in the history of television.

"Hi, Honey, I'm Home!!!!"

Welcome to our foray into sitcoms, a world of talking horses, precocious children, and houses with floor plans that would make Frank Lloyd Wright do a 360 in his grave. Everything can be found here: pathos, irony, farce, tragic hairdos—yes—but also bigotry, larceny, prisoners of war, all turned into hilarity by the best comic minds in television. In fact, one of the great benefits of a nice dose of situation comedy is that it makes you realize that anything can be funny. Divorce can be funny. Poverty can be funny. Family dysfunction, well that's downright hilarious. And physical injury? Stop, you're killing us!

Admittedly, there have been other reference books written on the fifty-plus-year history of sitcoms—but we wanted to take a different approach. This book isn't meant to be exhaustive (or exhausting). Rather, we've put together an opinionated, lighthearted—but seriously considered—celebration of 101 of television's most significant half-hour comedies, representative of each decade and every genre we could think of.

One thing we think distinguishes this book from some that have preceded it is the photographs. We dug deep and came up with many photos that go beyond the usual publicity still or scene shot to show sitcoms from unusual angles and—perhaps most exciting—many stunning color photos of shows that were broadcast in black and white.

As in our previous collaboration, *Broadway Musicals*, we feel we must define the word "greatest" in our subtitle. Some of the shows included in our 101 are irrefutable classics. Others are here not because they were as hilarious as *I Love Lucy* or as smart as *Frasier*, but because they were

Elizabeth Montgomery welcomes two new leading ladies to ABC's 1966 fall lineup. Marlo Thomas became America's sweetheart as *That Girl*, but Judy Carne, about to premiere in *Love on a Rooftop*, headed to beautiful downtown Burbank to become a star on NBC's *Laugh-In*.

groundbreaking for representing a segment of the American population previously invisible on the small screen. Others made our list simply because they were highly representative of a particular trend in television, or perfectly reflected the morality and social climate of their time.

These lists are always subjective and some of you may be shocked to find one of your favorites missing. Rest assured, we spent innumerable hours watching DVDs, refining our list, and arguing like Archie Bunker and Maude Findlay to come to our final decision.

In addition to the 101 shows, we've included special chapters covering such general topics as flops, sitcom pets, sitcoms based on movies, and our favorite unsung character actors. We've also included many biographical features throughout, paying tribute to the writers, directors, producers, and actors that have devoted their talents to entertaining and amusing us for half a century.

So, sit back, flip up the foot rest of your La-Z-Boy, and join us on our journey through the 101 greatest sitcoms. No doubt you'll find a nostalgic favorite from childhood and a recent show that has filled your TiVo. And you might even discover a previously unknown show from forty years ago that you'll want to track down and enjoy.

There will be no commercial interruptions in this Very Special Episode.

THE ADDAMS FAMILY

abc | **1964–1966** | **64 episodes**

Charles Addams's creepy cartoon family from *The New Yorker* comes alive in this domestic comedy with a macabre twist.

Let's get this straight, *The Addams Family* was neither spooky nor ooky. To be sure, they weren't the Cleavers (although Wednesday Addams played with cleavers, just for kicks), but they never caused trouble or did any harm; they were just… different. The best way to think of them is as citizens of some unknown foreign country. Though they spoke English perfectly (and a hint of French, in Morticia's case), their wardrobe was sort of nineteenth-century-meets-Goth (not unlike some Parisian couture in the '60s), and they enjoyed meals consisting of items we might find repulsive (like the French). So let's just think of them as the French—only friendlier. In fact, it was Morticia and Gomez's exaggerated bonhomie that put off visitors. Well, that and the hirsute, Cousin Itt—another example of fashion styling gone mad. A cross between Tattoo from *Fantasy Island* and one of Jean Shrimpton's wigs, Cousin Itt was the ultimate foreign tourist—easily excited and undecipherable.

"Normal" Americans, understandably, distrusted the Addamses. Their effusive personalities and generosity (Gomez tended to offer great sums to charity) made people uneasy. Their familiarity made them suspect, especially in a society that was all about conformity and red-blooded middle-class values. And, like their sitcom relatives the Munsters, the Addams family had no idea that anything they did was the slightest bit strange.

Above: The Family Addams in a Thanksgiving portrait. They like their turkey rare.

Opposite: Hollywood family trivia: Blossom Rock, who played Grandmama, was the older sister of movie musical soprano Jeannette MacDonald.

ethereal, the former Morticia Frump prided herself on her green thumb, cultivating beautiful roses and promptly cutting off the blossoms to arrange the stems. The Addams offspring were equally unique. Daughter Wednesday had an interest in decapitation, and her favorite toys were a Marie Antoinette doll with a functioning miniature guillotine. Her brother Pugsley was an

Gomez: Tish! That's *French*!

imp with a special fondness for things mechanical, perhaps having inherited his penchant for diabolical inventions from his Uncle Fester.

Played brilliantly by former child star Jackie Coogan, Fester had a thing for electricity—and with good reason: with his thick neck and bald pate, Fester looked like a human lightbulb, a resemblance that grew more pronounced when he put an actual bulb in his mouth—and lit it. He was fond of blowing things up in the basement, sending plumes of smoke upstairs. Grandmama, played by Blossom Rock (a perfect name for someone from Addams's world—or *The Flintstones*) was Gomez's devoted mother. Not really a witch, she was more of a clairvoyant hag-cum-fortune teller. Two of the show's most popular characters were played by the same actor, Ted Cassidy. As Lurch, the family butler, Cassidy was a ghoulish cross between Frankenstein and a zombie, but with tender feelings and a love for all things musical, especially playing his beloved harpsichord. Cassidy also played Thing, who might be described as Lurch's right-hand man or, more accurately, right hand. The house itself was a kind of character as well, from its growling polar bear rug to the hangman's

The series was based on the twisted cartoons Charles Addams created for *The New Yorker* for fifty years, beginning in the late '30s. Born in Westfield, New Jersey, Addams exhibited a fascination with old Victorian houses and cemeteries, and that slightly perverse obsession found its way into his cartoons, which featuring a macabre household (never identified as the "Addams family" per se—that came with the television series) and their interactions with visitors.

Creating a unique, self-contained world in these single-panel drawings, Addams was approached by producer David Levy to help adapt his cartoons into a television sitcom. The first job was to give the characters names. They initially called Gomez "Repelli" and son Pugsley "Pubert." Addams helped solidify the attributes of each character. Head of the household Gomez, played by the bug-eyed John Astin, was head-over-heels in love with his wife Morticia—sometimes literally so, as he habitually stood on his head while smoking a cigar. Apparently having made sound investments, Gomez didn't work (he passed the bar but didn't practice law). Morticia, played by the delectable Carolyn Jones in the best role of her career, was a vamp(ire) in a skintight black dress. Calm, cool, and almost

noose used to summon Lurch, to the model trains that Gomez loved crashing into one another.

Once the characters were established, writer Nat Perrin started laying the groundwork for each episode. It was decided early on

JOHN ASTIN

Those goo-goo-googly eyes were accentuated for the part of Gomez in *The Addams Family* but John Astin's fame rests solidly on his unforgettable work on that show. The character followed him into the animated TV series of the same name and *The New Addams Family*, in which he played Grandpa Addams, but Astin racked up several notable film credits as well, including *Bunny O'Hare*; *Freaky Friday*; and *European Vacation*. On television, in addition to doing voiceover work, he played recurring characters on *Night Court*, *The Adventures of Brisco County Jr.*, and *Operation Petticoat*, and made a slew of one-shot appearances. He had many TV directing credits as well. Should we mention his work on the *Killer Tomato* films? Perhaps not.

to give the series an "anything goes" feeling. Gomez might come downstairs walking a tiger; Morticia asked, "Mind if I smoke?" and then sat with arms folded as smoke emanated from her person. Thing, the disembodied hand, collected the mail. Of course, a lot of the humor came from the family's reactions to "normal" occurrences in the outside world. When Pugsley was assigned "Hansel and Gretel" and other fairy tales, Morticia promptly took him out of school. Gomez believed that taxes should be raised. Lurch's mother insisted the Addamses treat Lurch like a slave. Wednesday was reprimanded for playing with Uncle Fester's dynamite—when she should have been using her own. Needless to say, the outside world was equally dumbfounded by the Addams family.

After the original series went off the air, *The Addams Family* lived on in films, animation, and the occasional special. The less said about these the better, with the exception of the first film, which featured a wonderfully cast Angelica Huston and Raul Julia as Morticia and Gomez. To purists, there will never be as wittily subversive a series as the original *Addams Family*.

Creepy Carolyn Jones, kooky John Astin, and altogether ooky Jackie Coogan, on the set between takes.

Top: John Astin with the crew of the pink battleship (including a young Jamie Lee Curtis, whose father Tony starred in the original movie) in the shortlived sitcom version of *Operation Petticoat*.

CAST

Carolyn Jones	Morticia Frump Addams
John Astin	Gomez Addams
Jackie Coogan	Uncle Fester Frump
Ted Cassidy	Lurch/Thing
Blossom Rock	Grandmama Addams
Ken Weatherwax	Pugsley Addams
Lisa Loring	Wednesday Friday Addams
Felix Silla	Cousin Itt
Tony Magro	Cousin Itt's voice
Margaret Hamilton	Hester Frump

THE ADVENTURES OF OZZIE & HARRIET

 | **1952–1966** | **435 episodes**

Ozzie and Harriet Nelson, your typical 1950s married couple, watch David and Ricky, their typical 1950s sons, grow up, get married, and leave the nest.

Once in a while truth, which can be a rare commodity in television, is not only stranger than fiction, it actually becomes fiction. On *The George Burns and Gracie Allen Show*, George and Gracie played George and Gracie. On *Seinfeld*, Jerry Seinfeld played Jerry Seinfeld. Larry David plays Larry David on *Curb Your Enthusiasm*. Another example of the surreal joining of truth and fiction was *The Adventures of Ozzie & Harriet*—ironically named, as the whole point of the show was that there were no "adventures" at all. The focus was the family. Ozzie and Harriet, played by a real-life married couple, had two children, Ricky and David, who were played by their two real children, Ricky and David. And when the boys grew up and got married, their real wives, Kris and June, played their sitcom counterparts as well. So blurred was the line between fact and fiction that the Nelson's TV home had the same layout as the family's Hollywood house and (as on the *Jack Benny* and *Burns and Allen* shows), the exterior shots were of their actual residence.

It was the longest running family comedy ever, if you count the radio years 1944–54 (only *The Simpsons* has surpassed its television run). Outside forces seldom intruded on the Nelson household, and there was no mention of such front-page midcentury issues as rebellious teens, race relations, or the cold war.

Outside characters seldom made appearances, either. Thorny Thornberry, a holdover

from the Nelsons' radio show, came around to give Ozzie misguided advice. Neighbors Joe and Clara Randolph appeared as needed—but the emphasis was squarely on Ozzie and Harriet's mishaps with lost keys and broken appliances, midnight raids on the refrigerator, and what to do when the television broke down.

The show didn't pretend to be about a typical American family, some amalgam of what sitcom writers, network bosses, and pollsters might imagine the viewing audience wanted to see. There weren't any interventions by the network bigwigs, since the show had been such a big hit on radio. It was Ozzie's show, so when he made the groundbreaking decision that he and Harriet would sleep in the same bed, that was that. Even real-life marrieds Lucy and Desi didn't enjoy that luxury.

When real-life Ricky (birth name: Eric) started a rock group in the garage and became a teen idol, he played his latest songs on the show just before the final credits. Ozzie's background included leading a big band, and Harriet had been a singer under her maiden name, Hilliard, so the Nelsons didn't go to pieces when Ricky embraced the scary new music called rock-and-roll. In fact, Ozzie encouraged Ricky and helped manage his career. The Nelsons played against the family stereotypes that had taken hold over the short history of the sitcom. Ozzie wasn't a dope who was ignorant of his teenage children's feelings. He wasn't the wise, moralizing dad, either; he was just a regular guy trying to do his best. Harriet was neither the all-knowing mother figure nor a schemer dressed in the latest fashions. David and Ricky were

well-adjusted adolescents with the typical anxieties of red-blooded American boys, not twenty-somethings attempting to act like teenagers. Watching the show, it almost seemed as if a scriptwriter had sat in a corner of the real Nelson household and taken notes.

The only mystery was what the hell Ozzie did for a living.

He seemed content to pad around the house putting out the little brushfires that crop up in family life. On radio Ozzie had played himself, the leader of a band and producer of the show. When bands went out of style and radio followed, it was only logical that Ozzie continue to play himself, the producer of the television version of *The Adventures of Ozzie and Harriet*. Since he was already on the set and in the show he couldn't really be shown going to work—so, in a surreal sense, he was playing himself playing himself.

Though Ozzie's family sometimes seemed a little bemused

OFF THE SET

BEGINNING IN 1944 as a radio show, *The Adventures of Ozzie and Harriet* didn't change much over its twenty-two-year history. At the beginning, Ricky and David were played by actors, but when Bing Crosby's sons played themselves on a radio show, Ricky and David decided to join the Nelson radio family. On the February 20, 1949, episode, "Invitation to Dinner," Ozzie and Harriet's actual sons played themselves. The radio series ran until 1954, two years after the television program began.

by his laid-back charms, they never condescended toward him or talked back. This was not one of those shows that derived its energy from friction, as did *The Honeymooners* or *Car 54*. Problems were resolved in the gentlest, most logical ways, with Ozzie chuckling over the silliness of it all. And while the Nelsons never reached the top of the Nielsen ratings, the family was an integral part of American life for much of the twentieth century and the show continues to be seen as one of the hallmarks of midcentury sitcom life, its gentle, truthful innocence still able to touch modern audiences.

Left: Ozzie and Harriet with Don DeFore, soon to be "Mistah B." on *Hazel*.

Below right: Teen heartthrob Ricky Nelson with perpetual 1950s guest star Joi Lansing.

Bottom: Two Bobs and a Babe, with Jess Oppenheimer and their most faithful employers, Lucille Ball and Desi Arnaz.

Bob Schiller & Bob Weiskopf

The "two Bobs" met in the writing room of *Make Room for Daddy* and decided to form a partnership that lasted into the 1990s. Their collaborations included *Our Miss Brooks* on radio and *The Bob Cummings Show*, among others.

One day Schiller and Weiskopf were summoned to the Desilu lot on the old RKO Studios property. They were working on Janis Paige's sitcom *It's Always Jan*, but were not particularly confident about its potential. Weiskopf's old college roommate, Jess Oppenheimer, saw him on the lot and suggested that the team join *I Love Lucy*, thus beginning a long association with Lucille Ball.

The *Lucy-Desi Comedy Hour* followed, and at the same time the two Bobs worked on other Desilu offerings, including *The Ann Sothern Show*. In 1960, they created *Guestward Ho!*, and worked as writers on the *December Bride* spin-off *Pete and Gladys*.

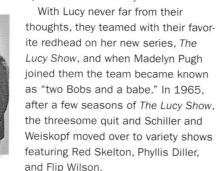

With Lucy never far from their thoughts, they teamed with their favorite redhead on her new series, *The Lucy Show*, and when Madelyn Pugh joined them the team became known as "two Bobs and a babe." In 1965, after a few seasons of *The Lucy Show*, the threesome quit and Schiller and Weiskopf moved over to variety shows featuring Red Skelton, Phyllis Diller, and Flip Wilson.

Enter Norman Lear, a new breed of sitcom producer. Weiskopf and Schiller may have seemed unlikely choices for the socio-political agenda of Lear's production company, but they thrived in the new atmosphere, joining the staff of *Maude*, then *All in the Family*. When their last sitcoms, *He's the Mayor* and *The Boys*, both failed, Schiller and Weiskopf recognized, after forty years at the top of their field, that the tide of television was turning once again, and decided to enjoy the benefits of retirement.

CAST

Ozzie Nelson	Ozzie Nelson
Harriet Hilliard	Harriet Nelson
Ricky Nelson	Ricky Nelson
David Nelson	David Nelson
Parley Baer	Darby
June Blair	June, Mrs. David Nelson
Frank Cady	Doc Williams
Lloyd Corrigan	Wally Dipple
Mary Jane Croft	Clara Randolph
Don DeFore	Thorny Thornberry
Lyle Talbot	Joe Randolph

ALICE

Newly widowed aspiring singer Alice Hyatt leaves New Jersey with her son, Tommy, heading for Hollywood but settling for the dimmer lights of Phoenix, where she slings hash at a greasy spoon.

There's a new girl in town: As the plucky Alice Hyatt, Linda Lavin became a heroine for pink-collar workers.

One of the few successful sitcoms based on a movie, *Alice* was a small-screen version of Ellen Burstyn's Oscar-winning movie *Alice Doesn't Live Here Anymore*, starring the talented Linda Lavin as the scrappy title character. She was supported by Vic Tayback (recreating his role from the movie) as cheapskate boss Mel Sharples, Philip McKeon (whose sister would soon be starring on NBC's *Facts of Life*) as her son Tommy, and the gangly Beth Howland as professional basket case Vera Gorman—plus a real corker, Polly Holliday, who played Alice's best friend and fellow waitress Florence Jean Castleberry. Gray-haired and soft spoken in real life, Holliday donned a red beehive and a pink polyester uniform and made one of the most remarkable transformations in sitcom history, into the gum-snapping, sassy Flo.

Flo was certainly one of the most popular aspects of the show (launching a bona fide catchphrase in "kiss my grits!"), and her departure after three and a half seasons, to try a spin-off that quickly sank, was nearly fatal to *Alice*. To fill the void, the producers called upon Diane Ladd, who had played the role in the original movie. Since Holliday had already staked a claim to the character on the small screen, producers created a new character named Belle for Ladd—but from the start, the magic was missing. Ladd never clicked with audiences or with the cast; Lavin wasn't happy with what she perceived were Ladd's attempts to steal the spotlight. Like other misguided replacements, including Julia Duffy on *Designing Women* and Jenilee Harrison on *Three's Company*, she was gone by the end of the season, replaced by the marvelous Celia Weston, who injected life back into the series as lady trucker Jolene Hunnicutt. Although no one could completely replace Holliday, Weston was extremely popular with the cast, and her fine acting and professionalism restored peace to the company. (Weston has had the most interesting career, post-*Alice*, playing supporting roles in some of the best independent films of the last twenty years.)

Although the writing was sometimes uneven, *Alice* has stood the test of time far better than its CBS Sunday cohort *One Day at a Time*. Maybe it was the fact that, although it did touch on serious issues, particularly the empowerment of working women, it didn't take itself as seriously as Bonnie Franklin's show did. In fact, plots were rarely more complicated than those of *I Love Lucy*, albeit with the addition of more modern technology: instead of a conveyor belt in a candy factory, a crazy ATM spouted thousands of dollars by mistake; instead of a wedding ring lost in cement, Flo lost a contact lens in a batch of green Jell-O.

Alice Hyatt became an idol to those stuck in the "pink-collar ghetto." It's not hard to see a direct correlation between the show and the hit 1980 movie *Nine to Five*, with Lavin, Howland, and Holliday precursors to the characters played by Lily Tomlin, Jane Fonda, and Dolly Parton. Alice was constantly trying to better herself, taking night classes in psychology, which she constantly spouted like Sigmund Freud in a hairnet. And let's face it. Linda Lavin really, really loves to sing. She recorded the show's theme song

Flo, Alice and Vera observe Vic Tayback preparing the daily blue-plate special: breaded Mel cutlet.

Linda Lavin

Best known to television viewers as Alice Hyatt, Linda Lavin has had a career as a superb character actress in nearly every medium, starting in the New York theater with the musicals *The Mad Show* and *It's a Bird...It's a Plane...It's Superman*. After a brilliant turn in the play *Last of the Red Hot Lovers*, Lavin moved to Los Angeles and landed a recurring role as Janice Wentworth, the only woman detective in the Twelfth Precinct on the first two seasons of *Barney Miller*.

Tapped for the title role on *Alice*, she became a role model for working women, gaining experience as a director during the show's nine seasons. She returned to her musical roots in the Emmy-winning special *Linda in Wonderland*. Appearing in numerous television movies, including *The $5.20 an Hour Dream*; *Another Woman's Child*; and *Lena: My 100 Children*, Lavin made a triumphant return to the New York stage in Neil Simon's autobiographical play *Broadway Bound*. Starring in two short-lived sitcoms, *Room for Two* (above, with a pre-*Everybody Loves Raymond* Patricia Heaton) and 1998's *Conrad Bloom*, she has continued to star on Broadway in such plays as *The Tale of the Allergist's Wife* and *Hollywood Arms*, also giving a memorable performance as a shrink on an episode of *The Sopranos*.

Above: Lavin with Philip McKeon, whose sister Nancy would soon become NBC's cycle riding chick Jo on *The Facts of Life*.

Below: Beth Howland and Linda Lavin flank the third blonde southern belle to fill the ranks of *Alice*, the versatile character actress, Celia Weston.

CAST

Linda Lavin	Alice Hyatt
Philip McKeon	Tommy Hyatt
Vic Tayback	Mel Sharples
Beth Howland	Vera Louise Gorman
Polly Holliday	Florence Jean "Flo" Castleberry
Diane Ladd	Isabelle "Belle" Dupree
Celia Weston	Jolene Hunnicutt
Marvin Kaplan	Henry Beesmeyer
Martha Raye	Carrie Sharples
Charles Levin	Elliot Novak
Victoria Carroll	Marie Massey
Dave Madden	Earl Hicks

OFF THE SET

THE SHOT OF the station wagon during the show's opening credits is film footage from the show's original source, *Alice Doesn't Live Here Anymore*.

IN THE SERIES pilot, the role of Tommy was played by Alfred Lutter III (recreating his role from the film), but he was replaced by Philip McKeon.

at least four times during its nine-season run and she worked her warbling into episodes whenever she had the chance.

Of course, the show was filled with the logic-challenging moments that befall most long-running shows: George Burns, Telly Savalas, Dinah Shore, and Donald O'Connor all found their way into Mel's, a place where ptomaine was the house special. Martha Raye, a presence too big for even a 54-inch diagonal, mugged her way through several guest appearances as Mel's mother, Carrie. Most unbelievably, the diner was destroyed numerous times—by a falling tree, a careening semi, a hot air balloon—yet it always rose like a phoenix (in Phoenix) from its greasy ashes.

The show ended with *Alice* getting her recording contract (back east, in Nashville…just think, she could've spared herself nine years of schlepping grub if her car had broken down 1,500 miles earlier), Vera getting pregnant, and Jolene opening a beauty parlor (the secret dream of most lady truckers). And, in an example of life imitating art, Linda Lavin became one of the show's main directors in its final seasons, realizing one of her dreams and elevating the status of women in a male-dominated field.

ALL IN THE FAMILY

  | **1971–1979** | **212 episodes**

Bigoted, cigar-smoking Archie Bunker rules the roost in Astoria, Queens, with an ever-patient dingbat wife, Edith; their feminist daughter, Gloria; and her ultraliberal husband, Mike. They all try to keep up with the changing times while sharing one terlet.

Imagine an unsuspecting television viewer tuning into CBS one January evening in 1971 and hearing the following disclaimer: "The program you are about to see is *All in the Family*. It seeks to throw a humorous spotlight on our frailties, prejudices, and concerns. By making them a source of laughter we hope to show, in a mature fashion, just how absurd they are." And with that, the sound of a toilet flush, the first ever heard in a situation comedy. It was a flush heard 'round the world, and the history of the medium would never be the same.

One of the major components of comedy is conflict, and in most of the shows that came before *All in the Family*, the conflict arose from two sources: situation—as in Lucy Ricardo and the candy factory; or character, as when the writers for *Dick Van Dyke*'s fictional *Alan Brady Show* lived in constant fear of their domineering boss. But in Norman Lear's new show, the conflict (as well as the comedy) came from a new source: a world of ideas, morals, and social conscience that had previously been touched upon in only the most gingerly fashion.

The journey of the show and its creator began in England, a surprising place for a show that is so American in its politics, both progressive and backward. Producer Norman Lear, along with his partner, Alan (Bud) Yorkin, bought the U.S. rights to the Britcom *Till Death Us Do Part*, which revolved around a bigoted blue-collar worker named Alf Garnett. Lear and Yorkin spent

Welcome to 704 Hauser Street, where guests are greeted by the cheery, gregarious grin of Edith Bunker and the skeptical eye of her husband Archie.

Carroll O'Connor

John Carroll O'Connor was born in the Bronx but grew up in the Forest Hills section of Queens, the borough where his most famous creation resided. Beginning his career as a supporting actor in the hourlong series of the

1950s and such films as *Cleopatra* and *Lonely Are the Brave*, he was considered for such varied roles as Dr. Smith on *Lost in Space* and the Skipper on *Gilligan's Island* (ironically, both about a group of marooned people). Having made a living as a dramatic actor for over a decade, the world of situation comedy was not the place O'Connor expected to find stardom. In fact, he was living in Rome when contacted by Norman Lear, and he figured the show would quickly be canceled and he'd soon be back in Italy. He couldn't have been more wrong.

After *All in the Family* morphed into *Archie Bunker's Place* (above, with Danielle Brisebois) for another four seasons, O'Connor took some well-deserved time off before returning to series television as Police Chief Bill Gillespie in the hourlong crime drama *In the Heat of the Night* which, in addition to a three-year run on CBS, spawned six television movies. After recurring roles on two series in 1996, as grandfather Jake Gordon on *Party of Five* and Helen Hunt's father Gus (opposite another television legend named Carol: Carol Burnett) on *Mad About You*, his health began to fail. O'Connor had never really recovered from the tragic death of his only child, Hugh, who had committed suicide in 1995 after a fierce battle with drug addiction. He spent his last years as a fiercely outspoken public advocate for the civil liability of drug dealers, something utterly un-Bunkerish but absolutely O'Connorish in nature.

two years making pilots that were rejected at ABC, when help finally arrived from Fred Silverman, then-programming head at CBS. Silverman was looking to shake up the network and get rid of its "rural" shows *The Beverly Hillbillies*; *Mayberry, RFD*; and *Green Acres*. He gave Lear and Yorkin a time slot, scheduling *All in the Family* as a thirteen-episode midseason replacement.

In anticipation of the show's premiere, the switchboards at CBS were on alert for the expected deluge of protests. But ironically, after all the build-up, *All in the Family* was met with little uproar; in fact, after some initial curiosity over its "adult" content, the show consistently lost its time slot, to the point where it faced cancellation. However (as

has happened with other sitcoms), summer reruns started word of mouth and the show won three Emmy Awards for its initial thirteen episodes. By the time it returned for a full season in the fall of 1971, *All in the Family* had firmly secured its place in the sitcom firmament.

The show was legendary on so many levels that the scope of its importance is difficult to grasp. It was the first series to be shot on videotape. (Up until then tape had been used only for variety shows and news programs, the immediacy of the format thought too aggressive for a sitcom.) But then, that was Lear's goal: to push the envelope so far that taboos would shatter—and shatter they did. Racism. Homosexuality. Rape. Draft resistance. Anti-Semitism. Breast cancer. Addiction. Watergate. Impotence. Menopause. Atheism. All perfectly natural subjects for comedy, no? Well, the answer lay in

Opposite below: The Bunkers and the Stivics, along with the chair that now sits in the Smithsonian Institution.

Jean Stapleton lends a sympathetic ear to Sally Struthers, whose agonized wail was one of her many comedic gifts.

of character comedienne Jean Stapleton that was the heart and soul of the show; the dizzying heights of exasperation that Rob Reiner was driven to; and the feisty and funny Sally Struthers, a relative unknown, as Gloria, the show's hardest role, superbly navigating the fine line between family loyalty and social conscience.

Behind the scenes, the show was equally impressive, staffed by the most talented writers and directors and employing the best character actors in the business, talents who by all rights should have been starring in their own series, in guest roles. (Many of them came straight from the New York stage, including Eileen Brennan, Marcia

the "how." Lear, along with the best writers, directors, and actors in the business, made these topics hilariously funny one minute, deadly serious the next, pulling the rug out from under the audience and making them face difficult truths. The chill was unavoidable when the Bunkers discovered a swastika painted on their door, meant for a Jewish family down the block. Then an activist from the Hebrew Defense League came to the house and, upon leaving, his car exploded, killing him as the Bunkers watched. *On a sitcom.* Not all of the story lines were as dramatic but they were often thought-provoking: Archie discovered that one of his buddies from Kelsey's Bar was gay; in another episode he went bonkers over the mere fact that a woman could pick up a chair flush against the wall and a man couldn't, due to a anatomical difference in pelvic structure. When Archie's friend "Stretch" Cunningham died and Archie was asked

to speak at the funeral, shocked when he discovered that his friend of many years was Jewish, he stood at the podium and let out one of his famously inappropriate remarks: "How could he be Jewish? He had 'ham' in his name!"

The key to the whole show was that by trying to explain the absurd reasoning and backward thinking behind his racism and bigotry, Archie continually exposed his own ignorance. Most of the time, he committed a hilarious malapropism that revealed his borderline illiteracy, or he resorted to name-calling: Edith the dingbat, Michael the meathead, and Gloria the little goil. Carroll O'Connor's portrayal of Archie was the absolute center of the show, and O'Connor, a fierce liberal in real life, never condescended to the character, making an impossible-to-like figure not only likable but legendary. The rest of the superb cast lived up to the standard he set: the touching genius

---

OFF THE SET

ALL IN THE FAMILY was the first of only three sitcoms to win Emmy Awards for all four of its main characters. The other two are *The Golden Girls* and *Will & Grace*.

HARRISON FORD TURNED down the role of Mike Stivic, feeling the show was offensive, and Rob Reiner's then-wife, Penny Marshall, was briefly considered for the role of Gloria.

ARCHIE AND EDITH'S chairs are now in the Smithsonian Institution.

John Rich

One of the most important and successful directors of sitcoms, John Rich, in his almost fifty-year career, has worked on nearly every influential series. He is one of the few people to have been present for the entire history of the sitcom. In addition to directing the opening ceremonies of Disneyland in 1955, he directed many hourlong shows, including fourteen episodes of *Gunsmoke*, five episodes of *Bonanza*, and many Westerns of the 1950s. He also served as executive producer of the 1990s hit *MacGyver*. But it was on half-hour comedies that he made his greatest contribution. In addition to directing more than seventy episodes of *All in the Family*, winning an Emmy for the famous Sammy Davis, Jr., episode, he helmed more than forty episodes of both *The Dick Van Dyke Show* and *Benson*, nearly thirty of *Gomer Pyle*, and numerous episodes of *The Brady Bunch*, *Gilligan's Island*, *Maude*, *Good Times*, *That Girl*, *Our Miss Brooks*, *Dear John*, *Newhart*, *Hogan's Heroes*, *Murphy Brown*, *The Andy Griffith Show*, *My World and Welcome to It*, *Barney Miller*, and *I Married Joan*. His most recent work was on the short-lived John Larroquette series *Payne*.

Now over eighty, Rich is still incredibly passionate about the future of television, concerned (and rightly so) about the dumbing-down of American audiences, and in particular the writing of most shows, which he has referred to as "a continuous stream of gags with no context."

Rodd, David Dukes, Barnard Hughes, Estelle Parsons, Roscoe Lee Browne, Jack Weston, Rue McLanahan, Charles Durning, Mary Kay Place, Cleavon Little, Elizabeth Wilson, Charlotte Rae, Robert Guillaume, Bernadette Peters, and Doris Roberts.)

Oh yes, and Sammy Davis, Jr. In a celebrity guest shot heard round the world, the self-proclaimed "hippest Jew in show biz" provided *All in the Family* with the longest single laugh in its nine seasons, and one of the funniest moments in television history. A huge fan of the show, Davis harassed creator Norman Lear until a script was written about Davis leaving his briefcase in Archie's cab. When Davis dropped by 704 Hauser Street to pick it up, Archie proceeded to put both feet and an arm in his mouth with his inappropriate remarks. Finally, when asked to pose for a photo, Davis said he would, but only if Archie would pose with him. Just as the photo was snapped, the African-American Davis planted a big, groovy kiss on O'Connor's lily-

CAST

Carroll O'Connor	Archie Bunker
Jean Stapleton	Edith Bunker
Sally Struthers	Gloria Bunker Stivic
Rob Reiner	Michael Stivic
Danielle Brisebois	Stephanie Mills
Mike Evans	Lionel Jefferson
Isabel Sanford	Louise Jefferson
Mel Stewart	Henry Jefferson
Sherman Hemsley	George Jefferson
Betty Garrett	Irene Lorenzo
Vincent Gardenia	Frank Lorenzo
Allan Melvin	Barney Hefner
Billy Halop	Bert Munson
Brendan Dillon	Tommy Kelsey #1
Bob Hastings	Tommy Kelsey #2
Burt Mustin	Justin Quigley
Ruth McDevitt	Jo Nelson
James Cromwell	Stretch Cunningham
Gloria LeRoy	Mildred "Boom Boom" Turner

white cheek, and the laugh that emerged from the look of shock on Archie's face was perhaps the best deserved in sitcom history.

All in the era when sitcoms could make you laugh hysterically and challenge you at the same time. Those truly *were* the days.

Jean Stapleton

Best known as the flighty yet devoted Edith Bunker, Jean Stapleton has been a character actress for half a century. Her early career in Broadway musicals included roles in *Damn Yankees*, *Bells Are Ringing*, and *Funny Girl*, before she headed west with many other New York actors. Appearing in several films, such as *Cold Turkey* and *Klute*, she received the call that the series she had been helping develop for over two years was finally going on the air, eventually being awarded three Emmys for her work on *All in the Family*. Turning down the opportunity to play mystery writer Jessica

Fletcher (giving Angela Lansbury her start as a huge television star on *Murder, She Wrote*), Stapleton returned to the sitcom in 1990's *Bagdad Cafe* (costarring Whoopi Goldberg, left), and has guest-starred on *Grace Under Fire*, *Caroline in the City*, and *Everybody Loves Raymond* (as aunts Vivian, Mary, and Alda, respectively), and as Miles Silverberg's grandmother on *Murphy Brown*. Like many yeoman actors who have a no-nonsense view of the business, she has never been one to wax reminiscent about the beloved character she created. When people call her "Edith," she politely corrects them, saying, "Edith is a character I played. My name is Jean." And when Norman Lear asked her if she had any feelings about how Edith should die when she left the show, she replied, "Just have her die off, she's only fiction." Lear paused, then said, "Not to me, she isn't."

THE AMOS 'N' ANDY SHOW

 | **1951–1953** | **78 episodes**

George "Kingfish" Stevens is always trying to get rich quick, usually employing Amos, a naive fellow member of the Mystic Knights of the Sea, in his schemes. Andy, the owner and sole operator of the Fresh Air Taxi Company, is the sensible one, usually relegated to the role of narrator.

Kingfish proposes a scheme to lawyer Algonquin J. Calhoun, who registers surprise. Later he'll acquiesce and join the Kingfish in another misadventure. And that, dear reader, is how the situation joins the comedy to make a sitcom.

Though few today have even seen the program, *Amos 'n' Andy* continues to stir up controversy a half century after its cancellation. Arguably the most popular radio show of all time, it was an enormous success in its first season on television, and its cancellation changed the course of television for more than fifteen years. The central question is whether it was a racist show. Notables on both sides of the color line still can't agree—but it's instructive to examine the history of the infamous series.

It all started in 1925, when two white Southern vaudevillians, Freeman Gosden and Charles Correll, created a fifteen-minute, weekday show, *Sam and Henry*, in which they improvised the dialogue and played all the male characters. By December 1927, the two were growing restless and joined WMAQ with a new series, featuring two extremely similar characters named Amos and Andy.

An immediate success, the series went nationwide on NBC on August 19, 1929. By 1943, after 4,000 episodes, the show expanded to a half-hour, adding an orchestra and a studio audience. Now *Amos 'n' Andy* was a true situation comedy. Established writers Joe Connelly and Bob Mosher, later known for their work on *Leave It to Beaver*, *The Munsters*, and *Nanny and the Professor*, came on board.

When the televised version of *Amos 'n' Andy* debuted on CBS in 1951, the radio show was still a successful enterprise. But while the radio version rolled on with two white per-

Bob Mosher & Joe Connelly

Joe Connelly and his writing partner, Bob Mosher, had a gentle comedic writing style that showed their great sympathy and love for their characters. Though their creations might be stupid or vain or immature, they were all too human.

Connelly and Mosher met at the J. Walter Thompson advertising agency and decided to strike out on their own. They were hired by the Edgar Bergen and Charlie McCarthy radio show. Following work for Phil Harris and Frank Morgan they joined *Amos 'n' Andy* when it grew from a fifteen-minute five-day-a-week series to a half-hour sitcom broadcast on NBC. The team followed the show into television and, over twelve years, wrote more than 1,500 scripts for the series.

They went on to conceive and develop *Leave It to Beaver*, and to write other shows, most notably *The Munsters* but also *Tammy*, *Blondie*, *Bringing Up Buddy*, *Pistols 'n' Petticoats*, and Gosden and Correll's animated version of *Amos 'n' Andy—Calvin and the Colonel*.

The ever exasperated Sapphire, in the grand tradition of sitcom wives throughout history, wastes her breath ordering Amos to get up off his duff and do something productive. We know she'll regret it if he does.

show's black audience—didn't see the series as demeaning. The NAACP, however, put pressure on the network to cancel the program and CBS finally relented to the protests.

After the uproar, many questions arose. Was the stupidity of Andy any worse than that of Ed Norton? Wasn't Kingfish a character close in motive to Sergeant Bilko? Was Lightnin's slow-as-molasses demeanor any more insulting than Gilligan's? On *Amos 'n' Andy*, just as on other sitcoms, the men were grown-up babies while the women were the rocks of the family with morals and brains. Was it because the performers weren't seen on radio that made that version acceptable? Certainly other shows and films were more racist in their depictions of blacks as maids, or butlers, or porters. Amos and Andy owned their own businesses, and the show encompassed a whole world populated by black doctors, teachers, ministers, and lawyers. Many black people of a certain age remember the television show as being the only depiction of blacks in a positive light.

In 1961, Correll and Gosden premiered their animated sitcom *Calvin and the Colonel*. In it, a bunch of animals from the South moved north to make it in the big city. The creators played the leads just as they had in the radio version of *Amos 'n' Andy*. Of course, this show had absolutely nothing to do with the previous sitcom, except for absolutely everything. When *Amos 'n' Andy* was canceled there was no regular work in TV for blacks. The networks were so gun shy they didn't schedule another black-centric series until 1968's *Julia*.

formers playing black characters, the TV series employed black actors. The excellent cast was made up of stars from black theater: Spencer Williams, who played Andy, was a producer, director, and writer of films that played the black movie house circuit. He was coaxed out of retirement with visions of thousands of dollars to be made on what was sure to be a smash-hit television series. Alvin Childress played Amos, and after the premature cancellation of the series, appeared occasionally on television shows in the usual demeaning and stereotypical black roles. Tim Moore, the brilliant comic and vaudevillian, was brought out of retirement to play Kingfish. It's ironic that the charges of racism that caused the cancellation of *Amos 'n' Andy* hurt its performers more than anyone else, both financially and professionally—and none of them believed that the show was racist. The black cast—and most of the

OFF THE SET

GOSDEN AND CORRELL first appeared on television as Amos and Andy in an experimental broadcast from the 1939 New York World's Fair.

EVEN THOUGH IT was canceled in 1953, CBS continued to syndicate the show until 1966, when the pressures of the NAACP and the burgeoning civil rights movement made its continuation politically incorrect.

AT ITS PEAK, the radio version of *Amos 'n' Andy* reached over 40 million listeners, fully one-third of the United States population at the time.

CAST

Alvin Childress ....Amos Jones

Spencer Williams ....Andrew Hogg Brown

Tim Moore ....George "Kingfish" Stevens

Johnny Lee ....Algonquin J. Calhoun

Ernestine Wade ....Sapphire Stevens

Nick Stewart (as Nick O'Demus) ....Lightnin'

Amanda Randolph ....Mama Ramona Smith

Lillian Randolph ....Madame Queen

THE ANDY GRIFFITH SHOW

 | 1960–1968 | 249 episodes

Andy Taylor serves as the sheriff and conscience of bucolic Mayberry. A widower, he lives with his Aunt Bee and son Opie. His deputy is the nervous, naive, and foolishly self-important Barney Fife.

Has any other sitcom so established an entire community in viewers' minds? The answer is, yes, *The Simpsons*. But *The Andy Griffith Show* did it first. In our minds, Mayberry, with its wide array of major and minor characters and guests, became a real town. We came to know everyone in it, some good, some venal, some drunk, some plain stupid—but all very human.

Most other shows of the '50s and early '60s had small casts. Think of *My Little Margie*, *The Honeymooners*, *Our Miss Brooks*, *I Love Lucy*, *Dobie Gillis*, well, the list goes on and on. Four or so main characters and one or two subcharacters were all that was necessary for a successful sitcom.

Because Mayberry boasted such a large and realistic population, it wasn't momentous when characters came and went. That's what happens in real towns. On other shows it has always seemed gimmicky when characters are added to small family units. Remember the addition of Leonardo DiCaprio as Luke Brower on *Growing Pains*? Not a good move. By contrast, think of Andy Taylor's girlfriends. First, there was Ellie Walker. She and Andy broke up after the first season and, though potential Mrs. Sheriff Andy Taylors tried their best, it wasn't until three years later that Andy and Helen Crump were, in the parlance of Mayberry, keeping company.

The breakup had not been a staple of early sitcoms. There was usually one pair of lovebirds for an entire season or longer, with the will-they-or-won't-they tension resolved in the last episode. Margie had Freddie, Dobie had Zelda, and Mr. Peepers had Nurse Nancy Remington. More recently, the denizens of *Friends* and *Will and Grace* changed partners here and there, but it all had little impact on the core group.

In Mayberry, although there was a large galaxy of supporting players, the core group remained small: Andy, Barney, Aunt Bee, and Opie. No romantic interest there, a very rare setup for a sitcom. So the will-they-or-won't-they sexual tension that drives so many shows had to be replaced by something else…emotion.

It was Andy and Barney who formed the yin and yang of Mayberry. Where would one be without the other? Dramatically speaking, they were the closest thing to married people: they were buddies.

Sidekicks have long been a staple of fiction—D'Artagnan had three—and sitcoms are no different. Loyal to the end though sometimes exasperating—and always subordinate—sidekicks provide sta-

Andy Griffith

Andy Griffith was born in Mount Airy, North Carolina, the model for Mayberry. He began his aw-shucks career as a comic monologist in clubs and on records, playing the role of a southern Will Rogers, commenting on the foibles of the north. Always smarter than people gave him credit for, he plumbed the darker side of the good ol' country boy in his first film, 1957's *A Face in the Crowd*, in which he played a Huey Long–type character. He repeated his Broadway success in the film version of *No Time for Sergeants* and conquered the Broadway musical in *Destry Rides Again*.

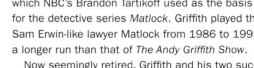

Griffith decided to try his luck in television, easily going through the door opened by another warm-hearted country boy who made it big, Tennessee Ernie Ford. Griffith's agents craftily got him 50 percent ownership of the series, in which Griffith wisely took on his more sophisticated Destry personality rather than the backwoods hick of his stand-up act.

Still in the top ten when Griffith finally called it quits, *The Andy Griffith Show* remained on the air through the decades following its 1968 demise in rerun heaven. Sponsor General Foods talked Griffith into executive-producing the sequel, *Mayberry, RFD*, which starred Ken Berry and featured many of the *Andy Griffith Show* supporting cast. In 1971, CBS decided to abandon its country-oriented lineup which also included *Green Acres*, *The Beverly Hillbillies*, *Hee-Haw*, *Petticoat Junction*, *The Jim Nabors Hour*, and *The Glen Campbell Show*. Griffith attempted a series titled *The Headmaster* (above), but it lasted only one season. His luck was no better with *The New Andy Griffith Show*.

Griffith went on to some movies-of-the-week and a mini series, *Fatal Vision* (1984), which NBC's Brandon Tartikoff used as the basis for the detective series *Matlock*. Griffith played the Sam Erwin-like lawyer Matlock from 1986 to 1995, a longer run than that of *The Andy Griffith Show*.

Now seemingly retired, Griffith and his two successful shows live on through the peculiar eternity of basic cable.

bility as well as friction. They illuminate the best and worst characteristics of the lead performer.

If Ralph Kramden had had to save one person from his burning brownstone would it have been Alice or Ed? Substitute Fred and Barney—Hanna Barbera did—and we're sure Fred would choose Barney over Wilma (Dino would have to save Wilma). Take Jerry and George…sometimes the

Opposite: Andy and Opie Taylor, hopin' the the trout are bitin'. You have permission to whistle the theme song now.

Top: Andy Griffith and Jerry Van Dyke in the one-season sitcom *The Headmaster*.

Left: Andy Griffith and Howard McNear, the male version of Marion Lorne, enjoy an off camera moment.

sidekick is around just to make the main guy feel superior.

Sometimes it's the titular star who functions as the sidekick. Gilligan got top billing but he took orders from the Skipper. A sidekick can be a kind of partner in crime. Would Lucy have been able to pull off her hair-brained schemes without Ethel? And occasionally sidekicks have sidekicks. Laverne had Shirley (or was it the other way around?) and in turn they had Lenny and Squiggy, the *ür* Laverne and Shirley.

A sitcom sidekick is always the main character's best friend. Mary had Rhoda (and was never as close to Phyllis), Alice had Flo for a few seasons, Jack Tripper confided in Larry Dallas on *Three's Company*, and when Will Smith was the Fresh Prince he had Alfonso Ribeiro's Carlton to kick around. Raj (Roger) on *What's Happening!* had two sidekicks, Dwayne and Rerun.

Ron Howard

Red-headed, freckle-faced all-American Ron Howard grew up in front of the film and television camera, and went on to a career behind it. He got his start at age five, guesting on a variety of sitcoms before hitting the big time, when he went fishing (over the credits) with Andy Griffith. As Opie, Howard spent his adolescence under the watchful eyes his Aunt Bee, Andy Taylor, and millions of TV viewers. Occasional side trips to River City (as Winthrop in the film version of *The Music Man*) and Manhattan (as the pint-sized matchmaker in *The Courtship of Eddie's Father*) occurred simultaneously.

Eight years later, Howard left Mayberry for good along with his TV dad. Maturing rapidly, he starred in the sleeper hit, *American Graffiti*, and kept the same character as Richie Cunningham in 1974's *Happy Days*. While Richie was idolizing the Fonz and trying to get to first base with the girls, Howard took his first tentative steps toward becoming a director. His career behind the camera began under the tutelage of the King of the B's, Roger Corman, on the film *Grand Theft Auto*.

In spite of its great success, Howard wanted to do more substantive work—and he has—going on to great fame and artistic success with *Splash*, *Apollo 13*, *A Beautiful Mind*, and *The DaVinci Code*, among others. Along with Brian Grazer, his partner in Imagine films, he has produced films as well as the sitcoms *Sports Night* and the underappreciated *Arrested Development* (which he also narrated).

And speaking of reruns, let's return to *The Andy Griffith Show*, one of syndication's longest-running, most lucrative hits. In addition to Griffith and Knotts's relationship, there were Andy Taylor's other two important relationships, with his son Opie (played by Ronny Howard, one of the greatest child actors in television history) and his Aunt Bee, played by Frances Bavier, as the surrogate mother we'd all like to have. In many ways, Andy was not only the law in Mayberry, but the moral compass. Though homespun and softspoken, Andy Taylor used textbook reverse psychology on his deputy, son, and aunt to get them to reconsider their behavior. He slyly undercut Barney's false bravado ("Barn" was always ready to throw the whole town into the hoosegow if necessary, because he wanted to "Nip it! Nip it

T. Bass. Andy was faced with a weekly crisis that threatened to disrupt the tempo of smalltown life—and very rarely, Andy himself got hornswoggled, occasionally by a city slicker but more likely by a gal with a well-turned ankle. Yes, it's true. Though Andy Taylor was romantically attached to Helen Crump throughout much of the series, he could still get rattled by a pretty face.

But suddenly, to the dismay of thousands of viewers, actor Don Knotts decided to leave the series. The previous season, fellow bumpkin Gomer Pyle had spun off onto his own series. He was replaced by Goober Pyle but it just wasn't the same. Andy needed another sidekick and the search was on. Several possible replacements were tried (including Jerry Van Dyke), and the writers finally settled on Jack Burns's Deputy Warren Ferguson—not an especially funny name and not an especially funny character. He lasted until 1966, and for the last two seasons there seemed to be a great big hole in the population of Mayberry. Sheriff Andy

Taylor became downright grumpy, short-tempered, and cranky. The series was still popular but it just wasn't the same.

in the bud!," a catchphrase that followed Don Knotts for the next forty years); he guided Opie through his growing pains; and he kept Aunt Bee from running off with the occasional shifty huckster. Then there were the other Mayberry residents to deal with, including Floyd the barber, gas station attendant Gomer Pyle, local booze hound Otis Campbell, town gossip Clara Edwards, and mountain man Ernest

CAST

Andy Griffith	Andy Taylor
Ronny Howard	Opie Taylor
Don Knotts	Barney Fife
Frances Bavier	Aunt Bee
Howard McNear	Floyd Lawson
Jack Dodson	Howard Sprague
Hal Smith	Otis Campbell
Elinor Donahue	Ellie Walker
Aneta Corsaut	Helen Crump
Betty Lynn	Thelma Lou
Jim Nabors	Gomer Pyle
George Lindsey	Goober Pyle

Sheldon Leonard

One of the most successful and influential producers of character based sitcoms, Sheldon Leonard began his career as an actor. After starting his writing career in radio, he moved to the quickly expanding medium of television. He began directing *Make Room for Daddy* in 1953, and was promoted to producer by its third season. He and Danny Thomas formed their own production company in 1961, developing and serving as executive producer on *The Andy Griffith Show* and *The Dick Van Dyke Show*. His greatest contribution was in the way he introduced spinoffs such as *The Andy Griffith Show*, which began as an episode of *The Danny Thomas Show*. Creating a "back door pilot," Leonard saved a fortune by folding the storyline into a pre-existing series without having to pay for a pilot. Five years later, Leonard did the same thing

with *Gomer Pyle, U.S.M.C.*, whose pilot was presented as an episode of Griffith's show. After producing the groundbreaking *I Spy*, Leonard's luck ran dry with the short lived *My World and Welcome to It*, based on the stories of James Thurber, which was hailed by critics but failed to find an audience.

Opposite left: Andy Taylor is so laconic, low-key, and laid back that Aunt Bee (Frances Bavier) has to hold the morning paper up for him to read.

Above: Traction Is Funny Part One: Barney Fife gets a very gentle peck from girlfriend Thelma Lou (Betty Lynn).

Top Left: Don Knotts as Barney Fife, not unlike the title of one of his films, was *The Shakiest Gun in Mayberry*.

Left: Television pioneer Sheldon Leonard (with Danny Thomas and Marjorie Lord) guest starring on *Make Room for Daddy*.

BARNEY MILLER

 abc | **1975–1982** | **170 episodes**

There's a daily parade of lawbreakers in New York City's Twelfth Precinct, where the detectives are as nutty as the perps.

With its distinctive bass-note theme song played over the skyline of New York City, the long-running hit *Barney Miller* was one of the most "street" sitcoms of the 1970s: gritty and often morbidly dark in its comedy. Resurrected from an unsold pilot created by Danny Arnold called *The Life and Times of Captain Barney Miller*, the show was revived by legendary director John Rich, who had been given a development deal with ABC after he directed the first few seasons of *All in the Family*. Rich saw the unsold pilot and requested that the show be picked up as part of his deal, but friction between Rich and Arnold forced Rich out after two episodes. Arnold viewed *Barney Miller* as his baby and exerted a great deal of control over every aspect of the production. The tapings became legendary, often lasting until three o'clock in the morning. (Arnold was notorious for doing massive rewrites after the first taping, stretching tape day to the point that it became unworkable to use a studio audience after the third season.)

The only actors retained from the original pilot were Hal Linden, straight from a long career on the Broadway stage, and the hangdog Abe Vigoda as the lugubrious Detective Phil Fish. Like those of *Mary Tyler Moore*, *The Bob Newhart Show*, *Taxi*, and *WKRP in Cincinnati*, *Barney Miller*'s expert ensemble signaled the demise of the character actor in modern situation comedies. In addition to Linden and Vigoda, the original cast included Max Gail as the hotheaded Detective

The detectives of *Barney Miller*'s Twelfth Precinct (clockwise from left): Jack Soo, Gregory Sierra, Abe Vigoda, Max Gail, Ron Glass, and (in the title role) Hal Linden.

Wojohowicz; Ron Glass as the suave Detective Harris; Gregory Sierra as the street-smart Detective Amenguale; and the hilariously deadpan Jack Soo as Detective Nick Yemana.

The squad room was a veritable melting pot of race and class, fueled by the most toxic coffee outside of Chernobyl. Often dropping in was the windbag Chief Inspector Luger, played by James Gregory, who possessed a borderline-sick obsession with the blood and guts of his own salad days pounding a beat. Rounding out the cast and providing the home-life facet of Captain Miller's life was the sensational Barbara Barrie as his wife, another New York stage transplant. Unfortunately for Barrie, the domestic side of things proved less colorful than life at the station house, and her character (along with the two Miller children) was phased out of the series; however her name remained in the credits until the end of the season.

Functioning almost as a character in itself was the precinct room, perhaps the most atmospheric set of any sitcom. The detail in the set decoration was extraordinary, light years more believable than the sprawling apartments of *Friends* or *Will & Grace* or the state-of-the-art workplaces of *Suddenly Susan* or *Just Shoot Me*. As the show evolved, it became more and more like a Broadway play, rarely straying from the precinct room and Miller's adjoining office. The cast of guest stars added a lot of flavor to the show, as neighborhood "regulars" getting booked and interviewed by the detectives. These included a gay couple, Marty Morrison and Darryl Driscoll; local liquor store owner Mr. Kotterman; Sidney, the local bookie; and ambulance-chasing attorney Arnold Ripner, in addition to a steady stream of pickpockets, hookers, and other assorted undesirables.

The show went through a series of cast

Hal Linden lays down the law to the droll Steve Landesburg on tape day of *Barney Miller*.

Ron Glass

The wry, effete Ron Glass set out to be a Shakespearean actor, working at the Guthrie Theatre in Minneapolis before heading west to California. After early appear-

ances on *Sanford and Son* and *Good Times*, Glass landed the role he was perfect for: the dapper, supercool Ron Harris. Better read, better spoken, and better dressed than any of his cohorts at the Twelfth Precinct, Harris was eternally bemused by the stereotyping he experienced as an African-American law officer. *Barney Miller* finished its run in 1982, and Glass returned the following season with *Sanford and Son* costar Demond Wilson (left) in a remake called *The New Odd Couple*. He guest-starred on many other shows and costarred on the short-lived sitcom *Rhythm and Blues*. His most recent appearance was on the Disney Channel series *Teen Angel*, playing God's cousin, Rod.

changes, but, perhaps because it took place in a workplace, like *M*A*S*H* and *Cheers*, other shows that centered around a group of people brought together by circumstance as opposed to a family unit, *Barney Miller* held up well under the shifts. Actress Linda Lavin briefly joined the cast as the only female detective on the squad, and Steve Landesberg and Ron Carey came on board in the third season, as the pseudo-intellectual Detective Dietrich and the pipsqueak Officer Levitt, respectively. The show lost two of its most beloved characters, first when Abe Vigoda was spun off into his own short-lived series called *Fish*, and later when Jack Soo died. So popular was Soo with the cast and audiences that the producers put together an unscripted tribute show where the cast reminisced about their favorite episodes featuring Soo.

And speaking of favorite episodes, one of the most memorable shows of *Barney Miller*'s nine seasons featured a plotline that might not survive the gauntlet of today's network censors. In the third season, "Wojo" brought in brownies baked by his

girlfriend. As it was the mid-1970s, the treats were, of course, laced with hashish, and each detective who sampled the magical baked goods had his own hilarious reaction. The episode was a triumph of comic character writing and acting.

Yemana: Then Fish runs in the alley and he leaps over us like one of those…what do you call those things in Africa that run and leap in the air?
Harris: Slaves.

Noam Pitlik

Character actor Noam Pitlik became familiar to sitcom viewers when he joined the ranks of such actor/directors as Jerry Paris, Peter Bonerz, and Dick Martin. He played a recurring role on the flop John Astin show *I'm Dickens, He's Fenster*, appeared on *Get Smart* and *Gomer Pyle*, and played seven different comic German officers on various episodes of *Hogan's Heroes*. Pitlik hit pay dirt with two recurring roles in 1972, as Officer Swanhauser on the first season of *Sanford and Son* and as the grouchy Mister Gianelli, a member of Bob Hartley's therapy group, on *The Bob Newhart Show*. When Gianelli was ignominiously killed by a truckload of zucchini in that show's second season, Pitlik began to pursue directing. Helming many episodes of *Barney Miller*, he was much in demand, and worked on such shows as *One Day at a Time*, *Alice*, *The Betty White Show*, and *Taxi* before joining the long-running *Night Court*. He made one final appearance as an actor before his death from lung cancer in 1999, on the Ted Danson series *Becker*.

Above: The setting of a neighborhood filled with local weirdos gave *Barney Miller*'s guest stars (including Mabel King as a voodoo high priestess) choice opportunities to chew some bigtime scenery.

Left: The racially and ethnically diverse ensemble that gave *Barney Miller* its sense of realism included Ron Glass and Greg Sierra.

Opposite: Jack Soo and James Gregory, back when networks weren't afraid of a sitcom whose cast was entirely composed of expert character comedians.

CAST

Hal Linden	Cpt. Barney Miller
Max Gail	Det. Stanley "Wojo" Wojohowicz
Ron Glass	Det. Ron Harris
Abe Vigoda	Det. Phil Fish
Jack Soo	Det. Nick Yemana
Steve Landesberg	Det. Arthur Dietrich
Ron Carey	Off. Carl Levitt
James Gregory	Insp. Frank Luger
Barbara Barrie	Elizabeth Miller
Gregory Sierra	Det. Sergeant Chano Amenguale
George Murdock	Lt. Scanlon
Linda Lavin	Det. Janice Wentworth
June Gable	Det. Maria Baptista
Florence Stanley	Bernice Fish

THE BEVERLY HILLBILLIES

👁 | **1962–1971** | **216 episodes**

Jed Clampett, a hillbilly backwoodsman from Bugtussle, Tennessee, accidentally finds oil on his property and becomes an instant mega-millionaire. So, as the song goes, he packs his fam-i-ly and moves to Bev-er-ly. Hills, that is.

The *Beverly Hillbillies* was the best sitcom ever to be reviled by the intelligentsia who claimed not to watch television. They shouldn't have let the terminally naive Clampetts, with their good-old country values, fool them. Though much of the humor sprang from the utter ignorance of Jethro, Elly May, and Granny, the show was consistently witty—and in the end, the city slickers showed themselves to be just as dumb as the Clampett clan.

Smart-as-a-whip creator Paul Henning made everyone on the show some kind of fool. He fought with the suits at CBS who wanted homespun homilies and warm, fuzzy conclusions to the episodes, intent on offering an antidote to the treacle offered by the likes of *Family Affair* and other happy-white-family shows. There would certainly be heart in the series but it wouldn't be laid on as thick as grits.

The press denounced the program as witless. David Susskind, a self-proclaimed expert on everything, urged "the few intelligent people left" to bombard their congressmen with letters denouncing the nadir of what Newton Minow had called "the vast wasteland." *The New York Times* wrote, "*The Beverly Hillbillies* is steeped in enough twanging guitar and rural no-think to make each half-hour seem like sixty minutes." No matter. It soared to the top of the ratings faster than any other show before or since. Two years later, the pundits at the *Times* loosened their moral suspenders enough to recant: "Folks who look down their noses at TV's number-one show have it all wrong. In truth, it mocks pretension—a spectacle the great American public has always enjoyed."

Even after striking oil, the lovably clueless Clampetts continued to tool around Beverly Hills in their broken-down 1921 Oldsmobile truck. Only Duke the bloodhound seems embarrassed.

In the very beginning the Clampetts often returned to their mountain roots, but after the first season they found enough folderol in California to keep them sitting around the cee-ment pond. Only when *Petticoat Junction* joined the Henning stable of shows did the family travel back to the hills and even visited the Shady Rest Hotel after the latter show had been canceled.

Above: Nancy Kulp and Raymond Bailey on location when the Clampetts and company visited Merry Olde England.

Below: Two fine specimens of pulchritude, Donna Douglas and Max Baer, Jr. (as Elly May and Jethro), lounge around the cee-ment pond.

PAUL HENNING

The 1960s was Paul Henning's decade. With *The Beverly Hillbillies* and its two companion shows, *Petticoat Junction* and *Green Acres*, Henning achieved the near-impossible: a television triple play.

Coming from the Midwest and a tradition of laconic, wry humor (as opposed to the cynical and self-reverent comedy of the left and right coasts), Henning celebrated the abnormalities of the normal, the surrealism beneath the surface of plowed fields. Before he came along, there had been spin-offs but they had never orbited around one another in such symbiosis, the casts regularly visiting back and forth. It was truly a mad mélange and it was all the idea of Paul Henning. He had gotten his start as a writer for the radio classic *Fibber McGee and Molly*, where he began by submitting a spec script and stayed for fifteen years. He then moved to television as a right-hand man to mentor Fred de Cordova, one of television's producing and directing pioneers. Henning's first project on his own was *The Bob Cummings Show* in 1955, in which he spoofed the ladies' man persona of Cummings himself. He reached his apex in Beverly Hills, Hooterville, and Pixley, and when CBS axed the three shows because they wanted to smarten up and de-countrify the network, he quit. That, for all practical purposes, was that. The Clampetts left the air in 1971 and with the new decade came new preoccupations. The public moved on and Henning quit while he was way, way ahead.

(Henning was a master of integrating his shows: the cast of *Green Acres* often crossed time slots to visit the cast of *Petticoat Junction* and vice versa.)

The premise of *The Beverly Hillbillies* was a noble conceit that can be traced back to the Greeks. Take someone out of his own world and plop him down in a completely foreign locale or situation. Henning used the formula again, in reverse, when he moved the city slickers of *Green Acres* to the country. Other shows have followed suit: Mork from Ork found himself a stranger on a strange planet on *Mork and Mindy* and the marooned day trippers of Gilligan's S.S. *Minnow* washed up (in every sense of the word) on an uncharted South Pacific island. The *Hill Street Blues* spin-off comedy, *Beverly Hills Buntz*, uprooted two New York cops and sent them to L.A., and the creators of *Fresh Prince of Bel Air* took the *Beverly Hillbillies* idea and substituted the black Will Smith for the hillbillies. Fathers are often "fish out of water," forced to raise their children in the absence of their wives. Think of *The Courtship of Eddie's Father*, *Bachelor Father*, *Diff'rent Strokes*, *Gidget*, *Major Dad*, *Family Affair*, and *My Three Sons*; double that and you've got *My Two Dads* and *Two and a Half Men*; triple it and you've got *Full House*.

Hillbillies owes a lot to the *Li'l Abner* cartoons of Al Capp and the resulting stage and film musical based on the comic strip. In *Abner*, the denizens of the Ozark community of Dogpatch are catapulted into the political maelstrom of Congress and the capitalist extraordinaire, General Bullmoose. The hillbillies just don't get the outside world, and the clash of their homespun traditions and logic with the modern status quo provides both the humor and the poignancy. That's a spot-on description of *The Beverly Hillbillies*, too, with Jethro equal to Abner, Elly May a close cousin to Daisy Mae, and Granny the counterpart of Mammy Yokum.

The actors could not have been better: Buddy Ebsen was a perfect Jed, the picture of sage country wisdom yet still able to cut loose with zany abandon; Donna Dixon was a down-home dish as Elly May; Max Baer, Jr. expertly played the peabrained Jethro, supremely confident in the fact that he was the Einstein of the family (after all, he had a sixth-grade education); and best of all was the wizened, pint-sized comic tornado Irene Ryan (in reality a woman of boundless class and grace) as Granny. Hunched over, her squinting, skeptical eyes forever sizing up strangers, Ryan's Granny was in a constant "show-me" state. Rounding out the cast were Raymond Bailey and Nancy Kulp, spot-on comic masters playing money-crazed banker Millburn Drysdale and his tweedy aide-de-campe Jane Hathaway.

Doing the laundry in the cee-ment pond and never discovering the source of those pesky bells that rang prior to someone showing up at the front door, the Clampetts created a universe that was often skewed, sometimes completely nutty, and always hilarious.

Unfortunately, the conceit had its limits and, as with most long-running shows, the original writers retired, burned out, and the new scribes made the show ever broader. It happened on *Gilligan's Island*, it's happening now on *The Simpsons*, and it happened on *The Beverly Hillbillies*. What was once social satire disguised as stupid, silly fun simply became stupid and silly—and not so much fun. One clue that a show is running out of steam is the onset of episodes filmed on location: the family goes to Europe or New York or even the corner store. When characters who have existed in the fake world of sets and backdrops enter reality, the jig is up and our willing suspension of disbelief is smashed. On the *Hillbillies*, the clan visited England and flirted with taking over Clampett Castle. (Reportedly, it was the first time an American sitcom was filmed overseas.) The episodes that took place in Silver Dollar City (whatever happened to Bugtussle?) were filmed in a real town, draining all charm from the hapless Clampetts. By the time the series concluded, Mr. Drysdale was just plain venal, Elly May was ridiculously enamored of her critters and her "frog man" boyfriend, Granny was unremittingly cranky, and even Jed seemed sapped of his signature wisdom. In its heyday, though, *The Beverly Hillbillies* was one of the most subversive comedies in the history of television, mocking capitalism, sophistication, and ignorance in one laugh-filled package.

Opposite top: At a party for the employees of the Paul Henning sitcoms, Irene Ryan and *Green Acres*'s Eddie Albert do an impromptu soft shoe for Donna Douglas.

Opposite bottom: Irene Ryan as an AARP Jayne Mansfield, accompanied by Lester Flatt and Earl Scruggs, who composed *The Beverly Hillbillies* theme song.

Lower left: Right purty Donna Douglas, who, when she wasn't possum wrasslin', cleaned up real nice.

CAST

Buddy Ebsen	Jed Clampett
Irene Ryan	Granny
Donna Douglas	Elly May Clampett
Max Baer, Jr.	Jethro Bodine
Raymond Bailey	Milburn Drysdale
Nancy Kulp	Jane Hathaway
Bea Benaderet	Cousin Pearl Bodine
Harriet MacGibbon	Margaret Drysdale

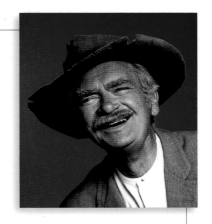

BUDDY EBSEN

The Beverly Hillbillies saved Buddy Ebsen from being known as the man who was almost the Tin Woodsman in the film version of *The Wizard of Oz*. He had had a notable career with his sister Vilma, as an eccentric dance team that rose from vaudeville to nightclubs and Broadway. On Broadway the pair introduced the Dietz and Schwartz song "A Shine on Your Shoes" in *Flying Colors*, and in the *Ziegfeld Follies of 1934*, they sang and danced to "I Like the Likes of You." The siblings then made the natural transition to Hollywood debuting on film in MGM's *Broadway Melody of 1936*, for which Buddy won the Oscar. It would be the first and last film for sister Vilma. A few more musicals, minus *The Wizard of Oz*, followed for Buddy, and then a series of cowboy films in the 1940s. He broke into television in a big way as Davy Crockett's sidekick, George Russell, in the Disney-produced series, *Davy Crockett*. That character, a slow but smart mountain man, was a clear precursor to Jed Clampett.

With his featured role in the 1961 film *Breakfast at Tiffany's*, Ebsen took another step toward the greatest role of his career. Clampett's creator, Paul Henning, recalled Ebsen's work in the film and offered him the role—but before he'd accept it, Ebsen demanded that Jed be smartened up a bit. Henning acceded to his wishes, providing the series with a solid center in the midst of all the shenanigans and misunderstandings. Ebsen was finally a star and when the show left the air in 1971, he was ready for more. Two years later he returned to television as the private-eye Barnaby Jones in the series of the same name. Ebsen retired for the most part in the 1980s but kept active into his 90s, writing his autobiography and making occasional guest appearances. His last television work was as a voice on *King of the Hill* in 1999.

FLOPS

And now, dear readers, we pause to remember those "Timeslot Turkeys," those "Nielsen Nightmares," and those "McLean Stevenson Mishaps."

Left: In the fall of 1965, all three networks were running series about the wacky goings on at various kinds of camps. Joining ABC's *F Troop* and CBS's *Hogan's Heroes* was the NBC flop *Camp Runamuck*.

Above: John Davidson with Sally Field in her last sitcom before movie stardom, the ESP-centered *The Girl with Something Extra*.

Top: Both with troubled futures ahead of them, Judy Carne and Peter Duel enjoy happier times as young marrieds in the romantic sitcom, *Love on a Rooftop*.

Left: Barbara Baxley, Lois Nettleton, and Anita Gillette in a fascinating failure: Norman Lear's gender-bending *All That Glitters*.

Below: Glynis Johns and Keith Andes search for their minuscule viewing audience in the 1963 wipeout, *Glynis*.

Right: Will Hutchins (here with Pamela Rodgers, Miko Mayama, and Sandy Baron) saw his big shot at sitcom stardom evaporate in 1966's *Hey, Landlord*.

McLean Stevenson

Starting out in radio, McLean Stevenson worked as press secretary for his cousin Adlai during his presidential bids in 1952 and 1956. Seguing into writing, he wrote comedy sketches for *That Was the Week That Was*, (featuring future *M*A*S*H* costar Alan Alda) and *The Smothers Brothers Comedy Hour*. Stevenson's acting breakthrough came when he was cast as Doris Day's boss on her constantly premise-morphing sitcom. Then came his memorable turn on *M*A*S*H*. After leaving that show, Stevenson had ten years of miserable luck, professionally speaking, during which he starred in no fewer than four flop sitcoms: *The McLean Stevenson Show*; *In the Beginning*; *Hello, Larry*; and *Condo*. Publicly, he was extremely good humored about his dismal track record (he was, in truth, a wonderfully gifted comedian), even making fun of it himself on talk shows. Privately, however, he admitted shortly before his unexpected death in 1996 that he regretted leaving the ranks of the 4077th.

Left: All dressed up with nowhere to go: Bette Midler in one of television's recent high-profile flops, creatively titled *Bette*.

Right: Flop-riddled McLean Stevenson with Broadway musical actress Priscilla Lopez (wishing she was back in *A Chorus Line*) in another black mark against the Roman Catholic church, the truly lousy *In the Beginning*.

BEWITCHED

 | **1964–1971** | **254 episodes**

Serene Samantha marries the tightly wound Darrin Stephens. The only hitch: she's a witch. Despite her best efforts, Sam turns Darrin's world upside down with her magical powers and the constant intrusion of her fractious family of witches and warlocks.

There was something funny going on inside 1164 Morning Glory Circle in Westport, Connecticut—or so insisted the neighbors, particularly nosy Mrs. Kravitz. People seemed to appear and disappear in a flash, things floated through the air, and Benjamin Franklin, Queen Victoria, and Mother Goose were all spotted in the front yard. And then there were Mrs. Stephens's relatives. Talk about a bunch of kooks!

Delightful, frothy *Bewitched* was a hit for ABC for eight seasons, but behind the scenes it went through a series of extremely bumpy patches. The first season was a more conventional black-and-white romantic comedy than were the color episodes most of us know from syndication, dealing with the problems faced by many newlyweds, and with only a few displays of magic per episode. But, at the urging of ABC, and after producer Danny Arnold left the show, the plotlines became wilder and wilder, constantly upping the ante of nutty behavior, characters, and situations. When Elizabeth Montgomery's husband, William Asher, took over as producer (and the show went to color), it became more reliant on special effects and the machinations of farce.

The true comedy of *Bewitched* lay in the constant collision of the mortal and the magical, with the delicious Montgomery serving as the calm in the eye of the hurricane. Wincing as she broke the news to a quivering Darrin that Christopher Columbus was in the kitchen, or that her cousin Esmeralda

The lovely Elizabeth Montgomery and Dick York, the first (and better) Darrin, with trouble never far behind them in the form of Agnes Moorehead.

Right: Darrin Stephens Deux, Dick Sargent, and the tremendous David White as the sycophantic Larry Tate, everyone's nightmare boss.

Below: Beatniks are funny. Paul Lynde and Phyllis Diller look for an answer blowin' in the wind on the flop series, *The Pruitts of Southhampton*.

had straightened the Leaning Tower of Pisa, or that their three-year-old daughter Tabitha had turned her playmate into a frog, Montgomery was the picture of patience, wide-eyed as she waited for the volcanic Mt. Darrin (also referred to as Durwood, Darwin, Dobbins, and Dustbin) to blow his top. Montgomery clearly understood the importance of imbuing her character with truth and believability, and she never played Samantha as either desperate or slapsticky. She was simply a woman (albeit with superpowers) trying to live the good suburban life with her family.

The cast included quite the roster of oddballs, and, along with *Green Acres* and *Barney Miller*, had the best casting of character actors in television history. Even the mortals were offbeat, with David White as the perfectly brownnosing boss, Larry Tate, Alice Pearce (and later Sandra Gould, after Pearce's death from cancer), and George Tobias as neighbors the

Kravitzes, the wonderful Mabel Albertson as Darrin's mother, and such classic types as Charles Lane, John Fiedler, and Edward Andrews as clients of Darrin's advertising firm. And the casting of Samantha's family was truly inspired: Marion Lorne as

the bumbling Aunt Clara, who usually made her entrance down the chimney; Alice Ghostley as the nervously disappearing Cousin Esmeralda; Paul Lynde as the fun-loving, pun-loving Uncle Arthur; the Shakespearean Maurice Evans as

Paul Lynde

No matter what character the comic wizard Paul Lynde played, he was always unmistakably Paul Lynde. Achieving attention with his comic sketches in the Broadway revue *New Faces of 1952*, Lynde went on to become a fixture on New York television in the 1950s, on the Buddy Hackett series *Stanley* and as a member of the stock company of comedians on Perry Como's *Kraft Music Hall*. With the role of the frazzled yet starstuck Harry McAfee in the Broadway musical *Bye Bye Birdie*, he moved to Hollywood and guest-starred on virtually every sitcom in the 1960s. Best-

known as the flamboyant, fun-loving Uncle Arthur on *Bewitched*, the creation of the "Paul Lynde persona" was a double-edged sword, for while he loved the work, Lynde had always wanted to be taken seriously as a dramatic actor. His appearances as the center square on the game show *The Hollywood Squares* from 1968–81 were legendary, and his head waggling, slightly smutty double entendres only solidified the Lynde persona. When he tried to star in sitcoms of his own, *The Paul Lynde Show* in 1972 and *The New Temperature's Rising* in 1973 (with the female version of his persona, *New Faces* and *Bewitched* costar Alice Ghostley, playing his sister), the efforts were met with indifference. Apparently, audiences preferred to sample Lynde in the measured doses of a second banana or guest star. Dealing with alcoholism and his own conflict over the fact that his homosexuality was an open secret in Hollywood, he died in 1982, having entertained audiences for thirty years without ever having a chance to show his range.

Pandora Spocks

The tragic story of Pandora Spocks has been oft-told in the heartbreak-riddled jungle of Hollywood. Born Sadie Feldman to Methodist missionaries in the wilds of the Belgian Congo, she became a runaway at sixteen, hopping a Turkish freighter bound for the states, determined to make it in Tinseltown. Floating like chum among the show business sharks, Spocks was working as a checkout girl at an Encino Alpha-Beta supermarket when she was spotted by an ABC casting director. Hired for her uncanny resemblance to *Bewitched* star Elizabeth Montgomery, Spocks became an overnight sensation as Samantha Stephens's supergroovy cousin Serena. Never really clicking with

Montgomery (indeed, many reported that the two refused to appear on set together), the experience was not the world of champagne and caviar that Spocks envisioned as a child in the underbrush of the Congo. After the show's cancellation in 1972, Spocks filmed no fewer than seven unsold pilots for sitcoms, hoping to build upon her success as Serena. But with titles such as *Oh, That Pandora!*, *It's Always Pandora*, and the one that spelled her downfall, the substance-fueled *The Pandora Spocks Experience*, Hollywood was on to her in a hot New York minute, labeling her a one-trick pony in go-go boots. Now a virtual recluse, Spocks scrapes by on her Screen Actor's Guild pension in a trailer park on the outskirts of Tempe, Arizona, spending her days combing out her Serena wig (the only memento from her acting career).

Samantha's father Maurice; Bernard Fox as the quackish family physician Dr. Bombay; and Reta Shaw, Jane Connell, and Estelle Winwood as occasional supporting witches.

And then there was Agnes Moorehead. Cast after bumping into Montgomery and Asher at Bloomingdale's, Moorehead, with her caftans, green eye shadow, and flame red hair (just imagine how much more potent her character became in the switch from black-and-white to color), Moorehead elevated the show from charming and quirky to an all-out campfest. Moorehead hadn't been known for playing comic roles, but she grabbed the opportunity and ran with it, playing the hilariously contemptuous, vindictive Endora with the utmost comic relish. And when

it was time for smoke and mirrors, both Moorehead and Montgomery became so adept at acting seamlessly throughout the stop-motion photography that the effects became uncannily convincing.

Boy: Are you a good witch or a bad witch?
Endora: *Comme çi, comme ça.*

If one really examines the psychology behind the show, *Bewitched* depicted what much of society was going through in the mid-1960s, with its attempts to open Darrin's mind to the blending of people from two vastly different backgrounds. Theirs was a "mixed marriage," after all, with many of the attendant problems (although Samantha's secret identity was desperately hidden from the "outside world"). This brings up another interesting theory about the subtext of the show, that of Darrin and Samantha's marriage serving as an allegory for a gay love story between a closeted homosexual and an "out" one. With the straitlaced Darrin constantly trying to hide and cover up

Mabel Albertson

The mother of all sitcom mothers-in-law, the brilliant Mabel Albertson made a career out of a vaguely pained expression of distaste. The sister of *Chico and the Man* star Jack Albertson, she had four recurring roles as mothers who always looked as though they smelled something foul. In addition to her hilarious appearances as Phyllis Stephens on *Bewitched*, whimpering, "Frank, I'm getting a sick headache" whenever she bore witness to a bizarre occurrence, she played Donald Hollinger's equally skeptical mother on *That Girl*, Howard Sprague's doting mother on *The Andy Griffith Show*, and Dick Van Dyke's mother on *The New Dick Van Dyke Show*. With a scene-stealing appearance as Mrs. Van Hoskins in the screwball film *What's Up, Doc?* (collapsing on the floor of a San Francisco hotel like Camille after her jewelry was stolen), Albertson's last television role was on *Mary Tyler Moore*, playing (you guessed it) a disapproving mother.

the flamboyant, outrageous behavior of his partner's "family," including the (let's face it) queeny Uncle Arthur and the bordering-on-drag-queen look and manner of Endora (if a reader doubts Agnes Moorehead's impact on the gay community, head down to Greenwich Village some Halloween and count how many Endoras you see, and compare it with the number of Jeannies, Morticia Addamses, Aunt Bees, and Lily Munsters spotted), it's not that much of a stretch, with suspicious and nosy neighbors certain of all kinds of unnatural acts taking place, and constant pressure from Samantha's family, who regard her mortal (read "straight") suburban life as "squaresville" (as Cousin Serena used to call it). Viewed in these terms, the show was very forward-thinking, socially speaking, especially in a famous episode in which Tabitha befriends an African American and twitches her into a white girl, at the same time turning her own skin brown. Ultimately, she realizes that the only good solution is to make them both striped—so there won't be any difference. Samantha puts a cap on it all by explaining to Tabitha that there was really no difference between the girls in the first place.

Behind the scenes, an unusual (some say jinxed) series of tragedies unfolded, including the death of two of its supporting actors (Alice Pearce and Marion Lorne), and the departure of Dick York after the show's fifth season due to crippling back pain. (Special furniture was used to accommodate his infirmity, and many times he had to be helped on and off the set.) Once the brilliant York left the show, *Bewitched* lived up to its magical title less and less, for

Opposite top: Erin Murphy as Tabitha, with Grandmama Agnes Moorehead, who possessed the greatest collection of caftans on television until Audra Lindley hit the scene on *Three's Company*.

Left: Elizabeth Montgomery holds her own amidst the two seasoned pros who played her parents, Agnes Moorehead and Shakespearean ham Maurice Evans.

CAST

Elizabeth Montgomery	Samantha Stephens
Dick York	Darrin Stephens (1)
Dick Sargent	Darrin Stephens (2)
Agnes Moorehead	Endora
David White	Larry Tate
Erin & Diane Murphy	Tabitha Stephens
Greg & David Lawrence	Adam Stephens
George Tobias	Abner Kravitz
Alice Pearce	Gladys Kravitz (1)
Sandra Gould	Gladys Kravitz (2)
Irene Vernon	Louise Tate (1)
Kasey Rogers	Louise Tate (2)
Marion Lorne	Aunt Clara
Alice Ghostley	Esmeralda
Bernard Fox	Dr. Bombay
Pandora Spocks	Serena
Paul Lynde	Uncle Arthur
Maurice Evans	Maurice
Mabel Albertson	Phyllis Stephens
Bernie Kopell	Apothecary
Roy Roberts	Frank Stephens (1)
Robert F. Simon	Frank Stephens (2)
Reta Shaw	Aunt Hagatha

while his replacement Dick Sargent was a perfectly fine actor, he lacked the comic exasperation of York, and the relationship between Darrin and Endora morphed from irritation to sheer loathing, thereby losing its comic punch. In addition, Montgomery was losing interest in the weekly grind and the writers were running on empty, with some episodes in the show's eighth and final season sporting recycled plots (and large stretches of dialogue) from earlier episodes.

Despite an awful movie adaptation that totally missed the charm (as well as the point) of the series, *Bewitched* has maintained its reputation as something

more than just a silly show for more than forty years, due in large part to the charisma and talent of Elizabeth Montgomery, who left our square, boring mortal world far too soon. Surely, with such an eternal charm Montgomery is hanging around someplace. In fact, next time you look out an airplane window, don't be surprised if you see a beautiful blonde hitching a ride on the wing, twitching her nose.

Above: Loyal *Bewitched* viewers were able to gauge Samantha Stephens's mood by her wardrobe. Housedresses, and later, hip huggers, signified smooth sailing. But, when she donned that black dress—Sam meant business.

OFF THE SET

TWO *BEWITCHED* ACTRESSES, Alice Pearce and Marion Lorne, were awarded Emmy Awards posthumously.

HELEN HUNT AND Jodie Foster auditioned for the role of Tabitha.

***BEWITCHED* MARKED THE** first time in sitcom history that a married couple played by unmarried actors was seen in the same bed together.

DICK SARGENT WAS the first choice to play Darrin when the show was pitched as a vehicle for Broadway actress Tammy Grimes. She turned the show down, but the two played husband and wife on *The Tammy Grimes Show*, which aired on ABC directly after *Bewitched* in the fall of 1966. It was canceled after four weeks.

THE BOB CUMMINGS SHOW

 | 1955 | 1955–1957 | 1957–1959 | **173 episodes**

Model photographer Bob Collins tries to bed every beautiful girl he meets.

Playing a fashion photographer, film and television's number-one occupation for unrelenting horndogs, Bob Cummings checks the lipstick of his model, Lisa Gaye.

What makes a sitcom great? Some of the shows in this book were innovative, some politically ahead of their time, some driven by a central brilliant performance, some long-running, award-winning favorites. And then there were a few that, while not exactly politically correct, were indisputably solid, well-crafted shows with good acting and an individuality that set them apart from the rest. Which brings us to *The Bob Cummings Show* or, as most of us remember it, *Love That Bob*.

This show was built around the self-deprecating charm of Bob Cummings. Never trying to send a message or teach a lesson, it was mainly concerned with photographer Bob Collins's constant need to bag a chick (at least that was the subtext). Collins lived with his sister, played by Rosemary DeCamp, who cluckingly disapproved of Bob's exploits; and his nephew, Chuck, played by Dwayne Hickman as a sort of junior horndog. It's interesting that Hickman went on to play the eternally vexed (at least when it came to the opposite sex) Dobie Gillis in another show directed by Rod Amateau. In fact, *The Bob Cummings Show* shared other similarities with *The Many Loves of Dobie Gillis*, as both Bob and Dobie had plain-Jane characters pining for them. Bob Collins had two: his secretary, Charmaine Schultz (played by Ann B. Davis) and Pamela Livingston (the equally frustrated Nancy Kulp) while Dobie was beset by Zelda Gilroy. Also, for all his huffing and

Bob Collins: Hold it! I think you're gonna like this picture.

Pamela wanted and needed, oh so badly. Pamela constantly threw herself at Bob, going to extravagant lengths to try and get him in the sack. (Kulp would later play another shamelessly aggressive woman, the Jethro Bodine–crazy Jane Hathaway, on *The Beverly Hillbillies*, also by Bob Cummings creator Paul Henning.)

There wasn't much more to the show but the writers kept our interest up with the help of good-natured wit, clever situations, and our own titillation. No one took themselves seriously and the fact that everyone was thwarted in his or her plans made it all palatable to '50s audiences. Credit is also due to the cast, all of whom seemed to be enjoying themselves immensely, treating even the most ludicrous situations with good humor.

Sexuality in sitcoms was a dicey thing in the first decade of their history, and *The Bob Cummings Show* was about as racy as it got. Of course, once Norman Lear opened the floodgates in terms of language and social commentary, sexuality moved to the forefront. Today, most sitcoms revel in explicitly sexual humor. Shows like *Friends*, in which it seemed that every character slept with every other character (of the opposite sex) at some point, and *Will & Grace* (in which only Grace seemed to score) treated the subject openly, with a matter-of-fact air. Perhaps the naughty subtext of *The Bob Cummings Show* opened the door for the more frank sitcoms to come.

puffing and scheming, Bob Collins ultimately fared no better with women than Dobie did.

In what we think of as the moralistic Republican society of the '50s, there was a whole lot of sex going on, albeit covertly. Understand, the word was never mentioned, but let's face it, underneath a veneer that seemed only slightly naughty, every character in this sitcom (except for DeCamp) was obsessed with S-E-X. Everyone knew what Bob was up to, and what Schultzy and

Bob Cummings

One of the first movie stars unafraid to turn his talents to television, Bob Cummings found his first fame on Broadway. Wanting to distinguish himself from the pack of young Broadway hopefuls, Cummings passed himself off as a young Englishman under the moniker Blade Stanhope-Conway. The ruse actually worked—and Cummings, or, rather, *Conway*, was cast in the 1931 drama *The Roof*. Next he tried his luck in Hollywood, this time as a Texan named Brice Hutchins. Again, the charade proved successful and Cummings, or rather, *Hutchins*, broke into pictures as an extra, leading to a series of small roles followed by a return to Broadway in the *Ziegfeld Follies of 1934*, in which he introduced the song "I Like the Likes of You." Fox eventually signed him to star opposite Betty Grable in *Moon over Miami*. His film roles grew in stature at Universal, then Paramount, alternating between the serious (*King's Row* and *Saboteur*) and the light comic. Television claimed him in

1950: he made appearances on *Your Show of Shows* and soon starred in his first series, 1952's *My Hero* (as the oddly named Robert S. Beanblossom). He still made time for the movies, appearing in his second Hitchcock film, *Dial M for Murder*, in 1954. *The Bob Cummings Show* followed the next year, making him a full-fledged television star. In 1961, he starred in a comedy/adventure series, *The New Bob Cummings Show*, in which he played a mystery-solving pilot, which he was in real life (a pilot, that is). His last sitcom was the cult favorite *My Living Doll* (right) in 1964, costarring Julie Newmar. They famously didn't get along, and Cummings quit the series with five episodes left to film. That same year brought his two notable big-screen appearances, *What a Way to Go* and *The Carpetbaggers*. He continued to work in film and television until 1986.

Cummings, a health food and exercise fanatic, looked fantastically fit on the show, an added bonus for female viewers. The male audience, likely just as thwarted in their own fantasies, had plenty of eye candy to keep them occupied, including busty cult icon Joi Lansing and Ingrid Goude (Miss Sweden of 1955, playing herself) as two of Bob's regular models. One got the impression that the writers perfectly captured Bob Cummings's offscreen personality (except for his wolflike behavior, that is. In real life he was a happily married man with five children). This made the character easy for him to play and a helluva lot of fun for cast, crew, and audiences alike. Though there are exceptions (Pearl Bailey and Danny Kaye come to mind), an audience can't usually be fooled into thinking a performer is nice when he or she is actually really, really mean. Cummings and company all came across as swell folks having a great time—and that inspired us to have a great time, too.

Nancy Kulp

Long, lean, and lanky Nancy Kulp was a sitcom veteran whose acting career was an unplanned detour. The Harrisburg, Pennsylvania, native started in show business as a studio publicist, but her—shall we call unique—look interested legendary director George Cukor and casting director Billy Golden. Kulp was smart enough to take the advice of the two veterans and, only three weeks after landing in California, found herself appearing in the film *The Model and the Marriage Broker* in 1951. Though she played minor parts in *Shane*, *Sabrina*, and *A Star Is Born*, it was as a character comedienne on television that she made her mark. Her appearance on *I Love Lucy* (as a British maid in the famous "Lucy Meets the Queen" episode) brought her into the Desilu family, and she soon appeared with her redheaded boss in the film *Forever, Darling*. Finding her niche as a WASPy beanpole of a Gal Friday, she became a semihousehold name playing Pamela Livingston on *The Bob Cummings Show*. Her second major sitcom role, the lovesick, high-strung Miss Jane Hathaway on *The Beverly Hillbillies*, became her stock-in-trade, and she continued to play variations of it throughout the rest of her career. In 1984, Kulp ran for a congressional seat in Pennsylvania but lost the bid after former *Hillbillies* costar, Buddy Ebsen, filmed a political ad opposing her extreme liberalism.

CAST

Bob Cummings	....	Bob Collins
Rosemary DeCamp	..	Margaret MacDonald
Ann B. Davis	....	Charmaine "Shultzy" Schultz
Dwayne Hickman	....	Chuck MacDonald
Nancy Kulp	....	Pamela Livingston
Lyle Talbot	....	Paul Fonda
Bob Cummings	....	Grandpa Collins
King Donovan	....	Harvey Helm
Mary Lawrence	....	Ruth Helm
Charles Herbert	....	Tommy Helm
Joi Lansing	....	Shirley Swanson
Lisa Gaye	....	Collette DuBois
Ingrid Goude	....	Herself
Gloria Marshall	....	Mary Beth Hall
Lola Albright	....	Kay Michaels

Opposite top: Rosemary DeCamp, the voice of reason on every television show on which she appeared, watches over her lothario little brother.

Top: The conservative Buddy Ebsen and dyed-in-the-wool liberal Nancy Kulp, in the only instance in which the two actors ever saw eye to eye.

Above: The forever frustrated Schultzy (Ann B. Davis) scowls at Bob and his nubile typing pupil.

THE BOB NEWHART SHOW

⬤ | **1972–1978** | **142 episodes**

Bob Hartley, a happily married Chicago psychologist riddled with almost as much insecurity as his patients have, stammers his way through life's puzzling contradictions.

Mild-mannered Bob Newhart, who had become a comedy star with several hit albums in the early 1960s (winning three Grammy Awards, including Album of the Year, for his first recording, *The Button-Down Mind of Bob Newhart*), might at first have seemed an unlikely person to anchor a situation comedy. His delivery was casual (deceptively so) and his trademark hesitations and stammers were at odds with the quick pace of half-hour television. In addition, Newhart's most famous routines were one-sided telephone conversations, so his material was not tailor-made for dialogue, as was the give-and-take act of George Burns and Gracie Allen. But, guided by the gifted creators David Davis and Lorenzo Music, *The Bob Newhart Show* became one of the wittiest, drollest comedies of the 1970s, pioneering a subtle form of humor that would later be the hallmark of such hits as *Taxi* and *Cheers*.

Davis and Lorenzo's angle was to cast Newhart as a psychiatrist, giving him ample opportunities for his deadpan reactive comedy. But before agreeing to the project, Newhart had two conditions: that they change his character from a psychiatrist to a psychologist so he would not be seen as making fun of the truly mentally ill (group therapy, all the rage in 1972, would plop Newhart smack dab in the middle of a whole pack of eccentrics); and that his character not have any children, to avoid what he saw as the pitfall of the "goofy dad."

The doctor is in: Bob Newhart as Bob Hartley, permanently (and rightly) memorialized by the TV Land cable channel in 2004 as a statue in downtown Chicago.

To support their unique star, Davis and Music were lucky enough to secure the talents of four first-rate light comedians, all of whom complemented Newhart perfectly, seamlessly falling in step with the very specific comic tempo that Newhart had been honing for over a decade. The major find was the beautiful, husky-voiced Suzanne Pleshette to play his wife. Until then, she had been known as a dramatic actress, but on *The Bob Newhart Show* she revealed a real flair for comedy, creating in Emily Hartley one of the smartest, sexiest, no-nonsense wives in sitcom history. As the workplace contingent, relative unknowns Peter Bonerz as swinging orthodontist Jerry Robinson and Marcia Wallace as their tart-tongued receptionist Carol Kester fueled the easygoing, "around the water cooler" camaraderie that was absolutely vital. And as the Hartleys' neighbor, airline navigator Howard Borden, the wonderful Bill Daily (already a legendary sidekick from five seasons as Roger Healey on *I Dream of Jeannie*) added his own fumbling, nervous delivery to the mix.

Newhart and company struck a singular tone in sitcoms: comfortable, low-key, with nary a raised voice. Though the show was rarely sexually explicit, with a childless married couple, a divorced neighbor (in some ways, Howard Borden was the Hartley's unofficial child, so dependent he was on them), and two single co-workers, it did reflect urban life in the swinging 1970s like none other. This was not the hard-hitting humor of *All in the Family* or even the heightened workplace reality of *Mary Tyler Moore*. Its closest cousin, tone-wise, was *The Dick Van Dyke Show*, with its equal balance of home and work life. (The comic bedroom scenes of Bob and Emily Hartley were, in terms of intimacy and naturalism, similar to the exchanges of Rob and Laura Petrie, and Wallace and Bonerz were the 1970s equivalents of Rose Marie and Morey Amsterdam.) And while it occasionally struck a more serious tone, the show was not out to tilt at societal windmills, mining the humor from the human condition in the gentle way that Newhart's observational stand-up did. Its zaniest moments occurred within the confines of Bob Hartley's office, with the loopy assortment of lonely malcontents that made up his group-therapy sessions:

Bob Newhart

Soft-spoken comic genius Bob Newhart was born in a suburb of Chicago (where he would later set his first sitcom) and went to college to pursue a business degree. Working as an accountant and an adman, he began developing comedy routines and submitting them to local radio stations. When a disk jockey introduced Newhart to a record executive at Warner Bros. Records, he was signed to the fledgling label and became the closest thing to an overnight sensation, knocking Elvis Presley off the top of the *Billboard* charts with his first album. Expanding his phone conversation routines into a full-length stand-up act, Newhart was an irreverent, slyly subversive breath of fresh air, and his career took off like a rocket with several more albums, a short-lived variety show, and many television appearances, including sitting in for Johnny Carson on *The Tonight Show* eighty-seven times. Tiring of the grind of the stand-up schedule, Newhart conquered series television with his eponymous sitcom. After *The Bob Newhart*

Show's six year run, he made a few films before returning to CBS with the *Newhart* series, running another eight years. In 1992, he tried series TV once again with the short-lived *Bob*, which, despite much promise and a superb supporting cast, was abandoned by CBS and relegated to no-viewers land. After another disappointment with *George and Leo*, starring alongside Judd Hirsch (another subtle comic actor who had made his mark in the ensemble sitcoms of the 1970s), Newhart decided once and for all that the tide had turned. Television had changed, evidenced acutely when some whippersnapper CBS suit chided Newhart for stammering too much, suggesting that he pick up his cues. We can only picture the brilliant, wordless "take" that Newhart gave that moron in response.

CAST

Bob Newhart .... Bob Hartley

Suzanne Pleshette .... Emily Hartley

Bill Daily .... Howard Borden

Peter Bonerz .... Jerry Robinson

Marcia Wallace .... Carol Kester Bondurant

Jack Riley .... Elliot Carlin

Florida Friebus .... Lillian Bakerman

John Fiedler .... Emil Peterson

Larry Gelman .... Dr. Tupperman

Renée Lippin .... Michelle Nardo

Pat Finley .... Ellen Hartley

Will Mackenzie .... Larry Bondurant

Noam Pitlik .... Victor Gianelli

Tom Poston .... Cliff Murdock, a.k.a. "The Peeper"

Left: Marcia Wallace and Peter Bonerz (later a successful director of *Murphy Brown* and *Friends*) as Bob Hartley's workplace comrades. Think of them as swinging '70s versions of *The Dick Van Dyke Show*'s Buddy and Sally.

Below: Bob tries to cure Emily of her fear of flying in a first-season episode. Penny Marshall as the flight attendant fails to instill much confidence.

Jerry: Have you ever been thrown over for a twenty-two-year-old guy? **Carol:** As a matter of fact, yes.

the milquetoast Emil Peterson (John Fiedler), the downright nasty Elliot Carlin (Jack Riley), the overweight and unhappy Michelle Nardo (Renée Lippin), and sweet old Mrs. Bakerman (Florida Friebus), who often seemed to come to group just to have a captive audience to knit for.

Yes, there was the wonderful support of its actors; its thoughtful, human writing; and its smart direction—but without a doubt, *The Bob Newhart Show* succeeded primarily because of the expertly blank, quizzical characterization of its star. The show became such an enjoyably com-

fortable destination for adult television viewers that the CBS programming block, which also included *Mary Tyler Moore* and the variety classic *The Carol Burnett Show*, turned Saturday from International Date Night into a great night to stay home and curl up with some good comedy.

OFF THE SET

THE BOB NEWHART SHOW spawned a popular beer-drinking game among college students. Whenever a character said "Bob," each player had to take one swig; whenever someone said "Hi, Bob," each had to chug the whole beer. Over the course of the six seasons of the show, the phrase, "Hi, Bob" was said 256 times, with Howard Borden racking up 118 of its utterances.

SUZANNE PLESHETTE WAS cast as Emily after appearing as a guest on *The Tonight Show*. Pleshette and Newhart sat next to each other on Johnny Carson's couch and the chemistry was immediate: the producers of the *Newhart Show* asked her to read for the role.

WHEN MURPHY BROWN finally got a competent secretary it was Marcia Wallace, reprising her role as Carol Kester from *The Bob Newhart Show*. True to form, the episode ended with Newhart appearing and begging Carol on bended knee to come back.

THE BRADY BUNCH

 | **1969–1974** | **117 episodes**

Carol Tyler Martin, a lady with three very lovely girls, marries Mike Brady, a widower with three boys of his own. They merge their families with the help of their wise housekeeper, Alice.

The whole bloomin' Brady Bunch, proving that honeymoons are for eleven (counting Tiger the dog and Fluffy the cat).

Here's the story: *The Brady Bunch*, the first TV series to be created and produced by Paramount Studios, was the brainchild of *Gilligan's Island* whiz Sherwood Schwartz. When Schwartz first pitched the premise of the Brady clan, it was rejected as too unbelievable. A year later, it suddenly seemed more plausible, thanks to the success of the 1968 Lucille Ball/Henry Fonda movie *Yours, Mine and Ours*, about a blended family with a total of eighteen children.

Living in a house designed by the family's own patriarch, who had flouted every known tenet of architectural reasoning in building it (there was an impressive cathedral-ceiling living room, yet only one bathroom—and no visible toilet—for six children), the Bradys were in many ways completely at odds with most American families of the time. Note, for instance, the furor that arose in the their household when oldest son, Greg, was sus-

Add to the mix six kid actors with refreshingly natural instincts who, in the thirty-five-plus years since the show went on the air, have all admirably managed to avoid lengthy prison terms. The writers understood that the Brady kids and their birth order mirrored the reality of many middle-class families. There was Greg, the oldest and grooviest; "Marcia, Marcia, MARCIA," the California Golden Girl; Peter, the prankster/schemer; Jan, the patron saint of the angst-ridden middle child; Bobby, who set a record for dream sequences…playing football with Joe Namath, becoming the billiards hustler of Clinton Elementary School, witnessing the slaughter of his entire family by that "mean, dirty killer" Jesse James…in fact, he was the only Brady kid who seemed to dream at all. And of course there was the lisp-impaired Cindy, the "youngest-one-in-curls."

pected of smoking a mere cigarette while, throughout the United States, many fourteen-year-olds were smoking somewhat stronger things. The Bradys were more reminiscent of the suburban American families of *Leave It to Beaver* and *Father Knows Best*, updated to 1969 by simply substituting the phrase "pizza parlor" for "malt shop" and the adjectives "heavy" or, better yet, "groovy" for "neato" and "keen," two of Theodore Cleaver's favorites. To the Brady kids, everything was groovy: clothes (a.k.a. "threads"), living in the attic, chicks with freckles, and Davy Jones. And although the show was "high concept," as were most of the sitcoms of its time (you know, astronaut meets genie in a bottle, nun discovers she can fly, Eva Gabor milks a cow), the plotlines of *The Brady Bunch* trod the well-worn territory of many of the shows that had come before it: a first kiss, catching the measles, losing one's favorite doll, having to get braces.

Of course, in the face of these weekly crises, there were always words of wisdom from Mom and Dad, and everything was tied up in a nice, clean, twenty-four-minute bow by the end. In roles originally intended for Gene Hackman and Joyce

Bulifant, the parental units were played by the perfectly matched Robert Reed and Florence Henderson. A recruit from Broadway, Henderson had shown off her comic flair as a guest on several *Dean Martin Shows*, and Robert Reed had proven a fine dramatic actor in such series as *The Defenders*. In retrospect, creator Sherwood Schwartz was exactly right in his ultimate choices, as he had been in the recasting of three out of seven roles after the first *Gilligan's Island* pilot, because for all of Robert Reed's complaints about the show (he was extremely vocal about his displeasure with what he felt were the unrealistic aspects of the series, constantly pushing it to be more "issue oriented"), he had the clean-cut looks and light comic touch that Hackman lacked, while Florence Henderson brought realism and a hint of glamour (after all, she invented the mullet!) to the role of Carol Brady that the pert Bulifant, though a thoroughly charming comedienne, didn't possess.

Balancing any potential tooth-rotting was the show's ace in the hole, Ann B. Davis, playing a variation on the persona she helped create (along with fellow *Bob Cummings Show* sidekick Nancy Kulp): TV's plain-Jane, perpetually single gal-confidante. As Alice Nelson, the Brady's faithful maid, Davis had the acerbic edge to offset any possibility of a "cute" overload that goes hand in hand with a pack of six children between the ages of seven and fourteen (see Eleanor Parker in *The Sound of Music* for the cinematic equivalent). Davis wore her blue uniform with pride, and at one time or other had a heart-to-heart with every member of the Brady family; indeed, in some ways, she was the ingredient that made the show work, for, as the only regular who was not a blood relation to either half of the Bradys, she could act as Switzerland in the United Nations conflicts of the household. Of course, Jan always felt she was Lichtenstein.

By the end of the fifth season, as the kids grew up and Greg got ready to graduate from Westdale High, the show brought on an annoyingly precocious younger relative, as many other shows did, to keep the age level from creeping up. So precocious was little Cousin Oliver that he was the first and only actor to utter the dreaded "S-E-X" word during the series' entire five-year run. Robbie Rist, a John Denver "Mini-Me," played Oliver, who came to stay with the Bradys while his parents went on an "expedition abroad." (Sure, sure…let's face it, nobody wanted to be around this kid.) By that point, Robert Reed had become so unhappy with the show that the powers that be were considering killing his character off if the show was renewed for a sixth season; in fact, he famously refused to appear in what turned out to be the final episode of the show, where Bobby sold "Neat and Natural Hair Tonic." Reed balked, saying kids didn't even know what hair tonic was in 1974, and his lines were divided up among other cast members.

Reed may have been right about the hair tonic but he was wrong about the show. There

OFF THE SET

THE HOUSE USED in the establishing shots of *The Brady Bunch* is located at 11222 Dilling Street (at the end of Klump Avenue) in Studio City, California. After the series went off the air, the house's owners did everything in their power (building a fence, landscaping, etc.) to mask the fact that they lived in one of the most famous houses in television history.

ALTHOUGH GREG WAS the family lothario, he never kissed any of the girls he dated. The only Brady child to have an onscreen kiss was Bobby. The object of his affection? Melissa Sue Anderson, who later played Mary Ingalls on *Little House on the Prairie*.

ON THE SHOW'S first day of shooting on the Paramount lot, Florence Henderson had her makeup applied sitting between Leonard Nimoy and William Shatner, who were preparing to shoot an episode of *Star Trek*. Neither Nimoy nor Shatner spoke to her.

Opposite Top: *The Brady Bunch* had TV's grooviest color scheme, with more prints per square inch than any show this side of *Laugh-In*.

Opposite bottom: The "boys' room." Note the dark panelling, the scattered toys on the floor, the blue bedspread, the painting of Emmett Kelly on the wall… in comparison to the Pepto-Bismol pink of the "girls' room." No breaking out of gender stereotypes here.

Left: The Bradys went on two three-episode-long vacations, one to the Grand Canyon and one to Hawaii, where, curiously, Robert Reed got on the plane with straight hair but disembarked with a Little Orphan Annie perm. Was it the humidity? Weird stuff like that never happened to Fred MacMurray.

is something about the lack of realism that about that contributes to the show's odd but undeniable charm. Approaching its fortieth anniversary, *The Brady Bunch* steadfastly refuses to fade away, with more people discovering (and rediscovering, for those of us who were there on Friday nights the first time around) its appeal through syndication. Corny? Sure. Square? Absolutely. But the Brady family has become permanently etched in the consciousness of most TV viewers born after 1960 in a way that is truly remarkable, because, despite its incongruities (a house with Astroturf in the backyard?), its reluctance to push the envelope creatively (the famous "Cindy is the next Shirley Temple" episode), and its modest success in its original run (it was never ranked higher than number thirty-four in any of its five seasons), it has stayed with us. This is a testament to the genius of Sherwood Schwartz. And remember, as Mom always said, "Don't play ball in the house."

CAST

Robert Reed	Mike Brady
Florence Henderson	Carol Brady
Ann B. Davis	Alice Nelson
Maureen McCormick	Marcia Brady
Eve Plumb	Jan Brady
Susan Olsen	Cindy Brady
Barry Williams	Greg Brady
Christopher Knight	Peter Brady
Mike Lookinland	Bobby Brady
Allan Melvin	Sam Franklin
Robbie Rist	Oliver Martin

Left: Florence Henderson's obsession with Mike Lookinland's fly away hair destroys his concentration as he prepares for the all-you-can-eat ice cream pig-out on the *Cartoon King* show.

Perhaps no other show became as much of a cottage industry as *The Brady Bunch*. In addition to *The Brady Bunch Variety Hour*, seen here (note Geri Reischl, second from the right, a.k.a. "Fake Jan"), there were two spinoffs (*The Brady Brides* and *The Bradys*), an animated series (just the kids, joined by a pair of talking pandas...huh?), reunion TV movies, two feature films, and a reality show, not to mention albums, lunch boxes, and other merchandise. Question: If Robert Reed was embarrassed by the plotlines in the original series, why did he fling himself with such abandon into a disco medley alongside Rip Taylor and the cast of *What's Happening*?

Ann B. Davis

As Alice on *The Brady Bunch*, Ann B. Davis was forever trying get a proposal from Sam the butcher, but wore duty shoes, no makeup, and could outrun any of the kids on the show. Indeed, Alice was so no-nonsense that at times her man-craziness seemed a bit suspect—until the episode where her cousin Emma (also played by Davis), straight out of twenty years as a sergeant in the WACs and tough as burlap, came on the scene and in one fell swoop, made Alice seem positively girly by comparison. A gifted comedienne with charm to spare, Davis was the television equivalent of the wise-cracking sidekick in the movies, a small-screen Mary Wickes or Eve Arden. (On TV, Arden wasn't really an "Eve Arden type" as she was the star of her show): Davis was cheerful, energetic, but with eyebrows permanently arched and never afraid to appear with her hair in curlers. She had helped blaze a trail as the loyal-to-a-fault assistant Schultzy on *The Bob Cummings Show* (below), and her charac-ter's lineage extends back to Zelda Gilroy on *Dobie Gillis* and Sally Rogers on *The Dick Van Dyke Show*, through Carol Kester on *The Bob Newhart Show* and Sergeant 'Gunny' Bricker on *Major Dad*. Sadly, it's a television archetype that is in danger of disappearing altogether, what with the beautification of the sitcom, and we are all the worse for it.

Jan: Well, all day long at school I hear how great Marcia is at this or how wonderful Marcia did that! Marcia, Marcia, Marcia!

Above: As she does at least four days a week, Marcia comes home from school (or as Maureen McCormick pronounced it, *skule*) to tell Alice her "superfantastic news." Note Jan's half-smile; she's clearly putting on a brave front. Soon the voices in her head will start again.

Right: Allan Melvin as doofus Barney Hefner, with Martin Balsam and Carroll O'Connor in *Archie Bunker's Place*.

Allan Melvin

The epitome of the word "galoot," character actor Allan Melvin made a career of playing slightly dopey sidekicks. In addition to his regular roles as Corporal Steve Henshaw on *The Phil Silvers Show* and Sergeant Charley Hacker on *Gomer Pyle*, he had recurring roles on two other sitcoms, as Sam the butcher on *The Brady Bunch* and as Archie Bunker's friend Barney Hefner on *All in the Family*. In addition to making many, many guest appearances, often playing military men or police officers, he was a member of *The Dick Van Dyke Show*'s group of repertory actors, playing such varied roles as Sam Pomeroy, Sam Pomerantz, Sol Pomerantz, and Harrison B. Harding. A highly successful animation actor, he was one of the mainstays at Hanna-Barbera Studios for thirty-five years. His most famous cartoon role? The voice of Magilla Gorilla ("Won't you buy him? Take him home and try him?").

CAR 54, WHERE ARE YOU?

NBC | **1961–1963** | **60 episodes**

Two New York police patrolmen—big, oafish Gunther Toody and lanky, shy
Francis Muldoon—have been partners as long as anyone can remember.

Believe it or not, *Car 54* was the first sitcom about policemen (not counting *The Andy Griffith Show*, which was about a sheriff and a deputy from a town that saw precious little crime). It was followed by such series as *Barney Miller, Arresting Behavior, Police Squad, Baker's Dozen*, and recently, *Reno 911!* Some feel that *Car 54* was the funniest of all of them and, for its die-hard fans, maybe even the funniest sitcom ever.

Of course, for full appreciation, you have to understand its New York Jewish style of humor, descended from vaudeville through radio to television. Creative visionary Nat Hiken didn't just write hilarious scripts for the show, he populated it with funny people who have all too recognizable quirks and faults. They are nice and kind and jealous and perpetually unaware, but the scrapes and misunderstandings they find themselves in never grow out of selfishness or greed. When Toody goes undercover with a gang of bank robbers, is it his fault he forgets himself and yells out, "Cops! Let's get out of here!"? Or that he forgets the name of the bank and helps the gang rob a different one? In fact, the one time Toody does solve a crime it's because he watches *Crimebusters*, the same television show as the criminals.

When a team of crooks rents a storefront next door to a bank with the intention of drilling through the wall, who do you think helps them? And when Muldoon robs a bank while trying to get money from the precinct health fund for Officer Schnauser, it's all a misunderstanding. Is it Toody's fault that when he

Officers Toody and Muldoon (Joe E. Ross and Fred Gwynne) attempt to figure out how they can be at a holdup in the Bronx, a fight in Brooklyn, and a traffic jam in Harlem all at the same time.

arrests pickpocket Wally Cox, he has his own pocket picked and Cox uses Toody's ID and badge to arrest other pickpockets? And isn't it an honest mistake when Toody and his wife Lucille rent out their spare bedroom to a counterfeiter disguised as a priest?

Toody and Muldoon were the rare sitcom leads who were not especially bright, though they had hearts of twenty-four-karat gold. Muldoon was smarter than Toody, but not smart enough to extricate himself from what can only be described as tortured situations. To compound matters, Muldoon was utterly hopeless around women, and more than a few episodes revolved around his acute shyness and insecurity.

Mention must also be made of Hiken's insistence that the 53rd Precinct, like Sergeant Bilko's platoon, be integrated as a matter of course. It was groundbreaking that such marvelous black performers as Ossie Davis, Frederick O'Neal, and Nipsey Russell were just members of the precinct, without comment. When the boys in blue help one of the kids living in the precinct with his bar mitzvah(!), all the members of the 53rd are in attendance, blacks and whites, Jews and gentiles.

Members of the supporting cast were given moments to shine, and most of them did their best work for Hiken and his crew. Particular notable was Charlotte Rae as Sylvia Schnauser. Over the top, vain, and a little zaftig, Rae became one of the funniest characters on any sitcom. When Sylvia decides she wants a real wedding and makes husband Leo woo her all over again, when she imagines herself a great actress, or when she goes on a crash diet only to lose her will power in an explosion of gluttony, her timing and characterization are so brilliant you can hardly catch your breath. (Sadly, by the time Rae got to *Facts of Life* her funny bone had been removed with the skill of a surgeon.)

Car 54 was canceled despite good ratings and replaced by the Imogene Coca bomb *Grindl*. The show had been scheduled against Ed Sullivan, a certain-death slot anyway, and Hiken felt burnt out and decided to quit. Almost immediately afterward, sitcoms abandoned the cities for the suburbs and families stopped bickering and having angst. The show featured the last of a proud line of urban,

RIGHT: Al Lewis and Paul Reed, two of New York's finest yet nuttiest.

Nat Hiken

Today, Nat Hiken is all but forgotten, but in his heyday, from the 1950s into the '60s, he was considered one of the funniest of all television writers. He first came to notice as the lead writer of two radio shows, the *Fred Allen Show* and the brilliant and astoundingly underappreciated *The Magnificent Montague*, starring Monty Woolley, Pert Kelton, Anne Seymour, and, in a variety of roles, Art Carney. Carney wasn't the only actor whose career got a boost by being associated with Hiken, who also helped Dick Van Dyke, Alan Alda, and Fred Gwynne with early career breaks. Hiken made the leap to television with two zany comics, Milton Berle on the *Texaco Star Theater* and Martha Raye on her eponymous show. He then created one of the greatest sitcoms of all time, *The Phil Silvers Show* (also known as *You'll Never Get Rich* and *Sergeant Bilko*, depending if you saw it in first run or syndication).

Even though Hiken left the series halfway through its run, he had cast the die from which all future episodes were struck. The thing that all of Hiken's characters had in common was that no matter how scheming they might be (like Bilko); forever trying to get something for nothing; trying to buck the system; or sweetly stupid like the members of *Car 54*'s 53rd Precinct, they all had undeniably big hearts. An avowed liberal, Hiken believed in colorblind casting, at least as much as he could get away with in the first two decades of television. And he named his characters perfectly. The slob in Bilko's platoon was named Doberman and the 53rd Precinct boasted an Officer Schnauser.

Hiken died at age fifty-four in 1968, a great loss to television and comedy. His only film, *The Love God*, premiered a year later.

CAST

Joe E. Ross .... Officer Gunther Toody

Fred Gwynne .... Officer Francis Muldoon

Beatrice Pons .... Lucille Toody

Paul Reed .... Captain Martin Block

Albert Henderson .... Officer O'Hara

Nipsey Russell .... Officer Anderson

Jerome Guardino .... Officer Antonnucci

Duke Farley .... Officer Riley

Shelley Burton .... Officer Murdock

Joe Warren .... Officer Steinmetz

Al Lewis .... Officer Schnauser

Bruce Kirby .... Officer Kissel

Hank Garrett .... Officer Nicholson

Jim Gormley .... Officer Nelson

Charlotte Rae .... Sylvia Schnauser

Frederick O'Neal .... Officer Wallace

Molly Picon .... Mrs. Bronson

Below: Joe E. Ross and Imogene Coca as prehistoric lovebirds Gronk and Shadd on the wacky cult flop *It's About Time*.

flawed, three-dimensional human characters that began with *The Honeymooners* and *I Love Lucy* and wasn't resurrected until Norman Lear's *All in the Family* and *Maude*. (After another hiatus, Larry David came along and gave us *Seinfeld* and *Curb Your Enthusiasm*.)

Finally, for you whippersnappers out there who think *The Simpsons* is so clever for having different openings under the credits, the idea originated with *Car 54*.

Joe E. Ross

"Ooh! Ooh!" Joe E. Ross's catchphrase, along with "Do you mind? Do you mind?" and "Jumpin' Jehosaphat!" made him one of the most imitated comics of the early 1960s. His early career consisted of nightclub and emcee appearances in New York, Miami Beach, and the Schuster burlesque circuit out of Chicago. Ross's film career could be generously described as abysmal. He made his debut as a burlesque comic in the 1955 schlockfest *Teaserama*, alongside such bodacious babes as Bettie Page and Tempest Storm. Still working as a "blue" comic and getting nowhere, he got his lucky break while appearing at the Café Ciro in Miami. Nat Hiken and Phil Silvers caught Ross's shtick and hired him to play Mess Sergeant Rupert Ritzik on *The Phil Silvers Show*, where he was paired with Beatrice Pons, who would later follow him to *Car 54*. Next, he was cast in the Sherwood Schwartz series *It's About Time*, opposite Imogene Coca. Playing two cavepersons (to briefly bow to political correctness), the show quickly went the way of the dinosaur. Ross went back to a series of "D" pictures, including *Linda Lovelace for President* and *The Happy Hooker Goes to Hollywood*.

CHEERS

NBC | **1982–1993** | **275 episodes**

Sam Malone, a former Major League relief pitcher, runs a friendly Boston bar where everybody knows your name, with a staff as goofy as its roster of habitués.

Before 1982, many television shows split their time equally between work and home life (*The Andy Griffith Show*, *The Dick Van Dyke Show*, *I Dream of Jeannie*, *Julia*, *Mary Tyler Moore*, and *The Bob Newhart Show*, to name a few). Sitcoms that spent the vast majority of their time in a place of business were rare, with *Barney Miller* and *Taxi* as two notable exceptions. And then there was *Cheers*, which filmed its first season (romance and all) entirely within the confines of the Boston

watering hole, with not a single scene taking place outside the confines of *Cheers*'s main room, pool room, and office.

Created and developed by James Burrows and brothers Glen and Les Charles, the show was initially conceived as taking place at an inn, a sort of Americanized *Fawlty Towers* (An actual Yankee-ization of the hit Britcom was attempted two years later, titled *Amanda's Place* and starring Bea Arthur as a somewhat more butch John Cleese. It was a resounding flop.) When someone suggested the hit radio series *Duffy's Tavern* as a template, the

Rhea Perlman, Nicholas Colasanto, and Ted Danson as the original staff of the Place Where Everybody Knows Your Name.

setting of a friendly neighbor-hood pub was substituted and *Cheers* opened for business. Casting began, and although Fred Dryer and William Devane were considered for the role of Sam Malone, a recovering alcoholic bar owner, the creators were ultimately won over by Ted Danson and switched his character from retired football player to retired baseball player to accomodate Danson's tall, lanky frame. In the role of the snobbish, infuriating Diane Chambers, the choice came down to two actresses, Shelley Long and Julia Duffy. The sly, subtle Long

won out and the most famous sparring lovebirds in sitcom history were born.

Abandoned by her fiancé, and (as the narration of *The Odd Couple* says) with nowhere else to go, Diane takes a job as a cocktail waitress at Cheers, though she didn't know her Amstel from her elbow. Almost immediately, the pseudo-intellectual *poseur* Diane starts to get under the skin of "Mayday" Malone, and

Shelley Long

With a natural sense of timing and innate intelligence, Shelley Long is one of the underrated masters of sitcom acting. Never afraid to point up the unlikable qualities in her characters, she played her best-known role, Diane Chambers on *Cheers*, as a person who saw herself as absolutely correct in her priggish behavior, making her simultaneously annoying and endearing (exactly the qualities that made Sam Malone want to either marry or throttle her). Born and raised in the Midwest, she worked in Chicago as a commercial actress and host of a magazine show. Moving west, she played a featured role in the very funny film *Night Shift* before becoming a full-fledged television star on *Cheers*. Making films during every hiatus, she starred in the well-reviewed *Irreconcilable Differences* and alongside Bette Midler in the women's buddy pic-

ture *Outrageous Fortune*. Leaving the cast of *Cheers* to become a full-time movie actress, she was in for a rude awakening. To put it mildly, the opportunities failed to materialize (with the bomb *Frozen Assets* representing the nadir of one of the fastest free-falls in show biz history), and within six years, Long was back on television in the short-lived sitcom *Good Advice*. They may have complained about her being difficult, but it certainly didn't stop the producers of both *Cheers* and its spin-off *Frasier* from calling on her for guest shots, as they knew what they had in both the character of Diane Chambers and the talent of Long. Rising again with a huge hit in *The Brady Bunch Movie*, Long tried her luck with yet another sitcom, the utterly lousy *Kelly Kelly*, which was canceled by WB after only seven airings. One gets the feeling that all she needs is some career traction and she'll be off and running again. Occasionally guest-starring these days (playing the wife of former *Cheers* castmate John Ratzenberger on *8 Simple Rules*), it's television's loss that no one can find a regular place for Long while so many of today's shows are riddled with actresses without her great gifts.

the fun begins. Coming at its humor from all angles, the show had the fish-out-of-water subplot, the comings and goings of the zany bar regulars, and the "opposites attract" romance between Sam and Diane. The spark that Danson and Long generated was the stuff that sitcom creators visit Lourdes in an attempt to achieve, and although the two actors may not have been great friends during filming, their chemistry propelled the show for an entire season on sexual tension alone. And with a razor-sharp supporting cast, including Nicholas Colasanto, playing Sam's former coach Ernie Pantuso; Rhea Perlman, who had played a recurring role as husband Danny DeVito's girlfriend, Zena, on *Taxi*, as the fertile cocktail waitress Carla Tortelli; and George Wendt and John Ratzenberger as bar fixtures Norm Peterson and Cliff Clavin, the show had the character-driven humor and ensemble acting that had helped propel such forerunners as *Mary Tyler Moore* and *Taxi* to success.

Cheers was not a ratings hit right off the bat, however, ranking dead last in the Nielsens and coming dangerously close to being canceled at the end of its freshman year. But with rave reviews and a growing base of fans, *Cheers* built its audience during summer reruns and, by the premiere of its second season, had a devoted following of educated, professional television viewers (then the target audience for sitcoms…today, networks aim for the coveted demographic of fourteen-year-olds with nonexistent attention spans who spend most of their time on MySpace and have complete control of their parents' Amex Gold card).

The show maintained a subtle yet insistent undercurrent of class conflict throughout its run, with Diane's highbrow aesthetic completely at odds with the working-class Carla and the clueless Coach. Later, husband-and-wife psychiatrists

Frasier and Lilith (played by Kelsey Grammer and the deadpan, cadaverous Bebe Neuwirth), tried to bring culture to the poor unfortunates at *Cheers*, and the gang of barflies responded by taking Frasier on a "snipe hunt." Diane's replacement, Rebecca Howe (Kirstie Alley), made it her goal in life to nab a wealthy, powerful man but ended up with a plumber, and the budding romance and eventual wedding of naive farm boy Woody Boyd (Woody Harrelson), Coach's replacement, and his equally naive but loaded girlfriend Kelly (the object of the hit love song, words and music by Woody Boyd, titled "Kelly") further explored class difference and friction.

Speaking of friction, amid rumors of not being the easiest person to work with and having an eye on movie star-

Ted Danson

Another natural for the sitcom form, Ted Danson is best known for his role as Sam Malone in the television series *Cheers* (1982). He and his wife, actress Mary Steenburgen, starred in and were executive producers of the CBS comedy series *Ink*. Danson came back in 1998 for a six-season run as the misanthropic doctor John Becker on the CBS hit *Becker*. Although he has proved himself as a fine dramatic actor, not only on some of the more serious episodes of *Cheers* but in such television films as *Something About Amelia*, his comic gifts have continually propelled him back to TV comedy. In the fall of 2006, he starred in the ABC sitcom *Help Me Help You*, playing a shrink (shades of both Bob Hartley and Frasier Crane) who leads a therapy group. Danson's great success on TV is all the more surprising when you consider that his heavy brow all but obscures his eyes, which are two of an actor's greatest tools. Unable to use his deep-set eyes in the way that a Lucille Ball or a Jack Benny did, Danson has honed his skills as a subtle physical actor, the tiniest change in his posture giving a punch line that extra oomph that he's unable to covey with an eye roll or double take.

Also a passionate environmentalist, Danson is one of the best-liked performers in show business, deserving every minute of his long career.

dom, Long decided to leave *Cheers*, then a bona fide smash, after its fifth season. People thought the show would never regain momentum, but cagily, the producers hired an actress totally at odds with the character of Diane Chambers. Kirstie Alley, brunette, curvy, and smoky voiced, took the show in a more blatantly sexual, yet somehow more touching, direction, and the emergence of Alley as a major comic force was frankly exciting to watch. After half a season of treading water, with Alley doing variations of a Bacall ice queen, the writers began to find her comic rhythm, and by the time she plopped herself into the back of Roger Rees's limousine in the eighth season, only to find another woman with him ("Ballerina, why don't you make like a swan and die?"), she had risen to the top of the class. In the last ten minutes of that episode, titled "Finally!" Alley ran a comic obstacle course of heights and depths not seen since Mary Richards went to Chuckles the Clown's funeral.

The Dick Van Dyke Show called it quits after five seasons and *Mary Tyler Moore* went off the air after seven years; perhaps the gang at *Cheers* outstayed their welcome by a year or two. By the show's ninth season, it had branched out in so many directions that it had as many supporting characters as *Dynasty* just prior to the Moldavia massacre. With eight actors billed at the top of the show (there were only five in the first season), the writers were juggling too many subplots, giving main characters short shrift. Sometimes they had only three or four lines in an episode.

So, after eleven seasons, the gang closed up shop to count their residuals, with Kelsey Grammer's *Frasier* spinning off to Seattle on his own series, becoming the longest-running character in sitcom history (an earlier *Cheers* spin-off, based on Carla's ex-husband and called *The Tortellis*, was canceled after thirteen episodes). A seminal show in terms of its smart writing, expert acting and all-around class, *Cheers* has become exactly like its setting: a warm, comfortable place into which to pop your head and have a few laughs with familiar faces.

Top: A passionate theatre buff, *Cheers*'s casting director Jeff Greenberg regularly called upon New York stage actors for guest shots, including the brilliant Frances Sternhagen as Cliff's mother, Esther Clavin.

Middle: Another import from Broadway, Harvey Fierstein, makes a guest appearance as Rebecca Howe's obviously gay high school boyfriend. Obvious to everyone but Rebecca, that is.

Bottom: Kelsey Grammer, on his way to an equally impressive run on his spinoff, *Frasier*, tries to determine if Bebe Neuwirth (plucked from a career in musical comedy), as wife Lilith, actually possesses a pulse.

Opposite top: Sawed-off spitfire Rhea Perlman landed her gig as Carla on *Cheers* after playing a recurring role as Danny DeVito's girlfriend on *Taxi*.

Opposite bottom: The gang at the far end of the bar includes comic cutups George Wendt, Woody Harrelson, and John Ratzenberger.

Norm: It's a dog-eat-dog world, and I'm wearing Milk Bone underwear.

CAST

Ted Danson	Sam Malone
Shelley Long	Diane Chambers
Nicholas Colasanto	Ernie "Coach" Pantusso
Rhea Perlman	Carla Tortelli LeBec
George Wendt	Norm Peterson
John Ratzenberger	Cliff Clavin
Woody Harrelson	Woody Boyd
Kelsey Grammer	Dr. Frasier Crane
Bebe Neuwirth	Dr. Lilith Sternin-Crane
Kirstie Alley	Rebecca Howe
Frances Sternhagen	Esther Clavin
Paul Willson	Paul
Dan Hedaya	Nick Tortelli
Jean Kasem	Loretta Tortelli
Jay Thomas	Eddie LeBec
Jackie Swanson	Kelly Gaines
Roger Rees	Robin Colcord
Tom Skerritt	Evan Drake
Keene Curtis	John Allen Hill
Alan Koss	Mike
Philip Perlman	Phil
Al Rosen	Al
Harry Anderson	Harry "The Hat" Gittes
Anthony Cistaro	Henri

COACH

| 1989–1997 | 200 episodes

Coach Hayden Fox and his bumbling assistants try to get a few wins out of the Screaming Eagles, the sorry excuse for a football team at Minnesota State University.

Not many sitcoms have successfully revolved around sports figures, unless you count *Cheers*, which focused on a retired baseball player, or the ones that feature a "Monday-morning quarterback" (also known as the fat, beer-swilling, unfunny guy in the flannel shirt seen on many current shows). *Sports Night* was admired by critics but short lived; *Phenom*, about a teen tennis star, was a quick flop for *Who's the Boss* star Judith Light; and *A League of Their Own* and *The Bad News Bears*, both based on hit films, failed to replicate their source material's success. Hourlong shows such as *The White Shadow* have fared better, as the lack of a studio audience makes the on-the-field action aspect much more feasible.

A notable exception is *Coach*, a staple of ABC's lineup for most of the 1990s. Created by *Newhart* producer Barry Kemp and starring the likeable Craig T. Nelson, *Coach* centered on the coaching staff at fictional Minnesota State University. Drawing from his own college days, Kemp based his lead on legendary football coach Hayden Fry, head of the team at his alma mater, the University of Iowa. Most of the establishing shots for the series were shot in Iowa City, on the campus of U of I.

Kemp wisely cast the appealing Shelley Fabares as the coach's love interest, Christine Armstrong (in a neat twist, Fabares's mother was played by her real-life aunt, Nanette Fabray), and Jerry Van Dyke—who finally found a sitcom hit—as assistant coach Luther Van Dam. Mining humor from the stereotype of the not-so-bright jock, many of *Coach*'s episodes revolved around the stupidity of the coaching staff. One of the funniest involved the methodical destruction of Christine's apartment by an increasingly idiotic Hayden and Luther. Spilling grape juice on her newly installed white carpeting, they tried unsuccessfully to clean it up by renting a steam cleaner—managing to lock themselves out while their dinner caught fire, destroying her kitchen. The fiasco

ended with Hayden breaking down the door just as Christine came home. In another disaster, Luther burned Christine's wedding dress. The dynamic duo's solution? Paint the dress white and hope she doesn't notice. And people thought Gilligan was moronic.

For a show that was built around such comic nitwits, *Coach* did deal with a few serious topics, including infertility: At one point, in an attempt to father a child with Christine, Hayden wore a device to increase his sperm count—which somehow started to leak while he was a guest on Christine's TV talk show. Ultimately, Hayden approached star football player Troy Aikman to be a sperm donor.

 SITCOMS: THE 101 GREATEST TV COMEDIES OF ALL TIME

Jerry Van Dyke

Stammering, banjo-playing Jerry Van Dyke was destined for sitcom stardom but, unlike older brother Dick, he'd need his share of patience before he'd attain the stardom he desired as a stand-up comic. Working his way up through nightclubs, he appeared on his brother's show, playing Rob Petrie's narcoleptic brother, Stacey. CBS immediately recognized his high-energy talent and began to look for a showcase for his clowning. This began a series of missed opportunities and downright bad luck that kept him on the fringe of television stardom for almost thirty years. First, he was cast on Judy Garland's tumult-fraught variety show. Then came two unfortunate moves: turning down the role of Gilligan and passing up the chance to replace Don Knotts on *The Andy Griffith Show*. Instead, he opted for *My Mother the Car*, a legendary dog that is the punch line of show business jokes to this day. Next starring in the flop *Accidental Family*, Van Dyke spent most of the 1970s doing stand-up. After *13 Queens Boulevard*, another short-lived series, he was an infrequent presence on television, taking an occasional cruise on *The Love Boat* or trip to *Fantasy Island*. He was the original choice for handyman George Utley on *Newhart*, and creator Barry Kemp made up for Van Dyke's loss of the role to Tom Poston by casting him as goofy assistant coach Luther Van Dam on *Coach*, finally achieving the fame he had richly deserved for three decades.

Of course, with such a testosterone-fueled cast, the battle of the sexes was frequently addressed. Gender-based challenges in poker, fishing, and golf invariably ended with the women—led by Fabares—triumphing and the men looking like complete boobs. (After all, any show that makes the blithely bubble-headed Georgia Engel, as recurring character Shirley Burleigh, seem like one of the smarter characters has to be doing something right.)

In the show's seventh season—so often the time when a show's creators unleash such plot devices as shark jumping or (shudder) the addition of a child—Hayden was recruited by the fictional Orlando Breakers, owned by the eccentric millionaire Doris Sherman (Katherine Helmond, fresh off a long run on another ABC sitcom, *Who's the Boss?*). Moving the show's setting from Minnesota was intended to afford new plot twists, but in actuality, the opposite happened. Once Hayden turned pro, the show, like its contemporaries *Murphy Brown*, *Roseanne*, and *The Nanny*, relied more and more on celebrity cameos, mostly from the world of sports, including Frank Gifford, Larry King, Al Michael, Walter Payton, Dan Dierdorf, Mike Ditka, Joe Theismann, Dick Butkus, and Bobby Vinton (if you count the polka as a sport). The final two seasons of the show are generally considered to have been the weakest, with many episodes running on the fumes of previous ones and rehashing major plot points from the show's glory days.

CAST

Craig T. Nelson	Hayden Fox
Jerry Van Dyke	Luther Van Dam
Shelley Fabares	Christine Armstrong Fox
Clare Carey	Kelly Fox
Bill Fagerbakke	"Dauber" Dybinski
Pam Stone	Judy Watkins
Kris Kamm	Stuart Rosebrock
Kenneth Kimmins	Howard Burleigh
Katherine Helmond	Doris Sherman
Georgia Engel	Shirley Burleigh

Opposite: Craig T. Nelson and Shelley Fabares, as Hayden and Christine Fox, made one of the most appealing and realistic couples of 1990s sitcoms.

Above: Jerry Van Dyke, as Dave Crabtree, re-enacts the difficult breech birth he experienced on *My Mother, the Car*.

Right: Pam Stone, Bill Fagerbakke, Jerry Van Dyke, and Craig T. Nelson in one of the show's many "battle of the sexes" episodes.

THE COSBY SHOW

An upper-middle-class black obstetrician, his legal aid lawyer wife, and their kids face the usual family vicissitudes with honesty, kindness, and a little bit of jazz. Oh, and sweaters.

At this writing, Bob Newhart and Bill Cosby are tied for the self-named sitcom record. Newhart has had *The Bob Newhart Show*, *Newhart*, and *Bob*. Bill Cosby has had *The Bill Cosby Show*, *The Cosby Show*, and *Cosby*. Fans of both comedians are still confused over which sitcom is which. Cosby made things even more confusing because his second and third sitcoms both featured Phylicia Rashad as his wife.

The Cosby Show, starring Cosby as ob/gyn Cliff Huxtable, was one of television's most popular shows, sitcom or otherwise, and it broke the sitcom mold in several ways. Though Cosby originally envisioned a series about a working-class family, the Huxtables were working professionals for whom money wasn't a problem. They were a close-knit and proud black family, and certainly not any kind of stereotype, especially as compared to the denizens of such shows as *What's Happening!!* or *Gimme a Break*. The show's plot evolved as the series continued: the children grew up, left home, returned, brought back husbands or boyfriends, and so on, much as in real life. And, unlike the many sitcoms that gave us "very important episodes" or (like the Norman Lear series) dealt constantly with "educational" hot-button topics, *The Cosby Show* taught its lessons in an entertaining, almost subversive way. It was never preachy, and the show's overseer, "William H. Cosby, Jr., Ed. D.," as he was credited, made sure that the emphasis was on humor and heart. *The Cosby Show* never

Bill Cosby, as Heathcliff Huxtable, wearing the results of a particularly unsatisfying Father's Day.

Cliff gardens with his wife Clair (Phylicia Rashad), perhaps the only person who could get the better of the sly, all-knowing Cliff.

and cozy, it proved a salutary role model for all kinds of families. Cliff Huxtable had Bill Cosby's alternately silly and wise outlook, sometimes exasperated and sometimes even wrong—father didn't always know best on this series—but he was unerringly human.

Perhaps because the show was filmed in New York, away from studio scrutiny and under Cosby's absolute authority, it prospered without too much interference from the MFAs who ruled the networks. Not everything was smooth sailing, of course. Forgetting that a show can never be all things to all people, especially a show about a minority family, Cosby was often criticized for being unrealistic, for ignoring problems between the races, for not representing the majority of the black population. These were many of the same complaints lobbed by critics at *Amos 'n' Andy*, critics that included Bill Cosby. True, *Amos 'n' Andy* dealt in stereotypical behavior and perhaps some of the characters couldn't be held up as role models at a time when we greatly needed them, but—had either show been cast with white performers, it wouldn't have received any criticism at all.

resorted to the kind of sniping and wisecracks of sitcoms that relied on easy, character-deprived humor. And, perhaps most important, the members of the show's family got along and respected themselves and others. There was never the kind of friction that marked such classics as *The Honeymooners* or *All in the Family*, and though the show might have strayed a little too far into the soft

Bill Cosby

One of America's favorite stand-up comics/television stars/hucksters, Bill Cosby was the star of the film *Leonard Part 6*. We offer that bit of information up front to prove that even the mighty fail occasionally; otherwise, Cosby has had a remarkably successful career. His natural gift for comic observation was noticed by Carl Reiner, and after stand-up appearances on television variety shows and successful comedy albums, he landed an historic part on *I Spy*. The hip, big budget buddy comedy/adventure/spy show paired Cosby with a white actor, Robert Culp. This multiracial casting raised eyebrows at the time but it would scarcely merit a mention today, proving how far we've come—though perhaps not nearly as

far as we should have. Unlike fellow black comedians Richard Pryor, Dick Gregory, and others, Cosby wasn't political or profane, and he didn't base his act on black culture. A large part of his stand-up routine was concerned with his childhood in Philly, and he further mined this material for the animated series *Fat Albert* and the *Cosby Kids*, which followed the two-year run of his first sitcom, *The Bill Cosby Show* (left). Fat Albert, Weird Harold, and their friends would eventually enjoy a decade as a staple of children's programming. Though he dropped out of school after flunking tenth grade, Cosby eventually got his high school equivalency certificate, graduated from Temple University, and earned a doctorate in education. When *Fat Albert* ceased production in 1984, *The Cosby Show* began its eight-year run. Following *The Cosby Show*, he starred in another sitcom, *Cosby*. He currently acts as a public speaker and was the spokesman for Jell-O Pudding.

The Cosby Show reinvigorated the sitcom scene in the mid-'80s, consistently coming in right behind Dynasty and Dallas in the Nielsen top ten. In fact, it was one of only two sitcoms in the top ten in the '84–'85 season, finishing third in its first season (Family Ties was number five). Surprisingly, in the top thirty shows for the season there were only seven sitcoms (Cheers, Newhart, Kate & Allie, Night Court, and Webster were the others). By the next season, the show had hit the number one slot and stayed there for five seasons.

The Cosby Show was a respite from prime-time soaps (Knots Landing and Falcon Crest were also in the top ten) and action/detective series such as The A-Team, Simon & Simon, Magnum, P.I., Cagney & Lacey, and Hill Street Blues. The series definitely changed the television landscape for, by its second season, there were thirteen sitcoms in the top thirty, seven of which were in the top ten.

The success of the show proved its broad appeal. While many ethnic shows have been popular only with their own ethnicity (especially shows on the WB [now CW] and UPN networks), The Cosby Show cut across a broad demographic. The fact that it featured a black family seems neither to have helped nor hurt its success, just as the failure of Margaret Cho's All-American Girl was neither helped nor hurt by the fact that it featured a Korean family. Bill Cosby and his extended family were role models for all Americans, but they were perhaps most instructive to other producers, writers, actors, and directors of situation comedies and network executives who had the most to learn from the success of The Cosby Show.

Rudy: This is woman stuff. I really need to talk to Mom.
Cliff: I'm a gynecologist, and you want to talk to a lawyer?

Jay Sandrich

The son of noted film director Mark Sandrich, Jay Sandrich is one of television's leading sitcom directors. His remarkable career began as a second assistant director with Desilu Productions, working on I Love Lucy, Our Miss Brooks, and December Bride. Following stints on The Danny Thomas Show and The Dick Van Dyke Show, he turned to producing as an associate producer of the series Get Smart. Worrying about all the aspects of production rather than concentrating on rehearsals and shoots didn't suit his temperament, however.

Sandrich honed his skills as a director on episodes of That Girl, the underappreciated He and She, and Julia. His real break came when he became the leading director of Mary Tyler Moore for its first two seasons, eventually directing more than one hundred episodes. Sandrich commented that he loved the way Grant Tinker "created this wonderful atmosphere of being able to have a lot of fun at your work—plus you were working next door to people who were interesting and bright." Sandrich followed Tinker's lead and is known for creating a fun, creative, low-stress atmosphere on his sets. After nurturing the spin-off Phyllis, Sandrich became the lead director on Soap and fulfilled the same role on The Cosby Show, eventually directing 103 episodes of that sitcom. Along the way, he also directed episodes of such fine series as The Odd Couple, The Bob Newhart Show, Laverne and Shirley, Rhoda, WKRP in Cincinnati, Benson, It's a Living, Night Court, and The Golden Girls.

Ed. Weinberger

As a writer and producer, Ed. Weinberger has enjoyed remarkable success. Weinberger began his television career as a writer for the Johnny Carson *Tonight Show* and *The Dean Martin Show*. His first success was a doozy, when he wrote thirteen episodes for the hat-tossing *Mary Tyler Moore (*above, Weinberger with Moore and Gavin MacLeod*)*. Working with Stan Daniels on the show, the team set up an informal partnership, leaving *Mary Tyler Moore* in 1975 to create and produce its spin-off *Phyllis*.

Success led to more success, with a few glitches along the way. *Doc*, starring Barnard Hughes, was a highly regarded yet little watched sitcom that Weinberger executive produced along with Daniels. Their next series as writers and executive producers was a little something titled *Taxi*, which ran from 1978 to 1983 (Daniels was also one of the creators). They filled the same roles for the succes d'estime *The Associates*, hailed by the critics but ignored by the public. *Mr. Smith* came next, which concerned "a talking orangutan with an IQ of 256 that worked as a political advisor in Washington." No. Yes! When Wallace Shawn turned down the lead role (the voice of the orangutan, that is), it fell to Weinberger himself. Pulling himself out of that ignominy, he followed it with *The Cosby Show*, which he cocreated with Bill Cosby and Michael Leeson. After that, he created *Amen*, another success featuring an all-black cast. The last three sitcoms on which Weinberger worked, *Baby Talk*, *Sparks*, and *The Good News* were not successes, but he remains one of the most successful toilers in the field, helping turn out smart, entertaining television comedy.

CAST

Bill Cosby	Dr Heathcliff Huxtable
Phylicia Rashad	Clair Huxtable
Sabrina Le Beauf	Sondra Huxtable Tibideaux
Lisa Bonet	Denise Huxtable Kendall
Malcolm-Jamal Warner	Theodore Huxtable
Tempestt Bledsoe	Vanessa Huxtable
Keshia Knight Pulliam	Rudy Huxtable
Geoffrey Owens	Elvin Tibideaux
Joseph C. Phillips	Martin Kendall
Raven-Symone	Olivia Kendall
Clarice Taylor	Anna Huxtable
Earl Hyman	Russel Huxtable
Deon Richmond	Kenny ("Bud")
Carl Anthony Payne II	Cockroach

Opposite: Cosby and Keshia Knight Pulliam, as his youngest daughter, in one of the simple and truthful moments that made *The Cosby Show* the most successful family sitcom ever.

Below: Two views of the Cosby kids wearing the mid-'80s fashions that keep such shows as *Family Ties*, *Growing Pains* and *The Facts of Life* from aging well. These duds are an unwieldy melange of acid-washed denim and Jennifer Beals's secondhand *Flashdance* legwarmers.

OFF THE SET

TWO SHOWS REACHED the number one position in the ratings five years in a row—*The Cosby Show* and *All in the Family*.

THE HUXTABLE HOUSE is really in Manhattan, not Brooklyn. It's at 10 St. Luke's Place in Greenwich Village.

A NUMBER OF music greats appeared on the show, including Sammy Davis, Jr., Lena Horne, Betty Carter, Dizzy Gillespie, Tito Puente, B. B. King, Alicia Keys, Tony Orlando, Nancy Wilson, Leslie Uggams, and Stevie Wonder.

BILL COSBY'S PARTNER on *I Spy*, Robert Culp, appeared on the third season as Scott Kelly. The name was a combination of their *I Spy* character names—Kelly Robinson (Culp) and Alexander Scott (Cosby).

CURB YOUR ENTHUSIASM

HB◎ | **2000– present** | **50 through Spring 2007 episodes**

The real Larry David plays himself, sort of, and gets into a seemingly endless loop of misunderstandings, insults, and embarrassments.

When he and Jerry Seinfeld created the sitcom *Seinfeld*, Larry David perfected characters whose ids ruled their lives. Misanthropic and self-absorbed, they occasionally attempted to help their fellow man but always, always, their good works turned ugly. So it is—but magnified to the tenth power—on *Curb Your Enthusiasm*. The difference is that on his own show, David plays the lead character and emits the bulk of the annoyance with the world and, in turn, bears the brunt of the world's annoyance with him. The other characters (save his long-suffering wife and manager/best friend) tend to take an instant dislike to David, often for good reasons and despite his best efforts to make things right.

David has surrounded himself with an ensemble of bright, talented performers who are called upon to improvise each scene based on general directions. There are no scripted laugh lines, quips, or bon mots, and no studio audience to cater to. The result is that the whole proceeding has an air of reality—though the "reality" of David's world just might make you want to blow your brains out.

As on *Seinfeld*, the plots take off from the most minuscule of observations—the perils, minor idiocies, and quixotic turns of everyday life. From there, the plots escalate, sometimes taking unexpected turns but always coming to a satisfying finish where the various plot strands are tied up neatly. David perfected the interweaving of multiple complementary storylines when he worked on *Seinfeld*, but the technique has reached its apex with *Curb*

Constantly finding himself in the most painful, embarrassing situations, Larry David trips Shaquille O'Neal at a Lakers game while a horrified Richard Lewis looks on.

An understandably frustrated Ted Danson played himself on seven episodes of *Curb Your Enthusiasm*.

Your Enthusaism—and the freedom from censorship afforded by cable television has enabled David and company to attack themes that might have been verboten or at best disguised (remember "Master of His Domain"?) on network television. Thus, political incorrectness is the norm, as David inadvertently insults minorities, women, and religions with hilarious results. Nothing—*nothing*—is sacred, not even the Holocaust. Sex and sexual dysfunction provide another mother lode of Davidian humor: the very first episode concerned a tenting of David's pants that was misinterpreted by the world at large.

David's is the kind of humor that separates those who like to keep their minds engaged with a healthy dose of irony from those who prefer their brains to seep through their ears as they sit stupefied in front of the screen.

CAST

Larry David	Himself
Cheryl Hines	Cheryl David
Jeff Garlin	Jeff Greene
Susie Essman	Susie Greene
Richard Lewis	Himself
Shelley Berman	Nat David
Antoinette Spolar	Larry's receptionist
Paul Dooley	Cheryl's father
Julie Payne	Cheryl's mother
Wanda Sykes	Wanda

Larry David

Like many of his generation and the next, Larry David began his career as a stand-up comedian. He broke into television as a writer on *Fridays* and joined the *Saturday Night Live* writing team, though he insists that only one of his sketches ever made it onto the program. He spent the late '80s as an actor, appearing in a couple of minor films. With the turn of the new decade his career took off. He was the cocreator of *Seinfeld* and stayed with the series for six seasons, occasionally appearing on the show. When he left *Seinfeld* in 1996, he wrote and directed the film *Sour Grapes*. But television was his métier and in 1999, he wrote and appeared in an HBO comedy special, *Larry David: Curb Your Enthusiasm*. The success of that show led to the sitcom.

DECEMBER BRIDE

 | **1954–1961** | **157 episodes**

The ups and downs of Lily Ruskin, a widow who lives with her daughter, Ruth, and her husband, Matt. Next-door neighbor Pete and his unseen wife, Gladys, and Lily's best friend, Hilda, also feature in the comedy equation.

The 1950s was a turbulent decade in show business. Technology was changing the face of almost every medium, and the new ways in which Americans would receive their entertainment were throwing professionals for a loop. Recording formats slowed from 78 to $33^{1}/_{3}$; the heyday of radio was drawing to an end with the emergence of television; the end of the studio system saw the thinning of the rosters of stars and supporting players. For the first time, actors were drawn to what they had previously considered a sign of being washed up: the small screen.

In a day before the word "demographics" had been coined, television played host to a series of actors of a certain age. In those heady days of the new medium there was no particular imperative to tailor prime-time shows for a particular age range. There was just one demographic, the family (or, more accurately, the middle-class white family). It was taken for granted that the whole family would switch on the black-and-white console and be equally amused; and, surprisingly, teenagers were content to watch family shows starring performers decades older than they were.

The American public was entertained by the likes of William Bendix, Gertrude Berg, Stuart Erwin, Walter Brennan, Eve Arden, Ann Sothern, and Spring Byington, all stars of their own television series. Like most of them, Spring Byington began her performing career on Broadway, segued to Hollywood, and finally ended up on television. By the time *December Bride* rolled around, she was

Spring Byington and Verna Felton in a tug of war with neighbor Harry Morgan.

recognizable, even if not by name, by the majority of the public.

By today's standards, Spring Byington played the most outlandish, most unbelievable character on television—more jaw-droppingly unreal than a couple of ghosts who come back to give advice, or a talking beagle. Byington played a beloved mother-in-law. Get this: she lived with her son and his wife, and everyone got along just swell. In fact, Byington's character was the most popular gal in town, and that she only gently butted in on her daughter's marriage threatened to raise eyebrows into the stratosphere. This was an era in which a parent of a certain age was still allowed to be a vibrant individual, well regarded (well, regarded at all), and with—dare we say it with younger readers perhaps stumbling onto this chapter?—a sex life. Some episodes of *December Bride* revolved around the idea that mom deserved a man!

OFF THE SET

SINCE *DECEMBER BRIDE* took place in Westwood, California, a variety of stars guested on the show as themselves—including Mickey Rooney, Zsa Zsa Gabor, Ed Wynn, Fred MacMurray, Rudy Vallee, and Edgar and Francis Bergen.

Byington was surrounded by a particularly adept cast, with special homage to Verna Felton. Her entrances gave the show a jolt of energy and her wisecracks and do-anything spirit turned her into a kind of noncurmudgeonly William Demarest. This is no surprise, as *December Bride* was a product of the Desilu factory. Parke Levy, who created the series as well as writing, directing, and producing most of the episodes, made his one and only foray into television with the series. Like many series in the early '50s, *December Bride* concerned itself with the everyday matters: fighting a ticket, the arrival of a new baby (the mother was the unseen Gladys), a woman's role in the home. At the center of it all was Spring Byington, exhibiting gentle humor and self-deprecation.

Perhaps that's why *December Bride* isn't on reruns on some sort of retro "family channel," the type that picks up the shows that Nick at Nite and TV Land won't show. Maybe it's just because it's in black and white. Maybe it's because the lead isn't prepubescent. Or maybe it's just because audiences today wouldn't accept its outlandish premise and sweet demeanor.

Above: Spring Byington, Dean Miller, and Frances Rafferty, the stars of *December Bride*.

CAST

Spring Byington ....Lily Ruskin
Frances Rafferty ....Ruth Henshaw
Dean Miller ....Matt Henshaw
Verna Felton ....Hilda Crocker
Harry Morgan ....Pete Porter

Harry Morgan

Harry Morgan was actually Henry Morgan, but the popularity of the same-named comic satirist/commentator/game-show panelist forced him to change his name first to Henry "Harry" Morgan and then just Harry. Best known today as the brusque but fair Colonel Potter on *M*A*S*H*, Morgan went easily from light comedy to drama. He graduated from devil-may-care Pete Porter of *December Bride* to its spin-off, *Pete and Gladys*. Through his fifty-seven-year film career, which began in 1942, he ably juggled life on both the big and small screens. In fact, as Detective Bill Gannon, first appearing on the revival of *Dragnet* in 1967, he made an appearance in the film version twenty years later and in a 1995 episode of *The Simpsons*. He was the rare actor for whom success and identification with a popular television character didn't hurt his ability to be cast in a variety of roles.

He fulfilled the basic tenets of character acting: be recognizable to audiences (if not always likeable), be non-threatening, and create a vivid character. From roles in films as diverse as *The Ox-Bow Incident*, the musical version of *State Fair*,  *Madame Bovary*, *The Glenn Miller Story*, *How the West Was Won* (in which he played Ulysses S. Grant!), and *The Apple Dumpling Gang*, it seems there was never a role that couldn't be embodied perfectly by Harry Morgan.

DESIGNING WOMEN

 | **1986–1993** | **164 episodes**

The five members of an Atlanta interior design firm take on life's challenges while going through swatches.

In many ways similar to its contemporary, *The Golden Girls*, *Designing Women* had four main female characters, each unique. At its best, particularly during the first five seasons, its writing also mirrored *The Golden Girls* in its smart, witty, character-driven dialogue.

The anchor character, the wise, fiery, and outspoken Julia Sugarbaker, was played by the sassy Dixie Carter, while her sister, the vain, much-married Suzanne, was played by Delta Burke—a former beauty queen in real life and on the show. The two actresses had worked together four years earlier on another show created by *Designing Women* writer Linda Bloodworth, the short-lived 1982 sitcom *Filthy Rich*. The other two members of the Sugarbakers design firm were played by Jean Smart and Annie Potts, two of the best actresses on television, who brought the essential warmth factor to the show. Rounding out the cast was Meshach Taylor, who played Anthony, the Sugarbakers ex-con delivery man, the victim of an "unfortunate incarceration."

Unlike the characters on other shows set in a place of business, the cast of *Designing Women* spent precious little time actually working. Oh, sure, Charlene sometimes tapped a few numbers out on a calculator and Mary Jo lugged a portfolio around, but this was not the WJM newsroom, Barney Miller's 12th Precinct, or even Mel's Diner. Much of the time, the employees of Sugarbakers read magazines, kibitzed, and nibbled on a nice Bundt cake. In fact, if someone had turned on the show without knowing the premise and seen four attractive women lounging around a house with a long staircase heading upstairs, she might have thought it was a sitcom set in a high-class Southern bordello.

This is not to say that the show wasn't highly amusing, particularly in many of Carter's sharply written tirades.

Right: Overhearing a beauty contestant (Pamela Bowen) badmouthing her sister Suzanne, Julia Sugarbaker (Dixie Carter) launches into one of her legendary diatribes:

"You probably didn't know, *Marjorie*, that Suzanne was not just *any* Miss Georgia, she was *the* Miss Georgia. She didn't twirl *just* a baton, that baton was on *fire*. And when she threw that baton into the air, it flew higher, further, faster than any baton has ever flown before, hitting a transformer and showering the darkened arena with sparks! And when it finally did come down, *Marjorie*, my sister *caught* that baton, and 12,000 people jumped to their feet for sixteen and one-half minutes of uninterrupted thunderous ovation, as flames illuminated her tear-stained face! And *that*, *Marjorie*— just so *you* will know—and your *children* will someday know—is the *night* the *lights* went out in *Georgia*!

Opposite: The cast of *Designing Women*: Jean Smart, Annie Potts, Delta Burke, Dixie Carter, and, about to be wheeled out on a gurney and into traction, Meshach Taylor.

Julia Sugarbaker tended to voice the liberal political, moral, and social views of creator Linda Bloodworth-Thomason, a long-time friend and supporter of Bill Clinton. And many viewers identified with either Potts, as newly divorced Mary Jo Shively trying to support her kids on her own, or Smart, as the forever optimistic dreamer Charlene Frazier (later Stillfield, after marrying the man of her dreams, played by Doug Barr). Potts possessed that rare combination of great likeability and a dry delivery, and Smart provided genuine sweetness and the best Southern accent in the bunch, which was ironic considering that the other three women were all from below the Mason-Dixon Line whereas Smart was born and raised in Seattle.

By the third season, Delta Burke began to gain weight and her character broke out as one of the most over-the-top comic characters of the 1980s. When the show first went on the air, the slim, gorgeous Suzanne had seemed frivolous and, frankly, annoying. But her struggle with her weight humanized her and the writers went to town, pushing Suzanne into more and more outrageous territory, as in the classic episode where Suzanne, modeling a mink cape at a fashion show, got accosted by a group of antifur protesters.

Meshach Taylor was the prime beneficiary of Burke's blossoming. The perfect foil for the politically incorrect Suzanne, Anthony became a more important presence on the show, and many plots revolved around their unlikely friendship: Suzanne and Anthony are forced to share a motel room during a snowstorm; Suzanne tries to get Anthony to impersonate her maid, Consuela, at her citizenship test (where, in a wig and a house dress, the big question was whether he looked more like Jane Wyman or Mrs. Khrushchev); Suzanne accidentally shoots Anthony in the butt the night before his college graduation. As it developed, Burke and Taylor's relationship, though never remotely romantic, had the underpinnings of a great love story, a sort of Hepburn-and-Tracy match-up without the kiss in the final reel.

By the middle of the fifth season, the writing had become spotty, patched together around Smart's real-life pregnancy as well as Burke's personal problems and flagging reliability. When Smart announced she was not returning and Burke was fired, the show attempted to fill the void by tapping *Saturday Night Live* alumnus Jan Hooks to play Charlene's cousin Carlene, straight off the bus from Poplar Bluff, MO (in actuality, creator Linda Bloodworth-Thomason's hometown), and Julia Duffy, fresh from great success on *Newhart*, as Julia and Suzanne's cousin Allison. Hooks was an amusing addition but Duffy was an unmitigated disaster.

OFF THE SET

STARS JEAN SMART and Delta Burke met their husbands working on the show. Smart married actor Richard Gilliland, who played Mary Jo's boyfriend, J. D. Shackelford, and Burke married Gerald McRaney, who was guest-starring as one of Suzanne's ex-husbands. Dixie Carter's husband, actor Hal Holbrook, was a recurring character as well, playing Julia's boyfriend, Reese Watson. Carter's daughters, Mary Dixie and Ginna Carter, guest-starred as Julia and Suzanne's nieces.

talented actresses never to have a hit series (her 1990 sitcom *Down Home* couldn't find an audience, and 1994's *The Five Mrs. Buchanans*, with a dream cast that included Harriet Harris and Eileen Heckart, wasn't given a fair shake by CBS), helped in the attempt to regain the early magic, but as often happens with major cast changes, all momentum was lost and the show faded away. *Designing Women* was canceled at the end of its seventh season, and the women of Sugarbakers were no more.

Almost. Suzanne Sugarbaker made a reappearance two years later when Delta Burke, having conquered her demons and made up with Bloodworth-Thomason, starred in *Women of the House* (now that sounds like a show about a brothel), alongside Teri Garr and future *Everybody Loves Raymond* star Patricia Heaton. In this short-lived spin-off, Suzanne ran for Congress, won, and moved to Washington, D.C. Like *The Golden Girls*, *Designing Women*'s syndicated run on Lifetime has attracted new fans of the outspoken sisters and their associates.

Wonderfully droll as the spoiled, petulant Stephanie Vanderkellen on *Newhart*, she was about as funny as a leg cramp in her new surroundings. Her energy was completely at odds with the others', and the fish-out-of-water element (à la Diane Chambers on *Cheers*) just didn't work. She lasted only a season, to be replaced by Judith Ivey as millionairess Bonnie Jean "B. J." Poteet. Ivey, one of the most

Alice Ghostley

Mousy yet perpetually on the verge of busting loose, the dithery comedienne Alice Ghostley took the New York stage by storm after arriving from Oklahoma. In a moth-eaten sweater, she created a sensation singing "The Boston Beguine" in *New Faces of 1952*, alongside her comic cohort Paul Lynde. Their careers intersected many times, both on television and in movies, and when Ghostley played "snarky," which she did equally as well as "dithery," she and Lynde sounded like they were imitating each other, so similar was their delivery. Her first regular TV role was that of Esmerelda, the nervously disappearing cousin of Samantha on *Bewitched*. With her trademark quavery "Oh, dear…" she would vanish (usually from the feet up). One of her best *Bewitched* moments was when she made the Leaning Tower of Pisa stand straight, rectifying a mistake she had made when she had been dating Michelangelo back in her misspent sixteenth-century youth. She was also a regular on *Mayberry R.F.D.* and *Captain Nice*, and returned to her *New Faces* sketch comedy roots along with Rich Little on Julie Andrews's variety show, as well as making frequent guest appearances on shows such as *Maude*; *Mary Hartman, Mary Hartman*; and *Good Times*. Her greatest comic gift is her ability to switch from shrinking violet to scold, an asset she used often when she hit pay dirt once again as a semiregular on *Designing Women*. As the befuddled Bernice Clifton, she sported an "arterial flow problem above the neck" and enjoyed a bizarre love-hate relationship with Meshach Taylor's Anthony Bouvier.

Protester: Fifty animals died because of that coat! **Suzanne:** Wanna make it fifty-one?

Opposite top: The four Designing Women (with Delta Burke in oh-so-politically incorrect blackface) lipsynch to "Ain't No Mountain High Enough."

Opposite bottom right: Dixie Carter with the lovable Alice Ghostley, one of the only actresses who could sing "Black Man! Black Man! Where have you gone to?" to Meshach Taylor and get away with it.

Opposite bottom left: Alice Ghostley in panic mode, from the 1967 flop *Captain Nice*.

Right: The episode "Big Haas and Little Falsie" gave Annie Potts one of her best opportunities to showcase her comic gifts. Considering...ahem...augmentation, Mary Jo proudly models a trial pair of double D's for an upper frontally threatened Suzanne.

Below: Replacing the terminally unfunny Susan Dey, Annie Potts considerably spiced things up on *Love & War*, she's here with the brilliantly wry Joanna Gleason and former *Night Court* clerk Charlie Robinson.

Annie Potts

One of the most consistently employed actresses on television, Annie Potts has rarely been out of work over the last twenty-five years. She began her career as a series regular on the short-lived World War II comedy *Goodtime Girls*, then enjoyed a career in films with the hits *Ghostbusters* and *Pretty in Pink*. After her seven-year stint on as lovable Mary Jo Shively on *Designing Women*, she immediately came to the rescue of the flailing CBS series *Love & War*, prolonging it for another two seasons and receiving an Emmy nomination in the process. She then tackled her first hour-long, playing a Marine-turned-inner-city-teacher in the TV version of the Michelle Pfeiffer movie *Dangerous Minds*. Next came the very short-lived sitcom *Over the Top*, also starring Tim Curry. Potts spent four seasons opposite Lorraine Toussaint on the hit drama *Any Day Now*, one of the first

original series on the Lifetime network, and in 2005, joined the cast of *Joan of Arcadia*. Bursting with ability and equally at home in comedy or drama, Potts is one of the most talented actresses on the small screen. The Hollywood Freeway is jammed with talented actresses, of course—but the secret of Potts's great success is that she appears to be someone we would want to know in real life. All of the enduring television stars, including Potts, Dick Van Dyke, Ted Danson, and Betty White, possess that indescribable likeability that makes viewers welcome them into their living rooms week in and week out.

CAST

Delta Burke	Suzanne Sugarbaker
Dixie Carter	Julia Sugarbaker
Annie Potts	Mary Jo Shively
Jean Smart	Charlene Frazier Stillfield
Meshach Taylor	Anthony Bouvier
Julia Duffy	Allison Sugarbaker
Jan Hooks	Carlene Frazier Dobber
Judith Ivey	B.J. Poteet
Alice Ghostley	Bernice Clifton
Douglas Barr	Colonel Bill Stillfield
Richard Gilliland	J. D. Shackelford
Hal Holbrook	Reese Watson
George Newbern	Payne McIlroy
Sheryl Lee Ralph	Etienne Toussaint Bouvier

THE DICK VAN DYKE SHOW

 | 1961–1966 | 158 episodes

Despite an occasional tumble over an ottoman, Rob Petrie perfectly balances his home life in the suburbs with his job as a comedy writer for *The Alan Brady Show*.

A recipe for sitcom success must include a sense of the constantly shifting trends in viewers' taste; star power is often a key ingredient; and a cushy time slot doesn't hurt, either. Perhaps most important of all is writing, be it the weekly invention of unique story ideas, the precise blueprint of a sequence of slapstick comedy, or the canny development of chemistry that unexpectedly sparks between characters during a show's run, sometimes taking a show down unexpected paths. *The Dick Van Dyke Show* stands as the greatest example of top-notch writing, in terms of all of the above, led by the prescient brilliance of Carl Reiner, who sensed an opportunity and wrote for the increasingly sophisticated viewing audience, many of whom had moved to the suburbs (like the show's hero, Rob Petrie) in the mid-to-late 1950s.

An angle few television viewers have ever seen: from the other side of the Petrie bedroom, America's sweethearts Rob and Laura enjoy a suburban clinch while the studio audience (and director Jerry Paris, in the center rear) look on.

Left: One of the greatest directors in sitcom history, John Rich gives his star guidance on the care and feeding of child actors.

Below: Regulars on *The New Dick Van Dyke Show* included Hope Lange, Richard Dawson, and Van Dyke's *Bye Bye Birdie* leading lady, Chita Rivera.

After a bumpy first season waiting for audiences to discover the show (it was saved from the dustbin of cancellation by producer Sheldon Leonard, who convinced CBS executives of its potential), viewers responded to it as a television counterpart to the boulevard comedies holding court on Broadway, including *Desk Set*, *The Tunnel of Love*, and *Barefoot in the Park*.

With *I Love Lucy* providing slapstick humor on the level of Chaplin, and Burns and Allen perfectly showcasing the vestiges of vaudeville and radio, *The Dick Van Dyke Show* was a landmark in that it was the first sitcom to spend equal time exploring a character's home and work life. (Actually, this wasn't the show's original concept, but Reiner subtly added more emphasis on domestic life when he realized what a corker he had in

Dick Van Dyke

Dick Van Dyke, deservedly dubbed "Chairman of the Board" by Nick at Nite, had the Midwestern upbringing and traditional roots that one would expect from a clean-cut, wholesome-looking string bean of a comedian. Finding inspiration in the work of the legendary Stan Laurel, Van Dyke began working as a DJ after World War II. Working as a local TV host in Atlanta and New Orleans, his big break came in 1956 when he signed with CBS. Guest-starring on game shows, acting as a daytime television host, and developing a stand-up act, he made his acting debut on a 1957 episode of *The Phil Silvers Show*.

Conquering Broadway as a comic song-and-dance man in *Bye Bye Birdie*, Van Dyke was tapped by Carl Reiner and Sheldon Leonard to star in a revamped version of *Head of the Family*. Lightning struck, and Van Dyke became a television and movie star, on top of the world for much of the 1960s. After the failure of *The Comic*, and important film directed by Carl Reiner, Van Dyke played a composite of Stan Laurel and Buster Keaton, he became disillusioned with Hollywood, moved his life to Arizona, and teamed up with Carl Reiner again for a three-season run of *The New Dick Van Dyke Show*. The late 1970s were not the most rewarding for Van Dyke, yielding only the short-lived variety show

Van Dyke and Company and a brief stint replacing Harvey Korman on *The Carol Burnett Show*. By the 1980s, he was slowing his pace to enjoy life after a well-fought public battle with alcohol, briefly ducking his head out of retirement to costar, opposite son Barry, in the 1988 sitcom *The Van Dyke Show*. Nearing seventy, Van Dyke came out of retirement yet again and hit the jackpot that so few television actors do, that elusive second hit. Like Andy Griffith, who had a comeback with *Matlock*, Van Dyke went from sitcom star of the 1960s to lovably nosy sleuth in the mold of Buddy Ebsen's Barnaby Jones, Peter Falk's Lieutenant Columbo, and Angela Lansbury's Jessica Fletcher. As Dr. Mark Sloan, the crime-solving MD of *Diagnosis Murder*, Van Dyke became a force on television once again and ran for eight years. He recreated Rob Petrie on 2004's *The Dick Van Dyke Show Revisited*, and recently guest starred on Broadway in Chita Rivera's autobiographical show, where they reprised their number "Rosie" from *Bye Bye Birdie*. At eighty, Van Dyke is as congenial and loose limbed as he was when he tripped over that pesky ottoman forty-five years ago.

Carl Reiner

A true Renaissance man, Carl Reiner has done it all: writing, producing, acting, and directing. After an early career in the Catskills and on Broadway in musical revues, Reiner was tapped by producer Max Leibman to join the cast of sketch comedians on Sid Caesar's *Your Show of Shows*. Working alongside Mel Brooks and Neil Simon, Reiner developed his own writing style and an unerring sense of taste. In 1957, Reiner wrote a successful semiautobiographical book, *Enter Laughing*, which later became a hit Broadway play; and by the summer of 1958, after Caesar's show went off the air, Reiner was preparing a show called *Head of the Family*, intending to star in it himself. Drawing upon his days writing for the often difficult Caesar, as well as his domestic life in the suburbs and his military service at Camp Crowder in Joplin, Missouri, he shot an unsuccessful pilot—but, anxious to see the show happen somehow, Reiner took the advice of sage television producers Sheldon Leonard and Danny Thomas and looked for someone else to play the lead so that he could concentrate on the behind-the-scenes aspect of the show. The result, *The Dick Van Dyke Show*, changed the landscape of sitcoms—and Reiner even got his wish to appear in the show, taking the role of the egomaniacal television star Alan Brady. Voluntarily taking a final bow after five seasons, Reiner and Van Dyke hoped to conquer the big screen. Although he scored a hit as an actor in *The Russians are Coming, The Russians are Coming* and a critical success directing *The Comic* in 1969, Reiner, along with Van Dyke, found the movie world ultimately disappointing. Trying to make magic twice, the pair returned to television in 1971 with *The New Dick Van Dyke Show*. Even though it ran three seasons, there was turmoil off the screen, due in part to the network censors' constant interference. Moving back to the world of films, Reiner directed such hits as *Oh, God!* and Steve Martin's star-making *The Jerk* and *All of Me*. Reiner returned to sitcoms in 1995 as an actor, reprising his role as the impossible Alan Brady on the Paul Reiser/Helen Hunt series *Mad About You*, a highly appropriate show on which to make a comeback, as Reiser and Hunt's onscreen relationship most definitely showed the influence of Van Dyke and Mary Tyler Moore.

his young leading lady.) Reiner and the other writers created separate worlds with two distinct types of comedy for its lead character. In the writer's office of *The Alan Brady Show*, the scenes were straight from Reiner's days on *Your Show of Shows*, including the Borscht Belt put-downs of Buddy Sorrell and the wisecracks of man-hungry Sally Rogers. At home, a kind of realism was achieved that was as refreshing as it was funny; naturalistic, comfortable, and utterly human. Straddling both these worlds was a young comic actor from Danville, Illinois, via Broadway, whose comic gifts combined the physical dexterity of Stan Laurel or Harold Lloyd with the insouciance of Cary Grant or William Powell. Dick Van Dyke, given the opportunity of any actor's lifetime, took the best qualities of all of those legends and gave them a fresh spin for 1961. And his character, Rob Petrie, came home to a wife who was neither a patient June Cleaver nor a wacky Lucy Ricardo. Rather, twenty-five-year-old Mary Tyler Moore was a perfect blend of the two types, first showing her real star power in an episode that dealt with her dying her hair blond (filmed as episode number nine of the first season but aired as the second episode,

80   SITCOMS: THE 101 GREATEST TV COMEDIES OF ALL TIME

Richard Deacon

The real-life Richard Deacon was not at all like the fussbudget he so often played. Beloved by all who knew him, he began his career in the theater, moving to Los Angeles and becoming a highly sought-after character actor on radio and in movies, usually playing variations on the cranky manager or clerk. Recurring on two series, the Betty White show *Date with the Angels* and as "Lumpy" Rutherford's father on *Leave it to Beaver*, Deacon was cast in his best role, as the high-strung and much maligned Mel Cooley, on *The Dick Van Dyke Show*. After that show wrapped, he joined the cast of *The Mothers-In-Law* for its second season, replacing Roger C. Carmel as Kaye Ballard's husband. Appearing in *Hello, Dolly!* on Broadway, opposite Phyllis Diller (with whom Deacon had worked in *The Pruitts of Southhampton*), Deacon continued to work in television until his death.

so thrilled were Reiner and Leonard with the blossoming of the comically untested actress), and going from green-yet-gifted ingenue to top-notch comedienne in the course of the premiere season.

More than any show before, the sexual chemistry factor was palpable, for while Lucy and Ricky Ricardo had a baby, Bob Collins was a well-known wolf, and Connie Brooks an aggressive single gal, Rob and Laura Petrie formed the most attractive, flirtatious, sexy couple ever seen on the small screen. And when Laura wore her scandalous capri pants (at one point censored by CBS, their absence was the source of a fervent letterwriting campaign), the effect on her onscreen husband was startling when compared to other sitcom couples. Despite their single beds, this was a man and wife who unapologetically had a good time together, even though it was never spoken of. They were the perfect couple to usher in the 1960s on television, a kind of casually glamorous, small-screen John and Jackie Kennedy.

OFF THE SET

JOHNNY CARSON WAS one of the final contenders for the role of Rob Petrie.

THE RECURRING JOKE about Alan Brady wearing a toupee was based on *Your Show of Shows* producer Max Liebman, who also sported a "rug."

THE NAME OF the show's production company, Calvada Productions, came from combining the names of all of the key players: Carl Reiner, Sheldon Leonard, Dick Van Dyke, and Danny Thomas.

RICHIE'S MIDDLE NAME, "Rosebud," was an acronym for Robert, Oscar, Sam, Edward, Benjamin, and Ulysses David.

Above: Good friends off screen, Morey Amsterdam and Richard Deacon made perfect onscreen foils.

Left: Morey Amsterdam, Rose Marie, and Dick Van Dyke, as the Three Musketeer writing team of *The Alan Brady Show*.

Opposite: The Petrie bedroom as we never saw it—in glorious color.

would become one of the driving forces of sitcom direction in the 1970s) and Ann Morgan Guilbert. Reiner and his staff of writers, many of whom went on to long careers creating their own shows, intuitively provided human scenarios and dialogue, true to the characters and yet hilarious, taking many of their ideas from real life situations. They were very careful not to include any 1960s slang and used topical references very, very sparingly, a choice that has helped keep the show feeling current and fresh, even forty-five years later.

By the end of the show's run, Rob and his cohorts had changed television forever, largely due to the wit of the show's writers, a group who, in previous decades, would have been the Kaufmans and Harts of their generation. With an affable genius as star, led by the steady hands of Carl Reiner and Sheldon Leonard, *The Dick Van Dyke Show* proved, particularly to the skeptical urban television viewer of the early 1960s, that there was truly smart, sophisticated comedy to be found for free from the safety of their three-piece living room set.

And then there was the kid. Considering that the show was originally titled *Head of the Family*, Ritchie Petrie, played by little Larry Mathews, was the phantom child of sitcoms (though always billed at the top of the show), adorable when present but sometimes disappearing for three or four episodes at a stretch. Indeed, it was easy to forget that Rob and Laura had a child, since so many of their scenes took place after the commute home to New Rochelle, when Ritchie had already been shipped off to bed with a cupcake.

Adding to the mix was the steadfast, surefooted delivery of comic stalwarts Rose Marie, Morey Amsterdam, and Richard Deacon, and such up-and-coming character actors as Jerry Paris (who

CAST

Dick Van Dyke	Rob Petrie
Mary Tyler Moore	Laura Petrie
Morey Amsterdam	Buddy Sorrell
Rose Marie	Sally Rogers
Larry Mathews	Richard Petrie
Richard Deacon	Mel Cooley
Ann Morgan Guilbert	Millie Helper
Jerry Paris	Jerry Helper
Carl Reiner	Alan Brady
Jerry Van Dyke	Stacey Petrie
Frank Adamo	Various characters

Above: While it's always startling to see beloved black-and-white shows in color, Mary Tyler Moore is positively eye-popping in her Josephine and the Amazing Technicolor Brunch Smock.

Top right: Rose Marie as the perpetually single career girl Sally Rogers.

Right: The hilarious Ann Guilbert and Bob Crane, just prior to *Hogan's Heroes* fame, in the episode "Somebody Has to Play Cleopatra."

BRILLIANT BUT CANCELLED

Throughout television history there have been shows that were replaced by a test pattern long before they deserved. Some of these lost gems were too clever by half, too special ever to strike a chord with a large enough audience, or absolutely hilarious but ahead of their time. In addition, there were shows that were abandoned by their networks like foundlings, relegated to time slots where they had to face unstoppable juggernauts or, even worse, shuffled around the schedule to the point where fans needed to wield divining rods over their *TV Guides* to find them. Here, then, are some of our favorite overlooked sitcoms, shows that, had the roll of the Nielsen dice come up seven instead of snake eyes, would have been included in our 101 Greatest.

Above: The cast of the too-smart-for-its-own-good *He & She*, real life couple Richard Benjamin and Paula Prentiss, with Jack Cassidy.

Top: Meeno Peluce, Joel Higgins, and Carlene Watkins in the razor-sharp 1981 gunslinger satire *Best of the West*. Even the talents of producer David Lloyd, director James Burrows, and *The Simpsons* writer Sam Simon couldn't make this one stick.

Left: Jeffrey Tambor and Jason Bateman in *Arrested Development*, a show that did manage to run three seasons (on and off), but should have been one of the all-time great shows. Henry Winkler played the family attorney, only to be replaced by Scott Baio. Liza Minnelli played a character with chronic vertigo. 'Nuff said?

DIFF'RENT STROKES

  | 1978–1986 | 189 episodes

When the mother of two African-American boys dies, they are welcomed into her employer's Park Avenue penthouse, bringing upheaval and laughs into the lives of a starchy widower and his young daughter.

Diff'rent Strokes, a late-1970s sitcom, was in some ways an updated, funkier version of *Family Affair* (another sitcom revolving around a single, wealthy man on Manhattan's Upper East Side who takes in some orphaned children). The twist this time was that the children were black. Arnold and Willis Jackson, the two young sons of Philip Drummond's recently deceased housekeeper, were straight out of Harlem and wise beyond their years. *Strokes* starred the droll Conrad Bain, fresh from a six-year run on *Maude*, and that three-foot-three bundle of dynamite Gary Coleman, a ten-year-old who, due to a kidney defect that had stunted his growth, looked much, much younger.

Opening with a theme song written and sung by future *Growing Pains* star Alan Thicke, *Diff'rent Strokes* became an instant hit for NBC. The phrase "Whatchoo talkin' 'bout, Willis?" swept the nation and pint-sized wisecracker Gary Coleman became America's favorite TV kid. Like other shows of its time, *Diff'rent Strokes* tackled serious topics, perhaps too frequently, as it became the butt of many jokes about the proliferation of "very special episodes" dealing with child molestation, steroid abuse, and bulimia. Most famously, an antidrug episode was graced with an appearance by then-first lady Nancy Reagan exhorting kids to "just say no." (The show was apparently one of the president's favorites, prompting smart alecks to crack that the nine o'clock

A scene from the pilot episode of *Diff'rent Strokes* in which the Jackson brothers "move on down" from Harlem to an even scarier neighborhood, where men like Conrad Bain wear gaudy cravats.

Right: Gary Coleman (shown here actual size) became one of the most successful child actors in sitcoms since Jerry Mathers.

Below: Todd Bridges and Dana Plato, at this point still models of youthful innocence.

time slot was just early enough for Reagan to catch it before he nodded off.)

The show launched two spin-offs: *The Facts of Life*, which premiered the season after *Diff'rent Strokes*, sending Charlotte Rae, as the Drummonds' maid, Edna Garrett, away from Park Avenue and into the fray of many more "very special episodes"; and the infamous McLean Stevenson vehicle *Hello, Larry*, which featured far too many "very crummy episodes." With Rae gone, the Drummond family went through two more maids: Adelaide (Nedra Volz) and Pearl (Mary Jo Catlett). All three maids were variations on the grand, sassy tradition of *Maude*'s Florida Evans and Nell Naugatuck (in fact, Conrad Bain, having been a regular on *Maude*, seemed to attract these types like flies).

Widower Philip Drummond was finally given a love interest in the seventh season and got remarried to Maggie McKinney, a television aerobics instructor (quite a hip, cutting-edge character in 1984) played by Dixie Carter. Maggie had a child of her own, Sam (Danny Cooksey), and the plot development clearly showed the series grasping at straws. *Strokes* was

canceled by NBC in the spring of 1985 but was picked up by ABC for one last gasp. (Dixie Carter had moved on to *Designing Women* and was replaced by Mary Ann Mobley.) Having run its course, the show's attempts at hard-hitting drama reached the pinnacle of ridiculousness at the beginning of its final season, when young Sam McKinney was kidnapped by a psychotic man in an attempt to replace his dead son (the kind of plot device usually reserved for the over-the-top angst of *Little House on the Prairie*).

Sadly, in the twenty years since the show went off the air, one of the most unfortunate associations

modern audiences have with it is the perceived "*Diff'rent Strokes* Curse," as all three of the children on the show

---

OFF THE SET

CONRAD BAIN WAS promised his own series after *Maude* went off the air. When an updated television version of the *Our Gang* series, set to feature young Gary Coleman, was scuttled, NBC paired the two unlikely actors in their own vehicle.

MR. DRUMMOND PAID $3,500 a month for his Park Avenue apartment.

THE SHOW'S WORKING title was *45 Minutes from Harlem*.

Arnold (as Romeo in his school play):
What thou talking about, Juliet?

Conrad Bain

Born in Canada, the urbane, patrician Conrad Bain was a weekly presence on sitcoms for fourteen consecutive years. He had a successful career on the Broadway stage (appearing in the original production of Leonard Bernstein's *Candide*), but first became known to television viewers on the gothic soap opera *Dark Shadows*, playing hotel clerk Mr. Wells. Making the exodus to California to seek more consistent work, as many of his contemporaries did in the late 1960s and early '70s, he was "discovered" by Norman Lear and cast alongside fellow theater actors Beatrice Arthur, Bill Macy, Rue McClanahan, and Adrienne Barbeau in the groundbreaking *Maude*. Perfectly cast as a slightly weary upper-class straight man surrounded by bewildering chaos, Bain immediately segued from *Maude* into the starring role of millionaire Philip Drummond on *Diff'rent Strokes*. He returned to television immediately after that show's eight-year run concluded, costarring on George C. Scott's short-lived Fox sitcom *Mr. President*.

have suffered serious problems. Dana Plato was arrested for armed robbery, and battled drug and alcohol addiction before finally succumbing to an overdose in 1999; Todd Bridges waged a battle with drugs as well (ironic, considering the Nancy Reagan episode) and served time in prison on a weapons charge; and Gary Coleman sued his parents for mismanagement of his fortune and has been arrested for assault.

Ten years after *Diff'rent Strokes* went off the air, Conrad Bain and Gary Coleman reprised the roles of Philip Drummond and Arnold Jackson, as potential buyers of the Banks's mansion on the finale of *The Fresh Prince of Bel-Air*.

Above: Conrad Bain and his "Maudie," Beatrice Arthur, in typical standoff mode.

Left: Tape day at *Diff'rent Strokes* (note the camera at right), with Dana Plato, Conrad Bain, Mary Jo Catlett (as Pearl, the third and final Drummond housekeeper), and Todd Bridges holding still in anticipation of a "Whatchoo talkin' 'bout?" from their teeny costar, Gary Coleman.

CAST

Conrad Bain .... Philip Drummond

Gary Coleman .... Arnold Jackson

Todd Bridges .... Willis Jackson

Dana Plato .... Kimberly Drummond

Charlotte Rae ...... Edna Garrett

Nedra Volz .... Adelaide Brubaker

Mary Jo Catlett .... Pearl Gallagher

Dixie Carter .... Maggie McKinney (1)

Mary Ann Mobley . Maggie McKinney (2)

Danny Cooksey .. Sam McKinney

Shavar Ross .... Dudley Ramsey

Le Tari .... Ted Ramsey

Dody Goodman .. Aunt Sophia

Janet Jackson .... Charlene DuPrey

THE DONNA REED SHOW

 | **1958–1963** | **275 episodes**

Donna Stone, her pediatrician husband, Alex, and their teenage son and daughter lead extremely wholesome, normal lives in small-town America.

"To me, the phrase 'situation comedy' conjures up inane plots, blundering TV husbands, and overbearing TV wives. It's everything we try to avoid on our show. I would call *The Donna Reed Show* a realistic picture of small-town life—with an often humorous twist. Our plots revolve around the most important thing in America—a loving family. In this family there's everything from belly laughs to near tragedies. Now, how can you call all that simply 'situation comedy'?" So stated Donna Reed to the *Chicago Daily American* in 1962. She couldn't exactly come up with a term to describe the show, but she obviously didn't like "sitcom." And maybe she was right: the show wasn't exactly funny; rather, it was a kind of mirror, reflecting what viewers imagined their lives to be. "Humorous" is a better word for it than "comic." Never sweet or pandering, the show was comfortable—and Reed had a lot to do with the tone. She was the star, of course, and her husband, Tony Owen, produced it. Most of the episodes revolved around her character's attempts to keep the family on an even keel.

Given Reed's personality, this was one of the gentlest sitcoms, at times making *The Adventures of Ozzie and Harriet* seem positively radical. And, like Ozzie and Harriet's son Ricky, who became a breakout rock-and-roll star, two of Donna Reed's television children had successes on vinyl. Paul Petersen ("Jeff"), one of the first heartthrobs of the newly emerging teenage class, had hits with "My Dad," "Lollipops and Roses," and "She Can't Find Her Keys" (which was introduced

Donna Reed, Paul Petersen, Carl Betz, and the daughter who materialized from the ether, Patty Petersen.

in a dream sequence on the show). And most viewers of a certain age remember Shelley Fabares's (Mary) big hit, "Johnny Angel." But unlike Ricky Nelson, neither Petersen nor Fabares had "legs" in the recording industry, a disappointment for Paul Petersen, who came to regret the years he had spent as a child actor in Hollywood.

In fact, in 1990, Petersen started an organization to draw attention to problems inherent in using child actors in the entertainment industry. The history books (well, the Hollywood history books) are full of horror stories of children who were abused by their parents (Jackie Coogan), by the studios (Judy Garland), or just weren't

Shelley Fabares

From the beginning of her career, Shelley Fabares established herself as a television star. Her beauty, appealing demeanor, and vitality made the cool medium of television a little warmer. Like a female Michael J. Fox, she made audiences feel comfortable and happy in her presence. Maybe it was genetics, since she was the niece of Broadway/Hollywood/television star Nanette Fabray (same last name, different spelling). By the time she appeared as Mary Stone on *The Donna Reed Show*, Fabares had three films under her belt, as well as television appearances on the preteen favorite, *Annie Oakley*.

When she outgrew the series and her character went off to college (returning to the family fold only occasionally), she appeared in three Elvis Presley films: *Girl Happy*, *Spinout*, and *Clambake*. Stretching her talent in the TV tearjerker *Brian's Song*, she remained gainfully employed on *The Brian Keith Show*, *The Practice* (the 1976 Danny Thomas sitcom, not the 1997 Dylan McDermott legal drama), *Forever Fernwood* (the title of *Mary Hartman, Mary Hartman* after Louise Lasser left), and as Ann

Romano's business nemesis on *One Day at a Time* (alongside her beloved Aunt Nanette). She spent most of the 1990s opposite Craig T. Nelson on *Coach*, as the grounded, sensible Christine Armstrong, a character that must've made her television mother Donna Reed burst with pride from her berth in sitcom heaven. Now married to fellow sitcom star Mike Farrell, she spent much of the last decade as the voice of Clark Kent's mother on the animated *Superman* series. Health problems led to her semiretirement as the century turned, but she has remained as luminous as ever.

career in porn films; and Patty Duke (although she has rebounded to have a most distinguished career), whose mother couldn't attend the Academy Awards since her manager's dog used the ticket instead.

Certainly many child stars have gone on to fulfilling careers as adult actors—Petersen's costar Shelley Fabares, for example, as well as Kim Fields, Ashton Kutcher, Valerie Bertinelli, Michael J. Fox, Nancy McKeon, Joseph Gordon-Levitt, Jodie Foster, Jason Bateman, Ron Howard, and the majority of the Cosby kids. (Special mention to Mayim Bialik of *Blossom*, who has a PhD in neuroscience.)

It's interesting that Paul Petersen's actual sister, Patty Petersen, came on the series as a one-episode guest and never left. With a mother as understanding as Donna Reed and a father as supportive as Carl Betz, who can blame her? That's what kept audiences watching for eight years. Besides, as Donna Reed averred, it wasn't really a sitcom at all; just a portrait of a loving family.

Left: Donna Reed proudly shows Carl Betz the result of six boxes of *Shake 'n Bake*. And, as she is the perfect housewife, *no one* helped.

Opposite top: Donna Reed dispenses sage motherly advice to Shelley Fabares about life, love, and the perfect navy pump.

Opposite bottom: Fabares grew up and went Hawaiian on *The Brian Keith Show*.

mature enough to handle the sharp drop in fame and fortune when they outgrew their acting careers. The sitcom world is full of troubled former kid stars like *Dennis the Menace* star Jay North (who was forced to be a child actor by his guardian), *Make Room for Daddy*'s Rusty Hamer (who committed suicide when his adult career failed to materialize), and *The Partridge Family*'s Danny Bonaduce, who is now a reality star because of his checkered past. Then there is the dysfunctional trifecta of *Diff'rent Strokes*: Gary Coleman, Todd Bridges, and Dana Plato; *Family Affair*'s Anissa Jones, who died of a drug overdose; *The Addams Family*'s Lisa Loring, who had a brief

CAST

Donna Reed	Donna Stone
Carl Betz	Dr. Alex Stone
Shelley Fabares	Mary Stone
Paul Petersen	Jeff Stone
Patty Petersen	Trisha Stone
Bob Crane	Dr. Dave Kelsey
Ann McCrea	Midge Kelsey

ELLEN

 | **1994–1998** | **109 episodes**

An affable single woman and her pals spend their days running a bookstore and their evenings looking for love of various kinds.

Has any show changed as much as *Ellen*? Two come to mind: *The Danny Thomas Show* lost Jean Hagan and gained Marjorie Lord, but that was peanuts compared to *The Joey Bishop Show*: halfway through its first season, five characters were dropped and, when the second season started, the entire cast (save Bishop) and the premise were new. *Ellen* also underwent drastic changes. The show premiered as *These Friends of Mine*, with Ellen working at a bookstore surrounded by that staple of '90s sitcoms—friends. The second season introduced a new title, *Ellen*, and a bunch of new friends. She bought the bookstore only to have it destroyed by an earthquake! Passing up their golden opportunity to change the setting, the writers decided to rebuild the store and sell it to a giant chain, with Ellen continuing as manager.

As the show went on, plot became less and less important as intimations of Ellen's sexuality (the character and the actress) took center stage. Ratings were respectable, if not meteoric, throughout the show's run until THAT EPISODE. Let your mind drift back to April 1997 and the "Puppy Episode" of *Ellen*. Though she had admitted to being gay in a *Time* magazine article and had confessed in person to Pope Oprah Winfrey, the viewing public was all agog when the show aired. What, you might ask, was the big

deal? There had been lesbian kisses on television before, including Amanda Donohoe and Michelle Green on *L.A. Law* and Roseanne and Mariel Hemingway on *Roseanne*, but for some reason, Ellen's coming out made headlines and caused a furor. Perhaps it was because of her girl-next-door folksiness. Perhaps it was because it wasn't just one crazy kiss for sweeps week—it was a forthright admission of who she really was. Interestingly, the following year saw the premiere of *Will & Grace*, a sitcom about

Ellen De Generes and Oprah Winfrey in the episode that landed the sitcom on the cover of every magazine on planet Earth.

homosexuals, and yet nary a same-sex kiss would be seen for the first seven years of that show.

Sitcoms are where television seems to expand its boundaries. *All in the Family* was the first series to utter the word "goddamn" on the air and *Maude* was the first prime-time character to undergo

David Anthony Higgins, Jeremy Piven, Clea Lewis, Joely Fisher, and Ellen DeGeneres, the second roster of regulars on *Ellen*.

CAST

Ellen DeGeneres	Ellen Morgan
Holly Fulger	Holly
Maggie Wheeler	Anita
Arye Gross	Adam Greene
David Anthony Higgins	Joe Farrell
Joely Fisher	Paige Clark
Jeremy Piven	Spence Kovak
Clea Lewis	Audrey Penney
Patrick Bristow	Peter Barnes

Paige: I still can't believe that Ellen is gay.
Spence: Well, I always thought she might be. I mean she could always run faster than I could, throw a ball farther, climb a tree faster…
Joe: Did you ever think maybe YOU were gay?

an abortion. (*Another World* had featured an illegal abortion as far back as 1964!) The word "condom" was first heard on *The Hogan Family*, and a forgotten 1972 sitcom, *The Corner Bar*, featured the first regular gay character. In a special arrangement with the FCC (and we're not kidding here), the first time a toilet was pictured on TV was in *Leave It to Beaver*—but calm down, only the tank was in view. Speaking of toilets, Archie Bunker's flush was also a television first.

Leading the way on social issues isn't the point of sitcoms, of course (unless they're produced by Norman Lear), and to much of the public, post-coming-out *Ellen* didn't have much to offer. Viewership declined after prurient interest was sated and right-wing groups began to exert pressure on the network. It was an easy decision to just cancel the show.

Lots of celebrities are afraid of unbolting the closet door but Ellen DeGeneres's career hasn't suffered a bit. Her award-winning talk show is a critical and ratings success, she represents American Express in ads, she has even hosted the Oscars. Not only is she accepted by the mainstream public—she is beloved. Perhaps it's easier for a woman to come out than for a man to—but recently Neil Patrick Harris, star of *How I Met Your Mother*, admitted he was gay and the great sucking of air was not gasps of amazement but yawns. *Ellen* may not have broken a lot of ground artistically, but politically—yes.

OFF THE SET

AFTER ELLEN CAME out, ABC put a parental warning at the beginning of each episode.

Maxine Lapiduss

Starting young in show business can be a blessing or a curse, and it's the lucky few who know when to jump in and when to get out. While she was in eighth grade, Dennis Miller urged Maxine to quit school and try her hand at stand-up in New York. Luckily, she decided to finish junior high, high school, and college before setting off for the Big Apple. She was a successful comic in New York clubs and wrote special material for the likes of Joan Rivers, Lily Tomlin, and Andrea Martin. After arriving in Hollywood, she wrote and produced such shows as *Roseanne*, *Ellen*, *Home Improvement*, and *Dharma and Greg*. She then left sitcomland to concentrate on a new company called VOXXY, Inc. that encourages teenage girls through Internet networking and other Web-based projects. She produced and cohosted the Bravo reality series *Situation: Comedy*, which follows various attempts to create pilots for NBC. On the other side of the coin was her autobiographical musical *Situation: Comedy: Observations on 10 Years in Hollywood… with Bongos*, which had a successful run in L.A.

EVENING SHADE

📺 | **1990–1994** | **98 episodes**

Former pro-football player Wood Newton returns to his hometown of Evening Shade, Arkansas, to become head coach at its hopeless, hapless high school.

Evening Shade, a short-lived but highly entertaining sitcom, revolved around a star turn by Burt Reynolds as football coach Wood Newton. Created by Harry and Linda Bloodworth-Thomason as the male-oriented counterpart to their woman-friendly hit *Designing Women*, *Evening Shade* was like its contemporary, *Coach*, in many ways. (In fact, Reynolds had been considered for that show's lead role, which ultimately went to Craig T. Nelson.) The place where the two roads diverged in an Arkansas wood, however, was in the laconic, leisurely pace of *Evening Shade*, akin to the aw-shucks days of Andy Taylor, Barney Fife, and Floyd the barber.

In fact, the show had its own version of Barney Fife, in the personage of the brilliant Michael Jeter as the assistant coach and mathematics teacher. It was a tightly knit group, with Reynolds sticking close to his own circle, and many episodes were helmed by Reynolds or one of his three of his best friends. In a testament to his un-Hollywood sense of loyalty, Reynolds has the most random group of friends ever: Charles Nelson Reilly, James Hampton (star of 1970s hit *Love, American Style*), and Robby Benson. This feeling of family translated onto the screen, and for the first three seasons, the show was one of the most charming, least assuming sitcoms in years.

One of the classic episodes was a subtle nod to Reynolds's hit movie *Deliverance*. Jeter, Reynolds, and Charles Durning found themselves in the woods, nekkid as jaybirds and desperately trying to find enough shrubbery to cover their meat and potatoes. When the three wanderers finally returned home, only to be told they'd have to reimburse the county $10,000 for the search-and-rescue team, they returned to the woods so the search team could "find" them. Another particularly touching episode revolved around Ossie Davis's character, who owned the café where much of the show's action took place, reuniting with a former political activist (played by Davis's wife, Ruby Dee) to reminisce about the 1960s march on Washington.

Evening Shade stars Hal Holbrook and Burt Reynolds, whose affability and low-key comic talent made him a perfect candidate for sitcom stardom.

Going on to win an Emmy and critical acclaim as Wood Newton, Reynolds was set to conquer television in a true Hollywood comeback story. But trouble arose when he had a very public breakup with his wife, Loni Anderson. The quality of the show was undeniably affected by his off-screen drama (which involved a cocktail waitress, according to the gleeful tabloids), and in the show's final season the story lines slid into a parade of guest stars, mostly country music singers such as Reba McEntire, Tammy Wynette, and Vince Gill. In addition, the ever-increasing politicizing of the show by the creators Harry and Linda Bloodworth-Thomason was at odds with the demographic of the show, preaching a blue-state message to a red-state audience. While the show was still in its adolescence, CBS wielded the ax with a merciless hand, and the show was canceled after its fourth season.

Disheartening to the Thomasons, the abrupt cancellation was all the sadder for the show's cast, which was expert: Marilu Henner, a textbook example of sheer charisma triumphing over the lack of true comic genius (that may sound harsh, but

the likeability factor that Henner possesses is a gift that is as laudable and unlearnable as the sense of timing of a Shelley Long); and, in addition to the aforementioned Jeter and Durning, such Southern specialists as Ann Wedgeworth, Hal Holbrook (whose wife Dixie Carter was the star of the Thomasons' other mint-julep hit *Designing Women*), Elizabeth Ashley, and Ossie Davis, whose narration closed each episode. Every one of the actors, totally at home in the Southern milieu, was given prime opportunities to shine, and the show, with its homey ensemble feeling, was one of the most comfortable places on the dial for several seasons.

Above: The brilliant Michael Jeter modeling the latest in backwoods lingerie.

Left: Michael Lombard and two future *Designing Women*, Dixie Carter and Delta Burke, in Linda Bloodworth-Thomason's *Dallas*-inspired spoof, *Filthy Rich*.

Linda Bloodworth-Thomason

The creator of two very successful sitcoms in the 1980s and '90s, Linda Bloodworth (later Bloodworth-Thomason) was never a woman to let her political beliefs take a back seat to her work. On her biggest hit, *Designing Women*, Dixie Carter's Julia Sugarbaker patently espoused Bloodworth's liberal, no-nonsense views. Born and raised in Arkansas, she was a staunch and early supporter of Bill Clinton, serving as his unofficial media advisor during his 1992 presidential run. Moving to Los Angeles from Poplar Bluff, Missouri, (later the hometown of Jean Smart's character Charlene on *Designing Women*) and teaching English in the Watts district of Los Angeles, she went from Crenshaw Boulevard to Sunset Boulevard when she sold scripts for such shows as *Rhoda* and *M*A*S*H*, ultimately writing the original pilot for *One Day at a Time*.

Setting up shop as an independent at Columbia Pictures Television in 1977, her first series as a producer was the short-lived *Filthy Rich* in 1982, costarring Delta Burke, Dixie Carter, Charles Frank, and Ann Wedgeworth (all of whom Bloodworth would use later to better advantage). After she married producer/director Harry Thomason, the pair became one of the most successful husband-and-wife teams in sitcom history, with their two Southern-charm-filled hits for CBS. Their subsequent ventures, *Hearts Afire*, *Women of the House*, and *Emeril*, starring that knee-slapper, the world-renowned chef Emeril Lagasse, have been less successful, but like the world of politics she feels so passionately about, sitcom fortunes are constantly changing.

CAST

Burt Reynolds	Wood Newton
Marilu Henner	Ava Evans Newton
Michael Jeter	Herman Stiles
Charles Durning	Dr. Harlan Elldridge
Ann Wedgeworth	Merleen Elldridge
Ossie Davis	Ponder Blue
Elizabeth Ashley	Frieda Evans
Hal Holbrook	Evan Evans
Jay R. Ferguson	Taylor Newton
Jacob Parker	Will Newton
Melissa Martin	Molly Newton #1
Candy Hutson	Molly Newton #2
Charlie Dell	Nub Oliver
Ann Hearn	Margaret Fouch
Linda Gehringer	Fontana Beausoleil
Burton Gilliam	Virgil
Hilary Swank	Aimee Thompson #1
Ari Meyers	Aimee Thompson #2

EVERYBODY LOVES RAYMOND

 | 1996–2005 | 210 episodes

Raymond Barone walks the emotional tightrope between his wife and his parents, while his brother Robert constantly threatens to push him off balance. By the end of each episode, Raymond manages to regain his equilibrium with the help and love of his family.

This show is at the top of our list for the consistency of its characters and the quality of its writing. Plus, it had the good sense to end on a high note, before the writers began the slow, steady slide into desperation.

We're not saying that the premise itself was groundbreaking. *Everybody Loves Raymond* was yet another show about a bumbling, thick-headed husband who needs constant straightening out by his pragmatic wife. In fact, there were three dumb men on the series: Raymond, his brother Robert, and their father.

Ah, poor clueless and henpecked men...where would sitcoms be without them? Even the smartest of them, Jim Anderson, Ricky Ricardo, and Dan Conner, sometimes needed a little course correction by their wives. Another thing that *Everybody Loves Raymond, Father Knows Best, I Love Lucy*, and *Roseanne* had in common was the sense that the husband-and-wife relationship was a partnership strong enough to weather all of the vagaries of life (i.e., the wacky situations dreamed up by a bunch of Jewish guys around a writers' table).

The elegant writing on *Raymond* elevated it above its clichéd underpinnings. In-laws have been a source of humor in sitcoms since the Stone Age, when Fred Flintstone had to contend with his battle-axe of a mother-in-law. Ralph Kramden was constantly heckled by Alice's mother on *The Honeymooners*, and *Bewitched*'s Darrin could never appease Samantha's witch of a mother. In a slight twist, Oliver Douglas even had problems with his own mother on *Green Acres*. In-laws were actually appreciated on a few TV series, *December Bride* and *Cosby*, and they were tolerated on *Roseanne*. On *Raymond*, Debra endured the curse of living across the street to her in-laws and, to make matters worse, her husband and his brother were quite the mama's boys.

Brad Garrett, Peter Boyle, Doris Roberts, Ray Romano, and Patricia Heaton made up the funniest dysfunctional family since Roseanne Conner and company.

Left: The bedtime conversations of Romano and Heaton rivalled those of Bob Newhart and Suzanne Pleshette in terms of sharp comic writing.

Below: Brad Garrett and Peter Boyle in one of their hilarious Frank/Robert father/son talks.

Raymond's father, Frank, certainly fulfilled the archetype of a cranky, complaining, older male character. Think Lou Grant on *Mary Tyler Moore*, Archie Bunker on *All in the Family*, and Redd Foxx's Sanford. (Compared to them, George Jefferson and Frasier Crane were curmudgeons in training.)

Raymond's brother Robert was a hulking man-boy, whipped by both his mother and his brother. He was what Jackie Mason would call a schmendrik; somehow, in most every sibling battle, Robert managed to come out on the bottom. The sitcom pond is well stocked with these fish in a barrel—easy targets for their friends and co-workers. Loveable, yes, but also a bit pathetic. There was Bea Arthur's ex, Stan, on *The Golden Girls*; Ted Baxter on *Mary Tyler Moore* (though he was blissfully unaware); Cliff Clavin at the end of the bar on *Cheers*; and these days, there's Toby Flenderson on *The Office*.

Finally, we come to Raymond himself. He was a bright man who made a good living for his family, but he was clueless when it came to life in general and constantly had to be managed, reprimanded, and saved by his wife and mother. Raymond's wife, Debra, was his superior in every way—a woman who, in real life, would probably have been out of his league. Is this the fantasy of all nerdy, average-looking comedy writers? They all seem to match up their ordinary husband characters with beautiful wives. Think of Homer Simpson; Ralph Kramden and his doppelganger, Fred Flintstone; Robinson Peepers (married at the end of the series); and Doug Heffernan on *The King of Queens*. Roseanne Connor was just about the only sitcom wife who was realistically matched to her husband. In fact, Roseanne is the only nonbeautiful sitcom wife we can think of. Even Vivian Vance was a looker when she wasn't wearing those formless housedresses.

Raymond was one of those sitcoms where the children appeared and disappeared at the whim of the writers. One week you'd see them happily playing, then, for weeks at a time, they seemed not to exist at all. It was every parent's dream—hot and cold running children.

Raymond followed the traditional sitcom form in other ways. We knew the writers were nearing the bottom of the idea barrel when the cast took a vacation in Italy. Whether such episodes are an honest attempt to inject something new into the formula or an excuse for a paid vacation, taking characters out of their milieu seldom works. The Barone family's trip was no exception.

Although *Raymond* rode out its run without a significant dip in quality, just around the time of the Italy trip the characters got just a little bit bitchy—especially Debra. Hugging and learning seemed to give way to full-on snarkfests, and, in a twist on the "new baby in the household" trick, Robert gained a wife. But the series managed to leave the air before it lost its real virtues. It remained a better series than most, right up until quitting time.

Georgia Engel

That voice! A cross between Marie Wilson and Gracie Allen, Georgia Engel has made a career of the playing dim, dumb blonde. Like Doris Roberts, she transcends her roles' stereotypes. Her warmth and deer-in-the-headlights stare have endeared her to audiences beginning with her career-making role as Georgette in *Mary Tyler Moore*. She joined fellow cast member Betty White on the short-lived *Betty White Show* before achieving more success with *Coach* and *Everybody Loves Raymond*, where she was the omega mother-in-law to Doris Roberts's alpha. In between television gigs she has trod the boards on and off Broadway.

CAST

Ray Romano	Ray Barone
Patricia Heaton	Debra Barone
Brad Garrett	Robert Barone
Doris Roberts	Marie Barone
Peter Boyle	Frank Barone
Madylin Sweden	Ally Barone
Sawyer Sweden	Michael Barone
Sullivan Sweden	Geoffrey Barone
Georgia Engel	Pat MacDougall
Monica Horan	Amy MacDougall
Fred Willard	Frank MacDougall
Katherine Helmond	Lois
Robert Culp	Warren

OFF THE SET

RAY ROMANO HATED the title of the show, but once it premiered he didn't have the power to change it.

RAY ROMANO HAS a brother in the New York Police Department, just like his onscreen counterpart.

Doris Roberts

Projecting an innocent facade that covered a nagging, self-absorbed interior, Doris Roberts perfectly embodied the classic nightmare mother on *Everybody Loves Raymond*. Shuffling around the Barone house gently slinging zingers at daughter-in-law Debra, Roberts somehow managed to keep her character funny and human, avoiding the massive boulders of cliché that littered her path. Roberts enjoyed an early career on dramatic TV and on Broadway in *The Desk Set* and *The Last of the Red Hot Lovers*, among others. In the 1960s, she graduated to features, including *No Way to Treat a Lady* and *The Honeymoon Killers*. She showed her flair for comedy in three 1971 releases, *Such Good Friends*, *Little Murders*, and *A New Leaf*. The television series *Angie* followed (briefly) and then came *Remington Steele*, where she mothered Stephanie Zimbalist and Pierce Brosnan as the office manager of the brawling detectives. More mothers followed, including one on *Alice*, which reunited her with her *Red-Hot Lovers* cast-mate Linda Lavin, and one on *Full House*. She peppered her sitcom roles with the occasional film role and guest appearance, but Marie Barone will forever remain her greatest achievement in comedy.

Top: Georgia Engel, Lorna Patterson, and Annie Potts as three World War II single gals in *The Goodtime Girls*.

Middle: Doris Roberts, as yet another Italian Mama, this time to Donna Pescow and Debralee Scott on *Angie*.

Above: Doris Roberts and Georgia Engel as a 2005 version of *The Mothers-in-Law*, with Peter Boyle and Fred Willard as the hen-pecked husbands.

THE FACTS OF LIFE

NBC | **1979–1988** | **209 episodes**

Under the supervision of their wise housemother, Edna Garrett, four girls from different ethnic and social classes "take the good and take the bad" at the all-girls Eastland Academy in Peekskill, New York.

At one point or another, most long-running shows undergo what is generously called a "change of concept." Perhaps no other show went through as many as *The Facts of Life*. Conceived as a spin-off of *Diff'rent Strokes*, the show sent housekeeper Edna Garrett (played by the dotty Charlotte Rae) away from the luxury of Philip Drummond's posh duplex to the relative squalor of Peekskill. The revamping began almost immediately.

Change of concept number one: Initially revolving around no fewer than seven girls plus Rae, a headmaster (John Lawlor), and a teacher (the delicious Jenny O'Hara), the show was deemed to have too many characters. Their solution? Ditch everyone, including a young Molly Ringwald, leaving Rae and three young'uns: snobby Blair, cutup Natalie, and precocious Tootie (in vulgar parlance, the rich one, the fat one, and the black one). By hiring Nancy McKeon as the tough-talking, streetwise biker chick Jo Polniaczek, the creators balanced out the eternally upturned nose of Lisa Whelchel, the vinegar of Mindy Cohn, and the winsomeness of Kim Fields.

The show became a much tighter, focused enterprise and no subject seemed off limits, from teen suicide to child pornography, from abortion to disability. Stand-up comedienne Geri Jewell took a recurring role as Blair's cerebral palsy–afflicted cousin, offering Blair an opportunity to reconcile her Breck Girl status with a cousin who didn't fit into her honey-blond view of life.

After four years, the producers realized that they could no longer fudge that Blair and Jo were ready to matriculate. Change of concept number two: The two eldest girls graduated, while Mrs. Garrett left Eastland altogether to open a gourmet deli called Edna's Edibles, which became the show's new hub.

Tootie, Blair, Mrs. G., Jo, and Natalie arrive triumphantly in Paris. Eat your heart out, Charles Lindbergh.

After two seasons of Edna's Edibles, the producers celebrated Natalie's graduation by burning the place to ground. Change of concept number three: Like a phoenix rising from the ashes, the girls opened a tacky gift shop. Grasping at straws, the show featured musical guests such as El DeBarge, Michael Damian, and

CAST

Charlotte Rae	Edna Ann Garrett
Cloris Leachman	Beverly Ann Stickle
Lisa Welchel	Blair Warner
Mindy Cohn	Natalie Green
Kim Fields	Dorothy "Tootie" Ramsey
Nancy McKeon	Joanna "Jo" Polniaczek Bonner
Mackenzie Astin	Andy Moffet Stickle
George Clooney	George Burnett
John Lawlor	Headmaster Steven Bradley
Felice Schachter	Nancy Olson
Julie Piekarski	Sue Ann Weaver
Julie Ann Haddock ..	Cindy Webster
Molly Ringwald	Molly Parker
Jenny O'Hara	Emily Mahoney
Geri Jewell	Geri Tyler

Stacy Q, relegating it to the time-warped miasma of shows that cast their lot with pop stars with a shelf life of twenty minutes.

Another year, and little Tootie graduated. Rae saw the writing on the wall and Edna Garrett got hitched. The show wasn't dead yet, and along came the sublime Cloris Leachman, frankly too talented to slum it in a series on its last legs. In addition, they added a kid played by MacKenzie Astin, and a hunky young actor named Clooney. By the way, his first name was George.

Facing sagging ratings, a storyline was written in which Blair loses her virginity. Death knell of the series: Actress Lisa Whelchel, a born-again Christian, balked, and the story line was given to the unlikely character of Natalie sleeping with her boyfriend Snake ("Snake?!?!?!") was only slightly more believable than Shirley Booth's Hazel moonlighting as a dominatrix.

No other show has been the butt of more jokes or mean-spirited spoofs than *The Facts of Life*. With its endless exploration of alcoholism, teen prostitution, illiteracy, and Jermaine Jackson, the promo tagline "This Week: A Very Special Episode of *The Facts of Life*" begins to lose its punch. When was an episode *not* "Very Special"? Did Blair ever suffer from something as mundane as split ends? Was Tootie ever saddled with a minor blister from her constant wearing of roller skates? Shucks, no. For a few years in the early 1980s, week in and week out, these girls seemed to suffer more Sturm und Drang than denizens of *Peyton Place*. Even as young viewers, we could somehow sense its future potential as camp. Ultimately, though, we can't help feeling nostalgic for *The Facts of Life*, among the guiltiest of our guilty pleasures.

Charlotte Rae

Charlotte Rae, the tiny, buxom, carrot-topped comedienne, will forever be known to an entire generation of TV viewers as "Mrs. G." She dropped her last name (Lubotsky) upon her arrival in New York City, where she had success both off and on Broadway, in shows such as *Threepenny Opera*, *The Littlest Revue*, and, in her most famous Broadway gig, creating the role of Mammy Yokum in the hit musical *Li'l Abner*. Rae cut her sitcom teeth as the wacky, love-starved Sylvia Schnauser on the New York–based *Car 54, Where Are You?* Seeking employment in the booming world of Hollywood-based sitcoms, she joined a mass exodus of character actors from New York to Los Angeles in the late 1960s and early '70s. Talented and fortunate enough to work on some of the best shows going, with guest shots on *All in the Family*, *Good Times*, and *Barney Miller*, she garnered high-profile attention that wouldn't have been afforded other equally talented actors doing guest shots on *Arnie* or *The Dumplings*. Her big break came in 1978, when she was cast as Conrad Bain's housekeeper on the hit series *Diff'rent Strokes*. As the warm, grandmotherly Edna Garrett, she hit the jackpot with viewers and was justly rewarded with a spin-off of her own. Now sporting a shock of white hair, Rae is tinier and funnier than ever, still working in the theater and on television, most recently on an episode of *The King of Queens*.

Above: The final cast of *The Facts of Life*, where only Lisa Whelchel and Mindy Cohn have been spared the attack of the killer mullets.

Opposite top: The original cast of *The Facts of Life*, including Molly Ringwald on the bottom left. Soon, they'd be cut in half.

Opposite bottom: Geri Jewell proving once and for all that cerebral palsy is funny.

Mindy Cohn prepares to "lay hands" on Murray Matheson (as Mrs. G's boyfriend) in an emergency effort to regain his mojo.

OFF THE SET

THE THEME SONG was cowritten by future *Growing Pains* star Alan Thicke and then-wife, soap-opera vixen Gloria Loring, who sang it starting in the second season, after Charlotte Rae's initial warbling of it was deemed too, well, warbly.

SINCE KIM FIELDS was only nine years old when the show went on the air (playing twelve-year-old Tootie), producers put her in roller skates for virtually every episode in the first season to make her appear taller.

ON A "VERY Special Two-Part Episode of *The Facts of Life,"* Jo gets the call after a visit from Blair's sister, a nun. Playing Sister Meg? None other than our beloved Eve Plumb, once again trying to shatter the artistic shackle that was Jan Brady.

FAMILY AFFAIR

 | **1966–1971** | **138 episodes**

Bill Davis, a successful engineer enjoying the single life in New York City, undertakes the difficult task of raising the three children of his dead brother, with the help of his rather stuffy British valet/housekeeper.

Family Affair, a hit for five seasons on CBS, was one of the charming and gentle, family-centric sitcoms of the 1960s, the era immediately preceding the Norman Lear/MTM onslaught of adult series. Revolving around an unlikely family unit, it was a precursor to such shows as *The Brady Bunch*, *Diff'rent Strokes*, and *Nanny and the Professor*. Produced by Don Fedderson, who had previously created *My Three Sons*, *Family Affair* resembled Fedderson's earlier hit in the makeup of the family: three children living with a wise and mellow father and a stern and curmudgeonly housekeeper.

Central to the success of the show was the chemistry of the cast, headed by movie actors Brian Keith and Sebastian Cabot, both finding the transition to the world of the sitcom exceedingly smooth. Keith played swinging bachelor Bill Davis, who had been leading a perfectly uncomplicated life supervising the construction of bridges and bagging lots of attractive babes. Davis's only constant had been his faithful "gentleman's gentleman," the third-generation valet, Giles French, who was the picture of English civility and never without his trademark bowler hat and umbrella. But when Davis's brother and sister-in-law were killed in an accident and their three children split up among various rela-

The Davis family enjoys one of Giles French's mocha tortes. In truth, Buffy and Jody would've preferred popsicles.

tives, "Uncle Bill" decided to reunite them, undertaking their care and rearing.

Though the grumbly, ultra-American Keith and the rotund, veddy British Cabot complemented each other perfectly, the young actors playing the Davis children were equally important to the success of the show. The sweet-faced Kathy Garver, played the oldest, Cissy, as a typical fifteen-year-old dealing with the excitement of moving from Terre Haute, Indiana, to spend her high school years in exciting, glamorous New York City (the establishing shots of Manhattan made the concrete jungle of the mid 1960s seem like something truly magical). Six-year-old Jody was played by Johnnie Whitaker, who had a face full of freckles and a permanent grin, and was already a a showbiz veteran. (He had hit it off with Brian Keith when they worked together on the film *The Russians Are Coming, The Russians Are Coming.*) Cute as hell, whatever acting ability Whitaker lacked, he made up for in sheer enthusiasm. To most viewers, the best actor of the bunch was Anissa Jones, playing Jody's twin, Buffy. She had an emotional range that was startling, and though perhaps it seems like hindsight now (she died of a drug overdose at the age of 18), Jones possessed the saddest eyes on television, even at the age of eight.

Having two male authority figures created a unique dynamic. There was nothing remotely going on between Uncle Bill and French (although, in retrospect, Cabot constantly referring to himself as a "gentleman's gentleman" does raise an eyebrow—not

that there's anything wrong with it), but as Uncle Bill was often travelling around the world, Mr. French in some ways fulfilled the stereotypical mother's role.

While some of the episodes' heartwarming plots come off as overly earnest, there

Johnnie Whitaker and Anissa Jones, who had too many freckles to begin with, shade themselves from the aging effects of the sun.

were many genuine laughs to be had, particularly in the expert comic interplay between Brian Keith and "Sabby" (as he was known to friends) Cabot. One episode that everyone seems to remember is the one in which Mr. French inadvertently knocks Buffy's beloved doll, the truly bizarre looking Mrs. Beasley, off the terrace of apartment 27A (an apartment straight out of the September, 1966 issue of *Architectural Digest*). A dragnet on the level of the search for the Lindbergh baby

ensues, and just when all seems hopeless, the doll is found in a garbage can full of leaves and clippings, having fallen into the garden of the Davises' downstairs neighbor. Episodes dealing with tonsils, birthday parties, and imaginary friends

were prevalent, and, like the story lines of *The Brady Bunch*, rarely touched on the issues of the time. One exception was when a classmate of Buffy's (played by Eve Plumb, soon to become the legendary Jan Brady) participated in school only via an intercom, as she was bedridden and dying of leukemia. After Buffy met her mysterious classmate, she enlisted the help of her family to give her friend an early Christmas, knowing that she wouldn't live to see another. By the end of Season Five the kids were growing up and the times they were a-changing. Mary Richards had already been hired at WJM and America was about to be introduced to the Bunker family. With the show winding down, producer Fedderson, having learned his lesson from the *My Three Sons* "Dodie

Kathy Garver, on playing *Cissy*: They wanted somebody over 18 who could play a 15-year-old. Plus, I have the same shape face as Brian Keith—parallel trapezoid."

debacle," wisely fought the urge to bring on a new child to replace the rapidly aging Davises. Instead, he brought Nancy Walker aboard, who was as short as Dawn Lyn but had infinitely better timing.

Now forty years old, *Family Affair*, despite sometimes teetering dangerously close to the brink of the saccharine chasm, has an unshakeable, undeniable appeal that is missing from the crop of more recent smartass, cynical shows.

Right: The usually subtle and unflappable Sebastian Cabot, does a "phone take" of Danny Thomas-like proportions.

Below: Brian Keith as a Hawaiian pediatrician, making one of *The Little People* bite the bullet during his physical.

CAST

Brian Keith ....Bill Davis

Sebastian Cabot ......Giles French

Kathy Garver ....Catherine "Cissy" Patterson-Davis

Anissa Jones ....Elizabeth "Buffy" Patterson-Davis

Johnnie Whitaker ...Jonathan "Jody" Patterson-Davis

OFF THE SET

WHEN ANISSA JONES broke her leg the day before an episode was to begin filming, the writers instantly came up with a new script that involved Buffy breaking her leg while playing stickball.

THE ODD-LOOKING MRS. Beasley doll became a marketing phenomenon and was commercially available even after *Family Affair's* cancellation. In addition, Johnnie Whitaker had his own successful line of boy's clothing, based on his wardrobe on the show.

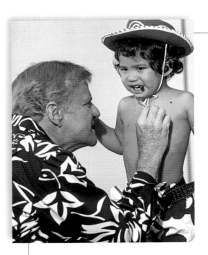

Brian Keith

With a gruff exterior covering a laid-back, easygoing charm, Brian Keith was the only child of stage actors Robert Keith and Helena Shipman. He travelled around the country with his parents until they divorced when he was five (his father remarried, to actress Peg Entwistle, who infamously leapt to her death from the Hollywood sign in 1932). After World War II, he became an actor in earnest (his debut was at the age of three in a 1924 silent film starring his father), with a small speaking part in the original cast of *Mr. Roberts* on Broadway (his father played the costarring role of Doc), before moving to California and becoming a consistently working actor, usually in "B" Westerns or war films. After starring in two short-lived series (*Crusader* in 1955 and *The Westerners* in 1960), Keith had his highest-profile job as Hayley Mills's (and Hayley Mills's) father in the hit Disney movie *The Parent Trap*. He began to pursue more comic roles at the urging of his good friend and *Parent Trap* costar Maureen O'Hara, landing his most famous part as the warmhearted Bill Davis on *Family Affair*. Nominated for an Emmy three out of the five seasons of its run, Keith found a permanent home in television and was a regular presence over the next twenty-five years. Along with a three-season success in the hourlong *Hardcastle & McCormick*, in the early 1980s, he also tried his hand at other sitcoms, coming back almost immediately after the end of *Family Affair* with *The Brian Keith Show*, also called *The Little People* during its two-season run. He starred in two other short-lived sitcoms, *Pursuit of Happiness* in 1987 and *Walter and Emily*, costarring Cloris Leachman, in 1991. Keith committed suicide in 1997, suffering from lung cancer and emphysema. (He had smoked often on *Family Affair*, which is odd to see today, in light of television's rabid anti-smoking stance.)

FAMILY TIES

NBC | **1982–1989** | **180 episodes**

Two former flower children of the 1960s try to raise their family in the era of Reaganomics. Home life becomes particularly nightmarish when dealing with their oldest child, Alex, a right-wing conservative.

The first sitcom to view the generation gap in reverse, *Family Ties* was, in some ways, liberal Hollywood's response to the renewed conservatism of the 1980s. Modeled after producer Gary David Goldberg's experiences as a former hippie dealing with suburban family life, the show was in many ways a gentle, upside-down version of *All in the Family*, with Mike and Gloria as the parents and Archie and Edith as the children.

Living in Columbus, Ohio, Elyse and Steven Keaton, products of the peace-loving 1960s, had three children: the eldest,

Alex, was a Republican who carried a briefcase to high school and read *The Wall Street Journal* over breakfast; middle child Mallory was a shopaholic who reveled in her lack of ambition; and the precocious youngest Keaton, Jennifer, constantly jockeyed for her own identity within the family. The situation was ripe for conflict, with Elyse, a successful architect, and Steven, who managed a public TV station, constantly bewildered by their children. A former folk singer, Elyse would get out her guitar and try to get the family to join in sing-alongs, usually featuring "If I Had a Hammer." Meanwhile, little Jennifer front-

ed a cutting-edge girl group named the Permanent Waves.

Not a hit when it debuted in 1982, the show picked up steam when the Reaganophile Alex ran off with much of the attention and many of the laughs. Never going for the slapstick antics of a *Perfect Strangers* or the bizarre characters of *Newhart*, two of its contemporaries, *Family Ties* can only be called "droll" (in the best possible sense of the word), with the sly, understated comic touch of Gross and Baxter-Birney, the dry, deadpan delivery of Yothers, and the yin-yang relationship of Fox and Bateman, who in particular had wonderful chemistry. Mallory's abject consumerism provided the perfect target for Alex's punch lines. In the show's seven-year run, the underrated Justine Bateman developed into a top-notch comedienne, learning how to get laughs on straight lines as Mary Tyler Moore had done twenty years before on *The Dick Van Dyke Show*. She also became a genius at setups (no doubt with the guidance of Goldberg and directors Will Mackenzie and Sam Weisman, who between them, helmed over half of the episodes), perfectly timing the lobbing of the comedic ball so Fox could knock the punch line out of the park. The family's unofficial sixth member was Alex's friend, next-door neighbor Skippy Handelman, played by the very funny Marc Price back when a geek from next door could be a welcome addition. (This was before Steve Urkel on *Family Matters*, who became so obnoxious that his mere appearance sent thousands of viewers diving for their remotes.)

Like many shows of its time, *Family Ties* dealt with its share of serious issues such as teen pregnancy, substance abuse (with Tom Hanks guest-starring as Elyse's alcoholic brother Ned), racism, suicide, and censorship. Many of the same topics had been dealt with ten years earlier on the Norman Lear shows *Maude* and *Good Times*, and those shows, produced in the 1970s, when the topics were truly "hot button," can still be riveting to watch. But with the rise of the Movie-of-the-Week, which had a luxurious two hours to deal with issues that a sitcom had only twenty-three minutes to address (well, forty-six for a two-parter), the 1980s' "Very Special Episodes" haven't stood the test of time well, coming off as slightly preachy and pat. A notable exception is the *Family Ties* episode "A My Name Is Alex," in which Fox, on a bare stage, talks to an unseen psychiatrist after his best friend is killed in a car accident. It's a true tour-de-force performance and it earned Fox one of the three Emmys he received for the show.

Bridget meets Birney: Meredith Baxter and real-life husband David Birney in the pilot of their controversial show about an interfaith marriage.

Meredith Baxter

The beautiful and versatile Meredith Baxter grew up in a television family, as daughter of actress/producer Whitney Blake (Mrs. B. on the 1960s staple *Hazel* and creator of the 1970s hit *One Day at a Time*). Her big break came in 1972, when she was cast as Bridget Fitzgerald, a wealthy Irish-Catholic girl who marries a struggling Jewish writer in the controversial and groundbreaking sitcom *Bridget Loves Bernie*. Marrying her leading man David Birney, she hyphenated her name and became a television star of the highest order when she joined the cast of one of the most prestigious dramas of the 1970s, *Family*, showing her dramatic abilities as the struggling divorcee Nancy Maitland. In 1982, cast on *Family Ties*, she got a rare opportunity to play comedy for the next seven years. She became one of the most gainfully employed actresses in Hollywood, appearing in more than thirty-five TV movies (twice playing convicted murderess Betty Broderick to critical acclaim). In addition to producing, she launched a very successful line of skin-care products bearing her name. Baxter still acts, reuniting with Michael J. Fox, once again playing his mother on the hit series *Spin City*, and a recent riveting turn on *Cold Case*.

The beginning of the fourth season was a full-length TV movie in which the Keaton family travel to England and become embroiled in an international spy scheme, complete with microfilm hidden in a hairbrush and concluding with Alex and Mallory bound and gagged. Almost as preposterous as *The Facts of Life Down Under*, in which Tootie, Natalie, et al. get involved in an international jewel heist (and critics accused *Mister Ed* of being unbelievable?), it was not among the show's finest two hours.

In 1985, Alex graduated from Harding High (Fox was already twenty-four). Steven and Elyse had a fourth child, and little Andrew (played by Brian Bonsall) became the fastest-growing child on TV, skipping from infant to preschooler over one hiatus. The show gained other regulars in successive love interests for Alex: budding ballerina Ellen (played by Fox's future real-life wife, Tracy Pollan) and psychology major Lauren Miller (played by a pre-*Friends* Courteney Cox). Mallory found romance, too, with Nick, an earring-wearing biker/sculptor/high school dropout played by Scott Valentine, whose charms were completely lost on the rest of the Keatons.

Michael J. Fox

Michael J. Fox, a gifted and inspiring actor whose sly sense of timing made him one of the most successful TV comedians of the 1980s and '90s, was born in Canada, quitting high school and heading to the United States to conquer Hollywood. Fox hit hard times and had sold his furniture when he auditioned for the role of Alex P. Keaton (the P was his ad lib). He was initially passed over, but casting director Judith Weiner convinced producer Gary David Goldberg to give Fox another chance. This time Fox nailed it and went from broke actor negotiating his sitcom deal in a phone booth to full-fledged television star. His performances on *Family Ties* won him three consecutive Emmy awards, and he became one of the few actors to make the transition from television stardom to movie stardom as Marty McFly in *Back to the Future*, filming at night while working on *Family Ties* during the day. He followed it with other agreeable film hits such as *Secret of My Success* and two *Back to the Future* sequels. It was at the age of thirty, during the filming of *Doc Hollywood*, that Fox was diagnosed with Parkinson's disease. He kept his diagnosis private, knowing it would limit his employment opportunities. He returned to sitcoms in 1996 on the hit *Spin City*, masking his progressing disease by keeping his right hand in his pocket. When this became too much, he revealed his nearly ten-year struggle to the world. Leaving the series to spend more time with his family, he has become a spokesman and advocate of stem-cell research (literally changing the balance of power in Congress), and still appears occasionally on television, most recently as a lung cancer victim on *Boston Legal* and a neurotic doctor on *Scrubs*.

By the end of the seventh season, Goldberg decided the show should go off the air while it was still doing well in the ratings (Fox had become a full-fledged movie star,

Bateman had those aspirations, and Valentine shot a pilot for a spin-off titled *The Art of Being Nick*, which was never picked up). In the spring of 1989, in a two-part episode titled "Alex Doesn't Live Here Anymore," the show wrapped up as Alex prepared to leave Columbus and join a Wall Street investment firm. The episode gave Meredith Baxter a chance to do some of her best work, struggling with letting her firstborn leave the nest. Definitely a product of its time, *Family Ties* still resonates today, not for its politics but for its truthful depiction of parents and children raised in very different eras.

CAST

Meredith Baxter	Elyse Keaton
Michael Gross	Steven Keaton
Michael J. Fox	Alex P. Keaton
Justine Bateman	Mallory Keaton
Tina Yothers	Jennifer Keaton
Brian Bonsall	Andrew Keaton
Marc Price	Erwin "Skippy" Handleman
Scott Valentine	Nick Moore
Tracy Pollan	Ellen Reed
Courteney Cox	Lauren Miller
John Hancock	Gus Thompson

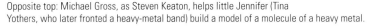

Opposite top: Michael Gross, as Steven Keaton, helps little Jennifer (Tina Yothers, who later fronted a heavy-metal band) build a model of a molecule of a heavy metal.

Above: Fox and Barry Bostwick share a warm, fuzzy moment in *Spin City*.

Left: In the capable hands of Michael J. Fox, Alex P. Keaton became one of the most popular sitcom characters of the 1980s.

FATHER KNOWS BEST

◉ ![NBC] | **1954–1960** | **203 episodes**

Father comes home daily from his job as an insurance man to address the little travails of suburban family life, greeted by his wife, son, and two daughters.

In the years following the Second World War, the family was America's most important asset. After years spent fearing that loved ones might return from overseas maimed—or not return at all—the stability of the 1950s was a blessed relief. It's no wonder that so many sitcoms emphasized family harmony. In the Goldbergs, the Nelsons, the Cleavers, the Rileys, the Aldriches, the Williamses, the Hansens—and *Father Knows Best*'s Andersons—America had role models of familial stability. The status quo was steadfastly upheld and the middle class was celebrated in half-hour time slots across the television dial.

Of course many of these families had been introduced on radio, and *Father Knows Best* was no exception. Robert Young had originated the role of Jim Anderson on radio, but the character was a stereotypical dunderhead with a sticky-sweet wife, played by June Whitley and later Jean Vander Pyl; a daughter, Betty, played by Rhoda Williams; a son, Bud, played by Ted Donaldson; and little Kathy, played by Norma Jean Nilsson. As the series progressed, Jim got smarter, Margaret got some backbone, and the kids matured. In 1953, when the radio show left the air to make way for television, only former film star Young made the transition. In every episode, he would come home from work calling to the kitchen, "Margaret! I'm home!" He'd change from his suit jacket to a comfy sweater (while keeping his tie on). The family was a community and it was all a little pat, but the sweetness and compassion overcame any cynicism.

In the Anderson family, everything was in its place and every problem could be solved. While Jim's contemporary, Ozzie Nelson, was often befuddled, Robert Young's Jim handled problems with gentility, logic, and kindness. And while there was tension, to be sure, it was of a mild sort, and everyone learned tolerance and understanding by the end.

It should be noted that memories of this series may be misleading. Though Father mostly knew best, on occasion Mother had to straighten him out. Even the kids could sometimes teach Dad a thing or two. He also had a temper, and though he never erupted like Ralph Kramden, he sometimes lost his patience—patience was one of the sterling traits to which all Andersons aspired. Mother was not exactly as we remember her, either. If you think of the lovely Jane Wyatt as the most kitchen-bound, traditional maternal figure on television, a look back at the show reveals a woman who is smart as a whip, and no simple domestic. She often took the reins after letting the men make fools of themselves. Elinor Donahue's Betty (or "Princess," as Father called her) had a backbone, too. When she decided to go to the state college instead of Mom and Dad's alma mater, she got her way and taught her parents that she was capable of charting her own course. Even Lauren Chapin's Kathy, her father's little "Kitten," sometimes figured out things that her older siblings and parents couldn't see clearly. On the other hand, Bud, played by Billy Gray and devoid of a fatherly nickname, was seemingly incapable of straight thinking. But what he lacked in common sense, he seems to have made up for in his appeal to the show's teenage girl fans. Betty had her share of admires of the opposite sex, too, and in an era when sex was seldom discussed, the charms of Bud and Betty helped propel the show's high ratings.

In subsequent years, TV families became more dysfunctional, if no less loving: the Connors, the Bundys, the Simpsons, and the Bunkers all made Americans feel superior. New kinds of families—made up of friends or co-workers—formed the center of such shows as *Mary Tyler Moore*, *Evening Shade*, *Alice*, *The Golden Girls*, and *The Drew Carey Show*, among others. Today, unrelated groups are the families of choice on TV: think *Friends*, *Seinfeld*, *Will & Grace*, *Sex and the City*, *Scrubs*, and *My Name Is Earl*. Cynical, self-aware, narcissistic, and sometimes downright venal but, at the center, family units composed of friends.

Some long for the days of *Father Knows Best*, when the outside world seldom encroached on the family unit. The Andersons never had to deal with changing mores, societal pressures, or world problems. Instead, they and their television cohorts existed to provide solace, enjoyment, and a sense of well-being to millions of hungry viewers.

Robert Young with Lauren Chapin, whose real life was anything but the picture perfect one of *Father Knows Best*.

CAST

Robert Young ...... Jim Anderson

Jane Wyatt .... Margaret Anderson

Elinor Donahue ... Betty Anderson ("Princess")

Billy Gray .... James Anderson Jr. ("Bud")

Lauren Chapin .... Kathy Anderson ("Kitten")

Sarah Selby .... Miss Thomas

Robert Foulk .... Ed Davis

Vivi Jannis .... Myrtle Davis

Yvonne Lime .... Dotty Snow

Paul Wallace .... Kippy Watkins

Jimmy Bates .... Claude Messner

Roger Smith .... Doyle Hobbs

Elinor Donahue

With a warm smile and a calm, wry demeanor, Elinor Donahue seemed to grow up before viewers' eyes, first on *Father Knows Best* and then on *The Andy Griffith Show*. She began her long career before the age of five, with appearances in vaudeville and on radio. After acting in a number of B movies, she turned to television and her best-known role, Princess, on *Father Knows Best*. When that series left the air in 1960, she moved to Mayberry for a one-season run as Andy Griffith's girlfriend Ellie. Other than costarring with John McGiver (left) on the short-lived *Many Happy Returns*, Donahue spent much of the 1960s raising her four sons (she had married *Bewitched* and *Gidget* creator Harry Ackerman, and appeared at times as Sister Bertrille's sister on Ackerman's *The Flying Nun*). She came back to the small screen as a semiregular on *The Odd Couple*, playing Felix's girlfriend, Miriam Welby, and followed that with a role on the flop early dramedy *Mulligan Stew*. Consistently employed in guest spots on sitcoms (including a recurring role on *Dr. Quinn, Medicine Woman*), voiceovers, and soap operas, Donahue is still active after six decades, appearing as recently as 2005 on *Cold Case*.

OFF THE SET

THE SHOW WAS not a success in its original run on CBS, but when the network canceled it, letters poured in, persuading NBC to pick it up. CBS came to its senses and bought the show back for its final two seasons.

WHAT IS IT about Springfield? More important, where is Springfield? In *Father Knows Best* as well as *The Simpsons*, it's never made clear in which state the family resides.

THE TITLE OF the radio version of the show was *Father Knows Best?* (with a question mark). The equivocation became unnecessary for the television version, in which father really did know best.

Left: Robert Young with Elinor Donahue, who was on her way to one of the longest careers in television.

THE FLINTSTONES

abc | 1960–1966 | 166 episodes

It's the year 10,000 BC, and "modern Stone Age family" Fred and Wilma Flintstone, along with neighbors Barney and Betty Rubble, have all the madcap misfortunes and adventures of modern-day sitcom families.

For six years, thanks in part to the patter of Fred's two substantial feet, American audiences embraced the first prime-time animated sitcom. Though adults had long embraced animated cartoons directed at children, including *Ruff 'n' Ready*, *Crusader Rabbit*, the *Looney Tunes* series, and *Rocky and Bullwinkle*, this was the first prime-time animated sitcom, and it owed much more to its sitcom brethren than to kiddie cartoons.

Bullwinkle had almost become the first prime-time animation, but they missed the mark by an hour, clocking in on NBC from 7:00 to 7:30 P.M. Once Rocket J. Squirrel and Bullwinkle Moose

proved that cartoons for grown-ups could work, Bill Hanna and Joseph Barbera decided to try their hand at a multigenerational animated sitcom. ABC, long accustomed to being in last place in the ratings, proved adventurous in this regard, ordering up a bunch of *The Flintstones*. Their gamble paid off in a big way for everyone concerned.

The limited animation style of Jay Ward's *Rocky and Bullwinkle* and UPA's *Gerald McBoing Boing* cartoons was adopted by Hanna-Barbera, who understood that the detailed drawing style of the Warner Brothers, MGM, and Fleischer studios was too expensive and labor intensive. The style might have been herky-jerky and crude, but audiences didn't seem to mind.

If there's any doubt that *The Flintstones* was directed at adults, keep in mind that its first sponsor was Winston Cigarettes. Early on, critics carped that it was simply *The Honeymooners* in cave drag—and they were right, just as *Top Cat* was, shall we say, inspired by *Sgt. Bilko*. As the series went on, the similarities to *The Honeymooners* became less pronounced, with Alan Reed and Mel Blanc subtly making the characters their own, rather than mimicking Jackie Gleason and Art Carney.

One of the show's cleverest conceits was its use of animals as Stone Age versions of modern appliances: a young woolly mammoth as a dishwasher, the tail of a live bird as a duster, brontosauruses as construction cranes, etc. And, à la George Burns, these characters would often break the fourth wall and deadpan, "It's a living."

Bea Benaderet

The warm and wonderful Bea Benaderet, one of the hardest-working women in the early days of sitcoms, could do more with a knowing smile and an arched eyebrow than most actresses can do with pages of dialogue. Strange, then, that she made her mark in radio, playing regular roles in such classics as *Fibber McGee & Molly*, *The Great Gildersleeve*, and as the hilariously named Gertrude Gearshift on *The Jack Benny Program*.

Highly in demand, she simultaneously played neighbor Blanche Morton on *The George Burns and Gracie Allen Show* and best friend Iris Atterbury on Lucille Ball's radio hit *My Favorite Husband*. Benaderet was already committed to starring in Burns and Allen's television version of their show when Ball called and asked her to play Ethel Mertz on *I Love Lucy*. (She did get to make a memorable appearance on the show, as a lovestruck spinster.) After all of her radio work, Benaderet was a natural choice for animation, voicing the character of Granny in the Warner Brothers cartoons and creating the role of Betty Rubble on *The Flintstones*. She was considered for the role of Granny Clampett, but old friend Paul Henning instead created the role of Cousin Pearl Bodine on *The Beverly Hillbillies* for her, and she appeared on the show for its first season, until Henning gave her her own series, *Petticoat Junction*. (When the show crossed plotlines with *The Beverly Hillbillies*, it was strange that Jethro never commented on Kate Bradley's strong resemblance to his mother.) Like so many of her contemporaries, Benaderet was a heavy smoker for many years and died from lung cancer at only sixty-two, never completing the run of her first and only star vehicle.

While the first seasons of *The Flintstones* took on typical sitcom subjects (work problems, bowling, the battle of the sexes, trying to make ends meet), the writers soon looked for other inspiration. Fred and Wilma had a daughter, Pebbles, then Barney and Betty begat Bamm Bamm, their superstrong son. Guest stars including Ann-Margret (playing Ann-Margrock) started showing up, and a prehistoric version of *Bewitched* (another ABC show) crossed over for an episode, with Elizabeth Montgomery voicing a sabre-tooth-clad Samantha Stephens. Other celebrity parodies included Stony Curtis, Cary Granite, and Ed Sullistone, and a new set of neighbors, the Gruesomes, obviously modeled on the Addams and Munster clans. Straws began to be clutched when a Beatles-type rock band (get it?) called the Wayouts came to Bedrock, along with a mischievous alien named Gazoo, voiced by Harvey Korman.

The show spawned multiple spin-offs, feature films, merchandising, DVDs, and even vitamins. Having lasted over 12,000 years (and proved what fundamentalists have been telling us all along, that man did coexist with dinosaurs), *The Flintstones* seems capable of lasting another few millennia.

Above: Alan Reed, Jean Vander Pyl, Bea Benaderet, and Mel Blanc gave voice to the most lovable cartoon characters in television history.

Opposite top: Even though she was a cartoon, Wilma's pregnancy unnerved the network censors. Did they think that Hanna-Barbera was going to show Dr. Stone cutting little Pebbles's umbilical cord with a pterodactyl beak?!

Opposite left: Bea Benaderet as Kate Bradley on *Petticoat Junction*, examining the ever-rising hemline of Pat Woodell (Bobbie Jo Number One).

Opposite bottom: *Gilligan's Island* drew the line between "Ginger men" and "Mary Ann men." *The Flintstones* forced us to cast our lots as well: Were you a Wilma man or a Betty man?

CAST (voices)

Alan Reed	Fred Flintstone
Jean Vander Pyl	Wilma Flintstone
Mel Blanc	Barney Rubble
Bea Benaderet	Betty Rubble (1)
Gerry Johnson	Betty Rubble (2)
Mel Blanc	Dino the Dinosaur
Jean Vander Pyl	Pebbles
Don Messick	Bamm Bamm
Harvey Korman	The Great Gazoo
Ann-Margret	Ann-Margrock

Actually, forget Wilma and Betty...all men are Ann-Margrock men.

Hanna-Barbera

Bill Hanna and Joseph Barbera's first cartoon was *Puss Gets the Boot* in 1940. Working as animation directors at MGM, they formed a partnership that lasted until William Hanna's death in 2001. When MGM shuttered its animation unit in 1957, the two animators turned their talents to television, hiring most of the MGM animation staff. Realizing that the techniques employed by MGM, Warner Brothers, and Paramount's Fleischer Studios was prohibitively expensive when faced with the weekly demands of television, the duo copied the techniques pioneered by Jay Ward's cartoon mini-empire. Hanna-Barbera concentrated on children's programming, beginning with *The Ruff 'n' Ready Show*. Other notable Hanna-Barbera shows include *The Huckleberry Hound Show*, *The Yogi Bear Show*, *Quick Draw McGraw*, *Top Cat*, *Magilla Gorilla*, *Jonny Quest*, *Scooby-Doo*, *SuperFriends*, *The Jetsons*, and *Wacky Races*. In 1967, the partners sold the company to Taft Entertainment but remained in control of operations. In 1990, Taft, renamed Great American Entertainment, sold Hanna-Barbera to Turner Broadcasting and the partners went into retirement, acting as figureheads for the organization.

THE FLYING NUN

 | 1967–1970 | 82 episodes

Sister Bertrille, a young novice at the Convent San Tanco in Puerto Rico, discovers that she can fly, vexing her Mother Superior every time there's an errant updraft.

she reconsidered, not wanting to burn a bridge with the studio that had discovered her; the producers were certain they had a long-running hit on the level of *Bewitched*.

The hitch was, unlike Samantha Stephens, Sister Bertrille had no magic powers—just a small frame and an aerodynamic cornette (heavy on the starch, please). It was an incredibly flimsy premise from which to wring three seasons worth of scripts, but there she went, zooming around Puerto Rico like a giant, drunken seagull with bangs. (In fact, a particularly funny episode dealt with a lovesick pelican who would simply not take no for an answer. And from a nun, yet.)

Parallels to *The Sound of Music* abounded, as well as to *The Singing Nun* (Field even released an album that charted in 1968, featuring a wimple-swinging single, "Felicidad"). When the show became a hit, the market was swamped with a wave of merchandise, from lunchboxes to paper dolls, Colorforms to board games.

The writers were hard pressed to come up with a weekly excuse to get their star airborne, and many of the plots dealt with Sister Bertrille (born Elise Etherington, a former surfer chick, in a tip of creator Bernard Slade's hat to Field's role as *Gidget*) saving the convent, which was constantly running low on money, with her quick wit and undying optimism. For the first season, much of the humor came from our heroine's trying to master her landings but often ending up in the top of a tree or careening onto the deck of the yacht owned by dashing playboy Carlos Ramirez (Alejandro Rey). It was never mentioned explicitly, but Carlos must've had some very interesting trips to the confessional, for although Sister Bertrille was a total pest, constantly crashing (in

The Flying Nun is the epitome of the high-concept sitcoms of the 1960s, right up there with *Mr. Ed*, *My Mother the Car*, and *My Living Doll* in terms of general silliness. But we forgive it its absurd plots and treacle—due in great part to the considerable charms of rising star Sally Field.

The show came about after Field's first sitcom, *Gidget*, was canceled after one season, only to catch fire during summer reruns and become a ratings hit. It was too late to revoke *Gidget*'s death sentence, so Columbia Screen Gems looked for another vehicle for their popular young comedienne. When they offered her *The Flying Nun*, Field turned down the rather ludicrous show. Then

Above: An unusually earthbound Sally Field as everyone's favorite novice, Sister Bertrille.

Opposite left: Field making up something really juicy to write in her diary on the set of her starmaking sitcom, *Gidget*.

the literal sense) his champagne-and-babe-filled evenings, there was a surprising, undeniable sexual undercurrent between the two. But there was to be no *Sound of Music* ending with Field kicking the habit and running off with the sexy bachelor. There were enough complaints from the Catholic Church already, and what was worse, Rey's character ran a gambling parlor, tamely named Carlos's Casino A-Go-Go.

There were an inordinate number of episodes concerning goofy animals, undoubtedly an attempt to capitalize on the Arnold the Pig craze that was sweeping the country. In addition to the afore-mentioned horny pelican, there was a depressed cow, a smuggled parrot, a frustrated donkey, and a kleptomaniacal monkey; some-times the show seemed like a cross between *Dr. Phil* and *Mutual of Omaha's Wild Kingdom*. And speaking of wild, the show dipped its toe into the psychedelic '60s when Sister Bertrille wrote a song titled "A Whole New World," which was bought and recorded by the group Sonny and the Sundowners (who she knew from her days hanging ten). Problem was, they reset and rewrote the song, and when the ladies of the convent arrived to see its world pre-miere, the lyrics included such phrases as "grow your own magic mushrooms," and was sung to a strobe light show, complete with caged go-go dancers. Wow. Peace and love, Sister Sixto.

The sisters of charity of the Convent San Tanco try to reason with a lovesick pelican who seems to have taken the starch out of their wimples.

As was typical of 1960s sitcoms, the cast was filled with excel-lent character actors supporting the young star. Rey, a sort of B-list Ricardo Montalban, was perfectly cast, clad in a smoking jacket and sporting a teased and sprayed pompadour that could withstand the gale force winds of Hurricane Bertrille. (Another interesting aside: *The Flying Nun* was probably the only series in television history where the male actors spent more time in the hair department than their female coun-terparts.) Madeleine Sherwood, straight from the film versions of several Tennessee Williams plays, had the disapproving glare of a Mother Superior down pat; Shelley Morrison, who enjoyed a career resurgence thirty years later as Karen's maid Rosario on *Will & Grace*, was the English-challenged Sister Sixto; and Marge Redmond (later known as Sara Tucker, the Cool Whip lady) was Sister Jacqueline, the show's nar-rator and the bemused voice of reason.

Sally Field

Though she can now be spotted doing commercials for osteo-porosis medicine, it seems unfathomable that Sally Field is sixty years old. The daughter of a B-movie actress and step-daughter of a stuntman, Field attended a Columbia Studios acting workshop designed to develop new talent. With her winning combination of all-American good looks and a natural flair for comedy, she was discovered within her first month in the workshop and tapped to play Frances Lawrence, better known as *Gidget*. When that show was abruptly canceled by ABC in 1967, Field spent the next three years flying the friendly skies above Puerto Rico (or against a blue screen on the Columbia lot, for those nonbelievers). Wanting to stretch herself after that, she found it very difficult to be taken seriously as an actress and returned to sitcoms (albeit finally as a true adult) in *The Girl with Something Extra*. Studying with famed acting teacher Lee Strasberg, Field finally broke out of the pigeonholing and won the challeng-ing title role in the television movie *Sybil*, forcing the show business establishment to take a very different view of the talented actress. Within two years she had won her first Academy Award, for *Norma Rae*, and has never looked back, becoming one of our finest character actresses. Recently, she has returned to television, with a recurring role on *ER*, and, back on ABC where it all started, on the family drama *Brothers & Sisters*.

CAST

Sally Field	Sister Bertrille
Marge Redmond	Sister Jacqueline
Madeleine Sherwood	Mother Superior Plaseato
Alejandro Rey	Carlos Ramirez
Shelley Morrison	Sister Sixto
Manuel Padilla Jr.	Marcello
Linda Dangcil	Sister Ana

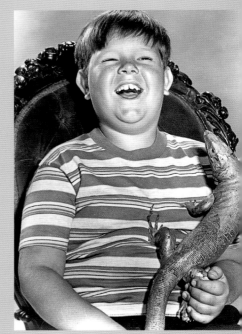

PETS

Pity the poor sitcom pets. While they tend to be very much in evidence in the pilot and premiere episodes, they often conveniently disappear for long stretches during the season, until called up for active duty in a specific episode. Come to think of it, they are a lot like sitcom kids. Tramp from *My Three Sons* and Richie from *The Dick Van Dyke Show* are just two examples of "here today...where tomorrow?"

Sitcom pets are almost always dogs. (We suppose fish are boring and cats are difficult to train.) Every once in awhile, a dog (or pig) has his day—and becomes a central character in his own right. These include Cleo, the talking dog on *The People's Choice*; Eddie, the remarkable Jack Russell terrier on *Frasier*; and Arnold the pig on *Green Acres*. These creatures were just as much a part of their respective households as their human cohabitants—and they exhibited just as much personality. In fact, Moose, who played Eddie, received more fan mail than any of his human companions (and earned $10,000 per episode!).

Clockwise from left: Eb (Tom Lester) checks Arnold the pig's pulse, which is racing after Doris Ziffel thoughtlessly serve him bacon for breakfast; Ken Weatherwax, who played Pugsley Addams on *The Addams Family*, is the nephew of Rudd Weatherwax, the legenday animal trainer who put Lassie through her paces (it is unknown who trained the iguana); Shirley Mitchell and woman's best friend from *Plea Don't Eat the Daisies*, Ladadog (real name: Lord Nelson).

FRASIER

NBC | **1993–2004** | **262 episodes**

Psychiatrist Frasier Crane moves from Boston to Seattle to host a radio advice show, enduring the constant interference of his father Martin, British nursemaid Daphne, his neurotic brother Niles, and Eddie the terrier.

One of the most literate, adult sitcoms ever to grace a major network, *Frasier* employed sophisticated repartee as well as the occasional slapstick divertissement. Even standard put-down humor was executed with great wit on this sitcom, and it was second only to *The Simpsons* for the depth of its humor, the jokes coming along at breakneck pace and on so many levels that if you didn't get one allusion, another was likely to come along shortly. *Frasier* was a social satire at its heart, with the pomposity of both Frasier and Niles skewered constantly, in the best tradition of Molière. The broth-

ers remained blissfully unaware of their own cultural snobbery, even as they sniffed their wine and discussed opera while their blue-collar father enjoyed a beer while relaxing in his beat-up recliner.

The series began as a spin-off from the long-running *Cheers*, as Frasier Crane (played on both shows by the Jack Benny of the new millennium, Kelsey Grammer) divorced his cadaverish wife Lilith and returned to his hometown of Seattle to begin life anew as a talk radio psychiatrist. Now the center of his own sitcom world, as Ted Danson had been on *Cheers*, Grammer was supported by a cast as adept as he was at witty banter. David

Kelsey Grammer as Frasier Crane, doing his trademark Jack Benny take at Moose (playing Eddie), the biggest scene-stealing pooch on modern sitcoms.

Hyde-Pierce, perfectly cast as Frasier's even fussier brother Niles, became the show's comic engine in many ways, edging closer to the line of over-the-top behavior than Grammer's character could. (Although still capable of utter silliness, Frasier became decidedly more grounded than he had been on *Cheers*, just as Rhoda and Benson did when they segued from supporting zany to title character.)

Just as expert were John Mahoney as father Martin and Jane Leeves as Daphne. Frasier's workplace was stocked with such brilliant comedians as Dan Butler, Edward Hibbert, Patrick Kerr, and Harriet Harris, playing a variety of characters who were a source of constant aggravation for Frasier. His only ally at work was his producer, the no-nonsense Roz Doyle (Peri Gilpin), who enjoyed more than her fair share of men while helping Frasier cope with the crazies who called in to his show. (In another similarity to *The Simpsons*, the callers included many celebrity voiceovers over the show's eleven-year run.)

It should be noted that Frasier wasn't your stereotypical sitcom blowhard, although much of the show's humor resulted from his comeuppance, making him akin to a highbrow Archie Bunker. Rival siblings Frasier and Niles continually tried to better their social standing, often at each other's expense. Where they banded together was in their disapproval of their father and his penchant for all of the things they considered beneath them.

One other thing they agreed on was the utter despicability of Niles's never-seen wife, Maris. First described as an emaciated "social X-ray," Maris had ballooned to mammoth proportions by the end of the series—or so she was described. The writers went wild in their descriptions of her, just as

Kelsey Grammer

Kelsey Grammer has made a career of playing Frasier Crane: Like James Arness of *Gunsmoke* fame, he portrayed the same character in prime-time television for twenty years and, remarkably, is the only actor in television history to be nominated for the same role in three different series (including a nod for his guest shot on *Wings*). Grammer began his career in the theater, specializing in Shakespeare, and got his big break through a flukish set of circumstances. Working as a theater actor in New York, Grammer played a small role on the Jane Curtin/Susan Saint James series *Kate and Allie*. The next morning, the show's casting director, Geoffrey Johnson, was called by the casting director of *Cheers*, who had caught the show but missed the actor's name (this before the days of IMdB and Google). He thought Grammer seemed right for the role of Diane Chambers's psychiatrist/boyfriend, then set to appear on only four episodes. The rest, as they say, is history. In addition to his appearances as Dr. Frasier Crane, Grammer has voiced characters in *Toy Story 2*, *Anastasia*, and other animated features.

Left: Shelley Long made welcome guest appearances on *Frasier*, irritating an entirely new set of characters as the pretentious Diane Chambers.

Opposite left: Dan Butler and Perri Gilpin, as 'Bulldog' Briscoe and Roz Doyle. The only thing the pair have in common are libidos the size of Montana.

another set of writers had done on *Mama's Family*, with Iola's unbelievably fat but never-glimpsed mother. Two other "funny fatties" were the wife of *Scrubs*'s Dr. Bob Kelso and *Karen*'s husband, Stanley, on *Will & Grace*—though in his case we did get a glimpse of his feet.

The proud tradition of unseen characters actually started on radio, with unheard characters. Though *Duffy's Tavern* was one of the most popular of radio shows, listeners never heard Duffy—only Archie, the bar manager, on the other end of the phone in a daily call from Duffy. Likewise, Mrs. Nussbaum's husband, Pierre, on *The Fred Allen Show*, and almost all the supporting cast of *Vic and Sade* were only spoken about.

The first unseen character in sitcoms was Pete's wife, Gladys, on *December Bride*. Other characters known only through third-party accounts include Norm's wife, Vera, on *Cheers* (she once actually appeared but she was hit by a custard pie so her face was not visible) and Archie's cousin Oscar on *All in the Family*. On *Friends*, Phoebe's roommate Denise never showed her face, nor did Barney Fife's girlfriend Juanita on *Mayberry*. On *Mary Tyler Moore*, Phyllis's husband, Lars, never made the scene, nor did an audience favorite who also didn't appear on *Rhoda*, Carleton the Doorman.

Carleton may not have been seen but we heard his voice—placing him in another category altogether. Those heard but not seen also include Mr. Schotz, the owner of the brewery on *Laverne and Shirley*; Peg's mother on *Married with Children* (from all accounts another plus-size character); Mork's boss Orson, back on Ork; and Wilson, the neighbor on *Home Improvement*, who was always partially hidden.

Maris, however, was the queen of the unseen, and an integral part of the *Frasier*

Three masters of light comedy, Jane Leeves, David Hyde Pierce, and John Mahoney, share the credit for making *Frasier* the classiest, wittiest sitcom since *Mary Tyler Moore*.

family. Her off-screen actions and Niles's descriptions of her made her as real as any of the other characters, all of whom were sharply written and beautifully played. Most sitcom characters seem somehow based on the actors who play them, but, like the characters on *Mary Tyler Moore*, the population of *Frasier* was a unique and complex ensemble of individuals who came together to bring us one of the greatest sitcoms of all time.

CAST

Kelsey Grammer	Dr. Frasier Crane
David Hyde Pierce	Dr. Niles Crane
John Mahoney	Martin Crane
Jane Leeves	Daphne Moon Crane
Peri Gilpin	Roz Doyle
Dan Butler	Bob "Bulldog" Briscoe
Edward Hibbert	Gil Chesterton
Patrick Kerr	Noel Shempsky
Harriet Harris	Bebe Glazer
Moose	Eddie

OFF THE SET

THE THEME SONG, "Tossed Salads and Scrambled Eggs," is sung by Kelsey Grammer.

THE CALL LETTERS of *Frasier*'s radio station, KACL, come from the names of the show's creators, Angell, Casey, and Lee.

PETER MACNICOL WAS the second choice to play Niles Crane.

THE FRESH PRINCE OF BEL-AIR

 | 1990–1996 | 148 episodes

Will Smith (played by Will Smith), West Philadelphia-born-and-raised, is thrown into Bel-Air hoity-toityness by his aunt, who is trying to get him out of the Philadelphia ghetto—and both the rapper and the upwardly mobile black family he lives with learn valuable lessons.

Will Smith jumped from singing to stardom with *The Fresh Prince of Bel-Air*, which rode the wave of new black sitcoms. After *Julia* opened the door, which had been firmly slammed shut and triple-locked by the response to *Amos 'n' Andy*, a raft of sitcoms featuring all-black casts inhabited the airwaves. Some, like *The Jeffersons*, were classy affairs in which the characters avoided black-sitcom stereotypes. Others might well have come right off the chitlin' circuit.

As many have pointed out, *Fresh Prince* is yet another example of the sitcom staple, the fish out of water. But, unlike *Diff'rent Strokes*, where black kids from the ghetto were thrown into an upper-class white milieu, *Bel-Air* featured an upper-class family that was black. And whereas Arnold and his brother were taught valuable lessons by the "great white father," on *Fresh Prince*, the hip, cool kid most often taught lessons to the uptight rich family.

The moniker "Fresh Prince" had been used by Will Smith as a recording artist and he sang the theme song, which he had written with DJ Jazzy Jeff. The song was imbued (quite a Bel-Air word for a rap song) with Smith's humor, and that quality made his character endlessly appealing.

Throughout the series, "Smith," or rather, Smith, kept his mood upbeat and sarcastic, instead of playing a tough hood from the ghetto. His happy-go-lucky, wry attitude toward the Banks family made him an especially charismatic character and was a key element to the series's success. Taking a leaf from the George Burns playbook, Smith would often break

Above: The success of *The Fresh Prince of Bel-Air* can be attributed in large part to one thing: The irresistible, electric charisma of its star, Will Smith.

Opposite left: Will Smith, Alfonso Ribeiro, and Tatyana Ali, three terrifically appealing young actors.

CAST

Will Smith	Will Smith
Alfonso Ribeiro	Carlton Banks
James Avery	Philip Banks
Karyn Parsons	Hilary Banks
Tatyana M. Ali	Ashley Banks
Joseph Marcell	Geoffrey
Janet Hubert-Whitten	Vivian Banks (1)
Daphne Reid	Vivian Banks (2)
Jeffrey A. Townes	Jazz

the fourth wall (or screen) and speak directly to the television audience. He was smart enough and talented enough to have it both ways, playing the character and commenting on the action at the same time.

The show employed sitcom clichés, but made them fresh by commenting on them with true wit. For example, take the old "new kid brought into the household" trope. The writers spun it so that young Nicky started out as a cute little baby but in just a few months turned into a kid. Will himself asked how the heck that was possible. When a new actress began playing Vivian, Nicky commented, "Man, I'm going back to the street, where things make sense."

Carlton, played by Alfonso Ribeiro, was a nerd, long a favorite sitcom staple. His favorite singer was Tom Jones, and Carlton went around singing and dancing (is that really a dance?) to "It's Not Unusual" in an extremely white-bread way. Then there was another classic type: the seen-it-all, sarcastic, blasé butler (or maid). Geoffrey carried on the grand tradition of *Soap*'s Benson and *Make Room for Daddy*'s Louise. He was always the farthest from the door when the doorbell rang. When nobody budged, he would ostentatiously proclaim, "Oh, please, allow me to get it."

The writers and cast made all of these familiar elements work because they never allowed us to take the whole affair too seriously. Rather, they loaded the

show with self-deprecating humor (Will got a haircut and the barber said, "Now you know I'm gonna have to charge you extra for cuttin' around these ears?"); breaks in the fourth wall (after making a basket, Will turned to the camera and proclaimed, "I'm goin' to Disneyland!"); self-referential humor (Philip commented to his wife, "Vivian, you are so naive. You would believe Will if he told you that he were some big rap star whose album just went platinum."); and downright silliness (Geoffrey's last name was Butler and his middle name was Barbara).

Its light attitude toward itself and its professionalism render *The Fresh Prince* almost beyond criticism. When the show was canceled, Will (the character) returned to Philadelphia. A letter-writing campaign actually revived the show, and the writers wrote a funny opening for the new season in which NBC suits kidnapped Will Smith, informing him that the show was the "*Fresh Prince of Bel-Air*, not the *Fresh Prince of Philadelphia*." They tossed him into the back of a van sporting the NBC logo and the words, "Star Retrieval Unit." You just can't hate a show like that.

Daphne Maxwell Reid

The beautiful Daphne Maxwell Reid, wife of the equally intelligent actor Tim Reid (who isn't quite as beautiful), has graced many series but has, inexplicably, never had that breakout role she deserves. She was the first black woman to appear on the cover of *Glamour* magazine and sometimes designs her own costumes. She and Tim Reid had a syndicated talk show, created the much-lamented sitcom *Frank's Place*, and developed their own production studio, Millennium Studios, in Virginia. She's appeared with Robert Conrad on *The Duke*, on the UPN network's *Eve* (right, with Jason George and Eve), and her husband on *Snoops and Linc's*.

FRIENDS

NBC | 1994–2004 | 238 episodes

A bunch of New York friends live together in various configurations, help one another in and out of various scrapes, and get increasingly friendly in various combinations over the course of ten seasons. Throw in a monkey, a duck, and a chick, too.

Take a deck of cards and a marker. On two of the kings, write the names Chandler and Ross. On the jokers, inscribe the names Joey and Phoebe. Give two of the queens the names Rachel and Monica. Shuffle the six cards and deal them out in pairs. When you've explored all of the plot possibilities suggested by the pairs, shuffle again and deal yourself some new pairs. Repeat until the series finally goes off the air. We don't actually know if that's how the writers of *Friends* came up with their ideas but, however they did it, the story of six urban twenty-somethings seeking love and happiness was a great success. (though siblings Monica and Ross never hooked up.)

In the olden days of sitcoms, each episode was a freestanding unit and the series had only the characters in common. In syndication they could be shown in random order. Many modern sitcoms have story arcs that last from four episodes to an entire season. Take *Will & Grace*, *Frasier*, and *Seinfeld* as examples. *Friends* was one of those ongoing sitcoms, with the characters' changing relationships providing the continuity—and the suspense from week to week.

The Friends lived in the mythical sitcom land of New York City. For most of the run, Monica and Rachel inhabited a ridiculously huge Greenwich Village apartment (with a great view and a wall of windows!) more likely to belong to the Olsen twins than to a

Opposite: The six friends of *Friends*, polar opposites in many ways yet comically bound together by life in the Big Apple.

Bottom: The sharply dressed young professionals Ross, Chandler, and Rachel, who have "real" jobs, as opposed to Monica (chef), Joey (actor), and Phoebe (space cadet).

Left: The producers of *Friends* never met a fat suit they didn't like. This time, Matt LeBlanc is the victim.

Friends was one of the most successful series in television history, and that success was worldwide. The reasons were many. Sharply delineated characters; provocative situations; and smart, funny writing with a determinedly young, contemporary view made the sitcom feel hip. Issues such as whether Chandler might be a little—gay—and what fabulous new hairstyle Rachel would bring to the world became the subject of many an impromptu water-cooler debate. Unlike the old-guard sitcoms, which were written by a phalanx of elderly, usually Jewish writers, *Friends* boasted a young stable of twenty-somethings writing for characters—and audiences—very much like themselves. Producers Kevin Bright, Marta Kaufman, and David Crane kept a firm hand on character development and plot lines, avoiding network interference and critics' suggestions. The result was a show that will shine in syndication for years to come.

struggling young chef and a would-be fashionista. (*Will & Grace* also lived in an imaginary New York. Never, on either of these shows, did the actual New York figure into the plot.) Central Perk, the name of the coffee shop where the Friends hung out, is one of the few details that rang entirely true. This is in contrast to shows like *Car 54, Where Are You?*, *The Honeymooners*, and, to cite a more contemporary example, *Seinfeld*. Those series featured relatively small, cramped New York apartments, and their characters interacted with the city itself. On *Friends*, despite the occasional guest-star boyfriend (Tom Selleck) or simian (Marcel the monkey), the Friends lived in a hermetically sealed world. It made sense that they would hook up with one another; everyone else was rather superfluous.

It seems that the same was true off screen. The actors banded together for all contract negotiations and insisted on being considered for the same award categories. Funny as the series was, our hearts never really went out to the characters. After all, what did they need us for? We were like outsiders watching the members of a very small cult.

Joey: How *you* doin'?

Maybe that's why Matt LeBlanc's spin-off series, *Joey*, was a no-go. None of the characters could exist without the others. You might have thought, as the writers obviously did, that the naive and self-absorbed Joey embodied enough sitcom clichés to make it on his own. But then again, think of Maynard G. Krebs, Woody Boyd, Rose Nylund, or Chrissy Snow. Could any of them have piloted their own series? Nope, and neither could Joey, or, for that manner, any of the other friends.

The otherworldly Lisa Kudrow played Phoebe Buffay (here with Jason Brooks), who occasionally went under the aliases Dr. Regina Phalange and Princess Consuela Bananahammock. Occupation: beefcake masseuse/folk singer.

Lisa Kudrow

Perhaps the most successful of the post-*Friends* Friends, Lisa Kudrow has shown a sophisticated talent for a variety of roles both comic and dramatic. Early on, she decided not to follow in her father's footsteps as a research doctor, but to instead pursue acting. Like many young comics of her generation, she began her career as part of an improvisational troupe, Los Angeles's the Groundlings. Her first television role came on *Mad About You* (below, with Helen Hunt), as the dimwitted waitress Ursula Buffay. Soon, Ursula had a twin sister—Phoebe, on *Friends*. Not content to stay in the run of weekly television, Kudrow has taken roles in series of films, both mainstream and independent. Mainstream highlights include *Romy and Michele's High School Reunion*, *Analyze This*, and *Analyze That*; indie favorites include *Wonderland* (a biopic of the immensely endowed porn star John Holmes) and the quirky dramedies *The Opposite of Sex* and *Happy Endings*. Kudrow returned to series television with the pseudo-reality show *The Comeback* on HBO, which she co-created, co-wrote and co-produced; it was a critical success but, as that phrase always implies, not a hit with audiences. Clearly, she has talents and interests beyond those of many TV actresses. Expect to see more great things from Kudrow on one side of the camera or the other.

CAST

Matthew Perry	Chandler Bing
Courtney Cox Arquette	Monica Geller
Lisa Kudrow	Phoebe Buffay
Matt LeBlanc	Joey Tribbiani
David Schwimmer	Ross Geller
Jennifer Aniston	Rachel Green
Elliott Gould	Jack Geller
Christina Pickles	Judy Geller
Jane Sibbett	Carol Willick
James Michael Tyler	Gunther
Maggie Wheeler	Janice
Tom Selleck	Dr. Richard Burke
Paul Rudd	Mike Hannigan
Helen Baxendale	Emily
Kathleen Turner	Charles Bing
Teri Garr	Phoebe Abbott, Sr.

THE GEORGE BURNS AND GRACIE ALLEN SHOW

 | **1950–1958** | **239 episodes**

George Burns, the cigar-smoking, bemused husband of scatterbrained Gracie Allen, hosts a weekly television program set in the couple's Beverly Hills home.

Keep your Gilligan, keep your Aunt Clara, keep your Lisa Douglas, and keep your Chrissy Snow (please!)—our vote for the ditziest sitcom character, the dizziest dame of all time, is the unparalleled Gracie Allen. It's no wonder she was confused on *The George Burns and Gracie Allen Show*: for one thing, her Beverly Hills home was on a stage in a theater; for another, her husband, George, had a television in his upstairs office on which he could view the proceedings downstairs; and finally, her spouse was the only one who could see the theater audience. Neither Gracie nor the other cast members were in on the premise—or at least that was the premise. As far as they were concerned, there was no *George Burns and Gracie Allen Show*: they were blissfully living in Sitcomland.

Burns and Allen had spent decades in vaudeville, movies, and radio so their personae were firmly established. They were among the first vaudevillians to decamp to radio, and, when television came on the scene, they helped lead the radio exodus. They played themselves on the TV series but, like the similarly bizarre *Jack Benny Show* (where Jack played himself and used a variety-show backdrop), the Burns/Allen sitcom borrowed from the couple's real life but took plenty of liberties for the sake of humor. In reality, George and Gracie were married with two children and, of course, they didn't have next-door neighbors like the Mortons. But their real history as performers was very much a part of the show. (In this way you could say that Burns was a direct precursor to Jerry Seinfeld.) The most radical difference between their life and the sitcom, of course, was that in real life Gracie wasn't remotely as scatterbrained as the eponymous character she played.

For its first two seasons, the show was broadcast live from New York and then it made the move to Hollywood, airing after *The Ed Wynn Show* and *The Alan Young Show*. Recognizing the power of television to devour a performer's creativity and sap him of his material, Burns insisted that the

Classic Gracie Allen logic meets with the appropriately blank looks of husband George, Bill Goodwin, Hal March, and Bea Benaderet.

show be broadcast only every other week. By the start of the third season it was filmed without an audience and the laughs were provided by a live audience viewing a film of the final cut, the same technique used by *The Phil Silvers Show* (and, much later, by *All in the Family*).

Though the show made the transition from radio, many of its elements were new to television. It was the first to show the home life of entertainers and the first to have a character break out of a scene and speak directly to the audience. The line between reality and show business became totally surreal in this, perhaps the most inventive of all television shows; where would *It's Gary Shandling's Show* have been without Burns and Allen's peculiar brand of wackiness? The series had its own logic and it succeeded because the writers never went overboard in their imaginings. For instance, the house was built on a soundstage, minus one wall. In one astounding sequence, a salesman, flustered as all were by Gracie's idiocy, tried to leave the house by stepping off the platform to the stage floor. George insisted he come back and go out properly, through the front door. Then, when he was "outside," George spoke to him through the nonexisting door. Needless to say, the salesman was in such a hurry to escape the Burns residence, he left his hat in the living room. Gracie, ever polite and practical, picked it up, gave it a number, and placed it in the closet with all the other hats left by

hasty salespeople. The sequence has to be seen (through tears of laughter) to be believed.

Burns began each show with a little monologue at the proscenium arch, at the end of which he introduced the particulars of the episode. At the end of each show Burns and Allen would take a kind of curtain call and perform another brief routine before Burns requested, "Say good night, Gracie." She responded with a simple, "Good night."

Unlike today, television shows of the time were sponsored by one company or, on occasion, two. In most cases, commercials were performed as part of the show. Burns and Allen did their own commercials, which were written by the show's writers, under the supervision of the sponsor, and were incorporated into the plot. Gracie, for example, often served George coffee with delicious Carnation Milk. When the show went into reruns the commercials were cut out—though some references could not easily be excised.

In 1958, Gracie pulled the plug on the show, as well as her career, when she decided to retire. What she didn't tell anyone, including George, was that her health was failing. Burns went on the next year, with much of the same cast, but this time Burns was a theatrical producer and the Mortons were his secretary and accountant. It lasted one season. Burns without Allen just wasn't the same. Funny. But not the same.

OFF THE SET

IN KEEPING WITH the loony nature of the show, when Fred Clark (as Harry Morton) left the show and was replaced by Larry Keating, George announced the change on the air. During a scene, Clark walked out, Larry Keating walked in—and the show continued.

BURNS'S MCCADDEN PRODUCTIONS produced other situation comedies, including *Mr. Ed*, *The Bob Cummings Show*, *The People's Choice*, and *The Marie Wilson Show*.

Ralph Levy

Another stage-struck lawyer, Ralph Levy's first job was managing the Massine Ballet Company. Levy next tried television, becoming an assistant director for CBS, supervising the birth of the 1949 variety show *The 54th Street Revue* from CBS's Studio 54 (yes, *that* Studio 54). He was sent to the unknown land of Hollywood, California, to direct *The Ed Wynn Show*, the first major TV show to come from Hollywood. Lucille Ball and Desi Arnaz agreed to be guests on Wynn's show and were so successful that CBS suggested that Lucy's radio show, *My Favorite Husband*, be adapted for television. Meanwhile, Levy directed *The Alan Young Show* and the pilot of Groucho Marx's *You Bet Your Life*. CBS then assigned Levy to *The George Burns and Gracie Allen Show*; and when Jack Benny decided to enter television, Levy directed four thirty-minute specials for the comic. Levy directed *I Love Lucy*'s pilot but was too busy to direct the series, instead concentrating on Benny's show. When one of Burns's writers, Paul Henning, got into producing, he asked Levy to direct the pilots of *The Beverly Hillbillies* and *Green Acres* and two years' worth of *Petticoat Junction*. After stints at the BBC and some half-hearted stabs at features, Levy retired. He died on October 15, 2001, fifty years to the day after the *I Love Lucy* pilot first aired on CBS.

Al Simon

No one in television history has enjoyed the track record of producer Al Simon. Born in New York, Simon left WHN radio in New York to join the army. After World War II, he was hired by Desilu Productions and, along with Desi Arnaz, was instrumental in creating the three-camera system. Simon became associate producer of *I Love Lucy* in 1951, moving to *The George Burns and Gracie Allen Show*, first as associate producer and later as producer of the hit series. Burns's McCadden Productions assigned Simon to help get *The Bob Cummings Show* off the ground, and when Simon and Burns decided to turn Walter R. Brooks's *Freddie the Pig* book series into a sitcom, the result was *Mr. Ed*, which Simon executive produced. He mentored other writers along the way: Paul Henning, a McCadden writer who had contributed to *Burns and Allen* and *The Bob Cummings Show*, created *The Beverly Hillbillies* and its sister sitcom, *Petticoat Junction*; Simon served as executive producer on both series. On another spin-off, *Green Acres*, Simon produced alongside Henning, around the same time creating Filmways Productions (remember Eva Gabor purring, "This has been a Filmways presentation, dahling"?), an important distributor of television shows to the syndication market.

CAST

George Burns	George Burns
Gracie Allen	Gracie Allen
Bea Benaderet	Blanche Morton
Hal March	Harry Morton (1)
John Brown	Harry Morton (2)
Fred Clark	Harry Morton (3)
Larry Keating	Harry Morton (4)
Harry Von Zell	Harry Von Zell
Ronnie Burns	Ronnie Burns
Bill Goodwin	Bill Goodwin

Above: The cameraman prepares George and Gracie for a scene in the kitchen.

Opposite: A triptych of a typical Burns-and-Allen moment: the setup, the punchline, and the take.

GET SMART

NBC | **1965–1970** | **138 episodes**

The bumbling Maxwell Smart helps keep the world safe for democracy with the help of his fellow C.O.N.T.R.O.L. agent, the beautiful Agent 99, and "The Chief."

In 1965, the world of international espionage was hugely popular, with the *James Bond* movie franchise in full swing and *The Man from U.N.C.L.E.* and *The Avengers* major television hits. At the same time, the archetype of the dashing, handsome secret agent who took himself oh so seriously (both as an expertly trained operative and as a suave lady-killer) was a perfect target for parody, as would be proved yet again in the later Matt Helm and Derek Flint films.

Premiering one week after *I, Spy* and the season before *Mission:* *Impossible*, *Get Smart* was the first sitcom to satirize the form. Created by comic geniuses Mel Brooks and Buck Henry, the show was originally supposed to star Tom Poston and air on ABC, but when it was rejected by that network, NBC gladly picked it up, on the condition that the bumbling Agent 86 be played by rising comedy star Don Adams.

Cleverly written and very well produced, the show was responsible for generating more catchphrases than any sitcom until *Seinfeld*, including the ubiquitous "Sorry about that, Chief,"

A rare behind-the-scenes shot of Don Adams and Edward Platt. Perhaps it was snapped just before the descent of the dreaded "Cone of Silence."

Right: "Chief" Ed Platt, incognito as "Your Waiter, Irving," gives Agents 86 and 99 their assignment along with the wine list.

Below: Don Adams and Barbara Feldon share an off camera laugh with Dick Gautier, who is getting a buffet table tuneup as Hymie the Robot.

"Ahhhhhh…the old [fill in the blank] trick," "Would you believe…?", and "Missed it by that much." (Of course all of these were nearly impossible to say without mimicking the unmistakable nasal voice of Don Adams.) The role of Max was physically demanding, involving stunts and fight scenes in addition to all the comic business; Adams was one of the hardest working actors on television, to the point where, by the fifth season, he was unable to film an episode due to exhaustion. He was ably supported by the dee-lish Barbara Feldon as Agent 99, his partner in crime-fighting (and Max's wife in the last seasons), and the fantastically droll Edward Platt as "The Chief." The show was an immediate smash.

With some of the best comedy minds behind it, the dialogue often jabbed brilliantly at the paranoid, supersecret, and self-important world of the CIA and FBI. The term "intelligence community" became an oxymoron on *Get Smart!*, for the show didn't do much to encourage faith in under-

cover operations on either side of the political spectrum. They were all boneheads and screw-ups, including Siegfried (Bernie Kopell), the vice president of public relations and terror at C.O.N.T.R.O.L.'s nemesis K.A.O.S.; the robot Hymie (Dick

Don Adams

The singular Don Adams started his show business career as a stand-up comic, winning *Arthur Godfrey's Talent Scouts* in 1954 with an act he wrote with childhood friend Bill Dana. Appearances on variety shows followed, including a regular job as one of Perry Como's troupe of players (alongside future sitcommers Kaye Ballard and Paul Lynde) on *The Kraft Music Hall*. In 1963, he made his mark with two great gigs: a supporting role on *The Bill Dana Show*, playing the bumbling house detective that constantly aggravated Dana's Jose Jimenez (a foreshadowing of the role that put him in the history books); and as the voice of animated penguin, Tennessee Tuxedo. After rocketing to stardom as Secret Agent Maxwell Smart, winning three consecutive Emmys in the process, he discovered that his most famous role was as much of an albatross as a blessing. His follow-up series, *The Partners*, was not successful, and by the late 1970s, he was hosting a cheesy game show called *The Don Adams Screen Test*. Adams was a part owner of the *Get Smart* franchise, and he returned to his shoe phone with the 1980 film, *The Nude Bomb*. He got a boost with another voiceover character, *Inspector Gadget* (yet another detective). Starring for three seasons on the Canadian series *Check It Out!*, which failed to catch on in the States, his final sitcom was yet another dip from the well, the Fox revival of *Get Smart!*

Bernie Kopell

The masterful comic character actor Bernie Kopell was made for situation comedies. Gifted at dialects, he guest-starred (using every kind of accent) on such 1960s stalwarts as *The Jack Benny Show*, *McHale's Navy*, *The Beverly Hillbillies*, *My Favorite Martian*, and *The Dick Van Dyke Show*. By 1969 he had recurring roles on three sitcoms: as Don Hollinger's co-worker on *That Girl*; as the horny apothecary on *Bewitched*; and as Siegfried, the loony KAOS agent, on *Get Smart!* His success waned a bit in the early 1970s, and he found himself playing Doris Day's Italian neighbor in *The Doris Day Show* and Alan-a-Dale in the highly underrated Robin Hood spoof, *When Things Were Rotten*. His longest-running hit was *The Love Boat*, on which he played the oft-divorced ship's physician. Appealing and congenial, he's still a presence on television, recently appearing on *Scrubs*.

Siegfried: This is K.A.O.S. We don't shush here!

Gautier); the perpetually unlucky Agent 13 (Dave Ketchum), always stationed in the worst possible place, from a steamer tray to a bus-station locker; and, the most hapless of them all, Agent Larrabee, played by Adams's real-life cousin Robert Karvelas. In addition to the spy genre, *Get Smart* brilliantly spoofed the bureaucracy and increasingly idiotic red-tape world of corporate America, with Max and Siegfried often stopping their gun battles to compare benefit packages at their respective agencies, or the flavors of the cyanide pills they've been given.

The thing that made the show more than just a goof was that, however ridiculous the proceedings and however supersized Adams's performance became, Barbara Feldon and Edward Platt grounded the show: Feldon with her catlike purr and enigmatic smile and Platt playing the whole thing absolutely straight. Their performances, replete with sober forbearance and slow burns, provided a subtle undercurrent of irony that perfectly offset nuttiness that included such contraptions as the Cone of Silence and Max's brilliantly awkward shoe phone. Then there were the downright certifiable plotlines, like the one in which Carol Burnett guest-starred as country singer Ozark Annie, who swallows a green olive with a KAOS transmitter inside (that episode was written by Jess Oppenheimer, the comic mind behind much of the success of *I Love Lucy*). Edward Platt seemed, at times, like an unwilling or unwitting participant in a bad LSD trip.

The subject of espionage is still ripe for parody and the show has never completely faded away, thanks to cable, DVDs, a TV-movie reunion, and a movie starring Steve Carell. The less said the better about the short-lived 1995 Fox series that reunited Adams and Feldon and featured the mystifyingly unfunny Andy Dick.

OFF THE SET

AGENT 99'S REAL name is never revealed. At one point she is referred to as Susan Hilton, but she later asserts that it was merely an alias.

BARBARA FELDON, A former model, was two inches taller than Don Adams. She spent the entire five seasons wearing flats and slouching. Occasionally, Adams would stand on something so as to appear taller.

DON ADAMS BASED his inimitable Maxwell Smart voice on actor William Powell's calling, "Asta! Asta!" in *The Thin Man* film series.

CAST

Don Adams	Maxwell Smart, Agent 86
Barbara Feldon	Agent 99
Edward Platt	Thaddeus, "The Chief"
Bernie Kopell	Siegfried
Robert Karvelas	Larrabee
Dick Gautier	Hymie
David Ketchum	Agent 13
Jane Dulo	99's Mother
Leonard Strong	The Claw
King Moody	Starker

MILITARY SITCOMS

together people of various ethnic, economic, social, and cultural backgrounds, creating a mini-melting pot that made the perfect petri dish for a hit comedy.

Even the most seemingly unfunny situations became fodder for the military sitcom. What could possibly be funny about a World War II German prison camp? *Hogan's Heroes* found the humor in its pompous commandant, clueless underlings, and wily assortment of prisoners, with even the threat of a stint in "the cooler" a setup for a punch line. From the army (*The Phil Silvers Show*, *Private Benjamin*) to the marines (*Gomer Pyle, U.S.M.C.*, *Major Dad*) to the navy (*McHales' Navy*, *Hennesey*, *CPO Sharkey*, *Operation Petticoat*) to the air force (*I Dream of Jeannie*, *Mona McClusky*) to the denizens of a post–Civil War fort (*F Troop*), every branch of the military has had its turn.

When you add in the unsold pilots that never found network berths, the number of military shows becomes staggering. There was *The Fighting Nightingales*, a pilot starring Adrienne Barbeau, about army nurses during the Korean War (shot for CBS during the run of *M*A*S*H*); *Handle with Care*, set in an all-female MASH unit in Korea, starring Didi Conn (also shot for CBS during the *M*A*S*H* era—talk about a Korean conflict of interest!); and—most tantalizing of all—*Charo and the Sergeant*, in which everyone's favorite "cuchi-cuchi" girl lived on a marine base (with her husband, played by *Green Acres*'s Eb, Tom Lester). Had it sold, we might have been lucky enough to witness Charo rousing (or a-rousing?) an entire barracks with a flamenco guitar version of "Reveille."

What is it about the armed forces that makes them so ripe for comedy? Even during the dark and controversial conflict in Vietnam there were an astounding number of television comedies that revolved around life in the army, navy, or some other branch of military service. (*M*A*S*H*, though ostensibly set during the Korean conflict, was a transparent comment on the absurdity and pointless waste of life in Southeast Asia in the 1970s.)

Perhaps the subject's attraction arose from the generally liberal attitude in Hollywood, where many writers viewed the military as an offshoot of big, bad government. They had a field day poking pointed fun at the guys who got us into war in the first place. And with the built-in hierarchy of lowly privates menaced by bullying sergeants who were in turn terrified of lieutenants (and on up through the chain of command), there was always a juicy possibility for subversion of authority. Finally, the military by nature brings

Upper left: Joe Flynn, Tim Conway, and Ernest Borgnine in a hokey publicity shot for *McHale's Navy*.

Top: The Jane-Hathawayesque efficiency of Beverly Archer and the hilarious bluster of Jon Cypher were integral to the Gerald McRaney sitcom, *Major Dad*.

Left: Frank Sutton as Sgt. Carter and Jim Nabors as *Gomer Pyle, U.S.M.C.*, about to get a "Surprise, surprise, surprise!!!!"

GILLIGAN'S ISLAND

 | 1964–1967 | 98 episodes

Five sightseeing tourists, along with the crew of the S.S. *Minnow*, are shipwrecked on an uncharted isle somewhere between Honolulu and Hoboken. The castaways are weekly thwarted in their attempts to be rescued, consuming large amounts of papaya and coconut in the process.

In the history of television, certain shows just don't coalesce, no matter how brilliant the concept, until all the stars are in perfect alignment. To wit: two pilots of *All in the Family* were filmed, with two different sets of Mike-and-Glorias; and *Three's Company* taped alternate pilots with two other sets of female roommates. As late as the 1990s, scenes in the pilot of *Frasier* were refilmed, with Peri Gilpin replacing Lisa Kudrow (who must've been heartbroken at the time, but got a honey of a consolation prize with a nine-year run on *Friends*).

For the seven woebegone castaways of *Gilligan's Island*, it was another example of *pilotus interruptus*. In 1963, producer Sherwood Schwartz, fascinated with the social implications of strangers from various walks of life thrust into an isolated microcosm, pitched and shot a pilot, but with only four of its final cast members in place: Bob Denver as the hapless Gilligan, Alan Hale Jr. as Skipper Jonas Grumby, and Jim Backus and Natalie Schafer as squillionaires Thurston and Lovey Howell. The rest of the cast was composed of the Professor, played by future soap star John Gabriel, and two secretaries named Ginger and Bunny, played by Kit Smythe and Nancy McCarthy.

When the first pilot was rejected, Schwartz recast and revamped three roles and hit upon that elusive alchemy that elevates a show from mere curiosity to reference point for an entire generation. Tina Louise left the cast of the Carol Burnett musical *Fade Out, Fade In* to play movie star Ginger Grant; Russell Johnson, a longtime Hollywood supporting player, was swapped in as Professor Roy Hinkley; and pert, charming Dawn Wells (a former Miss Nevada) was tapped to play naive farm girl Mary

SITCOMS: THE 101 GREATEST TV COMEDIES OF ALL TIME

Ann Summers. This time, everything clicked and the show was off and running.

The passengers and crew of the S.S. *Minnow* (drolly named by Schwartz after Newton N. Minow, president of the FCC, who famously referred to television as "a vast cultural wasteland") are now such archetypes that imagining the show with other actors is almost impossible. Yet, had there been a different roll of the casting dice, we might now be discussing Jerry Van Dyke as Gilligan, Carroll O'Connor as the Skipper, Jayne Mansfield as Ginger, Dabney Coleman as the Professor, and Raquel Welch as Mary Ann.

Filmed on the lagoon and jungle sets of the CBS backlot in exotic, tropical, Studio City, California (for its final season in 1966, it shared the set with another Schwartz series, *It's About Time*), *Gilligan's Island* was universally dismissed by critics as the most inane piece of dreck ever to grace the airwaves. Of course it was silly—that was half the fun. *Gilligan's Island* challenged the viewers' suspension of disbelief more than did any sitcom until *Mork and Mindy* (most of whose viewers didn't even question the extraterrestrial aspect of the show ... they just wanted to know what the dude playing Mork was on, and where could they get some?). Without even going into particulars of the toilet facilities on the island, how did Miss Ginger Grant launder her extensively beaded and sequined wardrobe, much less maintain the obvious henna rinse and set that she sported week in and week out?

In truth, there is no point in trying to find a Chekhovian subtext in *Gilligan's Island*; it was an oasis of silly, nonthreatening fun. The cast particularly loved doing the numerous dream sequences,

Above: Alan Hale, Jr. and his little buddy Bob Denver were the Laurel and Hardy of sitcoms.

Below: Bob Denver and Herb Edelman share a stogie in *The Good Guys*, one of Denver's post-Gilligan sitcom efforts.

Bob Denver

The character of Maynard G. Krebs catapulted Bob Denver to national fame. Fresh out of college, taking on his first role, Denver turned Krebs into one of the seminal characters in sitcom history. Between that job and his next starring role, as the title character in *Gilligan's Island*, he made guest appearances on several sitcoms. After that hit, he played a lead in *The Good Guys*, which managed a two-season run, and the syndicated *Dusty's Trail*, a Gilligan rip-off that followed seven wandering members of a wagon train. He appeared in other television shows, several movies, and even replaced Woody Allen in the Broadway production of *Play It Again, Sam*. But somehow he could never shake the character of Gilligan, returning in *The New Adventures of Gilligan*, *The Castaways on Gilligan's Island*, and *Gilligan's Planet*. He also guested, as Gilligan, on *The New Gidget*, *ALF*, *Baywatch*, and, in his last television appearance, on the Bronson Pinchot sitcom *Meego*.

Skipper: Ginger, I've got a problem ... I've got a real problem ... now, you're a girl, right?
Ginger: Well, if you're not sure about that, you have got a problem!

giving them a chance to escape the drudgery of the plastic palm trees and rattan furniture they faced week in and week out. To see Russell Johnson as a horny old geezer in the "Jack and the Beanstalk" sequence, Alan Hale as Gilligan's sweet little gray-haired mother in a James Bond spoof, or Natalie Schafer and Dawn Wells as Mary Poppins and Eliza Doolittle, respectively, it's clear these hambones got a real kick out of cutting loose. To add to the fun, Schwartz gave three of its regulars the chance to play dual roles, a commonplace practice for sitcoms of the day. Along with a Thurston Howell impersonator and a Gilligan doppelganger (in actuality a Russian agent), the campiest dual role on *Gilligan's Island* involved Tina Louise, doubling as the plain, nearsighted librarian Eva Grubb (a name straight out of Dickens). Arriving on the

island having to get away from a society that rejected her, the generous castaways do the Henry Higgins bit and give Eva a makeover, the likes of which would not be seen again until *Oprah*. Transformed into a Ginger look-alike, Ms. Grubb slips away from the amenable suckers, returning to Hollywood as Ginger Grant, the only

survivor of the shipwrecked *Minnow*.

In addition to the dream sequences, there were weekly opportunities (usually foiled by a well-meaning but bass-ackwards Gilligan) to make contact with the outside world, whether it was a phone line washed up on the shore or a carrier pigeon bringing news to civilization. Careful not to put all the blame on one character, Schwartz made sure that Gilligan had his share of truly inspired ideas, saving them all from danger as often as he fouled things up. He was the personification of the double-edged sword, one minute the Skipper's "little buddy," the next minute an absolute dodo bird.

And considering it took place on an uncharted island, a seemingly endless parade of visitors washed up on the island:

A mosaic of Gilligan's Islanders playing dressup in some of the show's many dream sequences.

Jim Backus

A master of the mumbled ad-lib, Jim Backus started his career in radio (where one of his characters, the snobbish Hubert Updyke III, would become the basis for Thurston Howell III), where so many of his contemporaries cut their comedic molars. While making his way in radio he began to do cartoon voices, and in one of his first attempts, 1949's *Ragtime Bear*, Backus created the character he would be identified with forever, the hopelessly nearsighted millionaire Mr. Magoo, appearing in more than fifty cartoon shorts (our personal favorite: 1959's *1001 Arabian Nights*, as Uncle Abdul Azziz Magoo) over the next decade. His first situation comedy role was as the harried Judge Bradley Stevens in *I Married Joan*, working with future *Gilligan* creator Sherwood Schwartz, then an up-and-coming writer. Married on that show to a character even crazier than Lucy Ricardo, Backus perfected his slow burn and trademark droll retort. During the run of *Joan*, he also made film appearances, surprising everyone with his fine dramatic abilities as James Dean's father in the 1954 classic *Rebel Without a Cause*. After a flop series called *Hot Off the Wire*, Backus answered Schwartz's call to portray the role he was tailor made for, on *Gilligan's Island*. After *Gilligan's* three-year run, Backus was rarely out of work, writing several books with his beloved wife Henny, and making guest appearances (including two characters on Schwartz's *Brady Bunch*). And of course there was the cottage industry of *Gilligan* animated series and reunion movies, as well Mr. Magoo. Backus made a career out of playing comic millionaires. Only a long battle with Parkinson's disease finally slowed down the lovable blue blood.

Zsa Zsa Gabor as socialite Erika Tiffany Smith; a prepubescent Kurt Russell as a jungle boy; and Phil Silvers as the sleazy Broadway impresario Harold Hekuba, trying to mount a musical version of *Hamlet* (sung to the score of the opera *Carmen*: immediately, drop everything and sing Polonius's "To thine own self be true" speech to the Toreador Song. It works!). Oh, and the head hunters. No fewer than eight times savage natives (of apparent Polynesian descent, half a world away from Hawaii) came to the island in search of heads to shrink.

Three seasons and they were off, into the world of afternoon reruns. In 1978, after twelve years in syndication, NBC bought the idea of TV movie reunion in which the stranded seven were finally rescued. The original cast, puzzled but ultimately flattered by the long-lasting appeal of the show, agreed to appear (save Tina Louise, replaced by Judith Baldwin), and the result, *Rescue from Gilligan's Island*, was a surprise runaway hit. Others followed, with diminishing results (Ladies and gentlemen of the jury, I give you Exhibit A: *The Harlem Globetrotters on Gilligan's Island*. The defense rests), but in the same way that another Sherwood Schwartz series, *The Brady Bunch*, made the leap from TV entertainment to cultural phenomenon, *Gilligan's Island* has become intractably ingrained in the consciousness of an entire generation.

Right: According to the show's creators, the delicious Natalie Schaefer was the best sport of them all when it came to the inane hijinks the cast had to endure. Here, she cuts up and swaps headgear with Bob Denver.

CAST

Bob Denver	Gilligan
Alan Hale Jr.	Jonas Grumby, "The Skipper"
Jim Backus	Thurston Howell III
Natalie Schafer	Lovey Howell
Tina Louise	Ginger Grant
Russell Johnson	Roy Hinkley, "The Professor"
Dawn Wells	Mary Ann Summers

THE GOLDBERGS

 | 1949-1951 | 1952-1954 | 1954 | *100-plus episodes*

Molly Goldberg, a warm and wonderful Jewish mother, presides over a family that includes her husband Jake, her son Sammy, her daughter Rosalie, and her beloved Uncle Jake, in a house at 1030 East Tremont Avenue in the Bronx.

"Yoo-Hoo!" Philip Loeb and Gertrude Berg as everyone's favorite neighbors. Note the product placement of sponsor Sanka, who pulled out of the show when Loeb was blacklisted.

This country may have suffered its share of homophobia, racism, and anti-Semitism, but, surprisingly, early radio and television embraced minorities (okay, not gays), and shows like *Amos 'n' Andy* and *The Goldbergs* were long-running successes for decades on both radio and television.

Gertrude Berg created the character of Molly Goldberg for audiences at her family's Catskill Mountains hotel, though she was originally named Maltke Talznitsky. Molly made her first national appearance on radio on November 20, 1929, on *The Rise of the Goldbergs*, broadcast on NBC's Blue Network. The plots and characters had already been fully fleshed out, with Berg wearing three hats, as writer, actress, and producer. The fifteen-minute program was a melding of sitcom and soap opera, and was an immediate smash hit. Though many of the listeners were not Jewish, all could relate to a family's struggles to make good in a new country.

By 1931, Pepsodent was sponsoring the show six nights a week. After a break in 1935, the show returned on CBS radio as *The Goldbergs*, with Colgate-Palmolive-Peet as sponsors. In 1939, the Goldberg family moved to Connecticut from their home in the Bronx. Assimilated into American society but still respectful of their Jewish roots, the Goldbergs mirrored the lives of their listeners; when World War II began, Berg, an ardent supporter of Jewish causes, sent the Goldberg's son Sammy off to fight. Other episodes dealt with anti-Semitism and the

Left: The Goldberg family in the house on Tremont Avenue.

Below: Gertrude Berg and Betsy von Furstenberg on the short-lived *Mrs. G. Goes to College*.

Goldbergs and Gertrude Berg are the progenitors of every overtly ethnic show that has come after it, from *The Nanny* to *All-American Girl*, from *Life with Luigi* to *Chico and the Man*, from *Bridget Loves Bernie* to *Everybody Loves Raymond*.

CAST

Gertrude Berg.........Molly Goldberg

Philip Loeb ....Jake Goldberg (1)

Harold J. Stone ....Jake Goldberg (2)

Robert H. Harris ....Jake Goldberg (3)

Larry Robinson ......Sammy Goldberg (1)

Tom Taylor ....Sammy Goldberg (2)

Arlene McQuade ...Rosalie Goldberg

Eli Mintz ....Uncle David

perilous Jewish situation in Germany, in addition to the social life of the family and husband Jake's travails in business.

The series took a two-year break beginning in 1948, during which time Berg appeared on Broadway in her own play, *Me and Molly*, as well as in a film version of the series. In 1949, the show returned, this time on the newly blossoming medium of television. It quickly became the third most popular show on the air. It was not without its bumpy moments, however. In 1951, Philip Loeb, the actor playing Jake Goldberg, was blacklisted, and both the sponsor (General Foods) and CBS dropped the show. It moved to NBC and Berg (exhibiting her true class) continued to pay Loeb his full salary though he had to be replaced by Harold J. Stone. Depressed by his lack of work and other personal circumstances, Loeb committed suicide four years later. For the first six months of its tenure on NBC, *The Goldbergs* reverted to the fifteen-minute format and was broadcast three times a week. After a final move to the DuMont network, the show was filmed for the first time and syndicated under the name *Molly*. Because it was broadcast live through most of its history, little record exists of it today, save its final, filmed season.

A groundbreaking show created by a groundbreaking woman (the first to produce her own television show), *The*

Gertrude Berg

Find what you're good at and stick to it. That certainly worked for Gertrude Berg, who devoted much of her life to playing the character of Molly Goldberg on radio, television, film, and Broadway for almost thirty years. Even when she appeared as characters with other names, the characterization was the same. She was born to Russian immigrants in the Jewish section of Harlem and married Lewis Berg, a chemical engineer. When Berg adapted her Molly Goldberg character for radio, the show was an instant success and her future held more of the same. Berg took time out from the Goldberg family to write film scripts for Sol Lesser and soon became one of the richest writers in show business, landing a $5-million contract to write, perform in, and coproduce *The Goldbergs*. She also appeared on Broadway in *Majority of One* and, beginning in 1961, starred in another television series, *Mrs. G Goes to College* (retitled *The Gertrude Berg Show* halfway through its only season on the air). It's no wonder, with the eternal association between actress and character, that when she appeared as the mystery guest on *What's My Line?* she was identified as Molly Goldberg, not Gertrude Berg.

THE GOLDEN GIRLS

NBC | **1985–1992** | **180 episodes**

Four women of a certain age live, love, and laugh together in a house in Miami Beach. Weekly crises ensue, resulting in consumption of numerous cheescakes around the kitchen table and the inevitable sense of closure.

Picture it: Burbank, 1984. NBC executive Brandon Tartikoff visits his elderly aunt and becomes fascinated with the love/hate relationship she has with her next-door neighbor, best friend, and constant source of aggravation. Through the arguing, kvetching, and pettiness, he sees the germ of an idea for a sitcom dealing with a heretofore ignored population of the viewing public, and contacts Susan Harris, creator of the '70s hit *Soap*. She, along with Tony Thomas (son of Danny, brother of Marlo) and her husband, Paul Junger Witt, have a production company and produce a pilot for the 1984–85 season. *The Golden Girls* becomes not only the first hit show

with an all-female cast but the first show populated nearly exclusively with characters over the age of fifty.

Once a pilot was written and casting began, Bea Arthur was everyone's first choice to play the dry, droll Dorothy (in fact, creator Susan Harris knew Arthur well, having written the controversial "Maude's Abortion" episode of Arthur's previous sitcom)—but she passed on the project. The producers then set about looking for a "Bea Arthur type" (Lee Grant also passed, not wanting to play a woman old enough to be a grandmother, and Elaine Stritch, as she recounts in her one-woman show *At Liberty*, blew her audition and her big chance at television stardom. One must view this admission with a certain amount of skepticism,

They weren't just "the sexy one," "the wise one," and "the naive one." Rue McClanahan, Beatrice Arthur, and Betty White, all veteran character comediennes, gave the characters of Blanche, Dorothy, and Rose increasing depth over the seven-season run.

though, as she talks of auditioning for the suits at *CBS* when the show was born and bred exclusively at NBC).

The pilot was also conceived with actresses Betty White and Rue McClanahan in mind—but not for the roles they ended up playing. Betty White, who had created a legendary character in the oversexed Sue Ann Nivens on *Mary Tyler Moore*, was originally envisioned as the perpetually horny Blanche Devereaux, while Harris had McClanahan in mind for the ditsy Rose Nylund, not unlike the slightly spacey Vivian she had played on *Maude*. When they met for a reading, it was Jay Sandrich, the brilliant director of the pilot, that made the suggestion to switch characters and shake things up. Magic.

Then, in a stroke of good fortune, McClanahan persuaded Bea Arthur to take another look at the pilot. When she reread the script she called Susan Harris and said she'd take a chance on it, and the three main characters of *The Golden Girls* were finally perfectly cast with three genius veterans of the half-hour form. Rounding out the team was Dorothy's eighty-year-old mother, Sophia Petrillo, played by Estelle Getty, fresh from playing Harvey Fierstein's mother in the Broadway play *Torch Song Trilogy*. In actuality three months younger than Bea Arthur, Getty was initially rejected as looking too young to play an octogenarian, but after convincing them to audition her again, Getty

Levin. Harris had created the first gay sitcom regular, played by Billy Crystal on *Soap*, so Coco seemed to hold great potential as a supporting character who was always on hand with a zinger. But on

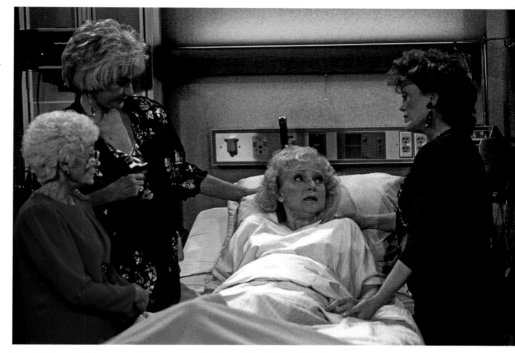

The girls in one of their more serious moments, when Betty White's Rose Nylund has to undergo open-heart surgery.

tape night of the pilot, Estelle Getty created such a smash as a perfectly outrageous octogenarian whose stroke had affected the portion of her brain that censors itself, the creators realized what a corker they had. The character of Coco, or, as Sophia

for their specific gifts. Arthur is a master of the unlearnable art of comic timing. A true genius of the unspoken reaction, on one episode she even attempted (without a net) a quadruple take, something sel-

dom if ever seen since the heyday of the Yiddish theatre. Of course she landed it flawlessly. White's genius is in creating a truly believable character of great naiveté, especially tricky for an actress who possesses one of the quickest and wickedest wits in Hollywood, yet never editorializes or passes judgment on the character of Rose. McClanahan is perhaps the best actress of the bunch in the sense that she always fills *every minute* of the scenes that she is in like an actress in a Broadway play. She made the producers' jobs considerably easier, for in choosing shots they could always cut to McClanahan secure in the knowledge that she would be fully energized and listening intently to the other

Blanche: My life is an open book.
Sophia: Your life is an open blouse.

showed up in a wig and old-age makeup and was immediately given the role.

The pilot was taped with the four girls and a fifth regular, the now notorious "Coco" the gay cook, played by Charles

called him, the "fancy man," was deemed excess baggage, and disappeared after the pilot, never to be seen again.

Every hardcore fan has his or her favorite Golden Girl but all four can be admired

actors. Getty is the most perplexing of the bunch, as she was not nearly as seasoned as the other three; in fact, on many episodes she can be seen glancing down at cue cards for her lines. And on the few occasions she had to play a dramatic scene she came across as, well, game at best. Still, she ended up getting the biggest laughs in many an episode, and it can hardly be attributed to the writing alone. In a wonderfully odd way, her seeming a bit out of step and over her head worked brilliantly. Any hesitations in her delivery ended up coming across as if Sophia's synapses were firing just a hair late.

The show lasted for seven successful seasons, its longevity due in large part to its strong writing. The writers, in addition to Harris, included Gail Parent, Marc Sotkin, Christopher Lloyd (NOT the actor from *Taxi*), and the teams of Barry Fanaro and Mort Nathan (vitally important to the development of the series over the first four seasons), Richard Vaczy and Tracy Gamble, and Jamie Wooten and Marc Cherry (later the wizard behind *Desperate Housewives*). Some of the best comic writers in the business, they knew the girls inside and out and wrote specifically for them, never supplying generic punchlines that could be swapped among characters, as in the later seasons of such shows as *Murphy Brown* and *M*A*S*H*. The four girls became like four points of a compass: each distinct and yet all four necessary to maintain a balance.

Not only did the show provide juicy opportunities for its four regulars, it was a wonderful showcase for many other greats over

The deadpan Beatrice Arthur and the twinkling Betty White approach comedy from opposite directions yet both arrive at the hilarious truth that is the hallmark of great sitcom acting.

Betty White

With her dimples and fresh scrubbed Midwestern cheer masking a rapier-like wit, Betty White has been a TV pioneer. She moved from Chicago to Hollywood when she was two years old, her family settling in a small house on Cahuenga Boulevard. Who could have guessed that more than sixty years later she would be taping *The Golden Girls* at RenMar studios, just three or four blocks down Cahuenga from where she grew up? After an early start as a television disc jockey, playing records and doing commercials on Al Jarvis's daytime show on KLAC, White attracted attention in her first sitcom, *Life with Elizabeth* (self-produced), which developed out of the sketches she had done on Jarvis's show. After producing and starring in another series, *A Date with the Angels*, costarring Bill Williams, White spent much of the late '50s and '60s playing herself on talk shows (she was one of Jack Paar's favorite *Tonight Show* guests) and game shows, after meeting and marrying her third husband, *Password* host Allen Ludden. In 1974, she was asked by Grant Tinker, an old friend of her husband's, to guest star on Tinker's show in the part of a sickeningly sweet TV homemaker. The show, of course, was *Mary*

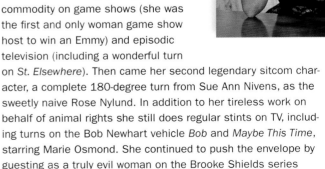

Tyler Moore, and as Sue Ann Nivens, White caused a sensation by bringing smuttiness delivered with a beatific smile to television in a wildly refreshing way. Her follow-up, *The Betty White Show*, lasted only thirteen weeks but White became a highly sought-after commodity on game shows (she was the first and only woman game show host to win an Emmy) and episodic television (including a wonderful turn on *St. Elsewhere*). Then came her second legendary sitcom character, a complete 180-degree turn from Sue Ann Nivens, as the sweetly naive Rose Nylund. In addition to her tireless work on behalf of animal rights she still does regular stints on TV, including turns on the Bob Newhart vehicle *Bob* and *Maybe This Time*, starring Marie Osmond. She continued to push the envelope by guesting as a truly evil woman on the Brooke Shields series *Suddenly Susan*, suing Susan for age discrimination, and a murderous secretary on the drama *Boston Legal*.

the age of fifty. Since all four women were single there were many suitors, including such masterful comedians as Dick Van Dyke, Pat Harrington, Jr., Hal Linden, John McMartin, Jerry Orbach, Robert Mandan, Paul Dooley, Eddie Bracken, Jack Gilford, Mickey Rooney, Ken Howard, and Robert Culp. Playing the girls' sisters, cousins, and friends were such gifted actresses as Nancy Walker, Polly Holliday, Geraldine Fitzgerald, Barbara Babcock, Marian Mercer, Anne Francis, Sheree North, Inga Swenson, Betty Garrett, Brenda Vaccaro, and the wonderful Lois Nettleton as Dorothy's college roommate Jean, whose lesbianism becomes an issue when she falls in love with a totally clueless Rose. The scene in which Dorothy and Sophia tell Blanche about Jean ("not *Lebanese*, Blanche. *Lesbian.*") is one of the classic sitcom scenes, ranking up there in writing and execution with Mary Richards's job interview and Felix and Oscar's appearance on *Password*.

At the end of the seventh season Arthur finally moved on (she had been threatening to leave since the end of the fifth), and her character married Blanche's Uncle Lucas, played by Leslie Nielsen. The show came back the following fall as *The Golden Palace*, with the three remaining girls now running a hotel in Miami Beach along with Cheech Marin and future movie star Don Cheadle. But with only three points of the compass remaining the magic was palpably gone. Hell, they even added a kid, a sure sign that they were foundering. Estelle continued playing Sophia on *Empty Nest* and *Nurses*, two other Witt/Thomas/Harris shows. She reprised her starmaking role as recently as 1999, when she played a now ninety-five-year-old Sophia on the show *Ladies Man*.

And still *The Golden Girls* chugs on in syndication, winning fans who missed it in its original Saturday night berth but have discovered it in its fantastically successful run on Lifetime Television for Women (and Gay Men). A hit in more than sixty countries, *The Golden Girls* will continue to find fans as long as people have affection for their zany aunt or salty grandmother, forever a testament to razor-sharp writing and the talents of its four masters of character-driven comedy.

Estelle Getty and Beatrice Arthur, in reality about as Italian as a bagel and a knish, as mother and daughter Sophia and Dorothy Petrillo.

Above: White, McClanahan, and Arthur in the kitchen, also known as crisis central on most episodes of *The Golden Girls*.

Right: Herb Edelman, as lovable shlemiel Stan Zbornak, in a nightgown that doesn't do a thing for his figure, and Estelle Getty, about to proclaim "There's a hurricane a'comin.'"

CAST

Beatrice Arthur .... Dorothy Petrillo-Zbornak

Betty White .... Rose Nylund

Rue McClanahan ... Blanche Devereaux

Estelle Getty .... Sophia Petrillo

Herb Edelman .... Stanley Zbornak

Harold Gould .... Miles Webber

Bill Dana .... Angelo Petrillo

Sheree North .... Virginia Hollingsworth

Scott Jacoby .... Michael Petrillo

Nancy Walker .... Aunt Angela

Lyn Greene .... Young Dorothy

Sid Melton .... Salvatore Petrillo

Herb Edelman

As Dorothy's ex-husband, Herb Edelman played one of the most lovable losers in sitcom history. In addition to his twenty-two appearances on *The Golden Girls*, Edelman costarred opposite Bob Denver and Joyce Van Patten in his own series, the short-lived cult show *The Good Guys*, in 1968. Beloved by all who worked with him, he was the picture of professionalism, as adept at drama as at comedy. He made over 100 guest appearances on such shows as *That Girl*, *It's About Time*, *The Mothers-In-Law*, *The Flying Nun*, *Bewitched*, *Barney Miller*, *Maude*, and *Welcome Back, Kotter* (playing Juan Epstein's father), but it is for his portrayal of Stanley Zbornak, the novelty salesman turned millionaire (with his invention "The Zborny," a baked potato opener), that he will forever be remembered. The interplay between Edelman and Bea Arthur (at 6'5", he was one of the few actors to dwarf the sequoia-like actress) in "The Monkey Show" episode, where Stan transfers his unrequited love for Dorothy to a traffic cone dressed like a monkey, is an all-time classic moment in situation comedy.

GOOD TIMES

 | **1974–1979** | **133 episodes**

The proud and loving Evans family, living in a Chicago housing project, manages to scratch out a good time or two through "temporary layoffs" and "easy-credit ripoffs."

Catch phrases. They have been a part of sitcoms from the very beginning. Their roots go back at least as far as vaudeville, where such beloved performers as Al Jolson coined his legendary "You ain't heard nothin' yet!" In radio, "Henryyyyyyy! Henry Aldrich!!!" swept the country. In the 1950s, on the small screen, Ralph Kramden's "Baby, you're the greatest" entered the general lexicon. In truth, catch phrases make a show seem formulaic on some level, and by the fiftieth time you hear Cousin Balki say "Don't be ree-dickoluss," it's frankly not that much of a knee-slapper, but these verbal trademarks enhance the familiarity that is the cornerstone of all hit sitcoms. "Missed it by that much." "What you talkin' bout, Willis?" "God'll get you for that, Walter." "Nip it in the bud!" And, along with Fonzie's "Aaaaaaaaaaaaaay" and Florence Jean Castleberry's "Kiss Mah Grits!," "Dyn-O-Mite!," made famous by J.J. Evans, the stringbean son on *Good Times*, became one of the most parroted phrases of the '70s.

Ironically, it was "Dyn-O-Mite" that caused much of the explosive atmosphere behind the scenes on *Good Times*. Created by Eric Monte and Mike Evans, the latter the actor who had played the Bunkers' neighbor Lionel Jefferson on *All in the Family*, the members of the Evans family were, in a way, step-grandchildren of the Bunkers. When Norman Lear spun off the character of Maude Findlay into her own sitcom in 1972, her housekeeper was Florida Evans, played by Esther Rolle. Around the same time, Monte and Evans created *Good Times*, set in

Esther Rolle and John Amos, the loving heads of the Evans family, in their humble apartment, where grits still fry in the kitchen and beans still burn on the grill.

the housing projects of Chicago. When Rolle was cast as the lead, the two shows were merged and the family matriarch of *Good Times* became Florida Evans. In the process, they gave her husband a new name, James (on *Maude* his name had been Henry), and three children: aspiring artist James Jr. ("J.J."), the sensitive and beautiful Thelma (BernNadette Stanis), and the politically active youngest, Michael, played by the fantastic Ralph Carter. In keeping with television's long-standing disregard for logic, it was never explained how Florida got from Tuckahoe, New York, to the projects of Chicago—but then again, it was never explained what seven stranded castaways used for toilet facilities.

Along with sassy neighbor Willona Woods, played by Ja'net DuBois with enough paisley headscarves to make Rhoda Morgenstern green with envy, the Evans family scraped by in a thinly veiled version of Chicago's notorious Cabrini-Green housing projects. In groundbreaking fashion, the show presented a situation that not only African American audiences could identify with, but also offered the entire country a look into life in the working class that was nothing like that of Ralph Kramden. The most important aspect of the show, however, at least for its first two seasons, was the deep pride the family felt, led by the moral compass of the parents, played by Amos and Rolle.

Good Times had without a doubt the most vocal studio audience of any sitcom: on one episode, a woman in the audience is clearly heard egging on Willona, shouting, "Hit him!!!!!" When the show dealt with real-life issues it was among the most compelling of its time. Gang violence, racial profiling, venereal disease, and alcoholism were all woven into the show, and, in a particularly sobering two-parter, J.J. eloped with his junkie girlfriend, played by a Debbie Allen. To make matters worse, the go-between to her supplier was a child younger than Michael, and the family's horror at finding a bag of heroin on him prompted the following exchange:

Florida: But James, he's still a baby!
James: Well, this ain't his talcum powder!

Norman Lear

A true television legend, Norman Lear is undoubtedly the most influential writer and producer in the history of sitcoms. After serving in World War II he set out as a comedy writer on such shows as *The Ford Star Revue* and *The Colgate Comedy Hour*. In 1959 Lear teamed with Bud Yorkin and founded Tandem Productions, and as early as 1968, Lear began developing an American version of a British television show called *Till Death Us Do Part*. After a slightly rocky start, *All in the Family* became a blockbuster, and Lear revolutionized the sitcom in appearance, tone, and subject, pushing the envelope so far beyond the merely countercultural *Smothers Brothers* and *Laugh-In*, that, in retrospect, those formerly controversial shows seemed like slightly naughty college skits. He followed up his smash with another retooled Britcom, *Sanford and Son*, and the first of eight *All in the Family* spinoffs, *Maude*. In Maude Findlay, Lear had the perfect mouthpiece for his own liberal views. After helping create two more spinoffs, *The Jeffersons* and *Good Times*, and two original shows, the hit *One Day at a Time* and the cult hit *Mary Hartman, Mary Hartman* (in which Lear pushed the envelope too far for the mainstream, so unrelenting was the mirror it held up to American hypocrisy), he became the busiest man in primetime television, at one point working on no fewer than six hit series. Lear began to lose his touch with such daring yet unsuccessful shows as *All That Glitters* and *The Baxters* (ahead of its time even today—a fifteen-minute sitcom dealing with current issues, followed by a fifteen minute talkback with a studio audience). As the 1980s dawned, He began to concentrate on other important issues. He founded a political action group called People for the American Way in 1982, to speak out for Bill of Rights guarantees and monitor violations of the Constitution. He returned to TV in the 1990s with the unsuccessful shows *Sunday Dinner*, *704 Hauser* (about an African-American family who moves into the Bunkers' old house), and the highly underrated political satire *The Powers That Be*. Norman Lear's greatest legacy is forever changing the timbre of the situation comedy, remaking it into an art form that uses laughter to challenge, inspire, and instruct viewers and get them to take a look at the world beyond their living rooms.

And then? Trouble. As the character of J.J., with his strut, his wisp of a moustache, and his toothy grin as wide as the mighty Mississippi, became more and more popular, his behavior became more and more buffoonish. Uncomfortable with the direction in which he saw the show going, Amos bitterly complained to producers, who responded by killing off his character (Florida famously reacted to the news by smashing a punch bowl with an anguished "Damn, damn, DAMN!"). After another season of ever more "Dyn-O-Mite!!!!!," Rolle left as well, claiming that Walker had become an unhealthy role model for young African Americans. With both Amos and Rolle gone, the Evans family was now supervised by neighbor Willona. Ja'net DuBois had first billing, with Walker in the final position (in a style usually reserved for the likes of Joan Collins: "and also starring Jimmy Walker as J.J.").

The show still tackled some important subjects, dealing with young Penny (played by a pre-"Nasty" Janet Jackson), a new character adopted by Willona, being abused by her birth mother. Then, in a truly surprising turn of events, Rolle returned to the show after a year's absence, having proved her point. Too little, too late. The show was yanked halfway through the sixth season, in the summer of 1979, and CBS dumped the remainder of its already taped shows. In a rare happy moment for the Evans family, in the final episode, everyone got out of the projects and all

was tied up in a perfect package for one of the only times in its six-year run. African-American sitcoms (in fact, most sitcoms) of the last twenty years would be wise to take a look at it for its combination of reality and family-driven humor.

Cast

Esther Rolle	Florida Evans
John Amos	James Evans, Sr.
Ja'net DuBois	Willona Woods
Ralph Carter	Michael Evans
BernNadette Stanis	Thelma Evans
Jimmie Walker	James "J.J." Evans, Jr.
Johnny Brown	Nathan Bookman
Janet Jackson	Millicent "Penny" Gordon
Ben Powers	Keith Anderson
Helen Martin	Wanda
Matthew "Stymie"	Beard Monty
Moses Gunn	Carl Dixon
Raymond Allen	Ned the Wino
Teddy Wilson	Sweet Daddy Williams

Opposite top: The Evans children, played by Ralph Carter, Jimmy Walker, and BernNadette Stanis, surround their matriarch Florida, played by Esther Rolle.

Left: Lanky scene stealer Jimmy Walker tries to charm a disapproving Esther Rolle, who publicly complained about the direction she saw the *Good Times* going.

GREEN ACRES

 | **1965–1971** | **170 episodes**

Wealthy New York City lawyer Oliver Wendell Douglas drags his loopy Hungarian wife, Lisa, kicking and screaming to the simple life on a ramshackle farm. Oliver soon finds that the insanity of the city was nothing compared to the residents of Hooterville, USA.

With some of the most surreal humor ever to grace the small screen, *Green Acres* was positively brilliant in its off-beat sense of reality. Let's face it: This show wasn't just odd, it was positively nutty. At the time, many called it idiotic, lumping *Green Acres* in with other 1960s shows such as *Gilligan's Island* and *The Munsters*. Its critics couldn't be more off base, though, for while the residents of Hooterville were undeniably crazy, they were crazy like a fox.

Paul Henning had created two hits with *The Beverly Hillbillies* and *Petticoat Junction*, so the suits at CBS gave him carte blanche to create a third show in the same vein. The new show was based on Henning's obscure 1950 radio series *Granby's Green Acres*, which had run for only thirteen episodes. Starring Gale Gordon and Bea Benaderet, it had also featured a handyman named Eb and a general store clerk named Mr. Kimball.

Green Acres featured some of the canniest casting of any series in the history of television. Eddie Albert and Eva Gabor were a crackerjack pair of comedians with a sexual chemistry that was refreshingly unlike any other married couple in its continental charm. (Gabor finished many an episode with, "When are we going

Above: TV magic revealed: With the proper perspective on a painted backdrop, a soundstage only four feet deep could be made to look like acres and acres.

Right: With the grips looking down from the catwalk, Eva Gabor concocts one of her lethal pots of coffee.

language and was absolutely no help on the farm, throwing dishes out the window rather than washing them.

These folks were no Ma and Pa Kettle, to be sure. The Douglases named their livestock, including a cow named Eleanor, a rooster named Bertram, and a pet duck named Drobney. How nutty was the show? Drobney was the offspring of a duck that had served in the Hungarian Underground with Lisa during World War II. (She had worked as a "tanks blower-upper" and met Oliver when he bailed out of a fighter plane over France, hiding in a haystack, when Lisa sticks him with a pitchfork, she became forever known as "Das Lumpenshticker.")

The most beloved cast member was a curly-tailed piece of porcine star quality named Arnold Ziffel. Adopted by Fred and Doris Ziffel, who didn't have any human children, Arnold watched television, played hooky, and won an occasional Halloween competition, so convincing was his pig costume. In fact, the entire county treated him like a human being, and part of the brilliance of the show was watching Eddie Albert, against his own better judgment,

to get to the shmooching?") Albert and Gabor were like skewed versions of William Powell and Myrna Loy in the screwball comedies of the 1930s. They were glamorous, madcap, yet living in an absolute dump of a house, with purple velvet chaise lounges in a living room with wallpaper dating from the Fillmore administration.

And then there were the loopy local yokels who made perfect sense to one another but drove Oliver straight up the telephone pole he had to climb to place a phone call. Watching Eddie Albert, as former Manhattan lawyer Oliver Wendell Douglas, deal with this bizarre world was frustrating fun at the time the show aired, but in retrospect it's clear that the subversive social satire of *Green Acres* was truly inspired, with hens that laid square eggs and a toaster that only worked when

someone said the number "five" ("seven" was an outdated model). Gabor's Lisa (née Granietz, whose father was the former king of "Hungaria"… according to her), decked herself out in a never-ending parade of gowns and peignoirs designed by famed Hollywood costumier Jean Louis. She was one of the most delightfully obtuse sitcom characters since Gracie Allen. A horrible cook (her "hotscakes," as she called them, were only useful to fix the gasket head on their tractor, or as smudge pots when the tomato crops in the Hooterville valley were threatened by an early frost), she constantly mangled the English

OFF THE SET

THE ONLY CAST member of *Green Acres* to win an award for his or her performance? Arnold the pig, of course, who received the coveted "Patsy" Award for best animal performance of 1967.

BEFORE EDDIE ALBERT was given the role of Oliver Wendell Douglas, the producers were considering Don Ameche.

GREEN ACRES WAS the first television sitcom in which the theme song was sung by the stars of the show.

Pat Buttram

Pat Buttram, whose yodel-like twang made him instantly identifiable, fell into show business in a most unlikely fashion. Attending the 1933 Chicago World's Fair from his native Alabama, he was interviewed by an on-the-scene reporter. So sidesplitting was his comic timing and folksy manner, he was offered a job with the station on the spot, hosting the long-running radio show *National Barn Dance*. On one episode, he charmed Gene Autry so much that Autry brought Buttram to Hollywood to be his film sidekick. He went on to appear on Autry's television show from 1950 to 1956. A natural for such bucolic sitcoms as *The Real McCoys* and *Pistols* and *Petticoats*, Buttram is best known as the huckster Mr. Haney on *Green Acres*, who had more hidden charges in his "deals" than anyone this side of Ticketmaster. Well known for his voice work in Disney movies, he was a regular member of the dais of Dean Martin's celebrity roasts, getting away with wicked potshots that others without his aw-shucks wit could never attempt.

Lisa: Why do you want to irritate your corn?
Oliver: Irrigate. It means put water on it.
Lisa: Won't that irritate it?

give in to the insanity and try to reason with a pig as if the latter were a ten-year-old Opie Taylor.

It's a show that got smarter when you perceived its many layers of reality. In particular, when Lisa "saw" the show's opening credits written in the batter of her "hotscakes," on the laundry she was hanging on the line, or on the eggs that their hen Alice laid, the show was positively Pirandellian. On one episode in which the characters were arguing at the top of the show, they stopped, sat down, and waited patiently while the credits rolled, then picked up their argument where they left off, as if nothing had happened.

Like the other Paul Henning shows, its on-the-nose casting was another key to its success. Like *The Beverly Hillbillies* and *Petticoat Junction*, *Green Acres* had a superb supporting cast: Tom Lester as the hopelessly incompetent farmhand Eb; Mary Grace Canfield and Sid Melton as brother and sister carpenters Ralph and Alf Monroe; Hank Patterson and Barbara Pepper as Fred and Doris Ziffel; Eleanor Audley as Oliver's mother, Eunice; and Pat Buttram, Frank Cady, and Alvy Moore as the trio of infuriating locals Misters Haney, Drucker, and Kimball. Here was

Above: Eva Gabor parading around in Jean Louis originals, a purple velvet chaise lounge crammed into the corner, and Kandinskys on the walls of a ramshackle dump just added to the surreality of *Green Acres*.

Opposite top: Tom Lester, as hopeless farmhand Eb; Eddie Albert; and Eva Gabor examine the results of an unfortunate case of cow-tipping.

an ensemble with hundreds of years of collective experience, timing, and sheer talent, and the scenes in Sam Drucker's general store are like versions of the Marx Brothers' comic riffs, so warped is their logic and quick as lightning their banter.

Where do you see a group of oddballs like this on television today? Pity the poor character type that tries to string together a career in sitcoms, for the roles (even as guest star) are few and far between. Hell, even the pig farmers are beautiful these days.

Alvy Moore

Indiana-born Alvy Moore dove into the acting profession after World War II, replacing David Wayne as Ensign Pulver in the hit Broadway play *Mister Roberts*. Moving to Hollywood, he began a string of countless uncredited bit roles in movies, working his way up to supporting roles on television as characters not unlike those played by his *Green Acres* costar Frank Cady: salesmen, ticket agents, and accountants. He scored a recurring role as Pete's friend Howie on *Pete and Gladys*, but as the perpetually contradictory county agent Hank Kimball, Moore hit the jackpot with his brilliant sense of comic confusion. Able to talk himself into (or out of) any opinion, Mr. Kimball was a self-contained debate team. When *Green Acres* went off the air in 1971, Moore never looked back, continuing to work through the mid-1990s on such shows as *Newhart*, *Evening Shade*, and *Frasier*.

Eleanor Audley

Only a year older than her onscreen son Eddie Albert, Eleanor Audley was best known as Oliver Wendell Douglas's mother, Eunice. Invariably playing society ladies with names such as Mrs. Teasley, Gertrude Van Dyne, and Millicent Schuyler-Potts, Audley was sometimes snobbish, sometimes dithery, but always a monied grand dame. A perfect example of her stock in trade was her three memorable guest shots on *The Dick Van Dyke Show* as Mrs. Billings, who always managed to lasso Rob Petrie into directing the New Rochelle PTA's annual talent show. A small-screen Margaret Dumont, she was often the target of comedy in her long career, except in her voiceover work for Disney animated films, where she let her dark side materialize as the voice of the evil Maleficent in *Sleeping Beauty* and Cinderella's evil stepmother.

CAST

Eddie Albert	Oliver Wendell Douglas
Eva Gabor	Lisa Douglas
Tom Lester	Eb Dawson
Frank Cady	Sam Drucker
Pat Buttram	Mr. Haney
Alvy Moore	Hank Kimball
Sid Melton	Alf Monroe
Mary Grace Canfield	Ralph Monroe
Hank Patterson	Fred Ziffel
Barbara Pepper	Doris Ziffel (1)
Fran Ryan	Doris Ziffel (2)
Arnold the Pig	Arnold Ziffel
Eleanor Audley	Mother Eunice Douglas

GROWING PAINS

 | 1985–1992 | 166 episodes

The Seaver family, with three wildly different children, is headed by "Mr. Mom," Jason, who runs his psychiatric practice out of the home, while mother Maggie works as a reporter for a local Long Island newspaper.

In many ways, *Growing Pains* was incredibly similar to *Family Ties*, with patient, attractive parents and three children (and eventually a fourth added for good measure): an oldest son who became the idol of the *Tiger Beat* crowd, a middle sister, and a youngest child (Jeremy Miller, who, like Tina Yothers, was adorable at seven but became less and less persuasive of possessing a true genetic link with the rest of their family the older he got). In no fashion pushing the boundaries or breaking the mold of the sitcom, *Growing Pains* was nevertheless a perfectly charming show, with witty writing and good performances from its five appealing cast members. Its added attraction was the bona fide future movie star Leonardo DiCaprio, who joined the show in its penultimate season as a troubled-child/last-ditch attempt to kick-start ratings. The popularity of *Growing Pains* and its role as a highly representative family sitcom of the early 1990s (post–*Family Ties* and pre-*That '70s Show*) more than qualifies it for inclusion in this list.

One of the most important dynamics of the show was the relationship of brother and sister Mike and Carol Seaver, an obverse of *Family Ties*'s most vital comic quotient. But where Alex and Mallory Keaton (played by Michael J. Fox and Justine Bateman) were a textbook case of the smart-brother/vapid-sister routine, *Growing Pains* featured dim but likeable Mike (played by Kirk Cameron, who became a teen heartthrob and the show's breakout star, the way Michael J. Fox had), whose only use for textbooks was to stand on to get a better view of the girls' locker room. Tracey Gold's Carol was the brain of the family, and while Fox would rake Bateman's character over the coals for her lack of gray matter, by the 1990s, making fun of intelligence was de rigueur, and the cool kid was the one who cared only about his lady-killer status and the way his hair looked.

The two actors were also the center of *Growing Pains*'s two notable off-screen dramas. The appealing young actress Gold fought a very serious battle with bulimia. Wearing intentionally baggy clothing to mask her condition, it was only through the intervention of onscreen mother Joanna Kerns that the subject was addressed, so worried was Kerns about Gold's ever-diminishing frame (happily, Gold recovered and returned to the show for its final season). Kirk Cameron's abrupt religious conversion to near-fundamentalism caused him to balk at many

 SITCOMS: THE 101 GREATEST TV COMEDIES OF ALL TIME

Left: Alan Thicke and Joanna Kerns have each worn many hats (director, composer, producer, and actor) over the course of their successful television careers.

Below: Alan Thicke and Cynthia Stevenson in the very funny yet overlooked *Hope and Gloria*.

CAST

Alan Thicke	Jason Seaver
Joanna Kerns	Maggie Seaver
Kirk Cameron	Mike Seaver
Tracey Gold	Carol Seaver
Jeremy Miller	Ben Seaver
Ashley Johnson	Chrissy Seaver
Leonardo DiCaprio	Luke Brower
Josh Andrew Koenig	"Boner" Stabone

of the story lines on the show. He had the actress who played his girlfriend fired when he learned she'd posed for *Playboy* and, at the height of his zeal, phoned the president of ABC and referred to the show's produc-ers as "pornographers." This final straw caused the three producers to throw up their hands and quit. The "pornographic" episode in question, by the way, dealt with a twenty-year-old's receiving a key to his girlfriend's apartment.

The show began to wobble on its axis and, as often happens in those situations, a new member of the family arrived: adorable little Chrissy Seaver, whose rapid aging from newborn to five-year-old over one hiatus should have prompted a visit from the Health Department to test the Seavers' drinking water—or at least a visit from the Sitcom Police for violating Ordinance Twelve of the Logic Code. In addition, after Cameron's religious conversion, he was not the stuff of *Tiger Beat* anymore, and the producers were trying desper-ately to hold on to the show's fan base of teenage girls. Thus, the aforemen-tioned addition of Leonardo DiCaprio as the homeless Luke Brower whom the Seavers take in. The new blood didn't help, though, and after a season of DiCaprio, his character was sent packing. After seven seasons, so was the show; interest-ingly, it was the transfer of Joanna Kerns's character that prompted the Seavers move to Washington, D.C., at the end of the series, something that would have been unimaginable in the days of Donna Reed and Barbara Billingsley. Maybe the show was more groundbreaking than it seemed.

Alan Thicke

The only actor featured in this book who also composed the theme songs to sit-coms, Alan Thicke is a highly underrated comic actor with a sly sense of timing and the good looks that make an actor click with the viewing audience. He began his career in his native Canada as a disc jockey and talk-show host. Marrying singer and soap opera actress Gloria Loring, he composed the theme songs to such shows as *Wheel of Fortune*, *Diff'rent Strokes* (which he also sang), and *The Facts of Life*. Though he was touted as a rival to Johnny Carson when he launched his own talk show, *Thicke of the Night*, in 1983, the show was a disaster and Thicke became the butt of industry ridicule rather than late-night king. He turned his fortunes around when he was cast as family patriarch Jason Seaver on *Growing Pains*, heading the family and the cast in a seven-season run. His most recent regular role was that of the unctuous talk-show host Dennis Dupree (clearly a wicked wink at his own attempt to rule the late-night airwaves) on the short-lived but funny *Hope and Gloria*, starring Jessica Lundy and Cynthia Stevenson.

HAPPY DAYS

 | **1974–1984** | **255 episodes**

The innocence of the 1950s is explored through the lives of Richie Cunningham, a freckle-faced high school kid, and his friends, including the leather-jacketed Arthur Fonzarelli, who lives above the Cunninghams' garage and teaches the entire city of Milwaukee the meaning of the word cool.

Happy Days—the sitcom world's entry in the 1950s nostalgia craze kicked off by the film *American Graffiti* (many assume the film spawned the series; actually, the pilot predated the film, and director George Lucas viewed it as Ron Howard's unofficial screen test for the movie) and the Broadway musical *Grease*—started out as an act of recycling, a decidedly 1970s notion. Centering on a middle-class

Midwestern family, the show originated as an unsold pilot titled *New Family in Town*. Rejected by Paramount, it was folded into the successful comic anthology series, *Love, American Style*, as an episode called "Love and the Happy Days." It starred Marion Ross, Ron Howard, and Anson Williams, all of whom ended

up in the final product. Producer Garry Marshall then partially recast it (Harold Gould, the talented actor who would later play Valerie Harper's father on *Rhoda* and Betty White's beau on *The Golden Girls*, was replaced for the second time after filming a pilot, having previously been bounced as Marlo Thomas's dad on *That Girl*) with Tom Bosley as the family patriarch, and sold the series to ABC under the new title *Happy Days*.

As with many shows, the proceedings were energized by a breakout character (think Don Knotts on *The Andy Griffith Show*, Jimmy Walker on *Good Times*, Polly Holliday on *Alice*, and Estelle Getty on *The Golden Girls*). *Happy Days* got its boost from a motorcycle-riding "tough" known as "the Fonz," played by a relatively unknown Henry Winkler, a Yale Drama School graduate who, in reality, was about as far away from a biker as a person could get. About the same time that Fonzie came along, *Happy Days* (like the other Garry Marshall/Jerry Paris sitcom *The Odd Couple*) switched from a single-camera film setup with a laugh track to a three-camera production shot in front of a studio audience. Both shows benefited greatly from the heightened immediacy, making them feel as if they might jump off the screen into viewers' living rooms.

The show had one of the most vocal, clap-happy audiences, and was perhaps second only to *Good Times* in the use (and abuse) of that audience to fuel the momentum. It proved a

SITCOMS: THE 101 GREATEST TV COMEDIES OF ALL TIME

double-edged sword, however, for the response became so predictable that writers had to figure a good two minutes of unwarranted applause into an episode's running time. Almost every character elicited an audible response upon his or her initial appearance, from the screams,

Every character at one point or another: Sit on it!

whoops, and hollers for Richie, Fonzie, and Chachi (even Potsie got wolfette whistles), to the warm, respectful round of applause for theater veteran Tom Bosley (the clapping upon his entrance was so reverential it was as if "Mr. C.," a hardware store owner, was being played by Sir Ralph Richardson). Eventually, the writers were stuck with something akin to a Broadway musical starring six Ethel Mermans. This affected the quality of the

Henry Winkler seems to be having some last-minute doubts as to whether jumping a shark is really a good idea.

OFF THE SET

THE POWERS THAT be at ABC feared that Fonzie would be perceived as a criminal, and insisted that he couldn't wear his trademark leather jacket unless he was on his motorcycle. The producers responded by keeping him astride his bike as much as possible, even inside Arnold's Drive-In. The jacket now hangs in the Smithsonian.

ROBBY BENSON WAS under consideration for the role of Richie Cunningham, and both Mickey Dolenz and Mike Nesmith, formerly of The Monkees, auditioned for the role of Fonzie.

IN ONE EPISODE, Mr. and Mrs. Cunningham are shown leaving the 1962 movie *The Music Man*, arguing about whether the character of Winthrop looks like their son Richie. Of course, that character was played by Ron Howard when he was eight years old.

THE SERIES WAS so popular that its theme song, "Rock Around the Clock," performed by Bill Haley and the Comets, hit the pop charts again nineteen years after its original release. Having reached number 1 in 1955, the song made it to number 39 in 1974.

plots, which sometimes took a good four or five minutes to get going. Then there was the rise of such catchphrases as "Sit on it!" Chachi's "Wa, wa, wa!" Ralph Malph's "I've still got it," and Fonzie's "Aaaaaaaaaaayyyyyyy," not to mention Ron Howard crooning "Blueberry Hill" every time he was feeling his oats. With all of this, the writers had more and more material but did less and less with it.

On the less illustrious side, *Happy Days* is responsible for one of the most famously accusatory phrases in television. It's not an actual quote from the show but a term that has come to represent the precise moment when a television show has forever gone around the bend, irrevocably straying from its original mission never to return to its original glory. The term is "jumping the shark," and it refers to a supposed nail-biter episode in the fifth season in which Fonzie, in swimming trunks and leather jacket and on water skis, jumps over a cage containing a man-eating shark (like there was ever any chance that the show's hero was going to be turned into chum. Never. Gonna. Happen.). While there were other episodes that tested viewers' patience, such as the burning down of Arnold's Drive-In, "jumping the shark" came to represent the

Jerry Paris

One of the premier sitcom directors of the 1960s and '70s, Jerry Paris started as a character actor in movies of the 1950s, such as *The Caine Mutiny*, *Marty*, and *The Naked and the Dead*. After a regular job on the series *The Untouchables*, Paris ran into producer Sheldon Leonard at an L.A. Dodgers baseball game and ended up auditioning for the role of Dick Van Dyke's neighbor on his new sitcom. Generous and congenial, Paris recommended and pushed for actress Ann Morgan Guilbert, the wife of his friend, to play his onscreen wife, and as Jerry and Millie Helper, the pair created the most memorable comic neighbors outside of Fred and Ethel Mertz. Given a chance by Carl Reiner to direct an episode

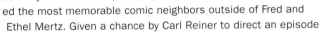

of *The Dick Van Dyke Show*, Paris found his niche and, with his easy-going manner and natural comic timing, ended up helming many of the most famous and beloved episodes of the show, following up with other series of the 1960s and '70s, including *The Munsters*, *Here's Lucy* (piloting the famous appearance of Richard Burton and Elizabeth Taylor), *Mary Tyler Moore*, *The New Dick Van Dyke Show*, and thirty-five episodes of *The Odd Couple*. After directing the pilots of *That Girl* and *The Partridge Family*, it was on *Happy Days* that Paris found a property to devote all his energy to, working with Garry Marshall on every aspect of the show. Just starting to hit his stride in films, with the second and third installments of the *Police Academy* franchise under his belt, Paris was struck down by a brain tumor at the age of sixty.

pinnacle of sitcom ridiculousness, entering the general lexicon to the point where many people under the age of thirty don't even know its origin.

The farther the show got away from the sweet high school dealings of clean-cut Richie, local crooner Potsie Weber, and corny jokester Ralph Malph, the more ludicrous the show became; and by the early 1980s, there were almost no remnants of the period-perfect detail that had graced its youth. By then, the cast was rebelling against the producers, refusing to wear their hair in a style that any respectable circa-1962 teenager would wear. Anson Williams and Scott Baio began sporting long, feathered "do's" straight out of Farrah Fawcettland, and "Short Cake" kid sister Joanie (Erin Moran) wore a loose perm that was more Glenn Close than Patty Duke. Only Marion Ross, who had worn sensible house dresses since the show's *Love, American Style* debut, seemed to hold on to the original spirit of the show until the bitter end.

In addition, with more and more subsidiary characters entering the picture, including Pinky and Leather Tuscadero, the crossover drop-ins of spin-offs Laverne and Shirley; Mork from Ork; and Nancy Walker, who starred in the worst of the *Happy Days*'s spin-offs, *Blansky's Beauties*, the show started to resemble the "cast of thousands" biblical epics of Cecil B. DeMille. After Ron Howard left, at

Above: Sitcom legend Jerry Paris, in his trademark red sweater, directs Tom Bosley and Ron Howard.

Left: Soon-to-be movie director Ron Howard, with Don Most and Anson Williams, sports hair that is far too long for upstanding young men in 1961.

the end of the seventh season, the show took on such actors as Ted McGinley, Crystal Bernard, Linda Purl, and Billy Warlock to replace the departed cast members. Although McGinley and Bernard would find subsequent fame on other sitcoms, they seemed like interlopers on *Happy Days*, totally out of sync with the show's concept. With the addition of Cathy Silvers (daughter of sitcom icon Phil Silvers) as Jenny Piccalo, the producers made the mistake of showing a character who had served as a long-standing punch line, often referred to but never seen.

Speaking of never seen, there was the great mystery of Chuck. For the first two seasons, there were three Cunningham children; older brother Chuck fulfilled the role of the lunkhead sports hero. Rarely adding anything to the proceedings, Chuck Cunningham spent more and more time at "basketball practice." Finally, with the switchover from one to three cameras, Chuck must have been mistakenly thrown out with the old set. He was never mentioned again.

Traction is Funny, Part Two: Marion Ross just hanging around the house.

Bottom left: Marion Ross as Polish émigré Sophie Berger on the cult series *Brooklyn Bridge*, with onscreen grandsons Danny Gerard and Matthew Louis Siegel.

Marion Ross

Something about the highly underrated character actress Marion Ross just doesn't jibe with the present, for she has forged a career on television yet rarely played a modern character. Growing up in Minnesota and moving to San Diego, she worked her way up in the theater, appearing in some films in the 1950s and nabbing her first television role as the Irish maid on the nostalgia series *Life with Father*. Appearing on other sitcoms while raising a family in the 1960s, including the doctor who diagnoses the Brady children's measles, she became employed for a decade as the sometimes dotty but always lovable "Mrs. C" on the '50's flashback *Happy Days*. She followed it up with her least challenging job, as Gavin McLeod's wife on the last season of *The Love Boat*, but her best work was as the peppery grandmother Sophie Berger on

still another nostalgia-com, the wonderful, critically acclaimed *Brooklyn Bridge*. Rarely out of work, Ross recently found herself in a recurring role as the star's mother on *The Drew Carey Show*. The apple-cheeked, forever sunny actress finally got a chance to play a villain, the evil Bernice Forman on *That '70s Show*. (Yes, another nostalgia series.)

CAST

Ron Howard	Richie Cunningham
Henry Winkler	Arthur "Fonzie" Fonzarelli
Tom Bosley	Howard Cunningham
Marion Ross	Marion Cunningham
Erin Moran	Joanie Cunningham
Anson Williams	Warren "Potsie" Weber
Donny Most	Ralph Malph
Gavan O'Herlihy	Chuck Cunningham (1)
Randolph Roberts	Chuck Cunningham (2)
Pat Morita	Matsuo "Arnold" Takahashi
Al Molinaro	Alfred Delvecchio
Scott Baio	Charles "Chachi" Arcola
Lynda Goodfriend	Lori Beth Allen Cunningham
Cathy Silvers	Jenny Piccalo
Ted McGinley	Roger Phillips
Crystal Bernard	K. C. Cunningham

HAZEL

NBC ● | **1961–1966** | **154 episodes**

Endearing buttinsky maid Hazel Burke rules the roost of the Baxter household, dispensing advice, solicited or not, with every batch of her world-famous brownies

Don DeFore and Shirley Booth went toe to toe each week on *Hazel*.

Household help has been used as comic relief since the days of Juliet Capulet's nurse. Accordingly, sassy maids, fresh-mouthed butlers, and wise governesses have been almost as prevalent on sitcoms as the single parent, another of the form's archetypes. Starting with the early days of *Beulah*, and Louise on *Make Room for Daddy*, the list of domestics is startling, not only in its length but in that they are often the most memorable and beloved characters on a given show. Mr. French. Lurch. Mrs. Livingston. Alice Nelson. Florence Johnston. Benson. Edna Garrett. Mr. Belvedere. Fran Fine. Rosario Salazar. All of them are instantly memorable—and if they weren't the most educated characters on their respective series, they were certainly the most practical and the wiliest, often restoring order to more than just cluttered closets. These indispensable domestics provided objectivity and, as honorary members of the families they served yet without blood ties, they were free to shoot from the hip and wrap things up quickly, a highly valuable trait in the shorthand world of sitcom storytelling. At the head of the long line of comic servants to grace the small screen, the title "Queen of Domestic Engineers" belongs to the wise, wisecracking Hazel Burke, as played by the incomparable Shirley Booth.

Based on a *Saturday Evening Post* comic strip by Ted Key, *Hazel* featured the first TV multitasker, executing her top-secret meatloaf recipe and bowling a perfect game simultaneously. Running the Baxter household ragged, Hazel helped the family navigate the many little things that typical middle-class American families faced: getting an unlisted phone number, fighting an unjust parking ticket, and being the first house in the neighborhood to own a color television set. (In a test of this relatively new technology, the episode in which Hazel bought her color set was the only one of the show's first season to be filmed in glorious color.) It was Booth's considerable charm and excellent acting that made Hazel far more than a meddlesome pain in the kiester.

With a cast that included Whitney Blake as Dorothy Baxter, invariably decked out like a centerfold from *Women's Wear Daily*, and little Bobby Buntrock as Harold, freckled and cowlicked like a *Dennis the Menace* also-ran, the show's main source of conflict was Hazel's run-ins with "Mr B," played by the portly, congenial Don DeFore. Considering the friction between the two, it was a miracle that Hazel wasn't toeing the line at the unemployment office. Forever reminding her boss that he was twenty pounds overweight and ten years too old, Hazel should probably have

been sacked the first time she opened her "big bazoo" (to borrow a phrase from that great wit, Fred Mertz). But as she was a part of the family, having raised "Missy" Baxter since she was a child, Hazel could (and often did) get away with murder. Adding to the fun were veteran actress Maudie Prickett as Hazel's best friend Rosie, and the delightfully dotty Norma Varden and Donald Foster as the Baxters' next-door neighbors the Johnsons, who went through maids like Kleenex and were so utterly helpless they had to call upon Hazel to find out how

long to boil a three-minute egg.

The show ran out of steam when it moved to CBS after the fourth season. DeFore and Blake left, so the writers sent Missy and Mr. B off to Saudi Arabia and stuck little Harold with his brother's family (shades of *The Brady Bunch*, where the dreaded Cousin Oliver, another towheaded moppet straight out of *Village of the Damned*, was abandoned by his parents). Plagued with bursitis brought on by five years of her trademark jog to answer the door, Booth found the notion of whipping an entirely new family into shape too much of a strain, and after one season of the revamped cast, Hazel hung up her apron for good.

Mel Brooks is quoted as saying "If I ever had a maid like Hazel, I'd set her hair on fire!" To be sure, the character could be downright infuriating; after all, she

Above: Symbolism in a press shot: Hazel Burke holds the Baxter family together.

Left: Always ready to jump into the fray, Hazel (with Harold riding shotgun) commandeers the Hydesburg Fire Department's Hook and Ladder.

Shirley Booth

Although best known for playing working-class women, Shirley Booth was one of the most versatile actresses to conquer three media, with perhaps only Angela Lansbury rivaling her successful and varied career. Hitting Broadway in 1925, Booth worked steadily on the stage, moving among comedies, dramas, and musicals with ease. In 1941, she conquered radio in the hit *Duffy's Tavern*, written and created by her first husband (who also starred as Archie, the tavern's manager). Turned down for the role of Connie Brooks, the role that made Eve Arden a household name (Booth couldn't find humor in the character of an underpaid teacher), Booth won a Tony and an Oscar for her legendary portrayal on stage and screen of tragic housewife Lola Delaney in *Come Back, Little Sheba*. In reality fifty-four-years-old when she became a full-fledged star (she had successfully shaved a full decade off her age, a secret not revealed until after her death), Booth starred in the Broadway hits *A Tree Grows in Brooklyn* and *The Time of the Cuckoo*, and films such as *The Matchmaker*. Winning two Emmys as Hazel, Booth returned to Broadway in the late 1960s, and played in her last TV sitcom in 1973, *A Touch of Grace*. Ridiculed by other legitimate actors when she took the role of Hazel Burke, Booth replied, "She's my insurance policy," knowing the potential for a hit, owning a piece of the action and providing security to enjoy her well-earned retirement, which lasted more than twenty years.

CAST

Shirley Booth	Hazel Burke
Don DeFore	George Baxter
Whitney Blake	Dorothy Baxter
Bobby Buntrock	Harold Baxter
Ray Fulmer	Steve Baxter
Lynn Borden	Barbara Baxter
Julia Benjamin	Susie Baxter
Maudie Prickett	Rosie
Norma Varden	Harriet Johnson
Donald Foster	Herbert Johnson
Ann Jillian	Millie Ballard
Robert B. Williams	Barney

Left: Shirley Booth as Grace Simpson in her final sitcom, *A Touch of Grace*.

Below: Although she was a total softie, Hazel would never allow "Sport" to spoil his dinner with anything more than a carrot stick, to tide him over until her top-secret meatloaf was done.

was always right. Yet that rightness was the show's most significant characteristic. As opposed to a show like *The Honeymooners*, which, for all its hilarity, never gave the audience any hope that the little man might get some respect, *Hazel* was one of the first sitcoms to make the working man or woman feel that he or she might speak out and make a difference.

OFF THE SET

THELMA RITTER WAS the first choice to play Hazel and wanted the role badly, but due to poor health could not be insured for the demands of a weekly series.

BOBBY BUNTROCK, WHO played Harold on *Hazel*, was killed in a car accident in 1974 at the age of twenty-one. Mysteriously, his mother had died in an automobile crash in nearly exactly the same spot a year earlier.

HOGAN'S HEROES

 | 1965–1971 | 168 episodes

Ah, scenic Germany, where five stalwart POWs set up an espionage outfit right under the noses of their bumbling captors.

In 1968, Petula Clark headlined an eponymous television special. Her guest star was Harry Belafonte, and during one of their duets, Clark took his arm. Because of concerns on the part of the sponsoring car company, the director asked for a retake. When Clark and her husband, the show's executive producers, discovered the reason for the retake, they insisted that the original be broadcast. Some members of the viewing audience were aghast and a much-publicized controversy followed.

Why are we telling you this? Because it occurred in 1968, smack dab in the middle of the run of *Hogan's Heroes*. In a year when a white woman couldn't touch the arm of a black man on national television without causing an uproar, a situation comedy about a Nazi prisoner-of-war camp inspired by the hit movies *Stalag 17*, and *The Great Escape*, was a big hit with the American public.

There was a painful irony at the heart of *Hogan's Heroes*. Many of the actors who portrayed its Nazi officers, including Werner Klemperer, John Banner, Leon Askin, and Howard Caine, were Jewish. Klemperer had fled the Nazis along with his father, the great conductor Otto Klemperer. Leon Askin had been held in a French camp (where his parents perished) and both Robert Clary, who played French POW Louis LeBeau, and John Banner, who played the moronic Sergeant Schulz, had been imprisoned in concentration camps.

American Jews, many of whom had lost family members in the Holocaust, were appalled by the very concept of the show, no

POWs are funny: The denizens of Stalag 13, dig a "trench" they'll use to come and go as if the camp were the Hammelburg Hilton.

matter how stupid the Nazis were made to appear or how many Germans were shot by Hogan. (Can you think of any other sitcom where the lead character actually kills people?)

Jews have often been noted as quite adept at making fun of their own travails over the centuries and, as Mel Brooks, the writer and director of that Nazi laff riot *The Producers*, has stated, "What better revenge is there than to laugh in the face of your enemies?" (He also said that he was the only Jew to make a dime off of Hitler—but clearly he was mistaken!) In spite of its controversial setting, the show was one of the unlikeliest comedy hits of all time. The probable reason is that *Hogan's Heroes* was an extremely well-crafted and funny series, very much in line with the other absurd sitcoms of its era, including *The Beverly Hillbillies*, *The Flintstones*, and *Get Smart*.

One side note: Bizarrely enough, the show was a hit in Germany in the early 1990s. It was first broadcast with the title *Stacheldraht und Fersengeld* (*Barbed Wire and Vamoose*) but that was later changed to *Ein Käfig voller Helden* (*A Cage Full of Heroes*). It replaced reruns of *Seinfeld* which, we guess, was just too Jewish for German tastes. However, the German broadcasts did differ somewhat from the originals. Since Nazi symbolism is outlawed in Germany, whenever the German officers gave the Hitler salute and bellowed, "Heil Hitler!" the German version dubbed in some stupid and incongruous line like, "This is how high the cornflowers grow." Anytime the show alluded to actual bombing and killing the dialogue was modified as well. For example, when the Americans destroyed a munitions factory, the German version made it a toilet paper factory. When Sgt. Schulz reported that the Allies had bombed Hamburg "flat as a pancake," it was miraculously transformed into the RAF dropping planeloads of candy as "a propaganda maneuver."

Bob Crane

As a disc jockey, Bob Crane was dubbed "The King of the Los Angeles Airwaves." Following two uncredited appearances in films, he made his real mark in television, thanks to his good looks and winning personality. First, he appeared as a guest on *The Dick Van Dyke Show* and then as a semiregular on *The Donna Reed Show*. *Hogan's Heroes* marked the apex of his career. His 1975 series, *The Bob Crane Show*, foundered quickly and Crane spent the rest of his brief life making the occasional guest appearance on TV and performing the play *Beginner's Luck* on the dinner theater circuit. He was notoriously murdered during that show's tour, a crime that was dramatized in the film *Auto Focus*.

Left: Nazis are funny. Werner Klemperer as Col. Klink, knowing that Col. Hogan (Bob Crane) got the better of him yet again.

Opposite right: Nazis are *really* funny. John Banner as the denial-ridden Sgt. Schultz.

Top: 1970s television favorite Jo Ann Pflug makes an incomplete pass at Bob Crane, on an episode of the 1975 flop *The Bob Crane Show*.

Sgt. Schultz: I see nothing! I know nothing!

CAST

Bob Crane	Col. Robert Hogan
Werner Klemperer	Col. Wilhelm Klink
John Banner	Sgt. Hans Schultz
Robert Clary	Cpl. Louis LeBeau
Richard Dawson	Cpl. Peter Newkirk
Ivan Dixon	Sgt. James Kinchloe
Larry Hovis	Sgt. Andrew Carter
Cynthia Lynn	Helga
Sigrid Valdis	Hilda
Nita Talbot	Marya
Leon Askin	Gen. Albert Burkhalter
Bernard Fox	Colonel Crittenden
Howard Caine	Maj. Wolfgang Hochstetter

The prisoners of Stalag 13: Ivan Dixon, Bob Crane, Robert Clary, Richard Dawson, and Larry Hovis, plotting their weekly mischief to foil the Axis.

OFF THE SET

MOST NIGHT SCENES were filmed during the day using a special "day for night" lens.

THE LEATHER JACKET that Bob Crane wore in the series was originally worn by Frank Sinatra in the 1965 film *Von Ryan's Express*.

WERNER KLEMPERER REPRISED his Colonel Klink role on *The Simpsons*, as Homer's guardian angel.

Gene Reynolds

One smart cookie, Gene Reynolds parlayed his early experience as a child actor into a career as one of the most important writer/director/producers on television. Reynolds first appeared on screen in 1936 at age eleven and continued to act in pictures until 1957, when he turned to directing television, helming such sitcoms as *My Three Sons*, *Leave It to Beaver*, *The Andy Griffith Show*, *F Troop*, and *Hogan's Heroes*. His second wartime sitcom was *M*A*S*H*, which he adapted for television and produced, along with writer Larry Gelbart, for its first four seasons. Reynolds and Gelbart were co-executive producers for the fifth season, after which Reynolds left to executive produce *Lou Grant*. Along the way, he also worked on such shows as *The Ghost and Mrs. Muir*, *Room 222*, *Blossom*, and *Anna and the King*.

CHARACTER ACTORS

You've certainly seen their faces, but as much as they've all worked (indeed, some of them have been series regulars), they have never become household names. We thought it important to pay attention to a vanishing breed and some of the hardest working people in sitcoms, the character actors who have made a career guest starring on show after show (in the 1960s and '70s some of them popped up on five or six series per season), often creating an archetype, whether it was a nagging mother-in-law, a kindly doctor, or a nosy neighbor.

Vito Scotti
Often seen as: Italian painters, mad scientists, and English-challenged seniors. Best known as: Gaspar Fomento, the bewildered Chief of Police who was constantly seeing a hovering postulant on *The Flying Nun*.

Doris Singleton
Often seen as: pushy neighbors and inscrutable secretaries. Best known as: Carolyn Appleby, the eternal thorn in Lucy Ricardo's side on *I Love Lucy*.

Jack Riley
Often seen as: neurotic yet subtly menacing oddballs. Best known as: Bob Hartley's unhinged patient Elliott Carlin on *The Bob Newhart Show*.

Joyce Bulifant
Often seen as: cheery sidekicks and strait-laced mothers. Best known as: Marie Slaughter, Murray's plucky spouse on *Mary Tyler Moore*.

Maudie Prickett
Often seen as: prying neighbors, stern schoolteachers, and sewing circle members. Best known as: Hazel's best friend and fellow domestic engineer Rosie.

Parley Baer
Often seen as: peppery beauracrats, small town mayors, and suspicious desk sergeants. Best known as: Arthur J. Henson, the exasperated insurance agent to the Addams Family.

Sandra Gould
Often seen as: snarky switchboard operators, secretaries, and harping landladies. Best known as: the second Gladys Kravitz on *Bewitched*.

Herbie Faye
Often seen as: sarcastic deli men, lethargic delivery men, and poker buddies. Best known as: hangdog Corporal Sam Fender on *The Phil Silvers Show*.

Pamelyn Ferdin

Often seen as: precocious offspring and slumber party guests. Best known as: Lucy Winters, who drives the haunted Jan Brady to wear a black wig on *The Brady Bunch*.

Burt Mustin

Often seen as: geezers, great-grandfathers, and crusty old codgers. Best known as: lovable octogenarian Justin Quigley on *All in the Family*.

Alison LaPlaca

Often seen as: brittle career women and materialistic yuppies. Best known as: Rachel's boss Joanna, who handcuffs Chandler Bing during a little workplace bondage on *Friends*.

Hal Smith

Often seen as: Santa Claus, goofy TV hosts, and beleaguered public servants. Best known as: Otis Campbell, the most frequent occupant of Mayberry's jail cell on *The Andy Griffith Show*.

Guy Raymond

Often seen as: country bumpkins and bucolic stringbeans. Best known as: Howard Hewes (note the spelling), who Mr. Drysdale mistakenly thinks is the reclusive billionaire, on *The Beverly Hillbillies*.

Amzie Strickland

Often seen as: kindly aunts, salty senior citizens, and mousy housewives. Best known as: Mrs. Bickner, the sweet little old lady who sues Murphy for 1.5 million dollars after a minor fender bender on *Murphy Brown*.

James Hong

Often seen as: wry doctors, laundry owners, and steely shopkeepers. Best known as: Bruce, the infuriating maitre d' in "The Chinese Restaurant" episode of *Seinfeld*.

Florence Stanley

Often seen as: hard-as-nails judges, Jewish grandmothers, and unflappable dames. Best known as: Phil Fish's deadpan wife Bernice on *Barney Miller*.

Helen Martin

Often seen as: proud grandmothers, hat-wearing church ladies, and strong-willed seniors. Best known as: window sitting sage Pearl Shay on *227*.

Edward Hibbert

Often seen as: fussy hairdressers, jewelry salesmen, and effete concierges. Best known as: restaurant critic Gil Chesterton on *Frasier*.

Elvia Allman

Often seen as: tough-to-please aunts, desperate old maids, and stern schoolteachers. Best known as: the candy factory forewoman, bellowing "Speed it up a little!!!" on *I Love Lucy*.

Ronnie Schell

Often seen as: pushy salesmen and slick publicity flacks. Best known as: skirtchasing private 'Duke' Slater on *Gomer Pyle, U.S.M.C.*

THE HONEYMOONERS

● | 1955–1956 | 39 episodes

Bus driver Ralph Kramden lives with his wife, Alice, in a tenement apartment. Their up-stairs neighbors are sewer engineer Ed Norton and his wife, Trixie. Ralph has a big heart and a quick temper, and is always looking for that big score—which never, some-how, comes.

Has any show with such a short run achieved such lasting success? *The Honeymooners* has never been off the air for any significant period since it was first broadcast fifty years ago—and yet the stand-alone sitcom version racked up only thirty-nine episodes. What might explain the show's longevity, and its absolutely rabid fan base (which includes many who weren't born until years after the show was first aired)?

The Honeymooners shares many of the same elements of other shows. Its fundamental underlying theme is the pursuit of the American Dream. Ralph Kramden wants nothing more than to improve his life, and a good number of the episodes find him pursuing the pot of gold via one wacky scheme or another. These elaborate capers were a hallmark of 1950s television. Think of Lucy putting on elaborate disguises that fooled almost nobody, Ann Sothern's Susie McNamera taking circuitous measures to help her boss, Gale Storm's Margie Albright roping her boyfriend Freddie into some baroque machination or other, or Eve Arden's

Connie Brooks cooking up a plot to cover a mistake before Mr. Conklin discovers it and blows his top. The proud tradition of characters' harebrained scheming continues through Laverne and Shirley and Al Bundy, all the way to Malcolm and his brothers.

Every manipulator needs a sidekick, and Ralph's partner in crime was the genially dumb Ed Norton who, like many of his sitcom counterparts, was forever being dragged, usually against his better judgment, into yet another cockamamie ruse. The sidekick is a staple of the sitcom world, of course. Usually, the second banana is, if not actually stupid, easily manipulated. Lucy had Ethel (and then Viv) in what was definitely the most fruitful of all sitcom partnerships. Gilligan had the Skipper, in a rare example of the stupid leading the smart, er, smarter. Eve (Arden) and Kaye (Ballard) sidekicked each other as Eve (Hubbard) and Kaye (Buell) on *The Mothers-in-Law*, a 1950s-style sitcom produced in the late 1960s.

The premise of *The Honeymooners* was supremely simple. Four characters led their lives in two small apartments. Of course, with only thirty-nine episodes, the writers weren't running out of ideas. The show began as a short segment on DuMont's *Cavalcade of Stars*, a variety show that was hosted successively by Jack Carter, Jerry Lester, Gleason, and Larry Storch. During the Gleason years, 1950–52, he featured many of the characters that would populate his later variety series, *The Jackie Gleason Show*, which basically transferred the elements of *Cavalcade of Stars* from DuMont over to CBS.

When the first *Honeymooners* segment aired on *Cavalcade*, on October 5, 1951, all the basic elements were in place except some of the casting. Alice was played by Pert Kelton and Trixie was seen, one time only, in the form of

Above: Audrey Meadows and Jackie Gleason share a playful moment during a script reading.

Right: The epitome of the complex, sad clown, "The Great One" at work in his office.

Opposite: Ed Norton and Ralph Kramden in glorious color, during the filming of *The Honeymooners*. At left is an Electronicam, developed by the DuMont network to provide better picture quality than that of other "live" shows of its time.

Jackie Gleason

"The Great One" was what Orson Welles called Jackie Gleason, and the sobriquet stuck throughout his long career on stage, screen, and television. Gleason first found success as the master of ceremonies of amateur shows in his native Brooklyn. He also tried his luck as a carnival barker, boxer, pool hustler, and daredevil driver in carnivals. He broke through in show business when he was cast in the Broadway musical *Follow the Girls*. Gleason's stage success brought calls from Hollywood, and the rotund comic appeared as a secondary figure in such films as  *Orchestra Wives* and *Springtime in the Rockies*. He didn't perform on screen for the next seven years, reemerging on television in 1949 as the star of *The Life of Riley*. He took over as host of DuMont's *Cavalcade of Stars* variety show the following year, introducing some of his most famous characters: Reggie Van Gleason III, the Bachelor, Joe the Bartender, Rum Dum the drunk, Charley Bratton ("The Loudmouth"), and the Poor Soul—and of course, Ralph Kramden.

Gleason soon left DuMont for CBS and greener (as in greenbacks) pastures, and took his variety cast with him, including *The Honeymooners* and other loyal Gleasonites Frank Fontaine, the June Taylor Dancers, and orchestra leader Ray Bloch, all of whom remained stalwarts throughout his television endeavors. In addition to his weekly television appearances Gleason took on film roles, most notably his Academy Award–nominated turn opposite Paul Newman, as Minnesota Fats in *The Hustler*. Gleason also had a lucrative moonlighting gig as conductor and composer of a series of successful Capitol easy-listening albums. But no matter what his other accomplishments, and they are impressive, it's as the beleaguered, bellicose bus driver with a heart of gold that he will always be remembered.

OFF THE SET

A SERIES OF specials appeared in 1976, '77, and '78 with Gleason and Carney in their usual roles and, most important, with Meadows rejoining the cast. Jane Kean retained the role of Trixie.

Another astonishing color shot of *The Honeymooners*, featuring the entire cast in the Norton apartment.

Elaine Stritch. Art Carney got the part of Ed Norton as a fluke, simply because he was a guest comic on that week's program, playing a policeman on the first sketch of the evening. In the earliest of episodes, the relationship between Ralph and Alice was much more vitriolic. When it was decided to turn the recurring sketch into its own full-blown half-hour sitcom, it needed a name, and *The Honeymooners* was chosen with a certain amount of irony. Kelton, who had been blacklisted, was replaced by Audrey Meadows, who still exhibited a take-no-crap attitude toward Ralph but also brought out his warmer side. In spite of his threats to send her to the moon, or Alice's impromptu visits to her mother, the two would invariably end with a hug and Ralph proclaiming, "Baby, you're the greatest!" Joyce Randolph came aboard in the rather thankless role of Trixie, and the classic *Honeymooners* quartet was in place.

It might surprise you to know that the show was not a success, perhaps because it was scheduled against Perry Como's relaxed crooning over at NBC, so Gleason returned to the hourlong sketch comedy format in 1956, making *The Honeymooners* an integral part of the proceedings. Carney left the following year and, as he was irreplaceable, that segment was dropped. The Gleason variety show returned to television in 1962. Carney was back and so was *The Honeymooners*, but with Sue Ane Langdon as Alice. She apparently clashed with Carney, and Sheila MacRae became the final Alice, with Jane Kean playing Trixie. In the 1967-'68 season, *The Honeymooners* went both color and musical! Surprisingly, the songs by Lyn Duddy and Jerry Bressler weren't bad—perhaps not Broadway quality, but skillful and entertaining nonetheless. And for the first time in its history, the luck of the hapless Honeymooners changed. Ralph and Ed

Audrey Meadows

Audrey Meadows and her older sister, Jayne, were born in Wuchang, China, where their parents were missionaries. The family moved to Connecticut, and Audrey moved to New York following high school. After an appearance on Broadway, in the chorus of the musical *Top Banana*, she achieved some notice as the sole female on television's *Bob and Ray Show*. Most of the remainder of her professional career was spent as Alice Kramden, the sharp-tongued yet loving wife of bus driver Ralph. She did make occasional appearances in such movies as *That Touch of Mink*; *Take Her, She's Mine*; and *Rosie*. Meadows did numerous TV guest shots and returned to series television as Nancy Dussault's mother on the Ted Knight sitcom *Too Close for Comfort* (right). In her private life, she was married to Bob Six, the president of Continental Airlines, and held many honorary posts with the airline.

struck it rich, winning a songwriting contest and traveling around the world on the proceeds.

One last word about the series. Chief among its assets was the drab apartment inhabited by Ralph and Alice. Don't underestimate the importance of that tiny apartment with its window to the fire escape, icebox, radiator, and unseen bedroom. Stage producer, director, and author George Abbott once opined that comedy was funnier when played within a cramped space—and the set of *The Honeymooners* proved him right. Within the main room, which served as living room, kitchen, and dining room, the characters were constantly in one another's faces and, given Gleason's girth (a lodestone of humor at his expense), his extravagant outbursts were all the funnier. Looking at the set against the mega-apartments of today's sitcom New York (think *Mad About You*; *Will & Grace*; *Caroline in the City*; and especially *Friends*), the home at 358 Chauncey Street in Brooklyn was a grim little closet—but a closet filled to the brim with laughs.

As in the case of *I Love Lucy*, the sitcom gods conspired to make every element—the acting, writing, direction, etc.—coalesce perfectly, making it a show for the ages. Its biggest asset of all was the heart behind all the shenanigans.

Leonard Stern

Writer Leonard Stern began his career at Universal Studios, working on films featuring the deathless teams of Abbott and Costello, and Ma and Pa Kettle. In 1952, he switched over to television with a post on *The Jackie Gleason Show*. He was a series writer on *The Phil Silvers Show* (a.k.a. *Sgt. Bilko*) and *The Steve Allen Show*. Stern was executive producer and one of the stable of writers on *Get Smart*, one of the most successful series of the 1960s. He was then associated with some lesser shows, including *Run, Buddy, Run*; *The Good Guys*; *The Governor and J.J.*; *Holmes and Yo-Yo*; and *Operation Petticoat*. He wrote the *Get Smart* movie *The Nude Bomb*, and a *Get Smart* special, *Get Smart, Again!* Stern also had a highly successful second career as a publisher. He cofounded Price, Stern, Sloan (along with "Droodles" inventor Roger Price and Leonard Sloan), a successful company specializing in humor and children's books. After the death of Roger Price in 2000, Stern and Sloan established the Tallfellow and Smallfellow Press.

Ralph: Norton, if a man in a white coat ever knocks on your door, don't ask for tutti-frutti, 'cause he ain't the Good Humor man.

Above: Comic genius Art Carney emerges from his subterranean office in the sewers of New York.

Left: Audrey Meadows and Joyce Randolph embark on a scheme of Lucy-and-Ethel proportions. Little known fact: Trixie Norton's real name was Thelma.

CAST

Jackie Gleason ....Ralph Kramden

Art Carney ....Ed Norton

Audrey Meadows ....Alice Kramden

Joyce Randolph ....Trixie Norton

I DREAM OF JEANNIE

NBC | 1965–1970 | 139 episodes

Astronaut Tony Nelson, returning from a space mission, splashes down into a Persian peck of trouble when he uncorks and unleashes a sassy minx of a genie named Jeannie. Released from two thousand years of bottled-up frustration, Jeannie does everything in her power to win her new master's heart.

I Dream of Jeannie was the perfect sitcom for the swinging 1960s bachelor: the guy with a sports car, a mock turtleneck, and a key to the Playboy Club. What other show featured a gorgeous, subservient woman in a harem costume who materialized from a bottle to grant every wish of a small-screen Rock Hudson? Oh, and what about the inside of that bottle? With its orange throw pillows, purple settee, the kind of flocked wallpaper seen nowhere north of a New Orleans bordello, and even a hookah, this was a pad that a guy and a chick could really swing in.

Yet, while having an undeniable sexual undertone, *I Dream of Jeannie* decidedly soft-pedaled the dominant/submissive subtext for Middle America, offering a paragon of straightforward manhood (an astronaut no less, an occupation on the same level of patriotism as Kate Smith) and an exotic yet wholesome dream girl. Starring Barbara Eden in a role that gave new meaning to the term "bottle blonde" and Larry Hagman, the son of Broadway darling Mary Martin, the show may not have challenged the boundaries of the art form but it was a sure thing in its quotient of out-and-out charm.

Created by Sidney Sheldon, *Jeannie* was NBC's answer to *Bewitched*; a mismatched love story between a mortal and a beautiful girl with magical powers. Darrin and Samantha trumped Tony and Jeannie for logic and wit, for while Samantha's magic kept showing itself no matter how hard they

Two of the most appealing actors ever to grace a sitcom, Larry Hagman and Barbara Eden, on screen (above) and off (opposite top).

tried to keep it hidden, no one (other than faithful sidekick Roger Healey) even knew Jeannie existed. In addition, there was a general classiness to *Bewitched* that *Jeannie* never achieved; after all, *Bewitched* boasted Agnes Moorehead, one of Orson Welles's Mercury Players, and Maurice Evans, a legendary Shakespearean, as primary cutups. Samantha never appeared silly, but Jeannie was sometimes so idiotic she was downright infuriating. She was invariably the culprit of the week's pickle, only to pop up as a teeny genie hiding behind a gi-normous pencil cup (one of those oversized props straight from the Screen Gems art department) while her beloved master did the improvising, sputtering out a frantic explanation of the camel in the living room.

The thing that kept Jeannie from being a feminist nightmare was Eden, who gave the character just enough of an impish mind of her own to offset critics who likened her role to white slavery. Besides, she and Hagman were so damned likeable they could get away with plots that were so transparent that Sherwood Schwartz over at *Gilligan's Island* would've rolled his eyes. The other regulars were the incomparable Bill Daily as Roger Healey and the perfectly long-suffering Hayden Rorke as everyone's nemesis Dr. Bellows, who always seemed to be in the right place at the wrong time, eternally on the verge of checking himself into a well-padded booby hatch.

The show's run was hardly all smooth sailing. Hagman, while an expert and highly underrated physical comedian, was anything but easy to work with, complaining constantly about the quality of the scripts. To make matters worse, in one of those bewildering

Barbara Eden

Barbara Eden has been charming television audiences with her spunk and sex appeal for over half a century. Her first big break came as a debutante vixen on an episode of *I Love Lucy*. Encouraged by Lucille Ball, Eden soon signed with Twentieth Century–Fox as a contract player. Taking the Marilyn Monroe role in the short-lived series *How to Marry a Millionaire* (left, with Lori Nelson and Merry Anders), Eden became known through guest shots on *Father Knows Best*, *December Bride*, and a memorable appearance on *The Andy Griffith Show* as a manicurist that turns the town of Mayberry upside down. Also starring in B films such as *Voyage to the Bottom of the Sea* and *The Seven Faces of Dr. Lao*, Eden, with her blond hair and turned-up nose, was the least obvious choice to play a veiled exotic from Baghdad, but Jeannie turned out to be the role for which she will forever be remembered and loved. Other series such as *Harper Valley P.T.A.* (where she recreated the role she played in the movie of the same name) and *A Brand New Life* failed to erase the iconic image of Eden in a harem costume, but she was more successful in many television movies. In 1991, Eden reunited with her *Jeannie* costar Larry Hagman when she landed a recurring role on *Dallas* as Lee Ann Nelson (a nod to Hagman's astronaut Tony Nelson). Her most recent recurring role was perfect casting: as Aunt Irma on the series *Sabrina, the Teenage Witch*. Always game for spoofing her iconic role as everyone's favorite harem girl, she bravely dealt with the tragic death of her son while keeping her class and her sense of humor intact.

Dr. Bellows: Major Nelson, some men dedicate their lives to science, some men dedicate their lives to politics. I'm dedicating my life to understanding you.

Above: Barbara Eden's Jeannie finally gets the white wedding she was dreaming of during those thousands of years she was trapped in a bottle.

Top right: Hayden Rorke and Bill Daily on location at NASA. (Although they were in costume, security was so tight that Major Healey's ID badge reads "William Daily.")

yet typical moves of clueless censors, the suited nitwits monitored the visibility of Eden's belly button to the point of obsession. After all, the human navel is offensively indecent, the most shockingly provocative part of the human body since Lillian Russell flashed her ankle in *Hitchy-Koo of 1903*; perhaps better to concentrate on a navel than the real issue, an unmarried man and woman living under one roof, something over which they really could've gotten their knickers in a knot. Compounding the challenges created by the navel patrol was the fact that Eden discovered she was pregnant immediately after being cast in the show's pilot. To hide her ever-expanding waistline, the producers spent most of the first season masking her situation with close-ups, referred to by director Gene Nelson as "ATB" shots (for "Above the Baby").

Mimicking its precursor, *Bewitched*, in numerous ways, the most blatant rip-off was Jeannie Two, a twin sister who had jet black hair just as Samantha's cousin Serena did (reinforcing feelings of low self-esteem in brunette children from sea to shining sea). This provided a juicy dual role for Eden, though Jeannie Two was more evil and not nearly as campy as Serena. And like *Bewitched*, the show included four-part episodes, including when Jeannie gets locked in a huge safe on its way to the moon, surrounded by matches and lipstick (to send a message of cosmic friendship to those makeup-deprived pyromaniac extraterrestrials).

With the network threatening to cancel the show if

there weren't Jeannie/Tony nuptials, the producers reluctantly gave in at the beginning of its fifth season, a huge mistake. NBC canceled it anyway—but that was not the end of the story. In 1991, they brought back the two lovebirds of Cocoa Beach for the TV movie *I Still Dream of Jeannie*. (Have you noticed that there was never a reunion movie called *I Still Love Lucy?*) Eden and Daily were back on board but Hagman declined and was replaced by former *M*A*S*H* star Wayne Rogers. Next up? A movie version of the series, which we can only hope will honor the show's legacy better than the big-screen adaptation of *Bewitched* managed to do.

CAST

Barbara Eden ....Jeannie

Larry Hagman ....Major Anthony Nelson

Bill Daily ....Major Roger Healey

Hayden Rorke ....Colonel Alfred E. Bellows, MD

Emmaline Henry ...Amanda Bellows

Barton MacLane .....General Martin Peterson

Vinton Hayworth .....General Winfield Schaeffer

Michael Ansara ......The Blue Djinn

JEANNIE AT WORK

OFF THE SET

***JEANNIE* DIRECTOR** Gene Nelson was a former movie hoofer who would later star in the Broadway musical *Follies*.

JEANNIE'S BOTTLE WAS actually a painted 1964 bottle of Jim Beam.

THE EVIL BLUE Djinn who had imprisoned Jeannie in her bottle for two thousand years was played by Eden's husband at the time, actor Michael Ansara.

SIDNEY SHELDON DREW his premise from the 1964 movie *The Brass Bottle*, which, perhaps not coincidentally, had costarred Barbara Eden.

Left: Even in comic publicity shots Barbara Eden had to cover up her scandalous, salacious navel.

Right: The inspired Bill Daily with Debbie Zipp, Jack Blessing, and Darren McGavin in the failed sitcom *Small & Frye*.

Bill Daily

A comic actor perfectly cast as the slightly jittery sidekick who fancied himself a ladies' man, Bill Daily started out as a jazz musician when he discovered his true talent and began doing stand-up. Daily became an announcer at the NBC affiliate in Chicago, and at the local Emmy Award telecast, he met a young comic named Bob Newhart. Moving to California, Daily played small roles on such sitcoms as *Bewitched*, where Sidney Sheldon, doing research for his own version of the mortal vs. the enchanted story, decided he was perfect for the role of astronaut Roger Healey on *I Dream of Jeannie*. After its five-year run, he was cast as airline pilot Howard Borden, the neighbor on *The Bob Newhart Show*, whose unannounced visits blazed the trail for such characters as Larry Dallas on *Three's Company* and Kramer on *Seinfeld*. Picking up where Roger Healey left off, the character of Howard Borden allowed Daily to find depth and poignancy in the character of an aging, lonely divorcé. Never able to parlay his success into a successful series of his own (*Small & Frye* and *Starting from Scratch* were fast misfires), Daily has continued to guest star on all of Bob Newhart's series, as well as playing the recurring role of Larry the Psychiatrist on *ALF*. Instantly identifiable by his faux swagger, all the while nervously fingering the brim of his hat in a cross between Oliver Hardy and the jazz musician he started out as, Daily is lovable to the core, with impeccable comic timing that perfectly complemented both the low-key style of Newhart and the more manic, physical comedy of Larry Hagman.

I LOVE LUCY

 | 1951-1957 | **179 episodes**

Much to the consternation of her Cuban bandleader husband, Ricky, crazy redhead Lucy Ricardo continually gets into a peck of trouble, usually with best friend Ethel Mertz at her side.

Lucy Ricardo. Lucille Ball. Has any actor's public persona ever been so at odds with her private self? Perhaps the ultimate testament to Lucille Ball's greatness was just how different she was from "Lucy," the most famous sitcom character in all of television history. Comparing actress and character reveals the true depth of Ball's brilliance.

Lucy McGillicuddy, hailing from Jamestown, New York, was a frivolous, scatterbrained nut—a true zany who was irresponsible with finances, a disaster with appliances, and starstruck to the point of paralysis. But in spite of it all, she had a loving husband who, although often exasperated, always forgave Lucy for her lovably loony hijinks. Lucille Ball, who also hailed from Jamestown, New York, was a serious, superprofessional pioneer. In private life she was anything but zany (in fact, husband Desi Arnaz was the one who had the wit and hearty sense of humor; to Lucille, comedy was nothing to laugh at). She was a fiercely intelligent businesswoman, and, by the late 1960s, with almost two decades of weekly training, knew more about the art of television acting than anyone. And as far as marital matters were concerned, Arnaz was the one who had the "splainin'" to do.

To some degree it's true of all actors, but no other sitcom star has hidden herself in a character as thoroughly as Ball did in Lucy Ricardo. While Lucy Ricardo was

Everyone's favorite redhead, Lucille Ball, "fakes it" with two trained conga drummers, Richard Keith and Desi Arnaz.

conniving, sneaky, and downright criminal at times, she was still an innocent at heart, usually wanting nothing more than a new dress, an opportunity to perform in her husband's nightclub act, or a chance to pick a grapefruit from Richard Widmark's tree. Ball, on the other hand, had one focus: hard work.

Every fan has his or her favorite episode, from the women's club elections to the brouhaha over a pair of hostess pants ("Happy birthday, Ethel. And I hope you live

Right: In one of the classic physical comedy bits in sitcom history, Lucy sets her fake nose on fire while trying to disguise herself from the dreamy William Holden, during one of the Hollywood episodes of *I Love Lucy*.

another *seventy-five* years."); grape stomping; *Little Red Riding Hood* in Spanish (truly sidesplitting, and without a doubt Arnaz's finest moment); the mirror routine with Harpo Marx; the Jacques Marcel potato sack originals; Aunt Martha's Salad Dressing; a cheese dressed like a baby; "mashies" in the golf episode; and on and on.

Much of its classic status can be attributed to the show's physical comedy, which Ball would spend hours perfecting, yet, when the actors did slip up, they

Lucille Ball

Born in Jamestown, New York, Lucille Ball was raised by her widowed mother and her eccentric grandparents. Attending acting school, she found herself in the shadow of another student by the name of Bette Davis. Dropping out when told she had no future, Ball regrouped and by 1932 had moved to New York City to pursue a career, working as a model for Hattie Carnegie and as the Chesterfield cigarette girl. Fired from three different Broadway shows (under the stage name Diane Belmont), she headed west, working as a Goldwyn Girl and at RKO (a studio she would one day own) in larger and larger roles, including a turn in *Stage Door* with Eve Arden, who remained a lifelong friend. Signed to MGM in 1943, by 1948 Ball met Cuban bandleader Desi Arnaz and fell in love. By 1948, not finding the stardom she wanted in film, Ball segued into radio, starring alongside Richard Denning in the comedy *My Favorite Husband*. When she turned the series into a television show costarring husband Desi, she became the biggest and most widely recognized star in sitcom history, reigning supreme on television until 1960, when *The Lucy-Desi Comedy Hour* went off the air. Her by then troubled marriage ended the following day. After an unsuccessful attempt to conquer Broadway in the musical *Wildcat*, Ball returned to her comfort zone, starring in *The Lucy Show* and *Here's Lucy*, the latter featuring her children Lucie and Desi Jr. After nearly twenty-five years on CBS, Ball looked for a lighter schedule, making the occasional film, and television appearances on variety shows. Looking to stretch herself, she played an elderly homeless woman in the television movie *Stone Pillow*, and the following year made a surprising return in a series with old cohort Gale Gordon. Alas, *Life with Lucy* was unsuccessful, and was unceremoniously dumped by ABC, whose treatment of the legend was rather shoddy considering her contributions to an industry she helped to build.

Desi Arnaz

One of the most unheralded pioneers in television history, Desi Arnaz came to America from the turmoil of 1930s Cuba, playing in various orchestras until getting a break from bandleader Xavier Cugat. Creating a sensation in the Broadway musical *Too Many Girls*, he appeared in the movie version a year later, falling in love with and marrying the movie's star, a flame haired comedienne named Lucille. He led his own orchestra in the mid 1940s, while Lucy had a hit with the radio show *My Favorite Husband*. In 1950, the couple formed Desilu Productions and pitched a television version of *My Favorite Husband*, with Arnaz now costarring. The network feared the pair was not believable as man and wife, so Arnaz and Ball put together a vaudeville sketch about a nutty wife trying to break into her husband's act, touring the country to prove their point. The show got the go-ahead, and Lucy and Ricky were born.

Involved in all aspects of the venture, Arnaz made the show more than just a run-of-the-mill situation comedy. Instead of broadcasting live and providing stations with kinescopes, Arnaz had the idea of filming the show with three cameras, so that all stations could air it on high-quality film, enlisting the services of cinematographer Karl Freund, the master behind *Metropolis* and *Dracula*. The network thought this was a waste of money, so Arnaz told CBS that Desilu would absorb the extra cost if he could maintain ownership of the show. Knowing that preserving shows on film made them more valuable with the passage of time, Arnaz, in effect, invented the rerun. Desilu Studios became one of the most successful in Hollywood, producing *Make Room for Daddy*, *December Bride*, and *Our Miss Brooks*. Additionally, hits such as *The Andy Griffith Show* and *The Dick Van Dyke Show* were filmed on its lot. Although their marriage ended, Ball and Arnaz remained close, speaking almost every day by phone. While he went on to produce *The Mothers-In-Law*, he spent the last twenty years of his life in semiretirement.

rarely stopped filming, talking their way out of missed cues and repeating fumbled lines. The atmosphere was one of studied casualness, with all hell breaking loose within the confines of a well-oiled machine, Ball convincing the audience that every situation she found herself in (usually with her partner in crime Vivian Vance in tow, ad-libbing an "Oh, honestly…" whenever she had the chance) was an absolutely spontaneous moment.

The support provided by Vance and William Frawley was invaluable. Sometimes they served as Lucy and Ricky's teammates in the inevitable battle of the sexes; other times they played the Hatfields to the Ricardos' McCoys. All the more to their credit was their believability as bickering but ultimately loving marrieds, for perhaps no other actors, with the exception of two stars of *The Golden Girls*, hid their contempt for each other better than Vance and Frawley.

Certain phrases instantly identify an episode to fans: "The Maharincess of Franistan," "The Friends of the Friendless," "Vitameatavegamin," "Ricky Riskerdoo," "Slowly I Turned," "Females are Fabulous," "El Breako the Leaso," and of course, "Speed it up a little!" the capper to the candy factory scene that is probably the most famous physical comedy routine in the history of television, one that everyone from Laverne and Shirley, Balki and Cousin Larry, Jack Tripper, and even Lucille Ball's subsequent characters, Lucys Carter and Carmichael, have forever been trying to duplicate in its innocent purity and genius sense of timing. In addition, the show was one of the most musical of any sitcom (with the exception of *The Monkees* and *The Partridge Family*), what with Ricky leading an orchestra, Fred and Ethel former vaudevillians, and our heroine Lucy representing every frustrated performer eternally trying to get into a show. (In fact, many young people only know such songs "Friendship," "Shortnin' Bread," "Carolina in the Morning," and "I'm an Old Cow Hand" from performances on *I Love Lucy*.)

Opposite, far left: Sitcom pioneer Desi Arnaz on the set of a show he produced, *The Mothers-in-Law*.

Opposite center: Two classic views of best-friendship: Lucy and Ethel hawking Aunt Martha's Old Fashioned Salad Dressing, and the two hanging out the window of 623 East 68th Street.

Left: Fred MacMurray guest stars on the *I Love Lucy* offshoot *The Lucy/Desi Comedy Hour* with Ball, Arnaz, Vivian Vance, and William Frawley (who would soon be costarring with MacMurray on *My Three Sons*).

Below: Great pals William Frawley and Desi Arnaz. Note the subtle presence of sponsor Philip Morris in the background.

OFF THE SET

THE RICARDOS' New York City address was 623 E. 68th Street. That would place their building approximately 150 yards into the East River.

THE ORIGINAL CHOICES to play Fred and Ethel Mertz were Gale Gordon and Bea Benaderet, the costars of Lucille Ball's radio show, *My Favorite Husband*.

William Frawley

Professional curmudgeon William Frawley began in vaudeville, singing "Carolina in the Morning" and "My Melancholy Baby" (which he claimed to have introduced) from coast to coast. A supporting character actor in more than one hundred films, he joined the ranks of the all-time greats when he was tapped to play landlord Fred Mertz on *I Love Lucy*. Almost rejected for the role because of a reputation for being a heavy drinker, he never came to work drunk and bonded with costar Desi Arnaz during the six-season run of the original *Lucy* series and three seasons of *The Lucy-Desi Comedy Hour*. He segued from Fred to the role of Uncle Bub O'Casey on *My Three Sons*, enjoying a five-year run before he became disgruntled with the bizarre shooting schedule of the show (which crammed a whole season of out-of-sequence scenes into a few weeks to accommodate star Fred MacMurray). In poor health, Frawley left the series when the studio couldn't insure him, and was replaced by William Demarest, whom Frawley publicly lambasted. He spent the last year of his life in the same studio apartment he had lived in for more than twenty years.

While the show began to wind down around the same time that Ball and Arnaz's twenty-year marriage did, the episodes of the show's original six-year run remain as sparkling as they were fifty years ago. One of the greatest testaments to the show is that, while lost in an episode, it is easy to forget that something so funny and so truthful was shot over fifty years ago and all the major players are long gone. Think about the show where Lucy got a loving cup stuck on her head and, as the girls were preparing to go out to have it removed, Ethel balked at riding the subway while wearing blue jeans. Yanked out of our reverie, we realize how timeless the show's comedy is, in spite of how much the world has changed. That is when *I Love Lucy* is at its most potent.

Right: Lucy and Desi comically express the pain and anger that often existed between them offscreen.

Below: Ball and Arnaz stroll the lot of their selfmade empire, Desilu Studios.

Ethel: I refuse to go to the theater with anyone who thinks I'm a hippopotamus.

Ricky: Did you call her that?

Lucy: No, all I did was intimate that she was a little hippy...but on second glance, she has got the biggest "potamus" I've ever seen.

CAST

Lucille Ball	Lucy Ricardo
Desi Arnaz	Ricky Ricardo
Vivian Vance	Ethel Mertz
William Frawley	Fred Mertz
Richard Keith	Little Ricky
Jerry Hausner	Jerry
Shirley Mitchell	Marion Strong
Elizabeth Patterson	Mathilda Trumbull
Doris Singleton	Caroline Appleby
Kathryn Card	Mrs. MacGillicuddy
Mary Jane Croft	Betty Ramsey
Frank Nelson	Ralph Ramsey
Barbara Pepper	various roles

I MARRIED JOAN

NBC | **1952–1955** | **98 episodes**

Joan Davis, what a girl, what a whirl, is married to Judge Bradley Stevens. What a life!

Though some confuse this title with the autobiography of Spanish artist Miro's wife, it was actually the Pontiac to Lucy's Cadillac of sitcoms. Although this was a relatively cheap show—even the theme song was sung a capella by the Roger Wagner Chorale—Joan Davis was billed as "America's Queen of Comedy." Well...she might not have been the queen but she was certainly a duchess. Davis was mentored by Eddie Cantor (as was Dinah Shore) and made a splash with him on radio and then in B movies.

Totally in the Lucy mold, Davis cooked up impossible schemes while her intelligent, emotionally balanced husband looked on with a mixture of shock and resignation. Davis didn't have a sidekick like Lucy did, though; she had to work twice as hard as Lucy since her nutty ideas were entirely hers to carry out. Two things the comediennes had in common were that they were both the producers of their own shows and, less significantly, Mary Jane Croft played a friend of the lead in both series.

Jim Backus's Judge Stevens didn't blow up quite as often as Ricky Ricardo did—he was far more patient. Just as Vern Albright had opened each episode of *My Little Margie*, Backus usually opened the show with a reminiscence of one or another zany adventure Joan had cooked up. The judge also closed the episodes with a wrap-up.

If the show had been produced by Norman Lear, Judge Bradley might have been on the Supreme Court and voting on *Roe v. Wade* while Joan decided to perform a home abortion.

Joan Davis, a four-alarm dingbat if ever there was one.

But this was suburbia in the 1950s, so there were no "very special" *I Married Joan* episodes. Here's a typical plot: Joan is preparing an intimate dinner for two when she finds out the judge has invited guests over. She takes a rolling pin to the fish course to try to stretch it. The judge keeps calling to say he's invited more people, and each time he does, she adds another cup of water to the soup, then attaches a bicycle pump to the chicken to inflate it. Believe it or not, the chicken trick works—until it rises into the air as if filled with helium. Finally, with nothing to serve for the dinner party, Joan invites everyone to a lavish picnic the next afternoon. Upon arriving at the picnic grounds, Joan is at first unaware that a stray dog has stolen all the food in the basket. Discovering this, she tries to steal food from other people's baskets, but she's caught and forced to admit to her guests

"I've kept going on a mixture of gall, guts, and gumption." —Joan Davis

Mary Jane Croft

The eternal best friend, the intelligent, bemused Mary Jane Croft was a member of the Lucille Ball stable of character actresses. After one small film role (she appeared in only two films ever—she was definitely a television gal), she first gained notice on *I Married Joan*, which ran concurrently with *I Love Lucy*. Croft made the transition to Lucy easily, playing the star's rival, Betty Ramsey. From *I Love Lucy* she moved to *The Adventures of Ozzie and Harriet* as Clara Randolph, a sort of precursor to her next role, as Mary Jane Lewis (her real married name, by the way) on both *The Lucy Show* and *Here's Lucy*. This time she was Lucy's best friend and sometime accomplice. Desi Arnaz was loyal to Mary Jane, too: he cast her in *The Mothers-in-Law*, which he produced. Mary Jane, Lucy, Vivian Vance, and Gale Gordon had one last hurrah, in the 1977 made-for-TV movie *Lucy Calls the President*.

that, again, there's no food. In the third act, she throws, yes, another big dinner party for her twice-disappointed guests—only to have them turn down the food, as they are pleased with all of the weight they've lost by not eating for two meals.

That, ladies and gentlemen, was the height of sitcom humor in the '50s and, thanks to the expert talents of Joan Davis and Jim Backus, it worked. The plots, idiotic as they were, existed only to let the stars do their shtick. Like the inflated chicken, the show had legs (and wings).

Opposite: Hope Emerson, Hal March, and Joan Davis puff away on set.

Top: Davis and Jim Backus are off to a costume party. Okay, we get that Joan is supposed to be Groucho, but who is Backus dolled up as? Norma Zimmer from *The Lawrence Welk Show*?

Right: Sitcom veteran Mary Jane Croft has yet to realize that Lucy's baby is actually a big old hunk of cheese.

OFF THE SET

JOAN DAVIS'S DAUGHTER, Beverly Wills, showed up on the series as Joan's younger sister.

DAVIS QUIT THE series because of health issues and died of heart problems at the young age of forty-nine; her daughter died only two years later in a fire.

CAST

Joan Davis	Joan Stevens
Jim Backus	Judge Bradley Stevens
Beverly Wills	Beverly Grossman
Hope Emerson	Minerva Parker
Elvia Allman	Aunt Vera
Hal Smith	Charlie
Geraldine Carr	Mabel
Dan Tobin	Kerwin Tobin
Sheila Bromley	Janet Tobin
Mary Jane Croft	Helen
Sandra Gould	Mildred Webster

IT'S GARRY SHANDLING'S SHOW

SHOWTIME | 1986–1990 | **72 episodes**

Fictional stand-up comedian Garry Shandling, played by real-life stand-up comedian Garry Shandling, parades his work and personal life in front of the camera.

Of course, the entire conceit can be traced back to *The Jack Benny Show* and, especially, *The George Burns and Gracie Allen Show*, two "backstage" comedies in which reality and fiction mingled.

Shandling's life, as portrayed on his series, left him no less neurotic than his real life, but at least on television he could manipulate his friends and family and events to suit himself. Unfortunately for him, they could also stop the action to beseech the studio audience for their advice and approval. And sometimes the audience preferred outcomes that weren't to Shandling's satisfaction.

He sometimes used his flashback machine to see just

The 1970s introduced a number of self-referential satires of television. *Fernwood 2-Night*, a parodic late-night talk show perhaps inspired by David Letterman's earliest incarnation, was itself a spin-off of the parody soap opera, *Mary Hartman, Mary Hartman*. Al Franken's *Lateline* was a spoof of *Nightline* on which real newsmakers appeared, as if the show within the show were real. The "fake" news show remains with us today, in the form of *The Daily Show* and its offspring, *The Colbert Report*. On these shows, stand-up comedians play talk show hosts and newscasters who interview real guests and report on real news… thereby becoming real talk-show hosts and newscasters. The mind reels.

why he had pissed off everyone at a party, or he fast-forwarded to see what his children would be like, if he had any. Everyone needs some time off and the fictional(ish) Shandling was no exception. Red Buttons once substituted for him on the show—and of course Shandling's friends and family preferred Buttons. On another occasion Shandling left his young, dorky neighbor Grant in charge while he went off on tour with Guns n' Roses! Once, when Shandling left town, he invited the studio audience to have a party in his apartment. Is it any wonder that his condo board tried to evict him?

It's Garry Shandling's Show morphed into Shandling's second series, this time for HBO, titled *The Larry Sanders Show*. Similar in concept to *It's Garry Shandling's Show*, Shandling's second

Garry Shandling

Dyspeptic, insecure Garry Shandling conquered the sitcom world with back-to-back brilliant sitcoms that broke all the rules. Taking a page from the George Burns playbook, Shandling played out his own neuroses on *It's Garry Shandling's Show* and *The Larry Sanders Show*. Reveling in his own nebbishness (as did many of his Woody Allen–influenced contemporaries), Shandling came from the world of stand-up. Unafraid of making fun of his less than matinee idol looks and the blunders of his personal life, Shandling created something fresh out of an idea stretching back to Jack Benny. Since his series ended, he's been featured in a few forgettable films: *What Planet Are You From?*, *Town and Country*, and *Trust the Man*. Gary, come back to sitcoms—we need you desperately!

outing was darker and the characters were more neurotic. This time, Shandling didn't break the fourth wall and address the audience, but the antics behind the scenes of the fictional *Larry Sanders Show* were more bizarre, often involving deeply insecure Larry's obsessive sexual pursuit of that week's female guest. A bonus was the parade of performances by top musical acts of the day—a reason in itself to tune in. The spectacle of Garry (as Larry) trying to "hang" with Old Dirty Bastard of the Wu Tang Clan has the makings of classic TV.

These two brilliant shows clearly helped inspire *Seinfeld* creator Larry David's personal vehicle, *Curb Your Enthusiasm*, in which he plays a barely fictionalized version of himself and the scripts are more like outlines around which the brilliant cast improvises "real" dialogue.

Backstage comedies and dramas have always been beloved staples of theater and film, but on TV, things get a bit more complicated. Real people playing characters who share their names and particulars; famous people playing fake famous people who interact with real famous people. Though the seeds of this conceit have been around almost as long as TV itself, the whole thing has become so confusing we just have to lie down.

Above: Shandling as the hilariously disturbed talk show host Larry Sanders, with sidekick Hank Kingsley (the amazing Jeffrey Tambor) and Bernadette Peters.

OFF THE SET

IN A MOVE that was unheard of at the time, Fox picked up *It's Garry Shandling's Show* while it was still running on Showtime, playing each episode a few days after it aired on the cable network.

HOWARD SPRAGUE, a beloved character from *The Andy Griffith Show* played by Jack Dodson, moved into Garry's building.

CAST

Garry Shandling	Garry Shandling
Barbara Cason	Mrs. Shandling
Molly Cheek	Nancy Bancroft
Michael Tucci	Pete Schumaker
Bernadette Birkett	Jackie Schumaker
Scott Nemes	Grant Schumaker
Paul Willson	Leonard Smith
Ian Buchanan	Ian
Jessica Harper	Phoebe Bass

Garry Shandling, unlucky at cards and unlucky in love, shares a scene with his best friend Nancy Bancroft, played by the droll Molly Cheek.

THE JACK BENNY PROGRAM

Comedian Jack Benny plays himself, taking us inside his work life (a network television show) and home life, where he is aided by his loyal if sometimes exasperated butler, Rochester.

crafted character, as were the other regulars.

On the show, when Benny wasn't "in one" (theater jargon for down at the footlights, in front of the first curtain), talking to the audience, he was at home with Rochester, his faithful manservant. His cronies from the studio, Dennis Day and Don Wilson, would drop by, as did Mary Livingston. (Clue number one: Livingston was Benny's real-life wife but played the role of his girlfriend.) Incorporating many gags from his long radio run, Benny was the same Benny audiences had grown to love: stingy, vain, exasperated at the stupidity

It's taken us until the letter *J* to bring up the most pressing of questions: What is a sitcom? When we chose *The Jack Benny Program* as one of the 101 greatest, we had our doubts as to whether it actually was a sitcom. When we told our friends it was included, we got quizzical looks. Some thought it was a variety show, some maintained it was some other form of comedy. It did have guest stars who performed their specialties (Jayne Mansfield played the violin!), and there's certainly no argument about the fact that it was one of the funniest shows of all time. But was it a sitcom? We say yes, based on the fact that the "Jack Benny" of the show, though he shared the star's name, was a carefully

of his inferiors, and a lousy violin player. (Clue number two: offscreen, Benny was generous, smart, played a very good violin, and was terrifically self-deprecating.)

Throughout his career, Benny played the persona he had developed through years of vaudeville, Broadway, films, stand-up, and radio. Like others who grew up along with show business in the first half of the century, Benny knew the power of creating a character. As director Ralph Levy noted, "These people were from another era of show business; one in which you took literally years to build your comedic character…" It's easy to confuse a performer with the character he or she plays. Once in a while, they are virtually one and the same—by all accounts, George Burns was

James V. Kern

Many talented people excel in more than one area. James V. Kern was one such hyphenate, whose career spanned performing, directing, songwriting, producing, and writing. He started out to be a lawyer but show biz grabbed him and he gave up on juries in favor of paid audiences. He started as a singer with the George Olsen band and with them he appeared in the Broadway musical *Good News*. He formed the singing group the Yacht Club Boys with three others, and wrote most of their original songs. (He had one standard to his name, "Easy Street.") Soon they had a Warner Brothers contract. In 1939, Kern went on to a job as screenwriter on such films as *Thank Your Lucky Stars* and *Shine On, Harvest Moon*. In 1945, he contributed the screenplay to the Jack Benny fiasco *The Horn Blows at Midnight*. No matter that the film was a bust, Benny and Kern hit it off and, when television called, Kern became a producer on *The Jack Benny Program*. It was as a television director that Kern really found his calling, becoming a house director on such series as *I Love Lucy*, *The Ann Sothern Show*, *Pete and Gladys*, *My Three Sons*, *The Joey Bishop Show*, *My Favorite Martian*, and, of course, *The Jack Benny Program*.

Jack Benny and two of his favorite things starting with the letter V: violin and vault.

pretty much the same on stage and off. On the other hand, some of the meanest performers in show business had the public completely fooled. The real Jack Benny had little in common with his persona, but at the end of the show, when he bid the audience good night, we got a glimpse of the real Benny. The truth, of course, is that no performer is exactly him/herself on stage or screen. Benny's television writers had forty years to perfect his persona, and they were masters of their craft. Radio writers are the unsung heroes of American entertainment, and we can categorically state that though some shows were as funny as *The Jack Benny Program*, no sitcom was funnier.

Opposite: Table reading day at *The Jack Benny Program*, with cast members including Mary Livingston, Eddie "Rochester" Anderson, and Don Wilson.

Left: Mr. Benny and Rochester evaluate the condition of his car, a 1918 Maxwell.

CAST

Jack Benny	Jack Benny
Eddie "Rochester" Anderson	Rochester
Don Wilson	Don Wilson
Dennis Day	Dennis Day
Mary Livingston	Mary Livingston

RECURRING APPEARANCES

Benny Rubin

Frank Nelson

Artie Auerbach

Mel Blanc

SITCOMS FROM RADIO SHOWS

Vaudeville begat radio and films which begat television. Radio had a particular relationship with television as the one medium replaced the other. Stars of radio like Burns and Allen and Jack Benny made the transition easily. Lucille Ball, Eve Arden, and other former movie stars with radio shows naturally turned to the small screen to further their careers. Shows like *Amos and Andy* continued on both television and radio. Few of the radio formulas didn't also work on television though the TV audience was shocked at the difference in appearance of their favorite stars from what they had imagined in their heads on radio. In addition to those in our list of the 101 greatest, forgotten successes include *Beulah*, *A Date with Judy*, *Ethel and Albert*, *Meet Millie*, *My Favorite Husband*, and *My Friend Irma*. Failures include *Blondie*, *Fibber McGee and Molly*, and *Meet Corliss Archer*.

Above: Jack Benny and Mary Livingston made the transition from radio to television but Mary, only begrudgingly a performer, didn't hang around the series for long. She was never an actress and only appeared with Jack because her rival (in her head only), Gracie Allen, appeared with George Burns and Mary was intensly jealous of Gracie.

Left: Marie Wilson, the original dumb blonde, seen here with co-star Cathy Lewis on the third incarnation of *My Friend Irma*. First came the radio program, then the film *My Friend Irma Goes West* (costarring Martin and Lewis), to be followed by the CBS television program.

THE JEFFERSONS

◉ | **1975–1985** | **253 episodes**

George and Louise Jefferson cross the river and move on up, to a deeluxe apartment on Manhattan's East Side, complete with a sassy maid, a peculiar British translator next door, and the Willises, an interracial couple, upstairs.

With the most infectious theme song of all time, *The Jeffersons* was one of the many spin-offs of *All in the Family*. In the first season of that landmark show, Norman Lear provided the Bunkers with African-American neighbors, the Jeffersons. Their son Lionel, a friend of Mike and Gloria's, served as a fifth member of the core cast during its first two seasons. Veteran actress Isabel Sanford began making appearances as Lionel's mother, Louise, developing a

touching and believable friendship with Jean Stapleton's Edith Bunker, and while Louise's brother-in-law Henry, (played by Mel Stewart) also guest-starred, for the first three seasons, the often-discussed Jefferson patriarch George, owner of a dry cleaning business, was never seen.

When he finally materialized, played by a perfectly cast Sherman Hemsley, George was a surprise. In a classic Lear twist, George Jefferson was just as conservative, cantankerous, and prejudiced as Bunker, albeit from the opposite end of the racial spectrum. After many episodes where the two butted heads about race, Lear came up with the brilliant idea of having George strike it rich in business, thereby making the bigoted Archie Bunker even more apoplectic as his neighbor delivered a coup de grace to the "honky" next door by moving to Manhattan and up the social ladder.

After the pilot, shown as an episode of *All in the Family*, many of the show's early installments revolved around George's trying to fit in with his new Upper East Side neighbors, including Mr. Wittendale, a rich banker who lived in the penthouse. The show gained another cast member in the first episode, when the wonderful Marla Gibbs, guesting as Florence, a maid hired to impress one of George's clients, created such a sensation that she soon became a regular.

The thing that made *The Jeffersons* click was chemistry. The volatile Archie Bunker needed a stabilizing force to keep him from being a raving one-note xenophobe, wife Edith provided that buffer. Similarly, Isabel Sanford's Louise was a perfect counterbalance for the mercurial George. Louise (or "Weezy," a nickname that perfectly evoked Sanford's gravelly, asthmatic voice) wasn't quite the pushover that Edith Bunker was. Weezy could kick the crap out of that pipsqueak George, and despite an age difference of more than twenty years, the spark between the two was strong, making them one of television's most believable married couples.

While Archie was the nucleus of *All in the Family*, around which all conflict revolved, on *The Jeffersons*, everyone seemed to have his or her own nemesis; in addition to George and the tart-tongued Florence, Louise had to contend with the withering asides of George's doting, sherry-loving mother, played by Zara Cully. The Willises, when not challenging George's view of interracial marriage, were taking on each other's views of race, gender,

and politics. Lionel and Jenny constantly battled with their parents, in-laws, and each other. Dropped into the midst of all this was Harry Bentley from next door, played by the pear-shaped, lantern-jawed Paul Benedict. The über-outré Mr. Bentley ranks alongside *Taxi*'s Reverend Jim Ignatowski and *Green Acres*'s Lisa Douglas as one of the most obtuse sitcom characters ever: eminently lovable, even when neither the audience nor the characters on the show knew what in the blue blazes he was talking about.

As in many other long-running shows, *The Jeffersons* sustained cast changes, including a Darrin Stephens/Becky Conner switch of actors that was perhaps the most confusing of all. Are you ready for this? Michael Evans, who had gone on to cocreate another *All in the Family* spin-off, *Good Times*, played Lionel on the first

Sherman Hemsley

Working as a New York City post office clerk while studying acting with the Negro Ensemble Company, Sherman Hemsley attracted attention in the musical *Purlie*. Norman Lear was looking for an

actor to play Archie Bunker's neighbor George Jefferson. He thought of Hemsley and took a chance, even delaying George's arrival on the show (he was referred to but unseen for three seasons) until Hemsley was done with *Purlie*'s Broadway run. The comic spark Hemsley generated set Lear to thinking about a spin-off, and Hemsley took the opportunity and ran with it. With the strut he created for George, arms swinging and chest puffed out, he could get a laugh just by entering a room, and he was perhaps the best door-slammer in sitcom history, so perfect was his timing. After *The Jeffersons* went off the air in 1985, Hemsley immediately came back as a character not too far afield from George Jefferson: the peppery Philadelphia church deacon Ernest Frye on the five-year hit *Amen*. In addition to a stint on the short-lived *Goode Behavior*, he has continued to make guest appearances with his "Weezy," Isabel Sanford, on everything from *The Fresh Prince of Bel Air* to commercials for Old Navy.

Marla Gibbs

Like costar Sherman Hemsley, Marla Gibbs, sitcom's queen of the sassy comeback, came to acting from another career. Working as a reservations clerk for United Airlines, Gibbs found herself transferred from Detroit to Los Angeles, where both she and her daughter Angela began studying acting. After some good reviews in L.A. theater, Gibbs landed the tiny role of the Jeffersons' temporary maid and became an overnight success. The character of Florence Johnston was soon a vital member of

the show's cast (though the pragmatic Gibbs continued to work for the airlines until she was sure of a steady gig), the only character truly capable of cutting the puffed-up George down to his true Napoleonic proportions. After the eleven-year run of *The Jeffersons* (during which Gibbs took only a brief hiatus for an unsuccessful spin-off called *Checking In*), Gibbs's daughter Angela produced the award-winning Christine Houston play *227* as a stage vehicle for her mother. So successful was the play that Gibbs bought the television rights and, along with former boss Norman Lear, developed it as a series for NBC, where she enjoyed a five-season run. In addition to running a Los Angeles jazz club/restaurant, Gibbs still appears on TV, most recently as mother Hattie Mae on the ABC series *The Hughleys*.

Left: Marla Gibbs and Isabel Sanford register their unique forms of stern disapproval of Sherman Hemsley.

Below: Roxie Roker and Franklin Cover, as Tom and Helen Willis, challenge Sherman Hemsley's George, the African-American version of Archie Bunker.

Opposite: Sherman Hemsley, as puffed up and cantakerous as ever, guest stars on Marla Gibbs's hit series *227*.

CAST

Isabel Sanford	Louise Jefferson
Sherman Hemsley	George Jefferson
Roxie Roker	Helen Willis
Franklin Cover	Tom Willis
Paul Benedict	Harry Bentley
Marla Gibbs	Florence Johnston
Mike Evans	Lionel Jefferson (1,3)
Damon Evans	Lionel Jefferson (2)
Berlinda Tolbert	Jenny Willis-Jefferson
Zara Cully	Mother Jefferson
Jay Hammer	Allan Willis
Ned Wertimer	Ralph, the doorman
Danny Wells	Charlie, the bartender

Florence Johnston: How come we overcame and nobody told me?

thirteen episodes of *The Jeffersons*. When it was renewed for a full season, Evans didn't return, preferring to concentrate on his behind-the-scenes duties on *Good Times*, so he was replaced by actor Damon Evans (no relation) for the next three seasons. In 1979, Damon left the show and Michael returned. Another two years and Michael left again, this time for good, the powers that be writing the character out of the show.

One of the most interesting shifts was the change in the character of George. Hemsley grew tired of the constant "honky" putdowns of Tom Willis and urged the producers to come up with something new. Hence, George mellowed and became friends with Tom, and *The Jeffersons* became more of a conventional two-couple show. The episodes often took on an *I Love Lucy* tone, with George and Tom trying to hide their Lucy-and-Ethel-like schemes from Weezy and Helen. In the final season the duo joined forces financially and bought Charlie's Bar, their favorite neighborhood hangout. (An ironic plot turn, as that is exactly what George's nemesis Archie had done near the end of his own series.) Finally, in one of the most bizarre turns in television, after its eleventh and final season, the cast, upset at finding out about the show's cancellation by reading it in the newspaper, spited the network by going on tour with a stage adaptation of the series, playing to sell-out houses.

JULIA

NBC | 1968–1971 | 86 episodes

Julia Baker, an African-American widow whose husband died in Vietnam, works as a nurse for a crusty doctor while raising her young son, Corey.

A show included in this book not for its knee-slapping comedy or its brilliant writing but for its groundbreaking status, *Julia* was the first sitcom to center on a nonstereotypical African-American character. Telling the story of Julia Baker, a recent Vietnam War widow who finds a job as a nurse to support her child, the show starred Diahann Carroll, a beautiful veteran of Broadway and nightclubs. She was the perfect actress to break down the barriers that had limited television opportunities for actors of color. *Julia*'s creator, Hal Kanter, had faced his own share of prejudice growing up Jewish in the Deep South.

Premiering five months after Martin Luther King, Jr. was assassinated, the show was considered an extremely risky move by NBC, its debut causing the network brass many a sleepless night. *I Spy*, costarring Bill Cosby and Robert Culp, which had premiered three seasons earlier, had certainly helped pave the way, but *Julia* was truly startling for many television viewers, particularly those in the deep south. While Cosby had merely been half of a team, Diahann Carroll as *Julia* was the sole center of the show, every bit as much as Connie Brooks, Samantha Stephens, or Ann Marie had been. She just happened to be black. Luckily, NBC's gamble paid off and the show caused an immediate sensation.

The action was evenly split between Julia's job in the clinic at Astrospace Industries and her struggles as a single parent. The wry Lloyd Nolan (wittily credited as "frequently starring Lloyd Nolan") appeared as her boss, the

Above: The elegant Diahann Carroll, with TV son Marc Copage, broke down racial barriers in sitcoms with her customary class.

Opposite: Carroll helps Betty Beaird, as next-door neighbor Marie Waggedorn, try on what looks like a castoff from the wardrobe department of another NBC hit, *Laugh-In*.

curmudgeonly Dr. Chegley, and veteran character actress Lurene Tuttle lent a sympathetic ear as co-worker Nurse Hannah Yarby. But outside of the supporting cast (including Mary Wickes as Nolan's wife, Melba, and Ned Glass as Julia's landlord), the show itself was far from top drawer. Much of the writing was "slice of life" to the point of banality, and without a laugh track one often wondered what the writers actually considered to be punch lines. In addition, young Marc Copage, who played Julia's son, Corey, was adorable, but one of the least natural child actors on television; it may sound cruel to pick on a little kid, but in comparison to the ability of the youngsters on *The Brady Bunch*, *The Cosby Show*, or the brilliance of young Ronny Howard, Copage came up short, reciting dialogue in a singsong manner that made it almost nonsensical. Perhaps it was the lack of a good dialogue coach, for Michael Link, who played Corey's best friend next door, the precocious Earl J. Waggedorn (who was always addressed by his entire name, even by his mother), was only marginally better—and even young Jodie Foster, appearing on one episode, came off so badly it sounded as if she'd learned her role phonetically.

Plots were simple, even quaint. Julia buys a new car; Corey needs a babysitter; Julia has to fill in at the last minute for a singer with laryngitis. And while many story lines dealt with Julia's struggles with prejudice, entire episodes would go by in which her race was never mentioned. Ironically, in Kanter's attempts to create a show that enlightened by treating race as a given rather than an issue, he ended up angering both ends of the spectrum. The more surprising reaction came from some in the African-American community, who condemned the show as being not nearly political enough and sidestepping the hard-hitting issues. Carroll dealt with criticism from both sides with customary class, but the constant stress of being under the microscope ultimately proved exhausting and she asked to be released from her contract in 1971, while the show was still a hit.

In three seasons, the two main forces behind *Julia*'s success, Hal Kanter and Diahann Carroll, had forever changed the face of television, opening the door for countless new shows and giving a voice not only to African-Americans, but also other groups previously not represented on television.

CAST

Diahann Carroll	Julia Baker
Lloyd Nolan	Dr. Morton Chegley
Marc Copage	Corey Baker
Michael Link	Earl J. Waggedorn
Betty Beaird	Marie Waggedorn
Lurene Tuttle	Hannah Yarby
Hank Brandt	Len Waggedorn

Hal Kanter

The son of the founder of "Classic Comics" (which provided many a student with the means to write a book report on a three-hundred-page snoozer they had no intention of reading), Hal Kanter began as a sketch writer for TV variety shows in the early 1950s. Joining the Emmy-winning team of *The George Gobel Show*, he branched out into film, writing screenplays for Bob Hope and the team of Dean Martin and Jerry Lewis. His first outing as a director was on the Elvis Presley movie *Loving You* in 1957, and he scored a cult hit by writing and directing the film intended to launch Dan Rowan and Dick Martin's big-screen career, the Western spoof *Once Upon a Horse*. Moving back to television, his most historic accomplishment was as creator of *Julia*, and he followed it up by becoming executive producer of *All in the Family*, further building upon his passion for dealing with important social issues through the humor of the situation comedy.

LAVERNE & SHIRLEY

abc | **1976–1983** | **178 episodes**

Arm in arm and trying to stay in step, bottle cappers Laverne De Fazio and Shirley Feeney make their dreams come true in 1950s Milwaukee.

Cast with two incredibly appealing and complementary actresses, *Laverne & Shirley* was a mix of the slapstick of *I Love Lucy* and the roommate scenarios of *The Odd Couple*, set in the 1950s milieu of *Happy Days*. Starring Penny Marshall, straight from her role as Myrna Turner on *The Odd Couple*, and Cindy Williams, a veteran of the nostalgia craze from her role in the movie *American Graffiti*, the pair was introduced

girls split their time between home, work as bottle cappers at the Shotz Brewery, and hanging out at the Pizza Bowl, run by Laverne's father.

Vital to the show's unique charm were Michael McKean and David L. Lander as the utterly greasy upstairs neighbors Lenny and Squiggy, flinging the door open with Squiggy's trademark "Hello…," a precursor to Michael Richards's comic entrances as Kramer fifteen years later. Musical interludes were offered by

former MGM musical star Betty Garrett as landlady Edna Babish, and Eddie Mekka as Shirley's on-again, off-again boyfriend, the dance instructor Carmine Ragusa, a.k.a. "The Big Ragu." Theirs must rank as the first "open relationship" in sitcoms (well, at least it was open on Shirley's part—as she told Laverne, "I can date other men and Carmine can date ugly women").

The first three seasons featured some truly inspired physical comedy, with the girls enduring a weekend of sleep and food deprivation at a psychiatric lab, to earn enough money to attend a swanky affair; sneaking into the Hotel Pfister dressed as maids in an attempt to meet their idol Fabian; and taking over the duties at a diner. In that episode, Laverne played cook and Shirley

on an episode of *Happy Days*, as friends of Fonzie's that double-dated with Richie Cunningham. Laverne, with her New York accent, ubiquitous embroidered *L*, and boisterous attitude, was offset perfectly by the fragile sweetness and undying optimism of Shirley (who ended more than one episode with a rousing version of "High Hopes"). Living in a basement apartment, the

(who Laverne insisted on calling "Betty" over the kitchen's microphone) played waitress, prompting the famous request, "Betty, pick up your hash blacks."

Episodes often ended with poignancy but rarely tackled serious topics, usually staying within the slice-of-life realm that was the hallmark of its sitcom parent, *Happy Days*.

Theatre, the La Brea tar pits, and Ed Marinaro, who joined the cast as the beefy stuntman living upstairs. But they also had lamer and lamer plots, the quality dipping with each successive season.

And when Cindy Williams, either pregnant or fed up with the show's decline, left the show in the middle of its eighth and final season, the show took a dive faster than Sister Bertrille with a case of wind shear. The opening credits were altered to feature Marshall all alone, watching a group of schoolchildren doing the old hopscotch chant, trying to do a buddy show with no buddy. Williams, Betty Garrett, and Michael McKean had all jumped ship, and the show died a rather ignominious death, with poor Laverne getting a job at an aerospace testing facility. The only person who landed on his feet was the Big Ragu, who finally got his long-awaited break in show business when he was cast in the Broadway musical *Hair*.

Like *Gilligan's Island*, *The Munsters*, and *Perfect Strangers*, in its prime, *Laverne & Shirley* was sometimes inspired, sometimes lame—but undeniably funny. Goofy as hell, but funny. Perhaps a clue to the show's peculiar appeal is that in Korea, Laverne and Shirley's behavior is explained by claiming that the two girls have just been released from a mental hospital and their bottle-capping jobs are a form of occupational therapy.

And speaking of *Happy Days*, *Laverne & Shirley* definitely jumped the shark after its fifth season, when the entire cast packed up and moved to California (our girls got jobs in a department store, Frank and Edna opened a restaurant called Buffalo Bill's, and Lenny and Squiggy were still weird, albeit with better tans). True, with the move to Burbank, the girls had more opportunities for fun, visiting such tourist attractions as Graumann's Chinese

Top: Virtually every script of the unsuccessful 1966 series *Hey, Landlord!* (co-produced by Garry Marshall) was reworked for *Laverne & Shirley*. Here the girls deal with their own landlady, the wonderful Betty Garrett.

Above: Their grins hiding their discontent, Cindy Williams and Penny Marshall "schlemiel" and "schlemazl" in the show's second setting, sunny California.

Penny Marshall

With the laugh of a braying donkey and the ability to be knowing and naive at the same time, Penny Marshall undoubtedly got an initial career boost from her brother Garry's success as a writer, director, and producer (as well as from the fact that she was married to actor/director Rob Reiner for a decade). But her own unique comic talent took her farther than nepotism ever could.

After playing Paul Sands's sister in-law on the short-lived *Friends and Lovers*, she immediately segued into the role of Myrna Turner (right), Oscar Madison's secretary on *The Odd Couple*, quickly becoming a regular. She first appeared as Laverne De Fazio on an episode of *Happy Days*, and while the spin-off was being prepared, Marshall made several appearances on *Mary Tyler Moore*, as Mary Richards's new neighbor Paula Kovacks, a pseudo-Rhoda. After *Laverne & Shirley*'s run, Marshall became a successful film director, scoring a huge hit with her second film, *Big*, and following it up with such fine films as *Awakenings* and *A League of Their Own*. Getting more and more offbeat in recent years, wearing bangs and dark glasses, her mumbling speech nearly indecipherable, Marshall voiced the evil nanny, Ms. Botz, on *The Simpsons* and recently appeared on the HBO series *Entourage*.

Lowell Ganz & Babaloo Mandel

Writing and producing partners Lowell Ganz and Marc "Babaloo" Mandel began their careers as writers on *The Odd Couple*, alongside Garry Marshall and Jerry Paris, which led to a long-running job with them on *Happy Days* and two of the hit show's spin-offs, *Laverne & Shirley* and *Joanie Loves Chachi*. With a keen sense of comic invention, they teamed up with *Happy Days* stars Ron Howard, who wanted to branch out into directing, and Henry Winkler, who was trying to break away from his Fonzie image, and wrote the very funny movie *Night Shift*. Ganz and Mandel were nominated for an Oscar for their second screenplay, the mermaid fantasy *Splash*, also directed by Howard and starring a young Tom Hanks. The greatest testament to their talent is that they have worked multiple times with their collaborators, including four times with Howard (including on *Parenthood*), four times with Billy Crystal (writing the hit *City Slickers*), and with old *Laverne & Shirley* costar Penny Marshall, director of their 1992 smash *A League of Their Own*.

OFF THE SET

LAVERNE & SHIRLEY'S theme song, "Making Our Dreams Come True," sung by Cyndi Grecco, hit the *Billboard* charts in 1976.

IN THE FIRST few episodes of the series, Cindy Williams adopted a much harder accent, sort of a cross between Milwaukee and New Jersey. It was almost immediately dropped.

CAST

Penny Marshall...... Laverne De Fazio

Cindy Williams...... Shirley Feeney

Eddie Mekka.......... Carmine Ragusa

David L. Lander..... Andrew "Squiggy" Squiggman

Michael McKean... Leonard "Lenny" Kosnowski

Phil Foster............... Frank De Fazio

Betty Garrett........... Edna Babish De Fazio

Ed Marinaro........... Sonny St. Jacques

Leslie Easterbrook. Rhonda Lee

Carole Ita White..... Rosie Greenbaum

Left: Michael McKean and David L. Lander started out as story consultants to *Laverne & Shirley* and ended up playing the positively ooky Lenny and Squiggy.

Above: Cindy Williams and Eddie Mekka, as the on-again-off-again Shirley and Carmine, in the basement apartment that was made up almost entirely of modified and repainted scenery from *The Odd Couple*, which had recently finished its five-season run.

LEAVE IT TO BEAVER

| **1957–1963** | **234 episodes**

Beaver Cleaver, his older brother Wally, and their friends grow up under the watchful eyes of their parents and teachers—but their most memorable lessons come from one another.

A charming series that helped pave the way for many more sitcoms revolving around kids, *Leave It to Beaver* entertained the entire family with its humor and warmth. Beaver was probably the first series in which the kids were the focal point. Sure, *The Adventures of Ozzie and Harriet* and *Father Knows Best* concerned nuclear families—but their titles gave them away. The kids were key to their plots but the parents got the last word. On *Beaver*, nothing June or Ward Cleaver did was as important as the schemes and feelings of their children.

Leave It to Beaver was all about Wally and Beaver and their friends, schoolmates, and teachers. There weren't any pesky neighbors or job-related adventures. At the start of the series, Beaver was only seven and Wally was twelve. Their relationship was not only heartwarming, it formed much of the basis of the series's humor. It was almost as though Wally was bringing up "the Beav" while the parents stepped in once in a while to save the day or teach a lesson. The boys shared a room, and their private discussions were a highlight of each episode, revealing Wally, in his preteen ignorance, trying to explain the world to Beaver and getting it all just a little bit wrong.

Then there were the friends. Was there ever a stupider child than Lumpy or as obsequious a young man as Eddie Haskell? These were revolutionary characters in the world of sitcoms, where previously all children had been either spoiled brats or perfect little

Jerry Mathers and Tony Dow on the fence. Mom, Barbara Billingsley, must have been looking the other way, for she never would have allowed them to perch on an unsteady structure while whittling.

angels. Eddie Haskell, one of the most memorable supporting characters in television history, was so transparent in his sycophancy ("and how is young Theodore today, Mrs. Cleaver?") that he was a breath of fresh air in the bland world of '50s sitcoms.

The adults were nothing if not even-handed. Ward and June were stern when they needed to be, but always totally loving; Beaver's teachers, Miss Canfield followed by Miss Landers and then Mrs. Reyburn, treated the boys with respect and a stern hand, even when baffled by their actions. Lumpy's father and Ward's boss, the pompous Fred Rutherford, seemed just as clueless about his surroundings as his son was. But there was always a

sense that Mayfield was populated almost entirely with children.

As the series went on, the kids grew up and the writers and producers were smart enough to allow them to develop. Wally discovered girls and grew more confused than ever, and then Beaver followed in his footsteps. Not all of the episodes provided innocuous little lessons about growing up. There were a few attempts to deal with serious matters (albeit gently) such as alcoholism and divorce—but always as these issues affected the children.

The show captured the imagination of young and old alike, each relating to the characters in his or her own age group. Surprisingly, the series became the subject of some urban legends. At one point,

playgrounds were abuzz with the news that Barbara Billingsley had broken her right arm and always carried a tea towel

Jerry Mathers

Known for one role and one role only (though he made a sweet impression in Hitchcock's film *The Trouble with Harry*), Jerry Mathers epitomized American boyhood as Theodore "Beaver" Cleaver on *Leave It to Beaver*. He was a natural actor, imbuing Beaver with sweet innocence and a cheery, inquisitive disposition. Wisely, he quit while he was ahead and retired from acting following *Beaver*'s cancellation. Mathers finished college and began a career in real estate development. When the nostalgia boom hit, he appeared as *Beaver* again, this time as the father of a son of his own on *Still the Beaver*. He made a few more appearances but has concentrated on public speaking, extolling the virtues of the American family and the positive role that television can play in our lives. He made his Broadway debut in the musical *Hairspray*.

CAST

Barbara Billingsley	June Cleaver
Hugh Beaumont	Ward Cleaver
Jerry Mathers	Theordore "Beaver" Cleaver
Tony Dow	Wally Cleaver
Ken Osmond	Eddie Haskell
Diane Brewster	Miss Canfield
Sue Randall	Miss Landers
Rusty Stevens	Larry Mondelo
Stanley Fafara	Whitey Whitney
Frank Bank	Clarence "Lumpy" Rutherford
Richard Deacon	Fred Rutherford
Madge Blake	Mrs. Mondello
Doris Packer	Mrs. Reyburn
Burt Mustin	Gus, the fireman

Beaver: Gee, Wally, that's swell.

over it to cover the fact that she could never straighten it out. After the series concluded, Americans were shocked to learn that Jerry Mathers had been killed in Vietnam and that Ken Osmond, who played Eddie Haskell, had grown up to be either the porn star John Holmes or the rocker Alice Cooper. We don't want to burst your bubble, but none of these stories is true.

By the time the series ended in 1963, Beaver was the age that Wally had been at the start and Wally was graduating from high school. Sitcoms also graduated that year and began to revolve around adolescents: *The Patty Duke Show* premiered, and a band named the Beatles would soon conquer America on behalf of teenagers everywhere. *Gidget*, *The Brady Bunch*, and a slew of other sitcoms about young people flooded the airwaves and never stopped, right up through *That '70s Show* and *Malcolm in the Middle*. But none can match the knowing wisdom and warmth of *Leave It to Beaver*.

Opposite: The Beav, once again flummoxing June and Ward with his skewed vision of 1950s life.

Right: Has there ever been a more All-American show than *Leave It to Beaver*? All that's missing from this scene is Betsy Ross sewing Alaska and Hawaii onto the Stars-and-Stripes.

THE LIFE OF RILEY

NBC | 1949-1950 | 1953-1958 | 212 episodes

Chester A. Riley can't seem to do anything right. If it weren't for the clear-headed guidance of his wife, Peg, Riley would continually be in hot water. Son Junior never listens to him and daughter Babs adores him but recognizes his limitations. Is it any wonder he's always exasperated?

Believe it or not, Groucho Marx almost starred as Chester A. Riley. Well, sort of. Marx played the part—completely straight—in a radio pilot of a show titled *The Flotsams*. The sponsor wouldn't buy Marx without the antics. The show's producer, Irving Breecher, happened to see the film *The McGuerins of Brooklyn*, starring William Bendix, and he knew he'd found his lead. The character was renamed, and the show went on the air on April 12, 1941.

When it was decided to create a television version of the show, Bendix was unavailable, due to the terms of his film contract, though he was allowed to continue in the radio version. A pilot starring Herb Vigran as Riley was aired on NBC in 1948. It didn't take off. In 1949, Breecher produced a film version with Bendix in the role, and later that year Jackie Gleason played Riley on TV—it was his first series. With Bendix continuing as the radio Riley, audiences had their choice of Bendix or Gleason, and Bendix won out: The Gleason version lasted only one season.

Three years later, Bendix was free of encumbrances and a new series of Riley adventures hit the small screen. With Bendix at the helm, audiences gladly tuned in, and the new TV *Riley* ran for five seasons.

Riley was a big lug, as was Gleason's later creation, Ralph Kramden, but without the insecurities, ego, and bluster. Like Kramden, Riley was resolutely blue-collar and had a best friend. On radio, film, and the original series, the friend was Digby "Digger" O'Dell,

Above: William Bendix and Marjorie Reynolds as blue collar lovebirds Chester and Peg Riley.

Opposite top: Bendix gets a wakeup call from Gloria Blondell (sister of Joan), as Honeybee Gillis.

Opposite bottom: Bendix and Tom D'Andrea, as best friends, neighbors, and co-workers Chester A. Riley and Jim Gillis, rivet their troubles away at Cunningham Aircraft.

an undertaker who existed mainly to spout such puns as "I've covered a lot of ground today" and "You're looking fine. Very natural." In the Bendix TV series, Digger was eliminated and a minor character named Jim Gillis was promoted to the role of best bud.

The Life of Riley was one of those easy-to-take and much-beloved series of the '50s. Audiences felt comfortably familiar with the comically confused Riley from his years on radio, and they felt an attachment to the characters that is rare in today's sitcom universe. Because radio and early television characters seemed so much like real people, audiences developed a genuine affection for them, as if they were cherished houseguests. Riley and family were always welcome. Many performers felt privileged to be so perceived, and actually thanked their viewers for their hospitality.

CAST

1949-50

Jackie Gleason..............Chester A. Riley

Rosemary DeCamp.....Peg Riley

Lanny Rees....................Junior

Gloria Winters..............Babs

Sid Tomack....................Jim Gillis

John Brown....................Digby "Digger" O'Dell

1953-1958

William Bendix..............Chester A. Riley

Marjorie Reynolds.......Peg Riley

Wesley Morgan............Junior

Lugene Sanders............Babs Riley Marshall

Tom D'Andrea..............Jim Gillis

Gloria Blondell.............Honeybee Gillis

Gregory Marshall........Egbert Gillis

William Bendix

William Bendix was one of popular culture's most beloved performers. His goofy grin, accessibility, and good nature endeared him to audiences on film, radio, television, and the stage. He began his career as a batboy for the Yankees, a job that stood him in good stead when he played Babe Ruth in the film *The Babe Ruth Story*. (Bendix had seen Ruth hit more than one hundred of his historic home runs.) He graduated from smaller character parts in film to a wide range of roles in such notable movies as *The Glass Key*, *Lifeboat*, *A Connecticut Yankee in King Arthur's Court*, and *The Time of Your Life*. Appearing in everything from film noir to musicals, Bendix portrayed an American everyman. In 1944, he premiered on radio in his most famous role, Chester A. Riley. He moved to television in the role, replacing Jackie Gleason and eventually playing Riley for over a decade. Ironically, Bendix also replaced Gleason in the Broadway musical *Take Me Along*—but in that case, once Gleason left, the show quickly folded.

THE LUCY SHOW/HERE'S LUCY

◉ | **1962–1968** | **156 episodes** | **1968–1974** | **144 episodes**

Wacky widow Lucy Carmichael works for the penurious Theodore J. Mooney.
Wacky widow Lucy Carter works for the penurious Harry Carter.

The *Lucy Show* and *Here's Lucy* are grouped together because, in fact, they were one and the same show, only changing the title and character names in the course of their twelve-season collective run, due to a business transaction. After appearing in the Broadway musical *Wildcat*, Lucille Ball wanted to return to television comedy, the medium she had helped invent and the form in which she'd achieved her greatest success. As owner of Desilu Studios, she was still an incredibly powerful player; she and her second husband, Gary Morton, approached CBS and wrote their own ticket. Shrewdly surrounding herself with many of the writers from *I Love Lucy*, Ball called

upon former costars Vivian Vance and Gale Gordon (whom she had known all the way back in her radio days, on *My Favorite Husband*) to join her. Vance came aboard, but Gordon was not available, as he had joined the cast of *Dennis the Menace* (after Mr. Wilson's original portrayer, Joseph Kearns's death). Fiercely loyal to those whose talent and professionalism she respected, Ball held a spot for him until he finished out his contract; he joined *The Lucy Show* in its second season.

In Ball's new show, she played Lucy Carmichael, a widow with two children sharing a house in Danfield, New York, with divorcée Vivian Bagley (Vance) and her son, Sherman. Lucy had been left a sizeable trust fund, managed by the stern Mr. Barnsdahl (played by the patron saint of character actors, Charles Lane) for the first season, until Gale Gordon hit the scene, as the penny-pinching Mr. Mooney. For the first three seasons, plots revolved around two basic themes: Lucy trying to get Mr. Mooney to loosen the purse strings on the principle of her late husband's trust, and Lucy and Viv getting stuck

Windbag Theodore J. Mooney expels hot air while Lucy simultaneously takes dictation and hatches her weekly plot.

in ridiculous situations and resorting to slapstick antics reminiscent of the *I Love Lucy* days (Lucy and Viv try to install a shower and get trapped inside, Lucy and Viv try to transport a model of the White House constructed of sugar cubes on a bumpy train to Washington D.C. . . . you get the idea).

After three seasons, Vance grew tired of the grind and left the show (the audience was told she had remarried), and Lucy Carmichael moved to Los Angeles. Coincidentally, Mr. Mooney turned up on the other coast as well, like the proverbial bad penny, and they continued locking horns as hot-headed boss and dithering secretary. Lucy's daughter, Chris, left for college and little Jerry exited soon thereafter, shipped off to military school. After the kids left, they were rarely mentioned. Without Viv, Lucy needed a partner in crime, so Mary Jane Croft (who had played Connecticut neighbor Betty Ramsey on *I Love Lucy*) joined the cast as best friend Mary Jane Lewis. (In addition, Ball's longtime friend Ann Sothern made

Lucy Carmichael and Vivian Bagley create a do-it-yourself drive-through window.

several appearances as Lucy Carmichael's childhood friend Rosie Harrigan, who had "married up" and was now known as "the Countess Framboise.") Just as the later years of *I Love Lucy* had, the next three seasons of *The Lucy Show* became

more and more a showcase for celebrity guest shots, and Lucy got to rub elbows with legends such as Danny Kaye, Mickey Rooney, Bob Crane, Joan Crawford, John Wayne, Sid Caesar, Dean Martin, Jack Benny, Carol Burnett, George Burns,

Vivian Vance

The epitome of the sidekick, the sardonic Vivian Vance perfectly balanced the two sides of her most famous character's persona: the disapproving voice of reason and the scheming co-conspirator; the angel on Lucy's right shoulder one minute, and the devil on her left the next. Starting out as a soubrette in musical comedy (she

understudied Ethel Merman in *Anything Goes*), she moved west to pursue films and television. While appearing in a play at the La Jolla Playhouse, Vance was seen by Desi Arnaz and cast as the legendary Ethel Mertz on *I Love Lucy*. Although Vance was eternally grateful for the break, the smash hit was

not without friction. Vance, who considered herself a potential leading lady, had misgivings about taking on the role of the sidekick, plus she had an extremely contentious relationship with the grouchy William Frawley, who played her husband, Fred. Rejoining Lucille Ball in 1962 on *The Lucy Show*, Vance agreed to take the job only if she could play a character named Vivian, so tired was she of being identified as Ethel. She made television history as the first series regular to play a divorced woman. Retiring to Connecticut after three seasons, Vance made appearances every season or so throughout the run of *Here's Lucy*, always generating a huge response from the studio audience upon her entrance. Also making infrequent guest shots on such shows as *Love, American Style* and *Rhoda*, she joined the ranks of middle-aged actresses turned advertisers—including Jane Withers (Josephine the Plumber), Marge Redmond (Sara Tucker, the Cool Whip lady), Jan Miner (Madge, the Palmolive lady), and Nancy Walker (Rosie, the Bounty paper towel lady)—when she played Maxine, the Maxwell House lady, in a series of commercials. Her last appearance was alongside old cohorts Ball and Gale Gordon on the 1977 CBS special *Lucy Calls the President*.

Ethel Merman, Danny Thomas, Robert Goulet, Milton Berle, and Phil Silvers.

In 1968, Ball sold Desilu Studios to Gulf & Western. *The Lucy Show* was still a ratings powerhouse (ranked number two in the 1967–68 season), but it was owned by Desilu. To retain ownership of the show, she ceased production on *The Lucy Show*, brought most of the creative team over to a new project, gave her character and Gordon's new names, and created a verrrrrrrrrry similar show titled *Here's Lucy*. As part of the new venture, Ball also saw an opportunity to engage in a little old-fashioned nepotism, casting son Desi Jr. and daughter Lucie as her children, thereby providing the two aspiring performers an education in comedy better than any college could provide.

Ball's character was now named Lucy Carter, and Gale Gordon played her brother-in-law, Harry. *Here's Lucy* was set at Carter's Unique Employment Agency, owned by Harry, with Lucy once again playing his incompetent secretary. The parade of stars continued unabated, with a headline-making celebrity coup in the third season opener when the most famous married (and divorced and remarried) showbiz couple of 1970, Richard Burton and Elizabeth Taylor, joined in the hijinks like the good sports they were. The wafer-thin plot revolved around Lucy's getting Liz's Krupp diamond (you know, the one the size of a bagel) stuck on her finger. (Surely no one bought the notion that the svelte Ball had a ring finger bigger than the Vienna sausage–like phalanges of La Liz—but anyway.) Hilarity ensued. Increasingly, it appeared that the show's casting director

Opposite top: This is another fine mess you've gotten us into: Lucy and Viv find themselves in a classic Lucy and Ethel situation.

Opposite bottom: Lucy (Ball) and Lucie (Arnaz) do the Don Ho bit on an episode of *Here's Lucy*.

Right: Lucy and her longest running foil, Gale Gordon, with Philip Amelio and Jenny Lewis in the ill-advised *Life with Lucy*.

was going door to door in Beverly Hills to hold auditions: the revolving star spot was passed around to the likes of Shelley Winters, David Frost, Petula Clark, Ruth Buzzi, O. J. Simpson, Buddy Rich, Ann-Margret, Donny Osmond, Dinah Shore, Johnny Carson, Liberace, Lawrence Welk, Vincent Price, and Flip Wilson. By 1974, both Ball and the show were winding down (she had broken her leg skiing two years earlier and had spent a good part of one season on crutches or in a wheelchair). The final straw came in a positively Pirandellian episode late in the sixth season, in which Lucy Carter entered a Lucille Ball look-alike contest. And…curtain.

Gale Gordon

The master of the slow burn and the explosive bellow, the lovable misanthrope Gale Gordon was one of the most gifted character men on both radio and early television. With his distinctive, cultivated speaking voice, he created such roles on radio as Mayor La Trivia on *Fibber McGee and Molly*, Rumson Bullard on *The Great Gildersleeve*, and Rudolph Atterbury on *My Favorite Husband*, in which he costarred with Lucille Ball, the actress he would be linked with for much of the next forty years. One of his most famous creations, and the one that helped solidify his persona of the pompous, short-tempered authority figure, was that of the stuffy principal Osgood Conklin on *Our Miss Brooks*, following it from radio to television over its eight-year run. Gordon was the first choice to play Fred Mertz on *I Love Lucy*, but he was already committed to Eve Arden's show and had to decline, making guest shots on *Lucy* instead, as Mr. Littlefield, the owner of the Tropicana Club. Starring in two

flops in the late 1950s, *The Brothers* and *Sally*, he had better success with a two-season run on *Pete and Gladys*. In 1962, Lucille Ball cast Gordon as her foil on her new CBS series. After eleven years of being brought to a boil by Lucy's Carmichael/Carter, Gordon went into semiretirement in 1974, coming out to join the crazy redhead one last time in the short-lived *Life with Lucy*.

OFF THE SET

ALTHOUGH *THE LUCY SHOW* was broadcast in black and white until the beginning of its fourth season, it was filmed in color as early as its second season as Ball, always thinking ahead of the curve, recognized that a show shot in color would be more valuable later on, in syndication.

WHEN SCREEN LEGEND Joan Crawford guest-starred on *The Lucy Show*, Ball became frustrated with Crawford's inability to remember her lines and unsuccessfully tried to have her replaced with Gloria Swanson the day before filming. When Crawford was asked about the experience in an interview, she replied, "And they call me a bitch!"

HIRED TO BE Lucy's neighbor and sidekick when Vivian Vance left *The Lucy Show*, Joan Blondell had such friction with Ball that her character was dropped after two episodes.

THE LUCY SHOW / CAST

Lucille Ball	Lucy Carmichael
Gale Gordon	Theodore J. Mooney
Vivian Vance	Vivian Bagley
Jimmy Garrett	Jerry Carmichael
Candy Moore	Chris Carmichael
Ralph Hart	Sherman Bagley
Mary Jane Croft	Mary Jane Lewis
Charles Lane	Mr. Barnsdahl

HERE'S LUCY / CAST

Lucille Ball	Lucy Carter
Gale Gordon	Harry Carter
Lucie Arnaz	Kim Carter
Desi Arnaz Jr.	Craig Carter
Mary Jane Croft	Mary Jane Lewis

MAKE ROOM FOR DADDY

 | 1953-1957 | 1957-1964 | 351 episodes

All-around entertainer Danny Williams's family and friends cause constant bewilderment, aggravation, and spit takes.

Danny Thomas was one of the last of a breed of all-around entertainers. He was a superior stand-up comic in the Sam Levinson mode: that is, a master of elaborate, humorous, heartfelt stories that pointed up the humanity in all of us. He could sing a song in the best Jolson sell-a-song tradition; and he could act, too, having appeared in the movie musicals *Call Me Mister*; *I'll See You in My Dreams*; and *The Jazz Singer* (the 1952 remake, not the original with Jolson—or the one with Streisand). But it was in television, both in front of and behind the camera, where he made his mark. In fact, Thomas is one of the great unsung forces in the history of television, having influenced many of its greatest sitcoms.

The eponymous *Danny Thomas Show*, better known to thousands of baby boomers as *Make Room for Daddy*, the name it used in its first four seasons and in syndication, was, in many

Common-sensical housekeeper Louise (Louise Beavers) serves breakfast to the Williams clan, played by Sherry Jackson, Danny Thomas, Jean Hagen, and Rusty Hamer.

Right: The Williams's station wagon breaks down in front of the cheesiest looking wilderness set outside of a kindergarten Thanksgiving pageant.

Below: Danny Thomas sees his future in the pate of an audience member.

ways, a remarkable sitcom. The storyline was fluid throughout its many seasons, while Thomas stayed firmly in the center of all the action.

The program began life when ABC wanted Ray Bolger to join its stable of talent. Bolger's agent, the legendary Abe Lastfogel, told ABC they could have Bolger only if they also took on Danny Thomas. Unbeknownst to the network, this was one of their luckiest shakedowns. ABC insisted that Thomas headline a sitcom rather than a variety show, and teamed him with producer Lou Edleman and writer Mel Shavelson, both television veterans. Thomas, who spent most of his time on the road entertaining in nightclubs, said he was relieved at the chance to stay home with the wife and kids. *Boing!!* A sitcom premise was born. The show's name was the idea of Thomas's wife. It seems that when he was away entertaining booze-soaked audiences, Rose-Marie Thomas would let their children move into the bedroom—and even the bed—with her. When Thomas would return from a long engagement, the kids were sent back to their rooms and told to "Make room for daddy."

The premise of the show was a smart one, showing at once the home life of a nightclub singer and allowing for a variety-guest- star element when he rehearsed his act. Thomas's wife was played by the wonderful comedienne Jean Hagen of *Singing in the Rain* fame. They had two kids, young daughter, Terry, and her younger brother, six-year-old Rusty, who certainly had a precocious streak—and we mean that in the best way. Danny tried to run his household like a good television father but he was often bested by his family as well as his manager, Charley Halper, and Charley's wife, Bunny.

Danny Thomas

Fate brought Danny Thomas and Sheldon Leonard together on *The Danny Thomas Show/Make Room for Daddy*. Leonard was tired of playing gangsters and tough guys and yearned for a role behind the camera. He was the chief director of the series and soon became its executive producer. As his friendship with Thomas grew, they founded a production company, Thomas-Leonard Productions. They hit the ground running and racked up success after success, beginning with *The Real McCoys* and moving on to *The Andy Griffith Show* (television's second spin-off—from *Pete and Gladys*), *The Joey Bishop Show*, *The Bill Dana Show*, and *The Dick*

Van Dyke Show. When Leonard left for *I Spy* and the partnership dissolved, Thomas joined up with another television genius, Aaron Spelling, to produce *The Mod Squad* (which some would describe as an unintentional sitcom). Thomas went on alone under the banner Danny Thomas Productions.

Worth noting: Thomas was the first to perform a warm-up act for the studio audience before the show, and it was Thomas who chose Mary Tyler Moore for *The Dick Van Dyke Show*. His daughter Marlo conquered sitcomland as *That Girl* and his son Tony, along with Susan Harris and Paul Junger Witt, was responsible for *The Golden Girls*, *Benson*, *Soap*, *The John Larroquette Show*, and *Empty Nest*, among others.

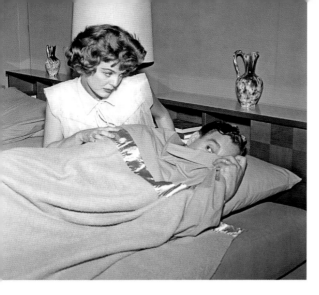

Things were going swimmingly, with the show at the top of the ratings, when Hagen decided to quit the show. Now, what would you do if your leading actress decided to leave? The creators seized the opportunity and killed her character off. It proved to be a boon to the series, and after Hagen's departure Thomas played the field for a season before settling down with the charming Marjorie Lord, who slid into the proceedings effortlessly, along with her television daughter, Angela Cartwright, and the show went on its merry way for an additional seven seasons.

Mention should also be made of the excellent supporting cast of character actors, including Sid Melton, Pat Carroll, Hans Conreid, Benny Lessy, Mary Wickes, Sheldon Leonard, Jesse White, Louise Beavers, and Amanda Randolph. The last two played the Williams's maid successively: Beavers was replaced by Randolph after one season. Just as Danny Williams's family and friends wouldn't give him a break, Louise never hesitated to speak her mind. Hey, if you're going to be subjected to a career of playing the maid, that's the kind of a maid you'll want to play.

CAST

Danny Thomas ....Danny Williams

Jean Hagen ....Margaret Williams

Marjorie Lord ....Kathy O'Hara Williams ("Clancey")

Rusty Hamer ....Rusty Williams

Sherry Jackson..............Terry Williams #1

Penney Parker ....Terry Williams #2

Angela Cartwright ....Linda Williams

Louise Beavers ....Louise #1

Amanda Randolph.......Louise #2

Benny Lessy ....Benny

Jesse White ....Jesse Leeds

Hans Conreid ....Uncle Tonoose

Mary Wickes.................Liz

Sheldon Leonard ....Phil Brokaw

Sid Melton ...."Uncle Charley" Halper

Pat Carroll ....Bunny Halper

Above left: The lovely Marjorie Lord became Danny Williams's second wife after Jean Hagen left the series, marking the first time that producers ever killed off a sitcom regular.

Above right: Sid Melton feels the squeeze from Marjorie Lord and comedienne Pat Carroll, as Barney's wife Bunny.

Sid Melton

Sidney Melton (né Meltzer) played an eternal optimist often shot down by reason and logic. He was born into a show biz family. His father was a comic and his brother was screenwriter Lewis Meltzer. Melton began his acting career in the road company of the Broadway hit *See My Lawyer*, soon decamping for Hollywood where he landed the part of "Fingers" in *Shadow of the Thin Man*. By the end of the 1940s, he was under contract to B-movie studio Lippert Pictures, making pictures for other studios throughout the 1950s, and entering the fledgling television industry in 1955 as a member of the cast of the sitcom *It's Always Jan*. He guested on many, many sitcoms, but is best remembered for his roles of Uncle Charley Halper on *Make Room for Daddy* and bungling carpenter Alf Monroe on *Green Acres*. Danny Thomas's son Tony cast Melton as Sophia's husband Salvadore Petrillo in flashbacks on *The Golden Girls*. He continued his long, long career until 1999, when he retired.

MALCOLM IN THE MIDDLE

FOX | **2000–2006** | **151 episodes**

Malcolm, a certified genius, deals with life in the middle of a family of serial underachievers.

One of the truly original and funny sitcoms of the twenty-first century, *Malcolm in the Middle* was the brainchild of former actor Linwood Boomer. Boomer, remembered by most couch potatoes for his three-year stint as an actor on *Little House on the Prairie*, playing Mary-the-blind-sister's-blind-husband-Adam-who-got-his-sight-back-after-getting-hit-on-the-head, went on to write and produce such worthy shows as *Night Court*, *3rd Rock from the Sun*, and the short-lived but very funny *Flying Blind*. The show deals with the life of middle child Malcolm Wilkerson (the family's last name was given only once, appearing on Francis's military school uniform in the show's pilot), who is discovered to have a genius IQ in a family of underachievers. Considering his early days on the cockle-warming prairie, Boomer would seem an unlikely candidate to create the cynical, subversive world of Malcolm and his family, but the show represented Boomer's skewed view of his own childhood as the second youngest of four boys who was enrolled in a gifted school.

Living in a dump of a house with an overgrown yard that was the embarrassment of the neighborhood, Malcolm had to deal with the double whammy of being an outcast both within his dysfunctional family and among "normal" kids, after being transferred into the dreaded Krelboyne class for the gifted. Even with the winning Frankie Muniz as the title character and narrator (the only one to address the camera directly), the true breakout of the show was alternately lovable and terrifying Lois, perhaps the most realistic portrayal of a mother on any sitcom. As played by the brilliant Jane Kaczmarek, Lois was the character that children and mothers alike could relate to, with her uncanny ability to read her children's minds and her unwilling role as the family's only true disciplinarian. Her dead-end job at a discount drug store (whose motto is "Lucky Aide: the *L* stands for Value") provided a setting for her own struggles under society's collective thumb, which of course Lois never failed to pass on to her own children and husband, Hal, (a hilariously hanging-by-a-thread Bryan Cranston), who lived in

Frankie Muniz, as Malcolm, gets the babysitting job of his dreams, only to discover—to his horror—that the family has been monitoring his every move with a Nannycam.

Lois: I just found out your family has a little nickname for me.
Hal: That's nice . . . what is it?
Lois: "Lois Common Denominator."

terror of Lois's wrath even more than the kids did.

Malcolm's brothers were just as important to the action as the title character: Second-oldest Reese was the bully of the family, due in large part to his frustration that all of Malcolm's extra IQ points seemed to have been deducted directly from his own. Justin Berfield did the clueless bit better than any TV actor since Woody Harrelson. Francis, the eldest (played by Christopher Masterson), was packed off to military school but was always available to his brothers via phone to provide seasoned advice on how to run the gauntlet with their control-freak of a mother; and the youngest (until the birth of fifth brother Jamie in season four),

Dewey, who had a truly tragic home haircut and spent many an episode in his flannel pajamas. In his singsong delivery, Erik Per Sullivan was the truth-teller of the family, and his fantastic non sequiturs provided many of the best laughs in the series. (Favorite Dewey line to his parents: "I just want you to know, if some crazy couple steals me and raises me as a girl, it's on your head.")

Never settling for mere punch lines, *Malcolm in the Middle* was true situational comedy where the inventive, sometimes bizarre, plotlines were the petri dish in which the characters could react. The first episode of the second season, which picked up immediately after the family's trip to a water park (Dewey, of course,

had an ear infection and had to stay home with a sitter. The babysitter? Bea Arthur), had the family stranded in a traffic jam due to an overturned oil tanker. Each of the four characters went off to have his own adventures: Malcolm met the girl of his dreams, Reese tried to get a reluctant ice-cream vendor to open his truck, Hal discovered the meaning of life by freeing a pigeon trapped in a six-pack holder, and Lois, ever the control-freak, decided to take matters into her own hands and clear the tanker off the blocked road herself. Dewey, meanwhile, followed a red balloon floating down the street and ended up on a Candide-like journey involving a convenience store holdup, an itinerant band of farmworkers, a scarecrow, and a group of Hells Angels (to whom Dewey says, "Thank you, Santa!"). With elements of slapstick, romantic comedy, and absurdist humor, *Malcolm* is a perfect example of the best things that twenty-three minutes of television has to offer.

Erik Per Sullivan, Justin Berfield, Christopher Kennedy Masterson, and Frankie Muniz wreak havoc from one of their favorite perches, the roof.

CAST

Jane Kaczmarek	Lois
Bryan Cranston	Hal
Frankie Muniz	Malcolm
Christopher Kennedy Masterson	Francis
Justin Berfield	Reese
Erik Per Sullivan	Dewey
Catherine Lloyd Burns	Caroline Miller
David Anthony Higgins	Craig Feldspar
Craig Lamar Traylor	Stevie Kenarban
Gary Anthony Williams	Abraham "Abe" Kenarban
Emy Coligado	Piama Tananahaakna
Kenneth Mars	Otto Mannkusser
Meagen Fay	Gretchen Mannkusser
Cloris Leachman	Grandma Ida
Daniel von Bargen	Commandant Edwin Spangler

Cloris Leachman

The only actress who has won five Emmys in five separate categories, the multitalented Cloris Leachman attended Northwestern University and started in New York theater, understudying Mary Martin as Nellie Forbush in *South Pacific* before appearing in the noir classic *Kiss Me Deadly*. She became one of the premier guest actresses on TV dramas, mostly on horseback; in fact, most of Leachman's career in the 1960s was one long spell of *Frontier Justice*, through a cloud of *Gunsmoke* on *The Road West* overrun by *Outlaws* who were *Wanted: Dead or Alive*, while on a *Wagon Train* through *Laramie* to visit *A Man Named Shenandoah* in *The Big Valley*. (After a decade of that, no doubt she had a *Rawhide*.) In the 1970s, Leachman's career went to a whole new level with a key role on *Mary Tyler Moore* (where she revealed a previously untapped flair for comedy), and parts in films as varied as the high-camp *Young Frankenstein* and the poignant *The Last Picture Show* (which won her an Academy Award). For theater buffs, it might be fascinating to discover that Leachman's family, including her sister, actress and singer Claiborne Cary, was the inspiration for George Furth's play *Twigs*. Her greatest work is to be found in "The Lars Affair" episode of *MTM*, where Leachman's character, Phyllis Lindstrom, discovers that her husband has been sleeping with Sue Ann Nivens, WJM's Happy Homemaker. Watching Leachman wearing an apron, hands covered with flour, having baked her first (and last) apple pie, is to see one of the true masters of situation comedy acting. After her spin-off, *Phyllis*, proved the difficulty in centering a series around a supporting character, Leachman returned in unworthy vehicles such as *The Nutt House*; *Walter and Emily*; and as Charlotte Rae's replacement during the last gasp of *The Facts of Life*. Finally, with vestiges of her hilarious work in the Mel Brooks comedies, she found a role perfect for her brand of unflinching comic honesty, that of the Teutonic Grandma Ida on *Malcolm in the Middle*.

Top: Jane Kaczmarek as Malcolm's mother Lois and Cloris Leachman as Lois's evil mother Ida share a rare moment of closeness as they perform a traditional dance for the St. Grotus festival.

Above: The gifted Bryan Cranston turned what was initially the straight-man role of Hal into a memorable comic character with his hilarious weekly crises of confidence.

Left: Cloris Leachman, as the nutty, impossible Phyllis Lindstrom, could make anything hilarious, even the act of mourning her late husband. Lisa Gerritsen played her far more sensible daughter Bess on the *MTM* spinoff *Phyllis*.

THE MANY LOVES OF DOBIE GILLIS

 | **1959–1963** | **147 episodes**

"My name is Dobie Gillis and I like girls. What am I saying? I love girls! Love 'em!"
But like his "good buddy," beatnik Maynard G. Krebs, Dobie can't catch a break.

Up to the time that *The Many Loves of Dobie Gillis* premiered, teens were invariably relegated to supporting roles in sitcom life. They seemed to exist only so that their parents could straighten them out and lead them down the road to adulthood. *Leave It to Beaver*, which premiered a year before *Dobie*, took the point of view of Beaver and Wally, but it was still a fam-ily comedy at heart, with the parents at the helm of the children's lives. *Dobie*, on the other hand, was concerned mainly with the lives of the title character and his friends, "beatnik" Maynard G. Krebs; Zelda Gilroy, the girl who had a crush on Dobie; his rich nemesis, Chatsworth Osborne, Jr.; and the unattainable Thalia Menninger. Dobie's parents were the secondary characters.

The whole point of life, for Dobie anyway, was finding love and companionship. The single man or woman in pursuit of a love object has long been a staple of situation comedies, and the problem has always been the same: The quest can only go on so long, but if boy gets girl (or vice versa), there's nowhere to go from there. The writers and the audience get confused and lose their bearings.

Thus, such perennial old maids as Connie Brooks, Susie McNamara, Ann Marie, and Margie Albright couldn't get their man until the end of the series. More recently, Sam Malone seemed doomed to a life of bachelorhood on *Cheers*, though at least he racked up some significant romances along the way. And think of all of the friends on *Friends*. Monica, Joey, Rachel, Ross, Chandler, and Phoebe spent years looking for love in all the wrong places, when in the end, all they had to do was go across the hall. *Will & Grace* at least put a twist on the cliché, since there was absolutely no chance that the two—married in every respect but actually, what with their sexual preferences at odds—could ever get married in the end.

Dwayne Hickman had an excellent mentor in his role as a single guy looking for the right (or any) girl when he was in the cast of *The Bob Cummings Show*: His uncle Bob was the original television horndog.

Left: Bob Denver and Dwayne Hickman were the sitcom world's poster boys of slackerdom.

Opposite: Denver and Hickman with Sheila James, as the lovestruck Zelda Gilroy.

on a book by Max Shulman, who created the series and contributed some of its scripts. Shulman had a dry wit, and that off-kilter sense of humor soon pervaded other sitcoms. Mention must also be made of the fine cast, which seemed to be made up entirely of archetypes and character actors. Bob Denver didn't just play a beatnik whose IQ was lower than his temperature— he inhabited the role so fully that he created a slacker role model for middle-class American kids. Similarly, Frank Faylen, Florida Friebus, Doris Packer, Sheila James, and Steve Franken filled out their characters in utterly unique ways. Though the straightest of the bunch, Hickman proved the perfect embodiment of Dobie, poised between adolescence and adulthood, grappling with the pressures to get a girl and make something of himself. *Dobie Gillis* introduced angst to the sitcom and, as the decade turned from the fabulous fifties to the turmoil of the sixties, it seemed to presage the national rift between the generations to come.

Dobie didn't play the field but he sure looked around a lot and, of course, he was always looking in the wrong places, while poor Zelda Gilroy waited patiently for him to get a clue, at least according to the proposed spin-off, which aired as a special in 1977. Titled *Whatever Happened to Dobie Gillis*, it showed Zelda had finally snagged Dobie. They're happily married, running Dobie's father's grocery, and the proud parents of a son, who is just like Dobie was as a teenager, giving credence to the old saw delivered by countless parents to their children, "I hope you have a child like you when you grow up, and see how you like it."

For those too young to remember it, we should point out that *Dobie Gillis* was a very, very popular and influential series. It was based

OFF THE SET

WARREN BEATTY PLAYED Milton Armitage for one season. When he left, he was replaced by a new nemesis for Dobie, Chatsworth Osborne, Jr. Both character's mothers were played by Doris Packer.

BOB DENVER WAS drafted right after the series started and it was decided that he would be replaced by Michael J. Pollard, as Maynard's brother. Luckily, Denver flunked his physical and returned to the series.

THE FIRST EPISODE had essentially the same plot (a scheme to rig a raffle) as the last episode. It was a witty way to show that, after all those years, the characters hadn't really changed.

Florida Friebus

The concerned mother of Dobie Gillis, Florida Friebus had a distinguished stage career before television. She worked extensively with legendary actress-director Eva Le Gallienne, including acting in and writing her legendary production of *Alice in Wonderland*. Television came calling and she logged many dramatic hours, including roles on *The Ford Theatre Hour*; *The Philco Television Playhouse*; *Kraft Television Theatre*; *Goodyear Television Playhouse*; and *The Hallmark Hall of Fame*. Friebus then turned to sitcoms, winning her first recurring role on *The Many Loves of Dobie Gillis*. In addition to doing guest spots on virtually every sitcom in the 1960s, she became a regular on *The Bob Newhart Show* as one of his patients.

CAST

Dwayne Hickman	Dobie Gillis
Bob Denver	Maynard G. Krebs
Frank Faylen	Herbert T. Gillis
Florida Friebus	Winifred "Winnie" Gillis
Sheila James	Zelda Gilroy
Tuesday Weld	Thalia Menninger
Warren Beatty	Milton Armitage
Darryl Hickman	Davey Gillis
William Schallert	Mr. Leander Pomfritt
Doris Packer	Clarice Armitage
Doris Packer	Mrs. Chatsworth Osborne, Sr.
Steve Franken	Chatsworth Osborne, Jr.

MARRIED...WITH CHILDREN

FOX | **1987–1997** | **262 episodes**

The ultimate in dysfunctional families, the Bundys fight, fight, and fight some more, proving that you only hurt the ones you love.

How low can you go? This premiere series of the Fox network set the tone for shows (and news programs) to come. It didn't just push the envelope—it shredded it. Even Buck, the family pet, didn't have anything nice to say about his human owners. In fact, Buck was probably the smartest member of the family: He had the good sense to die in 1995 but the bad luck to return soon after, reincarnated as the misnamed puppy, Lucky.

Buck wasn't the only one appalled by the Bundys, which was probably the whole point of the series. Sitcoms of the '70s were known for courting controversy with "Very Special Episodes," their groundbreaking producers trying to educate and inspire by broaching subjects that had previously been television taboos. *Married...with Children* pushed a different envelope—that of good taste. The purpose was laughs and, toward that end, anything went.

Hapless shoe salesman Al; his lazy, self-absorbed wife, Peg (the word housewife would indicate she actually knew how a stove or vacuum worked); daughter Kelly, a clueless hottie; and son Bud (named after Budweiser), a bright but nerdy kid, had many misadventures that viewers found either hi-larious or embarrassing to watch—but watch they did. The show became one of the most popular sitcoms of its day and put Fox on the map. Remember, this was a time when professional wrestling rose from the grave of Haystacks Calhoun into a ratings winner.

Somehow, despite the crude humor and lowest-of-lower-class characters (actually they were classless in every sense of the word), the show was somehow sweet. That's right, sweet. Yes, Al might

Ed O'Neill and Katey Sagal as Al and Peg Bundy, the most tender, gentle, loving married couple since Ralph and Alice Kramden.

have lusted after strippers and yes, Peg constantly cracked wise about his bedroom prowess, but they managed to hang together as only a devoted family can.

Was it Mark Twain or Robert Benchley who advised, "Lie when your wife is waking. Lie when your belly's aching. Lie

Katey Sagal tosses a delicious "mesclun salad with tar-and-nicotine dressing."

when you know she's faking. Lie, sell shoes, and lie"? No, it was Al Bundy, giving sage advice to his son, Bud. That encapsulates the general level of humor in the show. Though *Married...with Children*

CAST

Ed O'Neill	Al Bundy
Katey Sagal	Peggy Bundy
Christina Applegate	Kelly Bundy
David Faustino	Bud Bundy
David Garrison	Steve Rhoades
Amanda Bearse	Marcy Rhoades D'Arcy
Ted McGinley	Jefferson D'Arcy
Kevin Curran	Voice of Buck
Kevin Curran	Voice of Lucky
Shane Sweet	Seven Bundy
Tom McCleister	Ike
Pat Millicano	Sticky
Dan Tullis Jr.	Officer Dan

contributed to the general dumbing-down of American humor, that steep slide was in motion long before the show came along, mainly on film. Think of *Animal House* and *Porky's*. Still, once *Married...with Children* came along, it did seem that all of the "good work" done on sitcoms in the 1970s had been in vain. *Married...with Children* opened television's Pandora's box of crude sitcom humor, and contemporary shows like *In Living Color*, *Seinfeld*, and later, *Will & Grace* reaped the benefit.

A substratum of sitcoms celebrating booty and boobs emerged in the show's wake, especially on the Fox network. But at the same time, some of the best written, most intelligent sitcoms ever were sharing the airwaves, shows such as *Murphy Brown*, *Designing Women*, *The Cosby Show*, *Frasier*, *Evening Shade*, and *Mad About You*.

Here is the irony of ironies concerning *Married...with Children*. There were protests by conservative folk about the language and situations on the show and the general loosy-goosy morality of the Bundys. These were generally ignored until Michigan housewife Terry Rakolta

(no Peg Bundy, she) initiated a letter-writing campaign to sponsors. The press picked up on it, and soon Rakolta made the papers and appeared on talk shows and news programs. Fox did can one episode in response to a boycott by advertisers and generally negative publicity surrounding the contretemps. But—surprise, surprise—the ratings shot up, the controversy propelling the show into many more years of profit. Producers sent Terry Rakolta a fruit basket every Christmas.

Katey Sagal

Katey Sagal, the intelligent and beautiful actress behind the mask of Peg Bundy, grew up in a showbiz family. Her father, Boris, directed episodes of *Peter Gunn* and *The Twilight Zone*; her mother, Sara Zwilling, was a producer; and her twin sisters were...drum-roll...the Doublemint Twins! Katey was a Harlette, one of Bette Midler's backup singers, and briefly appeared on *Mary*, the failed Mary Tyler Moore sitcom. She followed that with *Married...with Children* and following that, to Hollywood's credit, they didn't typecast her as a sarcastic, self-absorbed wife. Fox stuck by her, featuring her on the cartoon *Futurama* as the Cyclops alien Leela, and as Hyde's mother on *That '70s Show*. She starred opposite John Ritter in the sitcom *8 Simple Rules for Dating My Teenage Daughter* (above, with Kaley Cuoco, Amy Davidson, and Martin Spanjers), which was canceled soon after Ritter's unexpected death. Most recently, Sagal has turned up on *Lost* and will return when *Futurama* rejoins the Fox schedule after a surprising success on DVD.

MARY TYLER MOORE

◉ | 1970–1977 | 168 episodes

Mary Richards, a spunky, thirty-year-old single gal, moves to Minneapolis and gets a job at the news station WJM. She lives in a sweet little studio apartment below the lovable yet tough Rhoda Morgenstern, and, through the support of her friends and co-workers, grows into a confident career woman.

In the history of the situation comedy, certain title-sequence images have been so iconic that they have become part of our collective consciousness: Rob Petrie tripping over an ottoman; Archie and Edith Bunker screeching out a tune around a piano; a swarm of choppers flying over the mountains of Korea; six friends sitting around a fountain and turning off a floor lamp. But perhaps no other image better personifies the spirit, humor, and pure joy of the sitcom form than a young woman spinning around on a frigid Minneapolis street and flinging her cap into the air.

That moment was, of course, the climax of the opening of *Mary Tyler Moore*, and in the final moment of the show's opening credits. The one thing that never changed during the show's historic, legendarily funny run of seven years was the image of everyone's ideal single working woman, staking her claim of independence and conquering the concrete jungle of Minneapolis–St. Paul.

The show was the first sitcom to allow its main character to grow exponentially during its run. Before it, Maxwell Smart and Agent 99 got married, Theodore Cleaver matriculated from grade school to high school, and the Ricardos moved to Connecticut—but no character before Mary Richards was permitted to develop so profoundly.

One of the reasons actors tend to grow dissatisfied with long runs is that their characters never change: *That Girl*'s Marlo Thomas was playing a struggling actress who, after five years, still hadn't gotten her big break; and even on a peerless show like *The Dick Van Dyke Show*, after five seasons and almost as many episodes as *Mary Tyler Moore* logged in seven (in the 1960s, thirty-two episodes per season were standard, as opposed to today's eighteen), the characters basically behaved in the same ways they had at the show's start.

Mary Tyler Moore had its genesis when, after a disastrous attempt at Broadway (in the musical version of *Breakfast at Tiffany's*), Mary Tyler Moore came back to television, in collaboration with her husband, the bril-

With love all around, Mary Richards turns the world on with her smile.

liant producer Grant Tinker. Together, they created a new showcase for her undeniable small-screen charisma. Premiering in September 1970, *Mary Tyler Moore*, as it was officially called, built upon the success of those independent career women Connie Brooks, Ann Marie, and Julia Baker, and ran it into the end zone. The result was something fresh and witty, with Mary Richards wedged between the two women in her home life, Valerie Harper as the Jewish, single, sexually active, and overweight (although her weight was more a matter of wardrobe and low self-esteem than actual poundage) Rhoda Morgenstern; and "special guest star" Cloris Leachman as Mary's landlady Phyllis Lindstrom, the friend that everyone wants to throttle but can't help loving.

That was only half of the riches to be found on the show, for Mary had an equally vibrant work life populated by Gavin McLeod as faithful confidant, Murray Slaughter; Ted Knight as the buffoonish yet sympathetic anchorman, Ted Baxter; and, most important, Edward Asner as that classically grouchy boss, Lou Grant. Although Moore was undeniably the focus of the show, her greatest gift is as a

Mary Tyler Moore

Even before graduating from high school, Mary Tyler Moore had begun to model and do commercials. Trained as a dancer, she was comfortably cast in minor roles on dramas of the late 1950s, parts whose main criterion was the adjective "leggy." After an uncredited role in the crime drama *Richard Diamond, Private Detective* (only her legs were shown), she auditioned for the role of Danny Thomas's daughter on *Make Room for Daddy*. Although not right for the part, she was remembered by Thomas when they were casting the role of Dick Van Dyke's wife on a new sitcom, and after reading for creator Carl Reiner, she was led by the top of her head to the offices of producer Sheldon Leonard and given the plum job within the day. It was her first crack at comedy, but the initial episodes called on the young actress to be little more than an understanding, plucky spouse. It was with the episode "My Brown-Haired Beauty" that Moore opened Reiner's eyes to her untapped sense of timing, as she began to develop the stammering, borderline hysterical characterization that would become her stock in trade. After *The Dick Van Dyke Show*'s five-season run, Moore hoped to work in films and on Broadway, but the phone wasn't ringing off the hook.

With her second husband, the television executive Grant Tinker, Moore formed the production company MTM Enterprises (which later produced *The Bob Newhart Show*, *WKRP in Cincinnati*, *Hill Street Blues*, and *St. Elsewhere*). The rest, as they say, is history, and after seven seasons and countless accolades, Moore finally got her shot at film and proved herself an actress of Shakespearean proportions in *Ordinary People*. She took another run at Broadway, too, in the play *Whose Life Is It, Anyway?* A third television success eluded her: *Mary*, *The Mary Tyler Moore Hour*, *Annie McGuire*, and *New York News* all failed to last a season, and the reunion television movie *Mary and Rhoda* lacked the magic of the characters' early days. With a hilarious performance in the film *Flirting with Disaster* and dramatic turns in such television films as *Like Mother, Like Son*, and *The Gin Game* (reuniting with Dick Van Dyke), Moore can still turn a comic phrase and tug at your heart strings like no one else, and still has the unerring taste and class to be a major force in the industry.

Above: Veteran character comics Shelley Berman and Jane Connell check in MTM and Valerie Harper in the first-season episode in which America's sweethearts masquerade as divorcees and visit the "Better Luck Next Time Club."

Top right: Mary Tyler Moore, age twenty-five, in her starmaking role as Laura Petrie on *The Dick Van Dyke Show*.

Edward Asner

One of the most talented, versatile character actors ever, Ed Asner hit the jackpot with *The Mary Tyler Moore Show*, achieving a level of recognition and success he had never known. He worked on the stage before heading west to work on many television shows of the 1960s. Like costar Ted Knight, Asner was not known for his comic chops when he was cast as the hard-bitten, hard-drinking Lou Grant. The gradual melting of his character into Mary Richards's best friend and closest confidant had the underpinnings of one of the great unrequited love stories of all time. Segueing from a sitcom into an hourlong format as the same character, an unprecedented coup, Asner continued playing Lou Grant on the eponymous dramedy for another five seasons. Along with Emmy Award–winning roles on the miniseries *Roots* and *Rich Man Poor Man* (he and MTM costar Cloris Leachman are the two most decorated actors in television history), he has continued to be a presence, on such sitcoms as *Off the Rack*, *Thunder Alley*, and *Center of the Universe*. Also a highly political animal, he served two terms as the president of the Screen Actors' Guild, and has publicly supported many liberal causes.

reactive comedienne, so the show was at its best when Moore was in the company of Harper or Asner, borderline-aggressive characters who shot from the hip. Even in the show's pilot, one of the best-written pieces of situation comedy ever, the scenes with Rhoda ("Get out of my apartment!") and Lou ("I hate spunk!") are the ones that cemented the show as a classic, providing the setups for our "Mare" to do her thing: flounder, flail, and stammer while securing her place as one of the greatest television comediennes.

As with such other classics as *The Dick Van Dyke Show*, *I Love Lucy*, and *All in the Family*, it's almost criminal to mention favorite episodes, for fear of leaving one out. Through its peerless writing, each of the show's actors had episodes where he or she took center stage: Ed Asner as Lou going on his first date after separating from his wife—and discovering it's with an eighty-year-old woman (the flower girl at Thomas Edison's wedding); Ted Knight as Ted Baxter suffering a heart attack on the air, momentarily softening his callous buffoonery; Cloris

Lou Grant: You know what? You've got spunk.
Mary Richards: Well… yes…
Lou Grant: I hate spunk!

Abovet: Ed Asner in *Off the Rack*, the short-lived garment trade sitcom costarring Eileen Brennan.

Right: Sharing one of the most complex relationships in sitcom history, Edward Asner and Mary Tyler Moore play out one of their classic Mr. Grant/Mary scenes.

Opposite top: Georgia Engel, Valerie Harper, and "Mare" examine the results of the Morgenstern green thumb in Rhoda's apartment, which looks like a cross between the set of *Laugh-In* and Belle Watling's bordello in *Gone With the Wind*.

Opposite below: Groom on my forehand, bride on my backhand: Ted and Georgette Baxter are married by John Ritter, himself just on the verge of sitcom stardom.

Leachman and Betty White (in her first appearance on the series) butting heads over a man in one of the masterpieces of sitcom writing and acting, "The Lars Affair;" Gavin MacLeod as Murray thinking he's in love with Mary; and the brilliant Valerie Harper, after three seasons of being the dumpy bridesmaid to her downstairs neighbor, losing twenty pounds and winning a beauty contest. And finally, there was the unparalleled comic character-acting of Moore as she tentatively sang "One for My Baby" for Mr. Grant in preparation for the talent portion of the "Teddy" Awards;

and her tour de force eruption of the giggles at the funeral in "Chuckles Bites the Dust" (named by many sources as the single greatest episode in situation comedy history), demonstrating in one segment her complete grasp of the dizzying heights and painfully hilarious depths of black comedy.

When Harper left after the fourth season, slimming herself into her own spin-off, the show wasn't quite the same: Mary seemed to lose some of her charming innocence as she gained confidence—but of course this was part of the show's point, evident even

at the beginning of the show's second season, when the first line of the theme song was rewritten from, "How will you make it on you own?" to "Who can turn the world on with her smile?"

At the beginning of the sixth season, the sitcom gods rewarded Mary with her own bedroom, moving her into an apartment building more befitting a professional career woman. By then, Harper and Leachman had been replaced by two women who weren't waiting for Mary at home but instead had ties to her workplace: the dotty Georgia Engel as Ted Baxter's wife,

MARY TYLER MOORE

Georgette, and the incomparable Betty White as the dimpled yet smutty Martha Stewart precursor, Sue Ann Nivens. White, in particular, personified the subtle yet insistent shift in the show's tone, from a comfortable, laid-back humor (after all, Mary and Rhoda used to sit and kibitz while doing needlepoint and painting their nails) to more pointed cynicism, paving the way for such workplace sitcoms as *Taxi* and *Cheers*.

Mary Tyler Moore was one of the first shows to leave the air while absolutely at the top of its form. (*The Dick Van Dyke Show* preceded it but it ended with little fanfare and no real conclusion to the story.) Closure came ironically, in an episode in which everyone at the station got fired except for the one true piece of dead weight, Ted. But it was touching, too, with the famous group hug that shuffled en masse to grab a Kleenex from Mary's desk. In a mere seven years Mary grew from a scared, hesitant girl applying for a job without the slightest qualifications into a confident television producer—and the show became an enduring reflection of the journey of the single American woman. Its importance cannot be underestimated.

Allan Burns

One of the smartest, most intensely creative writers in television history, Allan Burns started his career as a cartoonist, creating the character of Cap'n Crunch for Quaker Oats and working as an animator and writer on *Rocky and Bullwinkle*. Teaming up with Chris Hayward, Burns created the sitcom *The Munsters* and the notorious flop *My Mother the Car*, followed by the cult hit *He and She*, about a comic-book artist. In 1969, Burns began writing for the show *Room 222*, created by the television whiz-kid James L. Brooks. About this time, Grant Tinker contacted Brooks and Burns about developing a show for Tinker's wife, Mary Tyler Moore. Along with director Jay Sandrich, whom Burns had met on *He and She*, the trio created one of the greatest half-hour comedies in television history. Setting up shop at Paramount after the Moore show left the air, Burns co-produced *Lou Grant* with Gene Reynolds, and was nominated for an Academy Award for his screenplay for the 1979 movie *A Little Romance*. Amazingly level-headed and patient in the sometimes crazy world of situation comedy, Burns has maintained a low profile of late, his last projects the short lived *FM*, *Eisenhower & Lutz*, and *The Duck Factory*—another cult hit, dealing with a cartoonist at a small animation studio, starring a then-unknown Jim Carrey.

CAST

Mary Tyler Moore	...Mary Richards
Edward Asner	..........Lou Grant
Valerie Harper	.........Rhoda Morgenstern
Gavin MacLeod	.......Murray Slaughter
Ted Knight	................Ted Baxter
Cloris Leachman	....Phyllis Lindstrom
Georgia Engel	..........Georgette Franklin Baxter
Betty White	..............Sue Ann Nivens
John Amos	.................Gordy Howard
Lisa Gerritsen	..........Bess Lindstrom
Joyce Bulifant	..........Marie Slaughter
Priscilla Morrill	......Edie Grant
Nancy Walker	..........Ida Morgenstern

Top: The WJM gang during the tearful filming of the final episode.

Above: MTM and Betty White, great friends and consummate professio share a laugh during one of the few (very few) line fluffs that Mary ever committed during the show's filming.

SITCOMS FROM MOVIES

Hollywood has never, ever had any shame about squeezing every last drop from a good idea. In the same way that there have been many movie versions of successful TV series, many sitcoms are small-screen adaptations of big-screen comedies. The process continues to this day, with Showtime's *Barbershop* premiering in 2005—in spite of the fact that most of the sitcoms derived from movies have failed to achieve the success of their widescreen counterparts.

The classic exception is *M*A*S*H*, which ended up running five times longer than the Korean War that provided its setting. *Alice, Dobie Gillis, The Odd Couple,* and *The Courtship of Eddie's Father,* all based on films, also made the transition smoothly. Success to a lesser degree (more than one season, but far from achieving classic status) was to be achieved by the half-hour versions of *Private Benjamin, The Bad News Bears, Clueless, Nine to Five, Please Don't Eat the Daisies, House Calls,* and *The Ghost and Mrs. Muir.*

The batting average is relatively low for the process, however, with misfires aplenty: *Working Girl* (starring an unknown Sandra Bullock); *Paper Moon* (with a young Jodie Foster in the Tatum O'Neal role); *Adam's Rib* (with Blythe Danner and Ken Howard as in an updated version of Hepburn and Tracy); *My Sister Eileen* (with Elaine Stritch); *Bagdad Café* (Jean Stapleton and Whoopi Goldberg); *Ferris Bueller; Operation Petticoat; Uncle Buck; The Four Seasons; Parenthood; How to Marry a Millionaire;* and the triple strikeout of *Mr. Deeds Goes to Town, Mr. Smith Goes to Washington,* and *Mr. Roberts* (in fact, when you add in *Mr. T. & Tina* and *Mr. Terrific,* the only "Misters" who were successful on television were "Ed" and "Peepers," the two least likely candidates). Part of the problem is in the construction of the stories themselves. The structure of the original film of *M*A*S*H* was inherently episodic, so it adapted well into a weekly series. Compare that to *Working Girl,* to name one example. While delightful in movie form, the adventures of Tess McGill didn't lend themselves to an ongoing series.

Many ideas for shows based on films never made it past the pilot stage, and it's fascinating to explore the casts of these unsold pilots, imagining how the shows might have fared. A 1971 sitcom version of *Cat Ballou* with Lesley Ann Warren, Jack Elam, and Joel Higgins could have been a winner. A half-hour version of *Diner,* shot a year after Barry Levinson's movie, starring James Spader, Michael Madsen, and Paul Reiser (reprising his film role) is promising. *Bell, Book and Candle,* starring Yvette Mimieux, Michael Murphy, and Doris Roberts? Well…not so much.

Above: Playing the roles made famous in the original movie by Gene Tierney and Rex Harrison, the lovely Hope Lange is unaware she's about to be scared witless by ectoplasmic Edward Mulhare (who also replaced Harrison in Broadway's *My Fair Lady*) in *The Ghost and Mrs. Muir.*

Left: Mark Miller and Pat Crowley—small screen versions of Doris Day and David Niven—along with the rest of the fictional Nash family in the perfectly pleasant mid-'60s sitcom, *Please Don't Eat the Daisies.*

M*A*S*H

 | **1972–1983** | **251 episodes**

The 4077th Mobile Army Surgical Hospital (MASH), operating near the front of the Korean War, provides the setting for the often outrageous but always courageous behavior of its staff of mostly draftee doctors and nurses.

Many sitcoms hit a juncture during their run where they take a sharp turn and morph into something utterly different. Often, these shifts are due to cast changes, as in *Bewitched*, with the Dick York years followed by the Dick Sargent years; on *Cheers*, the Shelley Long era followed by the Kirstie Alley period; and *Mary Tyler Moore* with and without Rhoda Morgenstern. But perhaps no show made a more noticeable shift than *M*A*S*H*, which was based on the 1970 Robert Altman film and the earlier Richard Hooker novel. *M*A*S*H* did have its share of cast replacements, but they were accompanied by a night-and-day transformation of the comic tone between 1975 and 1978.

One of the few successful sitcom adaptations from a movie, the half-hour version of the 4077th was created by Larry Gelbart,

the brilliant wit who had worked on everything from Sid Caesar's *Your Show of Shows* to the Broadway musical *A Funny Thing Happened on the Way to the Forum*. The first three seasons of *M*A*S*H* are classic Gelbart: utterly subversive, often smutty, and frequently hilarious, with an antiestablishment subtext that echoed the anti–Vietnam War movement sweeping the country at the time. With a cast that played their characters as riffs on naughty fraternity brothers who could also perform open heart massage, the show took on the "inmates running the asylum" tone that had helped make the Altman movie a smash hit.

By 1975, McLean Stevenson, who played the lovably clueless commanding officer Colonel Henry Blake, had become increasingly frustrated with his role as third banana to Alan Alda and Wayne Rogers, and notified the producers that he would be leaving the series. In the final episode of the show's third season,

"Abyssinia, Henry," Henry got his orders to return stateside and boarded a plane after tearful farewells. The episode's final scene—a twist told to the cast only moments before filming a scene in the OR—revealed that Blake's plane had been shot down over the Sea of Japan. It was a moment that was at once shocking and perfectly true to the horrors of war, as viewers were slapped in the face with the reality of a situation they had been laughing at for three years (not to mention the poor actors, who were put through the wringer in the same way child actor Jackie Cooper had been when told that his pet dog had been hit by a car). The gamble paid off, though, and the show received the double perk of outcry from viewers and respect from critics.

Around the same time, actor Wayne Rogers, costarring as Trapper John McIntyre, saw the writing on the wall as Alda provided more and more creative input into the show. Sensing that *M*A*S*H* was revolving more and more around Alda's Hawkeye

Opposite: Mike Farrell, Jamie Farr, and Alan Alda in "The Swamp," the setting for many of the hijinks of the 4077th Mobile Army Surgical Hospital gang.

Left: Gary Burghoff (who went from playing Charlie Brown Off-Broadway to recreate his role from the film of *M*A*S*H*, as the naïve but prescient company clerk Radar O'Reilly, decides to save the 4077th's Easter dinner from becoming Lamb on a Shingle.

Below: In scenes in the OR, almost completely masked, Alan Alda expertly conveyed a full range of emotions with just his eyes.

Pierce, Rogers found a golden opportunity to slip out of his contract when he was asked to sign (of all things) a morals clause. The producers quickly replaced Rogers over the summer hiatus with a relative unknown, Mike Farrell, as the married, wholesome B. J. Hunnicutt. Stevenson was replaced by Harry Morgan, returning to television comedy for the first time since *Pete and Gladys*, as "regular army" colonel Sherman Potter. The transition was relatively smooth with viewers but after one season with the two new cast members, Gelbart left, unhappy with the direction of the show.

This was the turning point that would forever divide its fans into two camps: those who were fond of *M*A*S*H*: the wild and wacky Larry Gelbart/Gene Reynolds years, and those who preferred *M*A*S*H*: the deeply profound Alan Alda years.

As Alda took more control (if he sounds like a megalomaniac, he was anything but; he was an impassioned, sensitive, smart guy who saw a chance to make a real difference through mass entertainment), the show became increasingly moralistic, left-leaning, and sometimes annoyingly preachy. Often far too pleased with itself, the later episodes of *M*A*S*H* portrayed every character as having the same sharp intellect, tossing off puns and quips like members of the Algonquin Round Table (a sure sign that the writers had lost track of their characters), Maxwell Klinger lobbing bon mots as if he was Alexander Woollcott. After all, in a show that deals with characters embroiled in a three-year

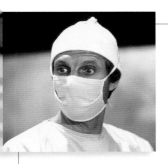

Alan Alda

A true Renaissance man, Alan Alda was raised in show business, the son of actor Robert Alda. After a stint in the army he played roles in New York theater and got a huge break when he was cast (at the age of thirty-two, amazing when you consider most actors today are washed up at eighteen if they haven't starred on a series) as Hawkeye Pierce on *M*A*S*H*. All told, he was nominated for twenty-one Emmys for his work as an actor, writer, and director, winning five. He cowrote more than twenty episodes of the show, directed nearly thirty, and by the show's fifth season was involved on every level, becoming one of the most powerful men on television in the late 1970s.

After the conclusion of *M*A*S*H*, Alda tried his hand at the movie business, writing and directing such films as *Sweet Liberty* and *Betsy's Wedding*. (He'd already written and directed *The Seduction of Joe Tynan* and *The Four Seasons*.) Recently, working more as an actor than a director, he has made memorable appearances in the films *Crimes and Misdemeanors* and *Manhattan Murder Mystery*, the Broadway play *Art*, and on the series *ER* and *The West Wing*, the latter garnering him his sixth Emmy. Turning in brilliant performances in the film *The Aviator* and the Broadway revival of *Glengarry Glen Ross*, Alda is enjoying the second stage of his career, as a highly sought-after character actor, having shaken the specter of the "sensitive man" that plagued him for much of the 1980s.

Left: Loretta Swit on set during the episode where the 4077th compiles a time capsule to be buried. Note Radar's teddy bear, a *M*A*S*H* prop now on view at the Smithsonian Institution.

Below: One of the perks of a long-running series is that nearly every cast member gets a chance to direct. Here, Mike Farrell supervises a scene with Alan Alda and William Christopher.

Frank Burns: I know I'm a real asset.
Hawkeye: You're only off by two letters.

war over an eleven-year span, credibility is bound to become an issue.

The core cast was a talented bunch: in addition to Alda, Rogers, Stevenson, and Morgan, Loretta Swit was head nurse Margaret "Hot Lips" Houlihan, whose character was one of the more unfortunate casualties of the long run, starting out as a hilariously starchy foil and ending up as a willing comrade. Also playing their roles with singular style were Jamie Farr, William Christopher, David Ogden Stiers, and Larry Linville, the last of whom was in many ways the unsung hero of the show's first five seasons, creating in villain Frank Burns one of the most complex, heartbreakingly ferret-faced doofuses in sitcom history. In fact, Linville's exit left a

huge hole in *M*A*S*H*'s later seasons: by the seventh or eighth year the only true enemy on the show was the North Koreans, while the conflict and infighting instigated by Burns and Houlihan took a backseat to antiwar messages.

After eleven years, the show packed up its old kit bag and went home to count its residuals (no doubt paid in scrip). In the two-and-a-half-hour "Goodbye, Farewell, and Amen," the Korean conflict came to a close. The finale, the first "television event" of its kind in sitcom history, was viewed by an astonishing 106 million Americans (almost 77 percent of the total viewership), ranking as the most-watched series episode in television history. In retrospect, the whole shebang was an incredibly

Above: Harry Morgan and Loretta Swit with Jamie Farr, dressed as Rebecca of Hairyback Farm.

Right: Jamie Farr with Dean Jones, John Banner, Marvin Kaplan, Art Metrano, and Huntz Hall in *The Chicago Teddy Bears*.

CAST

Alan Alda	Capt. Benjamin Franklin "Hawkeye" Pierce
Wayne Rogers	Capt. "Trapper" John Francis Xavier McIntyre
McLean Stevenson	Col. Henry Blake
Loretta Swit	Maj. Margaret "'Hot Lips" Houlihan
Larry Linville	Maj. Frank Burns
Gary Burghoff	Cpl. "Radar" O'Reilly
Jamie Farr	Cpl. Maxwell Q. Klinger
William Christopher	Capt. Father John Francis Patrick Mulcahy
Mike Farrell	Capt. B. J. Hunnicutt
Harry Morgan	Col. Sherman T. Potter
David Ogden Stiers	Maj. Charles Emerson Winchester III
Edward Winter	Col. Flagg
Allan Arbus	Dr. Sidney Freedman
Johnny Haymer	Sgt. Zelmo Zale
Jeff Maxwell	Pvt. Igor Straminsky
G. W. Bailey	Sgt. Luther Rizzo
Kellye Nakahara	Nurse Kellye
Sal Viscuso	PA announcer

drawn-out affair, with Alda having one last breakdown in a bid for an Emmy and every character provided with his or her own personal good-bye "moment," veering dangerously close to Maudlinville. After all, how many times can one witness Loretta Swit channeling Dorothy Gale's "I think I'll miss you most of all" speech? Remember, folks, she was a royal bee-yotch for the first seven seasons—when, why, and how did she turn into Loretta Young?

The show spawned either two or three spin-offs, depending on who you ask. The two that are beyond question were *After M*A*S*H*, a two-season misfire following the postwar, stateside life of the characters played by Harry Morgan, Jamie Farr, and William Christopher; and *W*A*L*T*E*R*, an unsold pilot about Gary Burghoff's Radar O'Reilly, back in polite society and working as a policeman. The third series, the hourlong *Trapper John, MD*, based on the character played by Wayne Rogers in the sitcom, was the subject of a lengthy court battle as to its source material, with a judge finally ruling that the show was based on the movie and not the sitcom, thereby cutting anyone connected with the sitcom out of potential profits. Hooray for Hollywood.

Jamie Farr

After Danny Thomas, Jamie Farr is the second most famous Lebanese sitcom comedian (with only a slightly smaller proboscis). The eternally amiable Farr was born in Toledo, Ohio, and was attending acting school at the Pasadena Playhouse where he was spotted by an MGM talent scout and cast in the movie *The Blackboard Jungle*. Because he was best suited to very specific character types, he was a shoo-in for variety shows and sketch comedy, and Farr became a semi-regular on both *The Red Skelton Show* and *The Danny Kaye Show*. After a regular role alongside Dean Jones and John Banner in the short-lived 1920s gangster spoof *The Chicago Teddy Bears*, Farr was tapped to play the cross-dressing Maxwell Q. Klinger on *M*A*S*H*, a draftee corporal who was constantly angling for a Section Eight psychiatric discharge. Originally slated to appear on only one episode, Farr was such a hit with both viewers and the show's cast and crew that he became a regular by the third season, one of only four actors to appear on all eleven seasons (along with Alan Alda, Loretta Swit, and William Christopher). As approachable and gregarious as one would expect from his cheery onscreen persona, Farr is actively involved in many charities, including an LPGA tournament that raises money for children in the vicinity of his birthplace, Toledo, Ohio.

MAUDE

 | **1972–1978** | **142 episodes**

The uncompromising, enterprising, anything but tranquilizing Maude Findlay fights the good fight for racial and gender equality while living in Tuckahoe, New York, with her fourth husband, her divorced daughter, and a seemingly endless parade of salty housekeepers.

The left-wing equivalent of Archie Bunker, Maude Findlay was Norman Lear's answer to himself, in a way, for creating a historic bigot in *All in the Family*. Even though Archie was invariably made to look the fool, Lear felt the need to tip the scales of free speech back into balance, creating in *Maude* a character that was as intractable in her liberalism as Bunker was in his conservatism.

Beatrice Arthur staked her claim on television with a guest shot as Maude in *All in the Family*, when a character actress closing in on fifty could still become an overnight sensation after twenty years in the New York theater. In some ways, *Maude* pushed the envelope even farther than *All in the Family* ever did, especially with the episode where Maude, finding out she's pregnant at the age of forty-seven, decides to have an abortion. There were precious few issues that were less "hot button" in 1972 than a

Beatrice Arthur, as Maude, directs her sarcasm at two of her favorite targets, Conrad Bain, as Arthur Harmon, and Bill Macy, as husband number four, "God'll get you for that Walter."

Beatrice Arthur

One of the driest wits in show business can be found in a five-foot-ten-inch drink of acid named Beatrice Arthur. Initially training as a medical technician, she served briefly as one of the first female marines during World War II. With a deep but highly musical voice, she came to New York to be a chanteuse, playing Lucy Brown in the legendary Off-Broadway production of *Threepenny Opera*. Revealing her talent for comedy as a semiregular on *Sid Caesar's Hour*, she spent the 1960s in two of Broadway's biggest hits, as the original Yente in *Fiddler on the Roof*, and winning a Tony Award as Vera "I was never in the chorus" Charles in *Mame*, directed by then-husband Gene Saks. Arthur traveled to Los Angeles to guest-star as Edith Bunker's cousin on *All in the Family*, creating a sensation as outspoken "pinko" Maude Findlay—and the resulting spin-off series made her a full-fledged television star. After a six-season run, she had a rare career misstep in the American version of *Fawlty Towers*, titled *Amanda's*. After its quick cancellation, Arthur vowed to never do another sitcom. She went back on her promise when she was presented with a fantastically funny script for a series about four women living under one roof. In *The Golden Girls*, Arthur spent another seven years flinging zingers as Dorothy Zbornak, joining the small club of actors who have had two hit sitcoms. More recently, she

had the misfortune of bringing a one-woman show to Broadway in the same season as Elaine Stritch and finding herself overshadowed by another whiskey baritone with an ax to grind. Continuing to do guest shots (most recently as Larry David's mother on *Curb Your Enthusiasm*), Arthur still possesses the timing of a Bulova.

Above: Two masters of deadpan delivery, Erik Per Sullivan and Beatrice Arthur, make for a hilarious episode of *Malcolm in the Middle*. Once they move on from the chaste activity of sorting her button collection, they'll be tangoing to the strains of ABBA's "Fernando."

---

woman's right to choose. (It was aired just months before the landmark *Roe v. Wade* decision.) What was more, it was the central character that was making the choice. On *All in the Family*, subjects like draft dodgers, homosexuality, free love, and anti-Semitic violence were dealt with, but always in conjunction with a guest-starring actor or supporting player. This time, it was Maude herself who was taking an extremely controversial stand. It was as if the entire enterprise were casting its lot with the pro-choice camp.

Many stations refused to air the abortion episode, providing the show with more free publicity than it could ever have hoped for. A subsequent three-parter dealing with Walter's alcoholism created almost as much of an uproar. As normally gentle Walter attempted to quit drinking cold turkey, he flew into a rage and hit Maude.

OFF THE SET

ON *ALL IN THE FAMILY*, the role of Carol was played by actress Marcia Rodd; she was replaced by Adrienne Barbeau when *Maude* premiered as a series.

ON AN EPISODE of *Seinfeld*, the cast is enjoying some sun in the Hamptons when Elaine walks in wearing a sundress, sunglasses, and a huge hat. Upon seeing her, Jerry says "And then there's Maude ..."

THE FINAL EPISODES of *Maude's* sixth season dealt with Maude getting elected to Congress and moving to Washington, D.C. The show was supposed to return for another season, but Bea Arthur changed her mind and the series ended.

MAUDE WAS BASED on the prickly, opinionated Frances Lear.

Now there's a man who's either stupid or nuts...for, despite her pantsuits, Maude Findlay (not to mention her portrayer Bea Arthur) wasn't a woman to be messed with. Walter's subsequent nervous breakdown (one of two he had on the show), as well as story lines dealing with menopause, face-lifts, and infidelity, became fodder for the controversy machine.

The show had a cast made up of the best New York theater had to offer, including Bill Macy as Walter, plus Conrad Bain and Rue McClanahan (both to soon be starring in their own sitcoms, *Diff'rent Strokes* and *The Golden Girls*, respectively) as best friends and neighbors the Harmons and Adrienne Barbeau, fresh from the Broadway musical *Grease*, as Maude's sexy and equally opinionated daughter Carol.

Oh, and there were the maids. While 1960s domestics like Louise on *Make*

Above: Just another hand-clenching crisis for Macy, Arthur, Rue McClanahan, and Adrienne Barbeau, in the most dysfunctional household in all of Tuckahoe, New York.

Below: Rue McClanahan and Dabney Coleman in Norman Lear's Depression-era sitcom, *Apple Pie*.

Room for Daddy and Hazel Burke were lovably meddlesome, and Mrs. Livingston on *The Courtship of Eddie's Father* was positively subservient, Maude's household help had even more opinions than she did. First was Esther Rolle, as Florida Evans, soon to decamp for *Good Times* in the Chicago housing projects; her replacement was Hermione Baddeley, as the hard-drinking Nell Naugatuck; and finally came Marlene Warfield as Victoria Butterfield, from the West Indies. All three of them were as fresh as paint—and silently bemused by the fact that Maude prided herself on being the picture of liberalism, yet she could be utterly naive about the issues she was taking on. This willingness on the part of Norman Lear to poke fun at the "knee-jerk liberal" showed not only complete open-mindedness but the desire to deflate self-importance on either side of the political fence.

It's surprising that while television has become much more explicit in so many ways, from violence to sexuality, sitcoms that truly challenge our morality have all but disappeared, in effect taking a step forward and a step backward at the same time. Maude Findlay, with her feet planted in the terra firma of Tuckahoe, New York, pulled no punches and took on all comers. She may have been the last sitcom character to change our minds.

CAST

Beatrice Arthur	Maude Findlay
Bill Macy	Walter Findlay
Adrienne Barbeau	Carol Traynor
Conrad Bain	Dr. Arthur Harmon
Rue McClanahan	Vivian Cavender Harmon
Brian Morrison	Phillip Traynor (1)
Kraig Metzinger	Phillip Traynor (2)
Esther Rolle	Florida Evans
Hermione Baddeley	Nell Naugatuck
Marlene Warfield	Victoria Butterfield
Fred Grandy	Chris

Rue McClanahan

When her *Golden Girls* character, Blanche Devereaux, received the dubious honor of *Maxim Magazine*'s "Number One TV Nympho," it must have made Betty White, creator of Sue Ann Nivens, positively green with envy. Rue McClanahan has led a colorful life, both on and off screen. Getting her start, as so many have, in the New York theater (in bra and panties, opposite Dustin Hoffman in *Jimmy Shine*), she gained major television notice as a homicidal nanny on the daytime drama *Another World*. Making a splash in prime time on *All in the Family*, as half of a couple of married swingers who try to have a "swap meet" with Archie and Edith, she worked again for producer Norman Lear as Maude Findlay's dotty best friend, Vivian Harmon. She had a flop in *Apple Pie*, a Depression-era sitcom costarring Dabney Coleman, then joined the cast of *Mama's Family*, working for the first time with Betty White. Reunited with both White and *Maude* star Bea Arthur on *The Golden Girls*, McClanahan gave middle-aged sexuality a patron saint. Now on husband number six, McClanahan has had an equally spicy private life, and has returned to the Broadway stage as a replacement in the musical *Wicked*.

MISTER ED

1961–1965 | 143 episodes

Wilbur Post finds himself the owner of Ed, a talkative palomino who doesn't seem interested in discussing things with anyone but Willllllburrrrr.

In the proud tradition of *Bewitched*, *I Dream of Jeannie*, *My Mother the Car*, and *The Addams Family*, *Mister Ed* took a surrealistic element and made it the focus of a sitcom. Of course, Ed wasn't the only talking animal on television. Cleo, the basset hound on *The People's Choice*, and Buck, the Bundy's mascot on *Married with Children*, were both "talking dogs"—but only the audience could hear them. It wasn't until *The Family Guy*'s inimitable Brian came along that a dog who conversed with humans became a central character again—and like Ed, Brian (though something of a dipsomaniac) acts as the voice of reason among a bunch of dithering bipeds. The loquacious equine Ed could talk to anyone—but he chose not to, preferring to talk only to his owner, Wilbur. That smartest of all dogs, Lassie, could rescue Timmy from a burning barn, put out a fire, or rebuild the barn like new—but she couldn't recite the Pledge of Allegiance. Likewise, Arnold the pig was a bona fide member of *Green Acres*' Ziffel family—but he never did more than grunt (albeit intelligently). In his day, and for a long time after, Ed was the only talking animal on the tube.

Silly premises only work if the surrounding reality is convincing and if the characters are likeable enough to make viewers suspend their disbelief. By those standards, *Mister Ed* was one of the best, if not always the funniest, of the bunch. When the show ran the risk of being con-

Alan Young and Bamboo Harvester, wearing one of Lovey Howell's hats from *Gilligan's Island*, enjoy a bright, sunshiny day.

Wilbur Post: What are you going to do with a straw hat?

Ed: I'll wear it till it goes out of style. Then I'll eat it!

fined to one setting, the writers came up with more and more outlandish excuses to get Ed away from the barn and corral: flying an airplane, driving a delivery truck, even riding a surfboard. Ed was also very handy at using the telephone, getting Wilbur into all kinds of trouble with his prank calls. And he looked great in a Beatle wig. *Mister Ed* also faced the same problem that had beset the writers of *Topper*: namely, how to stretch out the joke of Wilbur getting caught talking to Ed, in the same way that Cosmo Topper was constantly getting caught talking to the ghostly Kerbys. Topper tended to bluff his way through, but Wilbur unapologetically admitted he was talking to the horse. Still, the joke became a little repetitious.

Wilbur moved his office into the stable to be with Ed and it was their obvious love for each other—yes, love—that was at the heart of the series. Alan Young often proclaimed his fondness for Bamboo Harvester, the American Saddlebred palomino who played Ed. Their mutual admiration, call it chemistry if you will, was obvious on the screen in the same way that the fellow feeling among the cast of *Mary Tyler Moore* was evident to viewers of that show.

Yes, a horse is a horse, of course, of course, but we have to admit that Mister. Ed was a special horse, beloved not only by Wilbur Post but by millions of viewers throughout America.

Above: Ed scans the latest issue of *Good Barnkeeping* with the help of Wilbur and an ever-patient Carol Post (the lovely Connie Hines).

Below: Larry Keating, as the fourth and final Harry Morton, with the rest of the cast of *Burns and Allen*: Bea Benaderet, George, and Gracie.

Larry Keating

Cranky, pompous professional sitcom next-door neighbor Larry Keating began his acting career in 1945 with appearances in a series of B movies including *Francis Goes to the Races*, directed by *Mr. Ed* producer Arthur Lubin in 1947. While Keating toiled in relative obscurity in film, he could be heard on radio as the emcee of *The Fitch Bandwagon* (an immensely popular variety show) and as narrator of *This Is Your FBI*, another great success. Eventually, Keating broke into television, scoring a gaggle of character parts. He got his first regular gig as one in a line of Harry Mortons on *The George Burns and Gracie Allen Show*. He also appeared as Harry Morton on one episode of *The Bob Cummings Show* titled, aptly, "Bob Meets the Mortons." Keating's next and last series appearance was as short-tempered neighbor Roger Addison on *Mr. Ed*, thus assuring his immortality on reruns and DVD compilations.

OFF THE SET

WHEN LARRY KEATING died unexpectedly during the 1963-1964 season, the show created a new series of nosy neighbors, Gordon and Winnie Kirkwood, played by Leon Ames and Florence MacMichael.

ON JANUARY 5, 1961, *Mister Ed* became the first series ever to debut as a midseason replacement. The next wasn't for another five years, when *Batman* premiered.

CAST

Alan Young	Wilbur Post
Bamboo Harvester	Mr. Ed
Allan "Rocky" Lane	Voice of Mr. Ed
Connie Hines	Carol Post
Larry Keating	Roger Addison
Edna Skinner	Kay Addison
Leon Ames	Gordon Kirkwood
Florence MacMichael	Winnie Kirkwood

In one of the most bizarre guest shots ever (right up there with Liz and Dick on *Here's Lucy* and Andy Warhol's *Love Boat* appearance), Mae West conjures up unwelcome images of Catherine the Great in her scene with Ed.

THE MONKEES

 | **1966–1968** | **58 episodes**

Four zany guys—who should not be confused with the Beatles—live together, play music together (sort of), and have many madcap adventures together.

Hey, hey, it's the Beatles, er, Monkees. The success of the Beatles' zany movies, *Help* and *A Hard Day's Night* begged to be appropriated by American television. The answer was the totally fabricated group, the Monkees. Let's see, get together four cute boys of varying musical talents, write some jaunty tunes for them, pick a name of an animal and misspell it, and crank up the publicity and merchandising machines.

The result, surprisingly, was an eminently watchable and listenable series that transcended its formulaic origins. In fact, the show won two Emmys in its first season. Remember, the late '60s was an era of silly sitcoms such as *Gilligan's Island*; *Gomer Pyle U.S.M.C*; *The Beverly Hillbillies*; *The Pruitts of Southhampton*; *Get Smart*; and *F Troop*—and even tongue-in-cheek drama and adventure shows such as *Batman*; *Wild, Wild, West*; and *The Man from U.N.C.L.E.* The Monkees fit right in. *Batman* had his

Hey, hey they're *The Monkees*, here playing a life-sized version of the board game "Operation." Evidently Mike Nesmith lost the coin toss. His consolation prize? His mother invented Liquid Paper.

SITCOMS: THE 101 GREATEST TV COMEDIES OF ALL TIME

Batmobile and *The Monkees* had their Monkeemobile.

Lots of credit for the show's success should go to the four fellows who made up the group: Davy Jones (read Paul McCartney), Mike Nesmith (read John Lennon), Peter Tork (read Ringo Starr), and Micky Dolenz (by process of elimination, read George Harrison). Okay, so it wasn't an exact match with the Beatles, but the foursome did have the cute, charming, good-natured thing down. They differed from their more successful and talented English brethren in two ways. First, they didn't write their own songs; and second, they didn't play their own songs. Davy had been a child actor in musicals and Micky had played a little in local bands and appeared on television and in movies, but there was really no choice but to dub the music in the beginning. The boys supplied only the vocals (shades of Milli Vanilli, who played but didn't sing).

Just like *A Hard Day's Night*, *The Monkees* featured sped-up cameras, slow motion, distorted lenses, the cast addressing the camera directly, wacky editing, and all sorts of other nonsense. Luckily, the music was good and the group actually developed into a fine band, supplied with a surprising number of very successful songs, including, "(I'm Not Your) Stepping Stone," "I'm a Believer," "Last Train to Clarksville," "Daydream Believer," and "Pleasant Valley Sunday." The Monkees actually racked up several number-one albums and toured internationally. On one tour, the Jimi Hendrix Experience was the opening act! Briefly.

After the show's second season, the group grew tired of the lame scripts and decided to retire from television in favor of the concert circuit. The original episodes were rerun on CBS and later ABC on Saturday mornings, resulting in a new generation of fans. In 1976, long after Tork and then Nesmith left the band, the record *The Monkees' Greatest Hits* hit the *Billboard* chart.

In 1987, a new fake group called the Monkees was invented for a syndicated series titled *The New Monkees*. No go. It folded after thirteen episodes, proving that a new ersatz group can never replace the original ersatz group.

Top left: A grandmother's caption, circa 1966: It's ironic that those hoodlums would be photographed in front of a barber pole when they're all in need of a good haircut. Oh, and their pants are too tight.

Below: The Not-So-Fab Four, bummed out after missing the last train to Clarksville.

CAST

As themselves:

Davy Jones

Mike Nesmith

Peter Tork

Micky Dolenz

OFF THE SET

STEPHEN STILLS OF Crosby, Stills, Nash, and Young fame was almost cast as a Monkee. Instead, he suggested his former roommate Peter Tork for a part.

AS A CHILD, Davy Jones played the Artful Dodger in the musical *Oliver!* on Broadway.

ALMOST 500 ACTOR/MUSICIANS answered the Monkees casting call.

DURING A TOUR of Europe, after the series had ceased production, word leaked out that the band hadn't actually played on their early recordings, prompting the nickname The Pre-fab Four.

MR. PEEPERS

NBC | 1952–1955 | 69 episodes

Mild-mannered science teacher Robinson Peepers of Jefferson Junior High School, a do-gooder whose good deeds sometimes backfire, loves school nurse Nancy Remington. His best friend is the outgoing, go-getting history teacher, Harvey Weskitt.

We know a word you haven't heard used to describe any current television show, nor, we bet, any show of the last five years. The word is "gentle." Gentleness has gone out of fashion, far out of fashion. Today's sitcom protagonists are cool, edgy, ultra-hip, cynical, wisecracking masters of their domain. Or, when the men are not exactly masters (e.g., the married men in such series as *Everybody Loves Raymond* and *King of Queens*), they are buffoons. The women, often insecure or naive, are portrayed as ditzy scatterbrains. Take Phoebe in *Friends*, for example—she is really just a bit (and only a bit) smarter than Gracie Allen, the queen of confusion.

All of which is a long way of saying that *Mr. Peepers* seems like a relic of another universe. Robinson Peepers, especially as portrayed by that most benign milquetoast Wally Cox, was gentle. Today, he might be characterized as a nerd—but nerds today tend to be outcasts, as epitomized by Screech in *Saved by the Bell*, more to be pitied and ridiculed than embraced.

The success of *Mr. Peepers* was a surprise to the network, viewers, and, one would suppose, its creators. There was already a very popular sitcom set in a school, *Our Miss Brooks*, in which Connie Brooks yearned for Mr. Boynton with a wisecrack, not a whimper. She might not have been in her element pursuing the opposite sex but she was a mistress of her high school domain. Mr. Peepers, on the other hand, could never really get it together on any front. He wasn't as high-strung as Barney on *The Andy Griffith Show* (nor did he have Barney's delusional self-confidence), but he did his share of stuttering and fumbling. When he tried to do something, anything really, and screwed it up, his attempts wer e endearing. Female viewers loved him and wanted to be his mother. So did his longtime sweetheart, Nancy Remington. But, in the formalized 1950s, she had to wait till he made the first

Left: Professional nebbish Wally Cox, the voice of Underdog, a regular Hollywood Square, and the former roommate of Marlon Brando, during the filming of his starmaking role.

Opposite left : Marion Lorne as the stuttering, stammering English teacher (natch), Mrs. Gurney.

move. It's not surprising that at the end of the series, Peepers finally did pop the question and the two were united in holy matrimony. That episode was one of the most watched in television history, a gentle conclusion that suited the simple, early days of television.

Even the genesis of the show was tentative and gentle. Originally scheduled as an eight-episode summer series, *Mr. Peepers* was quickly renewed when NBC's *Doc Corkle*, whose stellar cast included Eddie Mayehoff, Billie Burke, Arnold Stang, and Hope Emerson, flopped after only three episodes.

The aforementioned *Andy Griffith Show* and *The Bob Newhart Show* were *Peepers'* successors in gentleness—but they were much more self-aware. It's the rare series that slowly but surely envelops its audience in the day-to-day travails of a character as benign and loveable as Robinson Peepers.

In a show built around such an extreme character type, an actor like the off-center Tony Randall (as Robinson J. Peepers's best buddy Harvey Weskitt) could seem positively mundane by comparison.

OFF THE SET

MR. PEEPERS **WAS** filmed at the Century Theater on Seventh Avenue and 58th Street in New York, formerly a Broadway theater. Among the musical shows that had premiered there were *Up in Central Park*; *High Button Shoes*; *Inside U.S.A.*; and *Kiss Me, Kate*.

CAST

Wally Cox	Robinson Peepers
Marion Lorne	Mrs. Gurney
Patricia Benoit	Nancy Remington
Gage Clark	Superintendent Bascom
Tony Randall	Harvey Weskitt
Ernest Truex	Mr. Remington
Ruth McDevitt	Ma Peepers
Sylvia Field	Mrs. Remington
Georgann Johnson	Marge Bellows Weskitt
Jenny Egan	Agnes Peepers
Jospeh Foley	Gabriel Gurney

Marion Lorne

Bewitched, bothered, and befuddled, Marion Lorne, a character actress who specialized in the stuttering, dithery and confused, became a late blooming television star on *Mr. Peepers*. After attending New York's American Academy of Performing Arts, she embarked on a Broadway career beginning with the 1905 play, *Mrs. Temple's Telegram*. She married playwright Walter C. Hackett and the couple moved to London, where they founded the Whitehall Theatre. Lorne returned to the States after Hackett's death, and in 1951, at age sixty, made her screen debut in Alfred Hitchcock's *Strangers on a Train*. The Lorne persona was by now fully formed and her turn as Mrs. Gurney on *Mr. Peepers* made her a star in the U.S. Television personality Garry Moore made her a part of his television family, chatting to great comic effect with the more than slightly confused Lorne. Her greatest fame, however, came as Aunt Clara on *Bewitched*. For four seasons, Lorne mixed up spells, and entranced audiences in the process. Sadly, Lorne suffered a heart attack in 1968, a short while before winning a well-deserved Emmy Award.

THE MUNSTERS

| 1964–1966 | 70 episodes

The Munsters of 1313 Mockingbird Lane creep out their entire town with their groovy but ghoulish hijinks.

Much broader than its counterpart, *The Addams Family* (the two shows premiered the same month in 1964 and were canceled the same week in 1966), *The Munsters* was equally funny in its depiction of the humorous goings on of the ghouls next door. In a strange way, both shows were lessons in tolerance and acceptance of one's neighbors' "differences."

Starring two cast members direct from *Car 54, Where Are You?* plus a B-movie bombshell with a wicked sense of timing, the show was like a burlesque version of the Universal horror films of the 1930s, with lead couple Herman and Lily Munster made up to look like the sitcom equivalents of Frankenstein and his bride; Grandpa a Borscht Belt takeoff on Dracula; and little Eddie (born Edward Wolfgang Munster) a cross between a werewolf in training fangs and Little Lord Fauntleroy. Fred Gwynne and Al Lewis, who had already developed a simpatico comic rhythm on *Car 54*, were the motor of the show, alternately feuding like Laurel and Hardy, then getting into a joint pickle like a Transylvanian Lucy and Ethel. In a role initially conceived as a straightwoman, the beautiful Yvonne DeCarlo revealed a fantastic flair for comedy and more than held her own with hambones Lewis and Gwynne.

The show greatly benefited from

its rich visuals, the moody cinematography (the original pilot was shot in color, but when the producers discovered they could save a whopping $1,000 an episode, they rediscovered the glory of black and white) deliberately mimicking the shadowy, cobweb-laden art direction of the early horror films of James Whale. In fact, *The Munsters* was an unlikely combination of a square, suburban family show running full-tilt-boogie into a dead-on

(voiced by the immortal Mel Blanc). And the Munsters' extended family (many of them never seen) made for some hilarious images. There was Grandpa's Cousin Humphrey, whom Grandpa hadn't spoken to since he stole an aspirin from him during the Black Plague; Uncle Gilbert, also known as the Creature from the Black Lagoon; Uncle Boris and Aunt Mina, who lived in Death Valley (where else?); and Lily's brother Lester, a werewolf, who perhaps explained some of the lycanthropic attributes of her son, Eddie. Which leads us to two strange, unexplained aspects of the show: if Marilyn Munster is the daughter of Lily Munster's sister, her last name shouldn't be Munster—unless her sister also married into the family? And Al Lewis's character is always referred to as Grandpa Munster, but—as he is Lily's father—shouldn't he be called Grandpa Dracula?

While all of Mockingbird Heights was wigged out at the sight of the Munster family, the Munsters themselves thought they were the picture of normalcy—and this was nowhere more evident than in their treatment of niece Marilyn. Played by Beverley Owen for the first thirteen episodes and then by Pat Priest, Marilyn was a pretty, blond college student not unlike Elinor Donahue on *Father Knows Best*

spoof of *Creature Feature*. For unlike the patriarch of *The Addams Family*, who was a nonpracticing lawyer, Herman Munster actually had a nine-to-five job (although probably nine P.M. to five A.M.) working as a gravedigger and hearse driver for the funeral parlor Gateman, Goodbury and Graves. And Lily was not a simple stay-at-home Mom (although she did do housekeeping, consisting of scattering garbage around the house). For a brief while she worked as a welder in a shipyard.

While the humor was never as sophisticated as that of *The Addams Family*, the show was full of witty touches. The opening sequence was a parody of *The Donna Reed Show*, showing matriarch Lily Munster lovingly giving the family their lunches as they went off to school and work. The family pets included Spot the fire-breathing dragon, who lived under the staircase; Igor the bat, who was Grandpa's lab assistant; and Charlie the raven

Fred Gwynne

The gentle giant Fred Gwynne is best known for his two starring roles on the 1960s sitcoms *Car 54, Where Are You?* and *The Munsters*, but his career was as varied and rich as most other talented character actors. A true renaissance man, he graduated from Harvard and worked as a cartoonist for the *Harvard Lampoon*. While also pursuing his acting career, Gwynne painted and wrote and illustrated several children's books. At six foot five, he was usually cast in roles that exploited his stature, as in the guest role he played on *The Phil Silvers Show*, as a ringer in a pie-eating contest, and of course in the role of Herman Munster, for which he will forever be remembered. Alas, Gwynne found it difficult to shake the specter of the flat-headed Herman. Despite his goofy persona on sitcoms, he was an excellent dramatic actor, appearing in everything from a 1974 Broadway revival of *Cat on a Hot Tin Roof* (as Big Daddy) and the musical *Here's Love*, to such movies as *Pet Sematary*, *The Cotton Club*, and *Ironweed*, and his last role, as a judge in the comedy *My Cousin Vinny*.

or Shelley Fabares on *The Donna Reed Show*. Trouble is, the Munsters viewed her as the poor ugly child of the family, so skewed was their idea of physical beauty. The other gag that found its way into every episode was the "reveal," when the door to the Munster home was opened and some poor, unsuspecting TV repairman, vacuum cleaner salesman, or date of Marilyn's got a gander at the inhabitants. Their reactions were the kind of comedy that viewers came to anticipate, week in and week out, just as viewers waited to see how the castaways of *Gilligan's Island* would be foiled in their attempt to get off the island, or who Murphy Brown's latest temp secretary would be, or what comic misunderstanding Jack, Janet, and Chrissy would set in motion on *Three's Company*. It's the kind of expectational humor that makes an audience feel comfortable. It may be formulaic—but it is necessary to an enduring sitcom.

Fred Gwynne and Yvonne DeCarlo, as Herman and Lily Munster, do their spring planting.

Al Lewis

Al Lewis was a man of mystery. He was born either Albert Meister or Alexander Meister, either on April 30, 1923, or April 30, 1910, in either Wolcott, New York, or Brooklyn. He claimed to have earned a PhD in child psychology from Columbia in 1941, but the university has no record of his ever attending. He also claimed that he was member of the Sacco and Vanzetti Defense Committee in 1927, impossible had he been born in 1923. He has said he

worked as a circus performer and a hotdog vendor at Ebbets Field but the particulars of Lewis's life prior to his taking up acting are all hearsay. Here's what's certain: after some work in the waning days of vaudeville and burlesque, he appeared in Broadway dramas and in the musical *Do Re Mi* in 1961. Racking up some minor television roles, he seemed to come out of nowhere when he was cast as Officer Leo Schnauser on *Car 54, Where Are You?* leading directly to his most famous role, as Grandpa Sam Dracula on *The Munsters*. For the rest of his life, he was rarely out of the spotlight. He hosted his own political radio show, opened an Italian restaurant in Greenwich Village, and ran for governor of New York on the Green Party ticket in 1998, at the age of either 75 or 88. Incredibly colorful, Al Lewis off screen just may have been wilder than the mad scientist vampire he played on *The Munsters*.

CAST

Fred Gwynne ....Herman Munster

Yvonne De Carlo ....Lily Munster

Al Lewis.....................Grandpa Sam Dracula

Butch Patrick ....Eddie Munster

Beverly Owen ....Marilyn Munster (1)

Pat Priest..................Marilyn Munster(2)

OFF THE SET

IN THE UNAIRED pilot of *The Munsters*, Lily Munster's was named Phoebe. She was played by actress Joan Marshall, who was replaced after being deemed too beautiful for the role.

THE WIZARD OF OZ'S "Cowardly Lion," Bert Lahr, was considered for the role of Grandpa.

AUTOMOBILE FANS FONDLY remember two custom-made cars from the show: "The Munster Koach," a hot rod built from the chassis of a 1923 Model T with the body of a hearse; and "Dragula," a drag racer that looked like a coffin.

MURPHY BROWN

 | **1988–1998** | **247 episodes**

Hardboiled, uncompromising investigative TV reporter Murphy Brown takes on all comers (including a vice president) with the help and hindrance of her fellow *FYI* staffers, her handyman-in-residence, the local bartender, and ultimately, her equally hard-headed mother.

How many sitcoms beget a national controversy? (And who knew the leaders of the political right were a bunch of couch potatoes?) When sitcom newshound Murphy Brown, a single mother, decided to have a child and raise it on her own, Vice President Dan Quayle decried her decision from the 1992 campaign stump. Perhaps feeling emasculated by the character's stand that it's so nice not to have a man around the house, Quayle ignited a societal debate about "family values," a key Republican catch phrase. As Quayle already had a reputation for planting his foot firmly in his mouth, the *Murphy Brown* writers had a field day striking back. In the 1992–93 season premiere, titled "You Say Potatoe, I Say Potato" (referring to Quayle's famous spelling gaffe), *FYI*, the *60 Minutes*–style show hosted by Brown, aired a special episode on the diverse American family.

As played by Candice Bergen, who got remarkable comic mileage out of acting with her neck and hitting her punch lines with a thrust of her chiseled jaw, Murphy Brown, like Dan Quayle, was in no way a perfect person; in fact, the series opened with her returning from the Betty Ford Clinic. And, as is usual in workplace-centric sitcoms, her fellow *FYI*ers were just as comically human: They included Jim Dial, the über-square, emotionally constipated anchor; reporter Corky Sherwood, as lustrous yet lightweight as her perfectly sprayed 'do; and Murphy's best friend and confidant, Frank Fontana. The terrific trio of Charles Kimbrough, Faith Ford, and Joe Regalbuto expertly developed their roles from broadly drawn portraits into

realistically complex individuals. Regalbuto, in particular, created in Frank Fontana a tragically insecure man, sharing with Murphy one of the rare, believable platonic male-female friendships in sitcoms. Handing out assignments was the nebbishy producer Miles Silverberg (played hilariously by Grant Shaud), who was strung as tightly as Andre Agassi's racket and constantly tormented by the entire staff. On the home front, Murphy had

Candice Bergen's unusual career path has taken her from fashion model to dramatic movie actress to sitcom cut-up.

housepainter Eldin Bernecky, a truly original sitcom character who insinuated himself into Brown's life through a series of home-design schemes that lasted six seasons. Played by Robert Pastorelli, Eldin eventually put down his paintbrush and became the day-care provider to Brown's baby son, Avery.

While very funny in its prime, *Murphy Brown* has not stood the test of time as well as some of its contemporaries. Since the writing often (too often, actually) relied on topical references—jokes about Fawn Hall, Tip O'Neill, Jerry Brown, and Donna Rice—the scripts feel less fresh with every passing day. And over the course of the series, the humor became less character-driven and started featuring garden-variety put-downs, interchangeable among characters. This sent *Murphy Brown* down the same path trod by other long-running shows that outstayed their welcome a season or three.

When Shaud left *Murphy Brown*, the show lost its footing. It helped that Lily Tomlin came on board in the final season, providing a ratings boost—and, as it turned out, *Murphy Brown* had one more trick up its sleeve, creating one more controversy. The entire final season was concerned with Brown's discovery that she had breast cancer. When she used marijuana to help counteract the nausea associated with chemotherapy, the Republicans again went on the attack. Though there was a remarkable 30

percent increase in women having mammograms, the Right was fixated on the dangers of encouraging marijuana use, even for medicinal purposes.

Whereas other series had "very special" episodes, *Murphy Brown* had a very special season. Maintaining its sense of humor while delivering a serious message, the show provided a classy, funny, insightful take on journalism, motherhood, and women's issues while managing to incite all the Right people.

Above: Faith Ford, Charles Kimbrough, and Joe Regalbuto, as the staff of the fictional *FYI,* give Grant Shaud's dweeby Miles Silverberg the old silent treatment.

Left: Martin Short, Joe Regalbuto, Alley Mills (later of *The Wonders Years*), Wilfrid Hyde-White, and Shelley Smith in the highly underrated *The Associates.*

Joe Regalbuto

Joe Regalbuto is graced with great comic timing and, as a bonus, he actually looks like a real person, someone you might encounter at work or in the neighborhood. His first job on television was as a regular on the short-lived cult hit *The Associates*, alongside Martin Short and Wilfrid Hyde-White. He spent the next decade guest starring on over fifty series, often as a villain on both sitcoms and hourlongs, before his ten-season run as Murphy Brown's best buddy, Frank Fontana. Since the show went off the air, Regalbuto has concentrated on directing more than acting, getting his feet wet with *Murphy Brown* before moving on to such shows as *Veronica's Closet* and *George Lopez*.

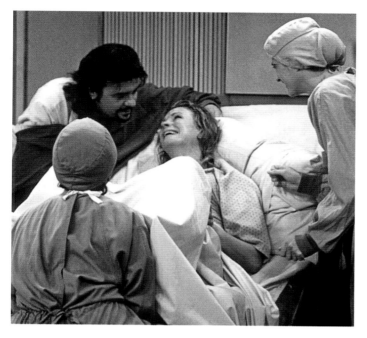

CAST

Candice Bergen	Murphy Brown
Charles Kimbrough	Jim Dial
Joe Regalbuto	Frank Fontana
Faith Ford	Corky Sherwood
Grant Shaud	Miles Silverberg
Pat Corley	Phil
Robert Pastorelli	Eldin Bernecky
Scott Bakula	Peter Hunt
Janet Carroll	Doris Dial
Dyllan Christopher	Avery Brown (1)
Haley Joel Osment	Avery Brown (2)
Garry Marshall	Stan Lansing
Paul Reubens	Andrew J. Lansing, III
Lily Tomlin	Kay Carter-Shepley

Murphy: Oh my god, I have milk coming out of my breasts! This is like having bacon come out of your elbow!

OFF THE SET

A RUNNING GAG on the show was Murphy's inability to keep a secretary. There were almost one hundred secretaries during the course of the series. One who was actually good at her job was Marcia Wallace, reprising her role of Carol Kiester from *The Bob Newhart Show*. Newhart appeared at the end of the episode, playing psychiatrist Bob Hartley, to beg Carol to come back to work.

Above: Murphy, with Eldin as Lamaze coach, gives birth to a huge controversy.

Right: Candice Bergen welcomes Lily Tomlin to the *Murphy Brown* family for its final season.

MY FAVORITE MARTIAN

 | **1963–1966** | **107 episodes**

Turning Tim O'Hara's world upside down, the lovably exasperating Exigius 12½, having let his intergalactic AAA card expire, crashlands on Earth and has to lay low until his ship is repaired.

Bill Bixby and Ray Walston in the place they first met, also known as Area 51.

spacesuit and got stuck firmly in the craw of unsuspecting schnook Tim O'Hara (a reporter, no less, who witnesses the greatest scoop of all-time yet keeps it a secret), played by one of the classic Everymen of television, the terrific Bill Bixby.

In the grand sitcom tradition of fish-out-of-water stories that has given couch potatoes so much amusement over the past sixty years, aliens have long been a tradition on television. Long before *The X-Files*, the space race of the 1960s spawned two sitcoms that made viewers look to the skies: *I Dream of Jeannie*, dealing with a 2000-year old harem girl wreaking havoc on the United States space program (paranoid types viewed Barbara Eden's dumb blonde routine as an allegory about a wily, sitcom version of a Russian counterspy, determined to ruin America's chances to land on the moon with a blink and a nod…True or not, Eden sure as heck didn't look like a typical girl from Baghdad); and the aforementioned *My Favorite Martian*, which capitalized on the fear of the little green men that had gripped America since Orson Welles was on the radio.

Walston's Uncle Martin blazed a trail for all those other half-hour space nuts, but he was definitely cagier than Mork from Ork or the Solomon clan on *3rd Rock*. In fact, the sitcom Visitor From Another Planet that most closely resembled Martin was ALF, that feline-eating Muppet with the Borscht-belt shtick. Even covered in "Fun Fur," ALF blended in with the locals much better than Robin Williams and his rainbow suspenders.

Like *Bewitched*, *Jeannie*, *The Addams Family*, and *The Munsters*, *My Favorite Martian* was a classic 1960s example of a show that relied on true situational comedy: getting Tim O'Hara and Uncle Martin into a weekly bind, where someone (usually that nosy Lorelei Brown from next door—who was as big a snoop

Exigius 12½, also called Uncle Martin on this 3rd rock from the sun but best known to television viewers as *My Favorite Martian*, was like one of the annoying gnats that try to burrow their way into your ear, only to disappear when you try to smack them. Played by the perfectly pesky Ray Walston, this antennaed know-it-all dropped out of the sky in a green lamé

as Gladys Kravitz—or her boyfriend, the flatfoot cop Bill Brennan) would witness a bundt cake floating across the room, forcing Tim and Martin to do some pretty fancy tap dancing to get out of that episode's pickle.

After two seasons in black and white, Tim and Uncle Martin sprang to life in color, which seemed to bring out even more of Martin's powers. Now able to sprout facial hair at will to disguise themselves, the pair often looked like the Smith Brothers peddling a new flavor of cough drops. He also built a time machine, and Tim and Martin went whisking through time, zipping from Merrie Olde England to the silent screen days of early Hollywood, or popping in to give Leonardo DaVinci an estimate on redecorating the rumpus room.

A show that appealed greatly to kids—I mean, what teenager wouldn't love to be harboring an extraterrestrial (*E.T.*, anyone?)—*My Favorite Martian* was the epitome of the silly yet fondly remembered sitcoms that made legions of fans in its initial run and subsequent syndication, and current converts through the miracle of DVD box sets.

CAST

Ray Walston....................Uncle Martin
Bill Bixby ....Tim O'Hara
Pamela Britton..............Mrs. Lorelei Brown
Alan Hewitt ....Det. Bill Brennan

Bill Bixby

One of the most personable performers in television history, Bill Bixby's notable television career was cut short by his untimely death from cancer. After a series of guest spots in many of the most popular shows of the 1950's and early '60s, Bixby got his big break with *My Favorite Martian*, leading to movies, including two with Elvis Presley, *Clambake* and *Speedway*. He solidified his great appeal as the star of *The Courtship of Eddie's Father*. He segued into the dramatic form with the cult series *The Magician* (Bixby was a magic buff in real life), and a role in the miniseries *Rich Man, Poor Man*. Playing David Banner, the guy you definitely don't want to tick off, on *The Incredible Hulk* solidified his status as one of television's most reliable and versatile stars. Turning to directing, Bixby became the principal director on the Mayim Bialyk series *Blossom*, working right up until his death.

Top: Ray Walston and Pamela Britton (as the nosiest sitcom neighbor since Gladys Kravitz), share a laugh when they discover they use the same shade of Clairol Nice 'n' Easy.

Above: Bixby with Brandon Cruz, on location for *The Courtship of Eddie's Father*.

Left: Uncle Martin sings "If I Had a Hammer" as Tim O'Hara begins to look for one.

MY LITTLE MARGIE

 | **1952-1955** | **126 episodes**

Tomboy Margie Albright, with the grudging assistance of her boyfriend, Freddie, tries to help her father—with hilariously disastrous results.

As in astronomy, sitcom stars are orbited by a small galaxy of minor characters who depend on the warmth of the star for their existence. The shows of the early '50s featured a bevy of cute little girls who got themselves and their satellites into lots of silly scrapes. These were dutifully cleaned up by the male members of the entourage. Margie Albright, played by the especially appealing Gale Storm, had two major planets in her orbit—her gently scolding father, Vern, played by film veteran Charles Farrell, and her milquetoast boyfriend, Freddie (Don Hayden), a classic in the mold of the hapless Chester A. Riley. Man, he was whipped! Freddie was Margie's Ethel, going along with every cockamamie idea against his own better judgment.

Margie knew she was a meddler but just couldn't help herself. But, unlike Lucy, she was never after her own gain. She was usually trying to help her father or to bolster Freddie in her father's affections. Every sitcom has to have some frisson, and on this one it was the tension between Vern Albright and the boyfriend, who was never quite good enough for his daughter. Tomboyish Margie never really won the approval of her father's sleek, sophisticated girlfriend, Roberta Townsend, either.

If Roberta didn't give Margie the approval she desired, there was always Mrs. Odetts, played by veteran actress Gertrude Hoffman, the elderly neighbor who was endlessly supportive of Margie.

Back in the dim, dark days of the '50s, elders were respected for their knowledge

Gale Storm, who just screams the adjective "pert," with her sitcom father, Charles Farrell.

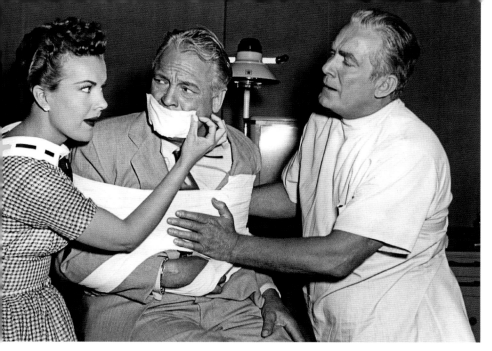

OFF THE SET

MY LITTLE MARGIE filled *Lucy*'s slot during the summer and was such a success, it was picked up for the regular season.

IN OPPOSITION TO the usual sequence of events, *My Little Margie* was adapted for radio at the end of 1952. The radio shows were original and ran simultaneously with the TV series.

and life experience. Several older character actors played pivotal roles in sitcoms. Think of Mrs. Davis, Connie Brooks's landlady; Mrs. Trumbull, Lucy's neighbor and babysitter for Little Ricky; and, a few years later, Aunt Bee in Mayberry. Sometimes, the elderly person actually became the lead of the sitcom. Walter Brennan on *The Real McCoys* and Spring Byington and Verna Felton on *December Bride* were thus elevated. On *Margie*, Mrs. Odetts wasn't your knitting-in-a-rocking-chair type of senior citizen. She zoomed around in race cars and kicked her heels up nightly while her dates tried to keep up.

My Little Margie is much beloved by those baby boomers who remember the show through the mists of time. It's surprising the impact it has had, considering that it ran only three seasons. Many series that lasted longer are practically forgotten, while sweet, simple, and inconsequential sitcoms such as *My Little Margie* live on in fond nostalgia.

Above: Gale Storm and Roy Roberts prepare Charles Farrell for the classic "medical tape tear-off" bit.

Below: Zasu Pitts with Gale Storm on her *Margie* follow-up, the far less successful *Oh! Susanna!*

Gale Storm

Mischievous, perky without being sticky sweet, Gale Storm began her career as a B-movie actress at RKO, Universal, and Monogram studios. When her film career went nowhere, she moved to television and found success with *My Little Margie*. Feistier than most ingénues, Storm's energy propelled the series. She was in the grand tradition of TV actors with whom audiences enjoyed spending time week after week after week. When *Margie* folded, Storm moved on to a new series, *The Gale Storm Show* (*Oh! Susanna!*), costarring venerable hangdog Zasu Pitts. Storm also enjoyed a brief but very successful recording career, topping the chart with "Dark Moon," "Memories Are Made of This," and "Ivory Tower." Like Pat Boone and other white performers who covered black hits, she recorded Smiley Lewis's R&B hit "I Hear You Knockin'" and Frankie Lymon's "Why Do Fools Fall in Love?" While still in her thirties she suffered the fate of hundreds of former movie stars: summer stock. Alcohol played its part in ending her career but, to her great credit, Storm recovered.

Unfortunately, her career never did. She's on our short list of former stars who deserve another chance to charm audiences with her ingratiating personality.

MY THREE SONS

  | 1960–1972 | 369 episodes

Widower Steve Douglas has to bring up his three sons, Mike, Robbie, and Chip (or Robbie, Chip, and Ernie, depending on when you tuned in) with the help of the cantankerous Uncle Bub (or Uncle Charley, depending on when you tuned in).

Single dads and moms have enjoyed high-profile lives on sitcoms. The menfolk have been featured on *Bachelor Father, Silver Spoons, Diff'rent Strokes, Family Affair, The Courtship of Eddie's Father*, and *Full House*, among others. Single mothers have ruled the roost on *One Day at a Time, Murphy Brown, Julia, The Lucy Show, The Ghost and Mrs. Muir*, and *Alice*. Significantly, most of these shows have been very successful.

Of course the single dads usually had help while the single moms were usually on their own. In the case of *My Three Sons*, Steve Douglas had Uncle Bub and later, Uncle Charley.

My Three Sons didn't have any "very special" episodes—in fact, unlike many of today's sitcoms (*Friends, Seinfeld*, and *Curb Your Enthusiasm* come to mind) no particular installment stands out for its plot or catch phrases. This is true of many of the mild-mannered shows of the '50s and '60s. Which girl Mike or Robbie was fighting over or what advice Steve or Uncle Bub doled out to the kids is completely forgotten and unimportant. Is it possible that the most significant thing about the fondly remembered *My Three Sons* is…its vibrant theme music by Frank De Vol?

Most of us can sing along to the title songs of *The Beverly Hillbillies, Gilligan's Island*, and *Green Acres*. Other memorable theme songs belong to *The Brady Bunch, Mary Tyler Moore, Three's Company*,

The five original Douglases in descending order of age.

and *All in the Family*. According to one newspaper poll, America's favorite sitcom songs come from *Cheers* and *The Jeffersons*. Though *I Love Lucy* had a lyric, few people remember it as the words weren't sung over the credits. Viewers of a certain age still hold the theme song to *I Married Joan* in high regard. Sometimes, the star would sing the theme song as in the case of Will Smith's rapping the *Fresh Prince of Bel-Air* and Linda Lavin's rendition of the theme song to *Alice*. Other favorites are *Growing Pains*, *Friends*, *Laverne & Shirley*, *Diff'rent Strokes*, *Perfect Strangers*, and *The Facts of Life*.

You'd think that instrumental theme songs wouldn't catch on as easily, but we can all whistle that *Andy Griffith Show* music and hum the tunes from *Barney Miller*, *Bewitched*, *The Dick Van Dyke Show*, *The Honeymooners*, *The Simpsons*, *The Odd Couple*, *The Cosby Show*, and De Vol's own *Get Smart*. A few shows didn't actually have theme songs. *Murphy Brown*, for example, featured a different Motown song at the beginning of each episode.

The theme to *My Three Sons*, catchy, simple, and repetitious, had all of the important elements of a classic TV theme—and the terrible animation that accompanied it is equally indelible. Even in 1965, when the show bolted ABC and began its color years at CBS, that cheap animation (it makes *South Park* look like Disney) was retained.

William Demarest

Grouchy, curmudgeonly William Demarest had an astoundingly long career in show business, beginning at age nine when he joined a carnival. He went on to vaudeville, then Broadway, movies, and television. In fact, he was there when the movies began to talk—as a player in *The Jazz Singer*. Demarest was a notable part of the Preston Sturges stock company at Paramount Pictures, where his explosive temper and electric energy helped propel the Sturges farces. He appeared in more than 150 films and was nominated for an Academy Award for Best Actor in a Supporting Role for his part in *The Jolson Story*. Despite his long career in films, Demarest is best remembered as gruff but sensitive Uncle Charley on *My Three Sons*.

OFF THE SET

THE VERY BUSY Fred MacMurray spent only sixty-five days a year filming *My Three Sons*, so continuity was all-important. All of his living room scenes would be shot at one time, then the kitchen, etc. For the rest of the season the other cast members filled in the blanks.

TIM CONSIDINE QUIT the show after an argument with producer Don Fedderson.

EDDIE ALBERT WAS considered for MacMurray's role.

Above: William Demarest and Jennie Lynn on the 1959 sitcom *Love & Marriage*.

Left: In a moment of extreme confusion, Steve Douglas proposes to Uncle Charley.

Frank De Vol

De Vol got his start in music during the Big Band Era. After playing violin in his father's orchestra, he turned to studio recordings and wrote arrangements for the greatest singers of the time, including Sarah Vaughan, Doris Day, Ella Fitzgerald, and Nat King Cole. That led to a job with Columbia Records and a series of easy-listening recordings under the name "Music by De Vol." He graduated to scoring movies, including the Doris Day hits *Pillow Talk*, *Lover Come Back*, and *Send Me No Flowers*. Then De Vol was assigned a series of sitcoms, including *Family Affair* and *The Brady Bunch*. De Vol's theme to *My Three Sons* became an instant classic and a hit single. De Vol also appeared as an actor in such sitcoms as *I Dream of Jeannie*, *Petticoat Junction*, and *The Jeffersons*. He had a recurring role on *Fernwood 2Nite* and *America 2Nite* as bandleader Happy Kyne.

To get back to our regularly scheduled program, when shows switch networks they usually don't last long—but *My Three Sons* thrived at CBS and lasted until 1972, in spite (or because) of the many changes that were made during its run. William Frawley was replaced by William Demarest, Tim Considine (Mike) quit, Ernie (played by Barry Livingston) came on board to keep the tally at three. Late in the series, Beverly Garland joined the cast as a love interest for Fred MacMurray, accompanied by the nadir of kiddie characters, the utterly tedious Dodie, and it was about time. Up until then, Mike and Robbie were the only ones getting any action.

The show was as comfortable to audiences as Steve Douglas's ubiquitous cardigan sweaters. It was typical of its era's undemanding, wholesome family entertainment—though it was smarter than some shows, and it did have that very catchy theme.

Above: Chip (Stanley Livingston) expresses extreme embarassment. I mean, it's okay to have your older brother play the guitar, and kind of cute to have little Ernie sit in on the bongos, but when Uncle Charley digs out his cello and Good Old Dad starts in on the sax when you're trying to make time with a cutie, it's a real drag.

Below: Playing the "Minuet for Annoying Child Actors," Victoria Meyerlink on the scratchy violin, future Oscar-winner Jodie Foster on the screechy clarinet, and Dawn Lyn as Dodie, obnoxious on any instrument she plays.

CAST

Fred MacMurray	Steve Douglas/Fergus McBain Douglas
Tim Considine	Mike Douglas
Don Grady	Robbie Douglas
Stanley Livingston	Chip Douglas
William Frawley	Michael Francis "Bub" O'Casey
William Demarest	Uncle Charley O'Casey
Meredith MacRae	Sally Ann Morrison Douglas
Barry Livingston	Ernie Thompson Douglas
Tina Cole	Katie Miller Douglas
Dawn Lyn	Dodie Harper Douglas
Beverly Garland	Barbara Harper Douglas
Anne Francis	Terri Dowling
Ronne Troup	Polly Williams Douglas

CHEESECAKE AND BEEFCAKE

TV was one of the last holdouts against blatant sexual content, but female pulchritude has always found its way onto the small screen. In the 1950s, *The Bob Cummings Show* offered a constant parade of gorgeous models, including the bodacious Joi Lansing, the object of many men's impure thoughts. On *The Donna Reed Show* in the late '50s and early '60s, Shelley Fabares represented a more chaste though no less alluring view of femininity.

The 1960s brought us Donna Douglas as Elly May Clampett, who was much more comfortable in blue jeans than in a bikini and who was totally unaware of her sex appeal. Laura Petrie created a furor in her scandalously tight capri pants, and *Gilligan's Island* drew a line in the sand, forever classifying men into two types: Ginger men and Mary Ann men. Barbara Eden gave everything but her navel to help fuel men's master/slave fantasies, while Julie Newmar, in the short-lived *My Living Doll*, took it all one step further, exploring the dark recesses of the tired businessman's inventor/robot fetish.

When Norman Lear, the ERA, and Mary Richards came into power, cheesecake on television took a backseat to more important issues—that is until Suzanne Somers brought "jiggle TV" bouncing back from the dead and suggestiveness reached its pinnacle. In the late 1970s there was enough cleavage in evidence to give new meaning to the term "boob tube." At one point, Somers and the impressively endowed Loni Anderson went toe to toe (well, they would have if they could have gotten that close) for the title of "Miss Décolletage 1979."

After that temporary boom of naughtiness, the 1980s brought about a shift, as *The Cosby Show* and other family sitcoms took hold of the remote. Sexuality moved to prime-time soap operas such as *Dallas* and *Dynasty*, on which Charlene Tilton and Heather Locklear could often be found lounging poolside. It seems that after the explosive, worldwide popularity of *Baywatch*, producers figured out that scantily clad women needed longer than twenty-three minutes to run across a beach in slow motion.

The male form hasn't been exploited on sitcoms as the female has. True, Gary Sandy wore the tightest jeans in Cincinnati, and Max Baer Jr.'s Jethro turned the heads of those who preferred brawn over brains. For teenagers, there was a steady parade of *Tiger Beat* heartthrobs starting with Ricky Nelson, Tony Dow, and two of the three sons, Tim Considine and Don Grady. Later, Barry Williams and Bobby Sherman turned post-pubescent girls' heads, and the reigning king of sitcom idolatry was *The Partridge Family*'s David Cassidy—who, in retrospect, looks the scrawny picture of androgyny. More recently, Kirk Cameron was a fan magazine staple, and *Saved by the Bell*'s Mark Paul Gosselaar and Mario Lopez had just as many fans as Tiffani-Amber Thiessen.

With cable shows such as *Sex & the City* shattering virtually every taboo, television has somehow become more graphic yet less sexy. There was something titillating (there, we said it) about praying that Elly May and Jethro would take a dip in the cee-ment pond, or that we might catch a fleeting glimpse of Barbara Eden's scandalous belly button.

Above: *Saved By the Bell*'s Mark-Paul Gosselaar and Mario Lopez, were evidently hitting the gym when they should have been hitting the books.

Below: Tropical dish Tina Louise, as "The Movie Star" Ginger Grant, one of the sexiest of the merry castaways of *Gilligan's Island*.

THE NANNY

 | 1993–1999 | 146 episodes

Like Mary Poppins in a miniskirt, Fran Fine becomes a "Noo Yawk" nanny to the three Sheffield children and turns their world topsy-turvy, skipping the spoonful of sugar and going right for the lip gloss and, in the process, falling for their widowed father, the handsome but square "Mistuh Sheffield."

Marriage-hungry women have been part of sitcoms from day one. Connie Brooks and Susie McNamara always hoped to nab a man, and *The Dick Van Dyke Show*'s Sally Rogers went so far as to make an appeal for a husband while a guest on a talk show (after all, as cohort Buddy Sorrell once told her, "Don't wait too long, Sal…I had an aunt who waited so long for her ship to come in that her pier collapsed."). Mary Richards, the epitome of the working woman, seemed content to remain single, but her best friend, Rhoda Morgenstern, was definitely on the prowl. But the most voracious husband-hunter on sitcoms, without a doubt, was *The Nanny*'s Fran Fine, played by Fran Drescher. The character was as close to Drescher's own comic persona as could

The Nanny's Fran Drescher, Charles Shaughnessey, Lauren Lane, and Daniel Davis made up two of the unlikeliest sitcom couples ever.

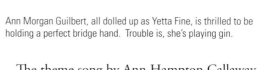
Ann Morgan Guilbert, all dolled up as Yetta Fine, is thrilled to be holding a perfect bridge hand. Trouble is, she's playing gin.

The theme song by Ann Hampton Callaway told the whole story, just as the title sequences to *The Brady Bunch*, *Gilligan's Island*, *Green Acres*, and *The Beverly Hillbillies* had done: Fran Fine, bridal consultant, gets dumped by her boyfriend, comes into Manhattan, and somehow ends up selling cosmetics at the East Side townhouse of Broadway producer Maxwell Sheffield. She charms her way into the job of nanny to his three children and sets her cap for the handsome widower.

Bringing street smarts into the stuffy family, Fran won over both the children and the adults of the Sheffield household (save for her nemesis, "C. C." Babcock, Maxwell's producing partner who also carried a major torch for the dashing Sheffield). Maxwell, played by the handsome Charles Shaughnessy with a dry wit that hadn't revealed itself during his long stint on *Days of Our Lives*, certainly had eyes for Nanny Fine, but, true to his veddy British roots, was unable to address it for four seasons, always referring to her as "Miss Fine." Our Fran was nothing if not patient, and by the end of the fifth season she hooked her hubby and soon gave birth to a pair of twins.

Although a typical sitcom on many levels, *The Nanny* was one of the few shows that wore its Judaism on its sleeve. This places it in a select group that

be, though in real life she was married to her high school sweetheart, Peter Marc Jacobson. The creators mined Drescher's sensibilities, manufactured though they might have been, and hung the entire series on the character.

Created by husband-and-wife team Rob Sternin and Prudence Fraser, who had previously been writer-producers on *Who's the Boss?* as well as several unsuccessful but promising sitcoms including *The Charmings* (a fairy-tale spoof that was both wickedly funny and unfairly dismissed) and *Oh, Madeline!* (starring the genius comedienne Madeline Kahn), the team hit pay dirt when they teamed up with Drescher, who had the germ of an idea about the clash of classes. After vacationing with good friend Twiggy, the 1960s fashion icon who had costarred with Drescher on the short-lived 1992 sitcom *Princesses*, the smart-as-a-whip Drescher saw comic gold in the dichotomy between the Brit and the Queen of Queens, New York.

Ann Morgan Guilbert

The wonderful comic actress Ann Guilbert has proven that a character type beats an ingenue any day when it comes to career longevity. Starting out in the comic ensemble of *The Billy Barnes Revue* (alongside other up-and-coming actors Ken Berry, Bert Convy, Joyce Jameson, and Len Weinrib), Guilbert first came to prominence on television as Millie Helper on *The Dick Van Dyke Show*, where, alongside onscreen husband Jerry Paris, she became the funniest, most lovable, and least annoying neighbor since Fred and Ethel Mertz. What's more, Guilbert and Paris even liked each other off-screen. Along with guest shots on such shows as *The Andy Griffith Show*, *The Partridge Family*, *Maude*, *Barney Miller* and *Newhart*, Guilbert was a regular on *The New Andy Griffith Show* and *The Fanelli Boys*, and had recurring roles on such shows as *Picket Fences* and *Seinfeld*. Without a doubt, Guilbert's second coming was as Grandma Yetta Rosenberg on *The Nanny*, paralyzing viewers with her blind, borderline-senile, chain-smoking, blue-haired old lady. Now in the prime of her worth as a character actress, Guilbert has recently returned to the New York stage after an absence of forty years, her sense of timing firmly intact.

Sylvia Fine: Trust me, there is only one man who can satisfy a woman in two minutes—Colonel Sanders.

includes *The Goldbergs*, *Bridget Loves Bernie*, *Rhoda*, *Seinfeld*, and *Will & Grace*. Of course, some of the Jewish characters on those shows were just playing a part (Valerie Harper is a nice Italian girl), but Fran was no shiksa, and many of the members of the fictional Fine family were named after Drescher's real-life relatives. Her real parents, Sylvia and Morty, actually appeared on the show as Aunt Rose and Uncle Stanley, and other family members were played by such brilliant character actors as Lainie Kazan, Marilyn Cooper, and Steve Lawrence, who, in the show's last season, finally gave a face to the unseen patriarch of the Fine family.

While certainly full of its share of setups and punch lines (particularly in the acid-laced zingers that Daniel Davis's butler, Niles, flung at Lauren Lane's socialite "C. C." Babcock, with whom he inevitably ended up by the end of the series), the humor of *The Nanny* was character-based, with running gags coming out of Nanny Fine's coyness about her age, mother Sylvia's voracious appetite, the comic senility of Grandma Yetta, and Mr. Sheffield's constant competition with Andrew Lloyd Webber (of all people!). The familiarity that audiences had with the lovable eccentrics, both Jewish and WASPy, turned *The Nanny* into a melting pot of quirky comedy.

A visit from mother, played like buttah by Renee Taylor, never failed to give Fran shpilkes in her genecktegessoink.

OFF THE SET

ON ONE EPISODE of *The Nanny*, Fran Drescher guest-starred as a character named Bobbi Flekman, the same name as the character she'd played in the movie *This Is Spinal Tap*.

WHEN *THE NANNY* was broadcast in Great Britain, many viewers wrote in to criticize actor Charles Shaughnessy's fake English accent, suggesting he study with actor Daniel Davis to hear what a true Brit sounds like. Shaughnessy was born and raised in England; Daniel Davis is an American, born and raised in Arkansas.

MANY, MANY CELEBRITIES did cameos on the show, including such disparate notables as Elton John, Carol Channing, Eydie Gorme, Bob Barker, Hugh Grant, David Letterman, Bette Midler, Monica Seles, Bryant Gumbel, Marvin Hamlisch, Eartha Kitt, Elizabeth Taylor, Donald Trump, Burt Bacharach, Patti LaBelle, Roger Clinton, Dr. Joyce Brothers, Celine Dion, Whoopi Goldberg, and, most famously, puppeteer Shari Lewis, in the episode where the Sheffields' dog tears apart the legendary sock puppet Lambchop. The one star that never appeared was the one most coveted by Fran Fine: the one and only Barbra Streisand. They had to settle for an appearance by Streisand's half-sister, Roslyn Kind.

CAST

Fran Drescher	Fran Fine Sheffield
Charles Shaughnessy	Maxwell Sheffield
Daniel Davis	Niles
Lauren Lane	Chastity Claire "C. C." Babcock
Nicholle Tom	Maggie Sheffield
Benjamin Salisbury	Brighton Sheffield
Madeline Zima	Grace Sheffield
Renèe Taylor	Sylvia Rosenberg Fine
Rachel Chagall	Val Troiello
Ann Morgan Guilbert	Yetta Rosenberg
Lainie Kazan	Aunt Frieda
Mort Drescher	Uncle Stanley
Sylvia Drescher	Aunt Rose

NEWHART

 | **1982–1990** | **184 episodes**

An author and his sweater-clad wife escape the insanity of New York City, hoping to find peace and quiet by buying an inn in Vermont. Out of the frying pan and into the fire, they find the local scene more colorful than anything they had experienced in the Big Apple.

Newhart, which had a very successful eight-year run on CBS, was a show that, despite its deftly drawn supporting performances, and its sharp-as-a-tack writing, solidified its place in sitcom history for one reason above all others: its final episode, which raised the bar so high in its final three minutes that it joined the pantheon of the greatest sitcoms of all time.

Revolving around an author of do-it-yourself books named Dick Loudon, the show started out very differently than it ended up, with the professional stammerer Newhart, Mary Frann as the angora-swathed wife Joanna, and Tom Poston as the dimwitted handyman, George Utley, the only constants over its entire eight years. The first season, shot on videotape, also featured actress Jennifer Holmes as the rich, shallow skier Leslie Vanderkellen and Steven Kampmann as pathological liar Kirk Devane.

The show exhibited promise but was misfiring in some respects. By season two, the show was filmed rather than taped, giving it a glossier look that helped it fit in better with the CBS sitcom lineup. Holmes was replaced by the delicious Julia Duffy as Leslie's even more spoiled cousin Stephanie. Also now a regular presence were three backwoods brothers, seemingly right out of the movie *Deliverance*, named Larry, Darryl, and Darryl, two of whom (the Darryls) never spoke a word until the final episode of the series.

Longtime friends Tom Poston (who had made periodic appearances on Newhart's first sitcom as Bob Hartley's college friend, "The Peeper") and Bob Newhart. Their comic rhythms perfectly complemented each other.

Kampmann's character finally ran out of steam after the second season. In retrospect, a pathological liar is a bad idea for a character, as the audience can become extremely impatient with someone they are unable to invest any faith in. Replacing him was the wonderful Peter Scolari, as stuffy, alliterative yuppie Michael Harris. Michael found a kindred spirit in the depths of Stephanie's shallowness, and their enduring courtship provided many of the biggest laughs on the series.

The show, which started out dealing with the guests of the inn, became more and more about the colorful locals, and Newhart's ever-increasing frustration with their eccentricities. After nearly eight years of wacky goings-on, *Newhart* was ready to go out on top. But not without a proper sendoff—with a twist dreamed up by, of all people, Newhart's wife Ginny (with a nod to *Dallas*). In the final episode, directed by Newhart's great friend and former *Laugh-In* host Dick Martin, the entire town is bought by a Japanese developer to be turned into a sprawling golf resort. The lone holdouts are Dick and Joanna. Fast forward five years and the now-wealthy townspeople are returning to stay at the Stratford Inn, still run by a now- apoplectic Dick Loudon, whose walls are constantly being pelted by golf balls. The show's regulars are more insane than ever (even the formerly steadfast Joanna is wearing a kimono and acting like a geisha), and the episode builds to a fren-

Julia Duffy

The deft and delightful comedienne Julia Duffy has been far too scarce of late. One of the original finalists for the role of Diane Chambers on *Cheers*, she was soon after rewarded with the role of the spoiled-rotten Stephanie Vanderkellen, cut off by her wealthy parents and forced to work as a maid at the Stratford Inn on *Newhart*. Nominated for an Emmy for her terrific work on the show seven years in a row, she went home empty handed every year. After *Newhart* went off the air, she suffered a fast flop with *Baby Talk*, a sitcom loosely based on the hit movie *Look Who's Talking*. The next year, she came in to fill the spot vacated by Delta Burke on *Designing Women*, as the Sugarbakers' spoiled-rotten cousin Allison—but unfortunately, for all of her gifts, Duffy didn't mesh with the mood or tempo of the show, her Yankee delivery at odds with the more leisurely paced world of an Atlanta design firm. Indeed, her character seemed a pale retread of the one she had played on *Newhart*. Another short-lived series, *The Mommies*, followed, and since then, Duffy has been woefully underused, given her expert timing, with only a few recurring roles on such shows as *Reba* and *Drake & Josh*.

zied finale with Dick screaming, "You people are ALL CRAZY!!!" and promptly getting hit on the head with an errant golf ball. The screen goes to black.

Cut to a lamp switching on in a bedroom in a Chicago high-rise, a room not seen in fourteen years. Bob wakes up next to actress Suzanne Pleshette, who had played his wife on the previous Newhart show, *The Bob Newhart Show*. Bob says he's had a terrible dream about running an inn in Vermont and—poof—à la *The Wizard of Oz*, the entire eight-year run of *Newhart* is dismissed. It was a sitcom first: an entire series reduced to the indigestion-induced hallucinations of one of the most beloved sitcom characters of all time. It was a brilliant stroke, drawing strands of television history together in a way that was at once shocking and hilarious.

Larry: I'm Larry. This is my brother Darryl. This is my other brother Darryl.

CAST

Bob Newhart	Dick Loudon
Mary Frann	Joanna Loudon
Tom Poston	George Utley
Steven Kampmann	Kirk Devane
Jennifer Holmes	Leslie Vanderkellen
Julia Duffy	Stephanie Vanderkellen
Peter Scolari	Michael Harris
William Sanderson	Larry
John Voldstad	Darryl
Tony Papenfuss	The Other Darryl

Opposite top: Newhart and the delightful Mary Frann, of the wide eyes and the fuzzy sweaters.

Opposite bottom: Julia Duffy, maid to order.

Below: Newhart and the legendary comic trio of Sanderson, Papenfuss, and Volstad.

NEWSRADIO

NBC | 1995–1999 | 97 episodes

Life at WNYX radio is delightfully unpredictable, thanks to a varied crew of workaholic kooks held together by mild-mannered boss Dave and the egocentric newscaster Bill McNeal.

straight man surrounded by kooks, that central character—Dave—became unhinged as the seasons wore on. Who can blame him, with the utterly zany goings-on around him?

The show also departed from other series when suddenly, in season five, Lisa up and married Johnny Johnson (played by Patrick Warburton as a variation on the character he played on *Seinfeld* and everywhere else). What about Dave? Didn't the writers know that by the last episode, the star-crossed co-workers must get together? It wasn't to be for Dave and Lisa, despite their discussions of whether to have kids after the marriage that even they assumed was a given.

Overshadowing that, and, frankly, everything that had come before it, was the murder

The sitcom gods have decreed that you, the viewer, can spend time with your favorite characters either at work or at home, but seldom both. There have been notable exceptions: *The Dick Van Dyke Show*, *My Little Margie*, *Mary Tyler Moore*, and *Frasier*, which featured characters both on the job and at home.

NewsRadio took place almost entirely in the workplace, and few personal matters entered the hermetic world of the studio. The writers stubbornly rejected the entreaties of NBC execs to create large story arcs, so most episodes were stand-alones. And the show was different from its sitcom brethren for another reason, as well: though it followed the familiar formula of the

of actor Phil Hartman (who played newscaster Bill McNeal) during the summer hiatus between seasons four and five. Hartman's death created a dilemma for the writers and producers. Should they replace the actor, eliminate the character, or just shut down the series? When *Petticoat Junction* lost Bea Benaderet, she was replaced by an entirely new character played by June Lockhart. When John Ritter died suddenly during *8 Simple Rules for Dating My Teenage Daughter*, the death was made a part of the plot and two new characters were added. Neither of those shows managed to recover. The one example of a show that thrived after the death of a beloved character was *Cheers*, where Woody Harrelson replaced the late Nicholas Colasanto and the series hardly skipped a beat. On *NewsRadio*, as on *Cheers* and *8 Simple*

CAST

Dave Foley	Dave Nelson
Maura Tierney	Lisa Miller
Phil Hartman	Bill McNeal
Khandi Alexander	Catherine Duke
Andy Dick	Matthew Brock
Joe Rogan	Joe Garelli
Vicki Lewis	Beth
Stephen Root	Jimmy James
John Lovitz	Max
Patrick Warburton	Johnny Johnson

Right: Dave Foley and the greatly missed Phil Hartman, whose performance as Bill McNeal fueled *NewsRadio*.

Below: Foley and Andy Dick, in what, for him, would be considered a subdued moment.

Opposite: The staff of station WNYX: Secretary Vicki Lewis…wait, I mean Kathy Griffin…no, I mean Vicki Lewis; co-anchor Khandi Alexander (not to be confused with a non-alcoholic drink); supervising producer Maura Tierney; news director Dave Foley, later host of *Celebrity Poker Showdown*; and hunky electrician Joe Rogan, later host of the creepy-crawly-eating reality show, *Fear Factor*.

Phil Hartman

His characters could be snarky and snide, but Phil Hartman embued them all with hearts of gold, which somehow made them hilarious. Hartman first came to prominence as a seven-year regular on *Saturday Night Live*, playing a wide variety of self-indulgent politicians, pop stars, and other smarmy characters. His expressive voice made him a natural for cartoons and his talents graced (if that's the word) *Scooby-Doo* and *Scrappy-Doo*, *Smurfs*, *Dennis the Menace*, and most important, *The Simpsons*, on which he triumphed as the ultimate insincere movie star, Troy McClure. He was featured on *Pee Wee's Playhouse* and co-wrote the film *Pee Wee's Big Adventure*. Hartman didn't fare as well in film, making appearances in such forgettables as *Fletch Lives*, *How I Got Into College*, and *Quick Change*. His energy and the way he managed to walk the line between totally obnoxious and sweetly sympathetic made him one of television's best-loved performers—and a prototype for such bigger stars as Jim Carrey and Will Farrell.

Rules, the writers decided to acknowledge the death. The first episode of the fifth season took place at Bill's funeral and was played for maximum poignancy.

Though the writing of the fifth season was up to the series's usual excellence, Hartman's death created a hole in the ensemble, and each week that empty news booth smack in the center of the office reminded the audience what they were missing. The show never made it back for season six.

It had never been a ratings favorite anyway, and had been bounced around the NBC schedule no fewer than eleven times. But *NewsRadio* attracted its own cult following and has done extremely well in reruns and syndication.

OFF THE SET

ONLY DAVE FOLEY, Stephen Root, and Andy Dick managed to appear in every episode of the series.

IRONICALLY, THE WRITERS included a number of fantasy sequences in which Bill McNeil died shortly before Hartman was actually killed.

EPISODE TITLES WERE random and bore no relation to the actual plots. The name of every Led Zeppelin album but one was used as an episode title.

THE ODD COUPLE

abc | **1970–1975** | **114 episodes**

Neatnik Felix Unger gets handed his walking papers (as well as his favorite frying pan) by his wife, Gloria. After aimlessly wandering the streets of New York, he surprises his old friend, the terminally sloppy sportswriter Oscar Madison, and the two mismatched roomies try to maintain their personal space along with their sanity.

Hit television shows based on movies are rare (*M*A*S*H* and *Alice* are among the few), but sitcoms based on original Broadway plays are even rarer. (*Mama*, based on *I Remember Mama*, and *Life with Father* were two exceptions.) *The Odd Couple*, based on Neil Simon's hit play (and later hit movie), was one of the standouts.

The show was never a ratings blockbuster; in fact, it was canceled at the end of every season of its run. But the show has thrived in syndication, where people have discovered its excellence, comparable to, yet subtly different from, the wildly successful play and movie upon which it was based. On a sitcom, actors have the chance (and the challenge) to build a character over a season, or, if they're lucky, six or seven seasons. Carroll O'Connor's Archie Bunker, Mary Tyler Moore's Mary Richards, and Ted Danson's Sam Malone all grew exponentially during the runs of their shows. Tony Randall and Jack Klugman made Felix and Oscar, the best roles of their careers, live, breathe, and grow week by week.

Randall possessed the ability to act (and react) with absolute, natural truth. Listening intently to Klugman, Randall would start to shake his head halfway through one of Oscar's speeches, so ingrained in his role of fussbudget that he knew exactly what Oscar's angle was going to be and was already preparing the perfect Felixesque response. Klugman expertly tossed off smart-ass retorts that only

Tony Randall and Jack Klugman just seconds before the inevitable "electrical tape tear-off," a physical comedy bit dating back to Aristophanes.

Above: Although *The Odd Couple* concentrated on laughs, it included many poignant moments dealing with the sadness that two middle-aged divorced men feel.

Right: Randall and Allyn Ann McLerie in Randall's *Odd Couple* follow-up, *The Tony Randall Show*.

Tony Randall

Born Arthur Leonard Rosenberg in Tulsa, Oklahoma, the marvelously eccentric Tony Randall came to New York and worked in the Broadway theater before his big break as gym teacher Harvey Weskitt on the Wally Cox sitcom *Mr. Peepers*. Moving into film, he became an archetype in the Doris Day/Rock Hudson romantic comedies as Hudson's best friend who invariably lost the girl. Perfectly cast as a fussy, fastidious micromanager, he returned to television in his trademark role on *The Odd Couple*. The season after Felix and Oscar were canceled, Randall came back as Philadelphia judge Walter Franklin on *The Tony Randall Show*, and while the series showed enormous potential, it was doomed by the good ole "time slot shuffle." After playing a middle-aged homosexual in the well-received television film *Sidney Shorr*, Randall gave series TV a final try in the groundbreaking *Love, Sidney*, based on the film. It ran for two seasons, but when the powers that be at NBC made the show's producers soft pedal his character's sexuality to the point that it wasn't even discussed, Randall became disenchanted with the show. With a perfect personality for talk shows, he often appeared on *The Tonight Show*, singing novelty songs from the 1930s and dressing down Johnny Carson for his chain-smoking. (A former smoker himself, Randall became a most militant antismoker.) One of his greatest contributions was founding the National Actors Theater in New York, a permanent company dedicated to presenting great classic dramas.

gifted comedians can make seem off the cuff, acting as the rumpled voice of reason to counteract Randall's flights of anal-retentive fancy.

With great support from Al Molinaro as New York's finest, Murray Greshler, and co-creator Garry Marshall's sister Penny (in no way an example of nepotism, for she was perfectly cast and hilarious) as Oscar's gal Friday, Myrna Turner, the show rolled along like a Broadway comedy with a different plot every week. *The Odd Couple* was always blessed with the best talent sitcoms had to offer, showcasing such actors as John Fiedler; Richard Stahl (who played a creepy minister better than anyone outside of a Stephen King novel); Ned Glass and Phil Leeds as various character types; Janis Hansen as Felix's beloved ex, Gloria; and Brett Somers (then Mrs. Klugman) as Oscar's ex, Blanche.

In its first season the show was much closer to the movie, featuring Oscar's poker buddies Murray, Speed, and Vinnie (only Murray stayed on as a regular presence), and upstairs neighbors the Pigeon Sisters (Carole Shelley and Monica Evans, recreating their delightfully dotty roles from both the movie and the play). As Garry Marshall crafted the kind of comic dichotomy that he further developed with Laverne DeFazio and Shirley Feeney, the yin and yang bottle cappers of *Laverne and Shirley*, he and co-creator Jerry Belson, partners since *The Dick Van Dyke Show*, began to make refinements. In the same way that Marshall's other project, *Happy Days*, was energized by the shift from film to videotape, *The Odd Couple* was invigorated by several changes after its first season; production switched from a single camera with a laugh track to a three-camera operation in front of a studio audience.

Felix: What do you dream about?
Oscar: Living alone.

The immediacy of a live response to Randall and Klugman made all the difference, and the show became a tightly produced twenty-four-minute weekly Broadway play: Oscar and Felix get arrested for scalping tickets to a Broadway musical (titled *Kiss My Nose*; Felix represents himself in court and deconstructs the word "assume" in a moment of legendary hilarity); Oscar and Felix appear on the game show *Password* (Felix gives the clue "Aristophanes" for the word "bird"); Felix writes a song for chanteuse Jaye P. Morgan called "Happy, and Peppy, and Bursting with Love;" Felix holds a séance to exorcise the poltergeist that he's

certain is living in the air conditioner. The plots all trod the same basic territory of the Prude vs. the Slob, but with enough originality—thanks to the sharp writing—that the show stayed fresh.

One less-than-stellar aspect of *The Odd Couple* was its increasing reliance on celebrity guest stars, a pitfall that shows like *Here's Lucy* and, more recently, *Murphy Brown* ultimately fell into as well. Having Oscar the sportswriter interact with Howard Cosell, Deacon Jones, and the battling tennis duo of Billie Jean King and Bobby Riggs was plausible; and with Felix's rabid interest in high culture, Marilyn Horne and Edward Villella were

Jerry Belson

Writer, director, and producer Jerry Belson's Hollywood career began right after high school, working as a magician and drummer. Starting his writing career with comic books, he teamed up with Garry Marshall to write for television, selling a script to *Make Room for Daddy* by the time he was 22. After becoming regular writers on *The Dick Van Dyke Show*, *Gomer Pyle, U.S.M.C.*, and *Hey, Landlord!*, Belson and Marshall developed *The Odd Couple* for the small screen in 1970, writing and directing many of the show's episodes. After a detour from television, writing the screenplays for the films *Smile*, *The End*, *Fun with Dick and Jane*, and an uncredited rewrite of *Close Encounters of the Third Kind*, Belson returned to television to produce *The Tracey Ullman Show* and *The Drew Carey Show*.

Jack Klugman (here, in his finest Oscar drag) went directly from playing slob extraordinaire Oscar Madison to another long-running hit as a nosy coroner on *Quincy.* ("It wasn't a reaction to a bee sting…it was MURDER!")

naturals—but when Rodney Allen Rippy, Paul Williams, Dick Clark, and Rona Barrett came out of the woodwork, the show started moving into the territory of "Lucy Carter gets stuck on a ski lift with Dinah Shore."

Randall and Klugman were deeply involved in the creative process of the show, adding new traits to their characters based on their own lives and interests. (Randall made Felix an opera buff; Klugman made Oscar a racing aficionado). Improvising dialogue on occasion, as Lucille Ball and Vivian Vance had done, the pair sometimes turned to a page in their scripts that read, simply, "Jack teaches Tony how to play football," allowing Klugman and Randall to make their own kind of comic magic. Together Marshall and Belson, main director Jerry Paris, Randall, Klugman, and, at the top of the family tree, Neil Simon, made the odd couple of Unger and Madison two of the funniest, most realistically detailed characters ever to grace the small screen.

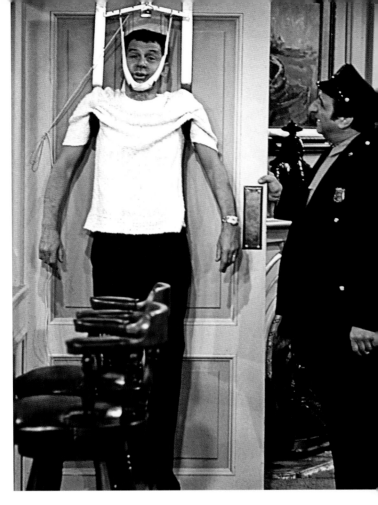

Right: Traction is Funny, Part 3: Al Molinaro, as Murray the cop, visits the alignment-challenged Felix.

Garry Marshall

A sitcom Renaissance man, Garry Marshall has done it all (and successfully, too): writing, directing, producing, and acting. Starting as joke writer for Joey Bishop and Phil Foster (who Marshall would hire to play Frank DeFazio twenty years later), Marshall moved to Hollywood and teamed up with Jerry Belson to write some the funniest episodes of *The Dick Van Dyke Show*, *Make Room for Daddy*, and *The Lucy Show*. After adapting *The Odd Couple* for the small screen, Marshall struck out on his own, creating three smash hits for ABC: *Happy Days*, *Laverne and Shirley*, and *Mork & Mindy* (as well as the misfires *Me and the Chimp*, *Who's Watching the Kids?* and *Blansky's Beauties*). He directed such hit films as *The Flamingo Kid*, *Beaches*, *Pretty Woman*, and *The Princess Diaries*. Good natured and beloved by all he works with, Marshall is such a great character type (and a true character in real life) that he has taken on more and more acting, most memorably playing a recurring role as network head Stan Lansing on *Murphy Brown* and providing the voice of Buck Cluck in the animated movie *Chicken Little*.

CAST

Tony Randall	Felix Unger
Jack Klugman	Oscar Madison
Al Molinaro	Murray Greshler
Penny Marshall	Myrna Turner
Janis Hansen	Gloria Unger
Brett Somers	Blanche Madison
Larry Gelman	Vinnie
Garry Walberg	Speed
Joan Hotchkis	Nancy Cunningham
Elinor Donahue	Miriam Welby
Pamelyn Ferdin	Edna Unger #1
Doney Oatman	Edna Unger #2
Andy Rubin	Monroe Hernández
Monica Evans	Cecily Pigeon
Carole Shelley	Gwendolyn Pigeon
Ryan McDonald	Roy

ONE DAY AT A TIME

1975-1984 | 209 episodes

Ann Romano divorces her husband and moves to Indianapolis with her two daughters, who suffer all the woes expected of sitcom teenagers. Constant advice, whether solicited or not, comes from the building's superintendent and perpetual drop-in, Schneider.

One Day at a Time was a groundbreaker in that it offered the first truly realistic portrayal of a divorced woman, played by Bonnie Franklin, on a successful sitcom. (Vivian Bagley on *The Lucy Show* had been the first.) The show was created by actress Whitney Blake, best known as Mrs. B. on *Hazel*, and her husband at the time, Allan Manings, and was developed by the legendary Norman Lear. The show was a favorite among teenagers in the late 1970s, who identified with the struggles and sibling rivalry of the daughters, and was recognized by women's groups as promoting positive feminist views. In retrospect, the show can be seen as a textbook example of the highs and lows of television stardom, with Mackenzie Phillips, who played eldest daughter Julie, fighting a very public battle with drugs during the series's run, twice being fired for her erratic behavior. At the same time, Valerie Bertinelli, as the levelheaded younger sister Barbara, became America's sweetheart and a full-fledged TV star.

Not surprisingly for a Norman Lear production, the show was one of the "message sitcoms" of the 1970s and early '80s, with many well-written two- (and four-) part episodes dealing with subjects such as suicide, alcoholism, and teenage sexuality. Other stories dealt with sexual politics, particularly in relation to Ann's career in advertising. In one episode, Ann convinced an attractive male assistant to work late. In a bold move, Ms. Romano, the heroine of our show, made a pass at him. To be sure, she was a modern woman, and Ann's sex life was not coyly hinted

at, as was Mary Richards's use of birth control. Ann went all the way, and not just with long-term boyfriends. Interestingly, it was with Bertinelli's character that Lear took a more chaste stance: Barbara remained a virgin until her wedding night.

Viewing episodes of *One Day at a Time* through modern eyes, Franklin's high-strung performance has failed to withstand the test of time perhaps more than any other sitcom character. While

Right: Bonnie Franklin, about to embark on one of her famous lectures to "Barbara, Barbara, Barbara…"

Bottom: Barney Martin, Matthew Perry, Craig Bierko, Valerie Bertinelli, and Daniel Baldwin in the short-lived *Sydney*.

she came off as a plucky, hip divorcée while the show was in its original run, Ann now registers as one of the most annoying television characters ever. Just what is it about her character that is like fingernails on a blackboard? Is it her catchphrase, a drawn out "Ohhhhhh. Myyyyyyyy. Gooooooodddddd"? Her twenty-minute monologue in the episode "Ann's Crisis," delivered into her bedroom mirror on her thirty-sixth birthday while she keeps an apartment full of guests waiting? The fact that she can't answer the door to the apartment, even from three feet away, without flipping her hair, clenching her fists, and breaking into a full run? But it's far too easy to lay the blame at the feet of Bonnie Franklin. There's something about the character itself that grates: her false bravado as she tries to stand up to injustice in a sexist world; her wry, sly way of seeming judgmental yet lascivious at the same time; her constant braless fashion parade of velour tops and cowl-necked sweaters…

well, it's everything.

Nevertheless, the show was a hit, and considering it went through more major plot twists than a Tolstoy novel, it remained a cornerstone of CBS's dominant Sunday-night schedule through the early 1980s. Many supporting characters came and went over *One Day at a Time*'s long run,

played by such talented actors as Richard Masur, Shelley Fabares, Nanette Fabray, Ron Rifkin, Mary Louise Wilson, Howard Hesseman, Boyd Gaines, and Michael Lembeck. In an especially cruel twist of plot straight out of *Chinatown*, by the series's end Ann Romano had become Barbara's mother-in-law as well as her mother.

Valerie Bertinelli

With an infectious smile and forever sunny disposition, Valerie Bertinelli is one of those actors whose likeability made her an instant television star. Moving with her family to Southern California after her father (an executive at General Motors) was transferred there, the young teenager enrolled in acting classes and began modeling. She had a perfect look for television and was cast as the level-headed, precocious kid sister Barbara on *One Day at a Time*, becoming one of the most popular actresses of her

era. With a huge career in made-for-TV movies and miniseries, she returned in two short-lived sitcoms, *Sydney* in 1990, with future star Matthew Perry as her younger brother, and *Café Americain* in 1993.

Her latest job was as a cast member of *Touched by an Angel* for its final two seasons, returning to CBS Sunday night lineup where *One Day at a Time* had been a staple for so many years. She provided tabloid fodder when she married rock star Eddie Van Halen. After twenty-four years of marriage and a child, they divorced in 2005.

After nine seasons, and three, count 'em, three episodes where the cast performed a variety show at a retirement home (Valerie Bertinelli thoroughly bewildered the oldsters with her infamous Elton John impersonation), the show had definitely run its course. Ann, newly married and sending a decidedly mixed message to viewers who looked up to her as a paragon of female independence, moved to London with her new husband while Schneider moved to Florida to care for his orphaned niece and nephew, the setup for a spin-off that never materialized.

Criticism may seem like hitting below the belt for any show that ran for nine seasons, and had noble intentions and legions of loyal fans. But on its 2006 reunion special, cast members themselves admitted that, looking back, *One Day at a Time* was one of those shows that, no matter how well-written and performed certain episodes were, fairly begs to be viewed with a cynical eye. Like *Family Ties*, *The Facts of Life*, and *Diff'rent Strokes*, it arose at the height of the sitcom's issue-oriented phase, providing an easy target with its ubiquitous and determinedly earnest "Very Special Episodes."

Pat Harrington, Jr.

The versatile comedian Pat Harrington, Jr. was born into a show business family, the son of a vaudevillian. After serving in Korea, he took a job at NBC while pursuing acting work. He finally got his break as part of Steve Allen's regular roster of comedians (which also included sitcom legends Don Knotts and Tom Poston), doing the "man on the street" interview sketches. His popular *Steve Allen* character, Italian immigrant Guido Panzini, also became a regular on *The Jack Paar Show*. Terrific with accents and an excellent mimic, Harrington was the voice of the animated Inspector Clouseau for much of the 1960s. Guest starring on most of the successful sitcoms of the 1960s and a regular on the 1969 flop *Mr. Deeds Goes to Town*, he will forever be remembered as the irritating yet lovable Dwayne Schneider on *One Day at a Time*, for which he won an Emmy Award in 1984.

CAST

Bonnie Franklin	Ann Romano Royer
Mackenzie Phillips	Julie Cooper Horvath
Valerie Bertinelli	Barbara Cooper Royer
Pat Harrington, Jr.	Dwayne Schneider
Richard Masur	David Kane
Mary Louise Wilson	Ginny Wrobliki
Shelley Fabares	Francine Webster
Michael Lembeck	Max Horvath
Ron Rifkin	Nick Handris
Glenn Scarpelli	Alex Handris
Boyd Gaines	Mark Royer
Howard Hesseman	Sam Royer
Joseph Campanella	Ed Cooper
Nanette Fabray	Katherine Romano

Left: Mackenzie Phillips asks herself the age-old question, "How many Schneiders does it take to screw in a lightbulb?"

OUR MISS BROOKS

● | 1952–1956 | 154 episodes

English instructor Connie Brooks (she of the dry wit) has the hots for a fellow educator at Madison High School, biology teacher Philip Boynton (he of the dim wit). Miss Brooks rents a room from Mrs. Davis (she of equal parts sugar and spice), cops a ride with Walter Denton (he of enthusiastic naïveté), and tries to keep out of the way of the school principal, Osgood Conklin (he of the short fuse).

When TV joined the entertainment firmament, the nascent networks needed product, and fast. They turned to Broadway, appropriating the revue format for variety shows, and turned to radio as a quick source of already established comedies and dramas. Sometimes, as in the case of *The Shadow*, transfer to the new medium proved impossible—the ability to cloud men's minds and become invisible was hard to dramatize visually. Other shows, such as *Gunsmoke*, required recasting—William Conrad's avoirdupois couldn't be overlooked on TV, though he continued to play the part of Marshall Matt Dillon on radio until 1961. Some radio shows, however, made the transition practically intact.

Our Miss Brooks, which started on radio in 1948, was one of them. In addition to Eve Arden, kept on board were Richard Crenna (who came across much younger when you couldn't actually see him) as Walter Denton, Leonard Smith as Stretch Snodgrass, Gale Gordon as Mr. Conklin, and Jane Morgan as Mrs. Davis. The original Mr. Boynton, Ira Grossel, went instead to his own television show, *Cochise*, and then to the big screen, changing his name to Jeff Chandler along the way. He was replaced on *Our Miss Brooks* by Robert Rockwell. (Chandler continued as Mr. Boynton on radio, still billed as Ira Grossel.)

Improving sentences – Developing style. In your own words tell how;
(a) Unity may be se
(b) Is most commonly
(c) Coherence may be s
(d) Is most commonly
(e) Emphasis may
(f) Is most commonly
(g) Define six
your sentence

The incomparable Eve Arden as sharp tongued, smartly dressed Connie Brooks, television's first career woman.

Like the aforementioned *Gunsmoke*, *Our Miss Brooks* existed on radio and television concurrently. Scripts were sometimes used for both versions, but often they differed. Amazingly, the radio *Our Miss Brooks*, which finally signed off for good in 1957, outlasted the television version by a year. The long run on two mediums (and one more to come later) is clear evidence of the great fondness the American public had for this kindly series. Were the jokes knee-slappers? No. Were the plots inspired? Again, no. What made the show so popular was its warmth and the perfect delineation of its characters, especially as performed by its crackerjack ensemble. Eve Arden's wisecracking masked her character's insecurities and, unlike the leads in many series who were fairly normal while the zanies orbited around them, Miss Brooks had her faults like everyone else. The energy came from the over-the-top, explosive bluster of Gale Gordon, who parlayed his basso bleat of "Miss Brooks!" into a well-honed career. Who can ever forget that same voice bellowing out "Mrs. Carmichael!" or "Mrs. Carter!" at Lucille Ball?

When the series started to wane in the ratings, an odd thing happened. All of a sudden, Madison High was torn down and Miss Brooks transferred to Mrs. Nestor's Private Elementary School. And who was the principal? None other than Osgood Conklin. Mrs. Davis was still around, too, though Walter Denton and Stretch Snodgrass had matriculated and Mr. Boynton—most missed of all—had disappeared. This time the proverbial shoe was on the other foot and Miss Brooks was being pursued by the phys ed teacher, Mr. Talbot, played by Gene Barry. It was a step up, romantically speaking—but not

to the audience. By the end of this, the last television season for *Our Miss Brooks*, Mr. Boynton had made a return visit but Miss Brooks never did catch him.

Was that the end of the story? Was Miss Brooks doomed to a life of old maid-dom? No! Warner Brothers came to the rescue and made a big-screen version of *Our Miss Brooks*. The whole cast returned for this last reunion, Walter Denton (though strangely here as a newcomer to the school) and Stretch Snodgrass included and, in a gift from the sitcom gods (namely writers Al Lewis and Joseph Quillan), Miss Brooks and Mr. Boynton were finally united in holy matrimony.

OFF THE SET

LUCILLE BALL TURNED down the part of Connie Brooks, urging her friend Eve Arden to take the role.

RICHARD CRENNA WAS twenty-six when he played the teenager Walter Denton on the first television season of *Our Miss Brooks*.

Above: Eve Arden, who could do more with a roll of her eyes than many comediennes can do with ten pages of dialogue, gives her silent critique of Jane Morgan's violin playing.

Opposite: Arden, Richard Crenna, as goofball student Walter Denton, and Robert Rockwell.

Right: Kaye Ballard and Arden as *The Mothers-in-Law*.

CAST

Eve Arden .... Connie Brooks

Gale Gordon .... Osgood Conklin

Robert Rockwell ...... Philip Boynton

Richard Crenna .... Walter Denton

Jane Morgan .... Mrs. Margaret Davis

Gloria McMillan ..... Harriet Conklin

Leonard Smith .... Stretch Snodgrass

Mary Jane Croft .... Miss Daisy Enright

Virginia Gordon .... Mrs. Martha Conklin (1)

Paula Winslowe .... Mrs. Martha Conklin (2)

Joseph Kearns .... Superintendent Stone

Daisy Enright: When I was in my teens, there weren't very many stars on television.
Connie Brooks: When you were in your teens, there weren't many stars on the flag.

Eve Arden

Eve Arden first made her mark on Broadway in the *Ziegfeld Follies of 1934*, returning in the *Follies of 1936* to introduce the standard "I Can't Get Started" in a duet with Bob Hope. The Kern and Hammerstein musical *Very Warm for May* followed, along with a leading role in the Cole Porter hit *Let's Face It* opposite Danny Kaye. Working in Hollywood for most of this period, Arden balanced her stage appearances with ever more important roles in films, first achieving notice in Hollywood the 1937 film *Stage Door* alongside another young comedienne named Lucille Ball, with whom she remained friends for the next fifty years. Inspired by her razor-sharp, uniquely modulated delivery, the writers expanded her role during filming. Though she wasn't usually the leading lady, she created her own archetype in the movies, the wisecracking sidekick, in such varied films as *At the Circus* (with the Marx Brothers), *The Doughgirl*s, and an Oscar-nominated role in *Mildred Pierce,* for which she bagged an Oscar nomination.

When William Paley beckoned with radio's *Our Miss Brooks* (after Shirley Booth was rejected for being too much of a downer), Arden created her most enduring character. Immediately following the end of that show, she starred in *The Eve Arden Show*, which lasted only a season. Though Arden was a natural for sitcoms, it would be ten years before she starred in another series, the guilty pleasure *The Mothers-in-Law*, opposite Kaye Ballard. In the meantime, she did guest spots on TV (memorably as Samantha Stephens's bewildered maternity nurse on *Bewitched*), and in the occasional film, and she returned to the stage in *Hello, Dolly!*, giving what was by all accounts one of the best performances of the role. Guest starring on such 1970s shows as *Maude* (as Maude's Aunt Lola) and *Alice*, she became known to a new generation and was finally promoted to school principal in the film musicals *Grease* and *Grease II*.

THE PARTRIDGE FAMILY

abc | **1970–1974** | **96 episodes**

Widow Shirley Partridge gets bamboozled into recording a song with her five children and, when it takes off, the clan begins a career on the road as a pop music group—still grappling with the more banal concerns of a typical suburban family.

Like its immediate predecessor, *The Monkees*, *The Partridge Family* was a "mu-sitcom," equally important for its contribution to the world of teen pop music as for its TV shenanigans. But while *The Monkees* was uniquely brilliant in its counterculture chaos, the Partridges somehow made the world of rock-and-roll seem hip and square simultaneously, like "A Very Funky Episode" of *The Lawrence Welk Show*. For while that lead boy had that long hair, the mother had been in the movie *Oklahoma!*, for goodness' sakes! And although their tour bus looked like it was painted during a particularly psychedelic acid trip, they sang songs about saving the whales. And, wearing burgundy velvet suit coats and ruffled tuxedo shirts, the three youngest children, exhibiting no musical talent at all, looked like every child who has ever been unwillingly recruited as ring bearer

at Cousin Irma's shotgun wedding. It was this constant blurring of suburban home life and pop musical moments that inspired its broad appeal.

The show was inspired by the success of the real-life family pop group the Cowsills, who were actually set to play the family on the show until Oscar-winning actress Shirley Jones was approached… and then it was throw Momma Cowsill from the train, along with the rest of the clan.

With lead vocals from Shirley Jones and David Cassidy, the only two cast members who could carry a tune in a wet paper sack; the beautiful Susan Dey, as oldest sister Laurie, on keyboards; the amazingly droll child actor Danny Bonaduce as bass player and all-around pest, Danny; and fraternal twins Chris and Tracy on percussion, the group somehow struck a chord of truth, even though, let's face it, the kid playing the drummer held his sticks like he was eating Chinese takeout and youngest sister Tracy played the tambourine like she was beating a dusty rug.

The amazing upshot of it all was that *The Partridge Family*, like *The Monkees* before it, became a recording success, with the single "I Think I Love You" hitting number one on the *Billboard* charts in the show's first season. Three other singles also charted, a development that must have made Barry Williams, who played Greg Brady on the other ABC squeaky clean-fest *The Brady Bunch* and had visions of becoming a pop star, go absolutely bonkers.

Dave Madden

Put-upon character actor Dave Madden had an early career in sketch comedy, getting his first break when he was cast as camp counselor Pruitt on the short-lived series *Camp Runamuck* (left). Gaining further fame as a confetti throwing curmudgeon on *Rowan & Martin's Laugh-In*, he was cast in his biggest role as the constantly headache-induced Reuben Kincaid on *The Partridge Family*. After the show's four-season run, he guest starred on such shows as *Love, American Style* and *Barney Miller*. After an eight-year recurring role as counter rat Earl Hicks on *Alice*, Madden continued in roles on such contemporary shows as *Married…with Children* and *Boy Meets World* (usually playing a Reuben Kincaid type, second only to Gale Gordon's Mr. Mooney as the most flummoxed, long-suffering character on all sitcoms).

The plotlines were often the wacky situations that led up to their weekly gig: the whole family gets gassed by a skunk and must come up with gallons of tomato juice to neutralize the odor; the bus breaks down and the family ends up performing at a benefit for a local Indian reservation; and the aforementioned "whale song" episode, complete with Bert Convy as a marine biologist. Only in sitcomland, folks, only in sitcomland.

In its fourth season, *The Partridge Family* definitely lost its footing with the addition of little Ricky Segall, playing the Partridge's new next-door neighbor Ricky. Vice President of the Utterly Annoying Child Actor Club (Cousin Oliver from *The Brady Bunch* is president emeritus, with Dodie from *My Three Sons* recently reelected sergeant at arms), his arrival marked the moment when the show tipped over into cloydom. And oh, the songs this little moppet sang. Spouting a lyric like "I'm not afraid of the dark/And I like to go for rides in the park," Segall sent many viewers screaming from their rumpus rooms, ears a-bleeding.

Cassidy, meanwhile, was on the brink of exhaustion, flying around the country on his days off to do concerts in stadiums packed with screaming girls. By the end of the third season, Cassidy had had it with the squares at ABC and wanted to get off of the show, giving a *Rolling Stone* interview where he tried to shake up his image, coming off like a small-screen Sid Vicious. (Note to Self: be careful what you wish for—Cassidy found himself in virtual obscurity within four years.) *The Partridge Family*, like other shows firmly cemented in their time, has not done well in syndication. It's a shame, for the show, both funny and tunefully groovy (or is that groovily tuneful?), deserves to be seen (and heard) again.

Above: The family in the kitchen, this time featuring Chris Partridge #2, Brian Forster.

Left: The Family Partridge, featuring Chris Partridge #1, Jeremy Gelbwaks, and the unparalleled tambourine banging of Suzanne Crough.

OFF THE SET

HAD *THE PARTRIDGE FAMILY* returned for a fifth season, the producers were set to replace David Cassidy with singer Rick Springfield.

THE EXTERIOR OF the Partridge house was a facade on the back lot at the Warner Brothers Ranch in Burbank. Look familiar? It was also used as Mrs. Kravitz's house on *Bewitched*.

CAST

Shirley Jones	Shirley Partridge
David Cassidy	Keith Partridge
Susan Dey	Laurie Partridge
Danny Bonaduce	Danny Partridge
Jeremy Gelbwaks	Chris Partridge (1)
Brian Forster	Chris Partridge (2)
Suzanne Crough	Tracy Partridge
Dave Madden	Reuben Kincaid

MOVIE STARS WHO TRIED TELEVISION

When the studio system came screeching to a halt in the mid 1950s, television provided an ideal destination for the scores of movie stars who found themselves without the security of guaranteed work. Even the MGM contract players, who had been forbidden by studio head Louis B. Mayer to appear on "that little box," attempted to cross over to the higher visibility afforded by the small screen. Some, such as Ronald Reagan, Dick Powell, Jane Wyman, Robert Montgomery, and Loretta Young, hosted anthology series, often appearing in the weekly dramas they introduced. Others, including Bob Hope, Judy Garland, Dean Martin, and Red Skelton, opted for the variety format.

Still others tried their hand at situation comedies, seeing an opportunity they had never been given during their years as movie actors: to play the same role week in and week out, building a character over a span of years. Since the world of sitcoms is much more welcoming to oddball types as long as they possess the requisite warmth, such actors as Eve Arden and Walter Brennan were naturals for their own vehicles. Others, such as Robert Young, Donna Reed, and Fred MacMurray, found comfortable niches as light comedians in family-based series. Doris Day, Ann Sothern, and Burt Reynolds found the transition easy, their amiable personas making them welcome in America's living rooms. And, of course, Lucille Ball was in a class all her own, breaking out to become a legend on the small screen, her talent expanding exponentially as a result of the freedom and inspiration she found in the half-hour form.

Some, however, never got the hang of it, and the road is littered with the carcasses of movie stars who tried and failed. Some, whose limitations had been masked by the multiple takes and careful editing of motion pictures, saw their shortcomings exposed by the relative rigor and fast pace of television.

Betty Hutton, Bing Crosby, Gene Kelly, Debbie Reynolds, Mickey Rooney, Ronald Colman, and Jean Arthur all failed in their attempts at sitcom success. In the 1970s, Shirley MacLaine and Jimmy Stewart were both let down by inferior vehicles, while the 1980s saw series featuring Ellen Burstyn and George C. Scott disappear after brief runs. With film roles drying up, Geena Davis and Bette Midler tried TV in the '90s, but both struck out. More recently, Heather Graham's heavily promoted series debut was canceled after one airing. The most tantalizing prospect for an unsold series? *Hello, Mother, Goodbye*, a 1974 pilot starring Bette Davis as Kenneth Mars's meddling maternal unit. Now that's a premise.

Top and above: Gene Kelly, trapped in the flop *Going My Way,* phones *Singin' in the Rain* costar Debbie Reynolds (with Patricia Smith in a shot from the stinker *The Debbie Reynolds Show*) to reminisce about the good old days at MGM.

Left: Mickey Rooney, with the wonderful Emmaline Henry (best remembered as Amanda Bellows on *I Dream of Jeannie*), Brian Nash, and real-life son Tim Rooney, strikes out with the foul ball family sitcom *Mickey*.

THE PATTY DUKE SHOW

abc | 1963–1966 | 104 episodes

Sweet, shy Cathy Lane comes to America from Scotland to live with her Uncle Martin and his family in Brooklyn Heights. A dead ringer for her cousin Patty, Cathy becomes Patty's reluctant partner in madcap adventures.

Patty Duke, on the show's wardrobe: "Not only did I hate those clothes, but they put my name on some and successfully merchandised them, so a lot of other poor girls were walking around with the same ugly clothes I had to wear."

Some actors are so well suited to the sitcom form, performing with such natural ability and ease that they seem to have been born to do it. Elizabeth Montgomery. Bill Cosby. Michael J. Fox. Betty White. John Ritter. Annie Potts. When a show is lucky enough to include two actors with that rare gift, viewers get to witness moments of utter magic; think, for example, of the almost casual yet perfectly executed high wire high-jinks of Lucille Ball and Vivian Vance on *I Love Lucy*; the eternal push-me-pull-you of Jack Klugman and Tony Randall on *The Odd Couple*; the spicy sparring of Ted Danson and Shelley Long on *Cheers*.

Add to that list Patty Duke and Patty Duke on *The Patty Duke Show*, as she was, in a way, two of the best actresses on television in the 1960s. As it was far from the happiest time in her life, Duke doesn't have a great deal of fondness for the show herself, but, having recently made her peace with her participation in the camp classic *Valley of the Dolls*, Duke should do herself a favor and revisit her work on the show, for much of it is quite extraordinary. The subtle delineation between Patty and Cathy in voice, manner, and physicality is so specific that it's easy to forget that there aren't two actresses playing the scene. Watching the split-screen scenes and seeing Duke doing subtle double takes to herself and then realizing they were actually shot separately and put together in the editing room is mind boggling. What's more, with subtle changes in her slight Scottish burr, she created four characters (five, if you count their Southern Belle cousin who appeared on one episode): Patty, Cathy, Patty impersonating Cathy, and Cathy impersonating Patty, performing on multiple levels, a truly impressive feat for a sixteen-year-old actress.

Created by Sidney Sheldon, the concept for the show was right in step with the other gimmicky sitcoms of the 1960s: identical cousins who, with the exception of their looks, were complete opposites. The show's catchy theme song explained it all: Cathy loved the minuet; Patty, rock and roll; Cathy, crêpes Suzettes; Patty, the hot dog (which she evidently feels so strongly about, it makes her lose control). Anyway, they were as different as night and day, providing the setup for endless cases of mistaken identity, teen angst, and "sibling" rivalry.

Yet another show retooled before going to series, the original pilot was set in San Francisco and had starred Mark Miller (father of actress Penelope Ann, and later sitcom patriarch on *Please Don't Eat the Daisies*). Handsome and appealing in the Carl Betz/Hugh Beaumont vein of fathers, Miller somehow didn't provide the slightly weary quality that charac-

Patty Duke

Born into a dysfunctional New York City family, Anna Marie Duke was roped into show business by her older brother's managers (a married couple who made Mama Rose in the musical *Gypsy* seem like June Cleaver) and renamed Patty. She got a life-altering break when she was cast as Helen Keller in the Broadway play *The Miracle Worker*, winning an Academy Award for the subsequent movie version. A bankable star at sixteen, she turned to television and became the youngest performer ever to have a TV series bearing her name. Married for the first time at eighteen, Duke began to experience a series of personal ups and downs attributable to severe manic depressive illness, exacerbated by years of abuse at the

hands of her managers. Hiding the fact that she was in personal turmoil, Duke became the queen of the made-for-TV movie, winning an Emmy for a brilliant performance in *My Sweet Charlie* and appearing in more than sixty other television films, including a 1979 remake of *The Miracle Worker* (this time in the role of Annie Sullivan). She returned to the world of the sitcom twice: in 1982's underrated *It Takes Two*, costarring Richard Crenna and a young Helen Hunt, and in the controversial but very funny *Hail to the Chief* in 1985. Having finally found inner peace and happiness with her fourth husband on a ranch in Idaho, Duke is entering her sixth decade as an actress, returning to Broadway after a forty-year absence, as Aunt Eller in the 2002 revival of *Oklahoma!*

OFF THE SET

SCREEN LEGEND BETTE Davis, who in 1964 played a double role in the film *Dead Ringer*, was offered a guest double role on *The Patty Duke Show*. The negotiations for her salary and other demands went on for so long that the producers finally ditched the idea altogether.

SINCE PATTY DUKE was only sixteen when the show went into production, it was filmed in New York City, where the child labor laws were much more lenient, allowing Duke to work a longer day in order to complete the special-effects–laden show on schedule.

ter needed—whereas his replacement, the wonderful William Schallert, with his bemused smile and sternly disapproving looks, was the perfect paternal figure for the rebellious teenybopper Patty. The cast was uniformly excellent, with the lovely Jean Byron as mother Natalie and Paul O'Keefe, another super-talented child actor, as kid brother Ross. (Ross and Patty shared a truly believable sibling relationship, a kind of Wally-and-Beaver dynamic that was both funny and touching.) And since the first two seasons were filmed in New York, guest stars included such Broadway stalwarts (and future sitcom stars) as Jean Stapleton, Kaye Ballard, Paul Lynde, and Charles Nelson Reilly—and, playing Patty's high school friends, future stars Marcia Strassman, Susan Anspach, and *The West Wing*'s late, great John Spencer.

A fourth season was planned but scuttled at the last minute when ABC crunched the numbers and realized how prohibitively expensive it would be to film the show in color. Duke, for one, was not sorry to move on, as she was now nearly nineteen and wanted to grow up, both on and off-screen. In 1999, thirty-three years after it went off the air, CBS aired a reunion TV movie subtitled *Still Rockin' in Brooklyn Heights*, reuniting Duke, Schallert, Byron, O'Keefe, and goofy Eddie Applegate, back as Patty's eternally famished high school boyfriend Richard, by now her ex-husband. Cathy also materializes, now a widow living in Scotland with a teenage son. Although the series was dusted off for Nick at Nite, it's been out of the rerun cycle for far too long. We can only hope that, thanks to the booming DVD market, everyone will be able to discover or rediscover *The Patty Duke Show*.

William Schallert

Racking up more than three hundred TV and film credits in his sixty-year career, William Schallert is one of the most recognizable faces in television. Born and raised in Los Angeles, he began with uncredited one-liners, steadily playing larger and larger roles. His first regular role in a sitcom was as teacher Mr. Pomfritt on *The Many Loves of Dobie Gillis*, followed almost immediately by his most famous TV role on *The Patty Duke Show*. Like all character actors, the passing years only increased his employment opportunities, with his kind face and avuncular demeanor. He practically cornered the market on doctor, scientist, professor, and minister roles, guest-starring on nearly every TV series from 1955 to 1990. His most recent regular stint was on 1991's *The Torkelsons*. If Schallert weren't so darn likeable, his fellow character actors might've taken out a hit on him long ago, he is so eminently employable. As it is, he is respected by his peers, serving as president of the Screen Actors Guild from 1979 to 1981 (a position held four years later by his former onscreen daughter, Patty Duke). Still active in his eighties, the one role that has brought him the most celebrity is that of Nilz Barris, Federation Undersecretary of Agricultural Affairs, in the legendary "Trouble with Tribbles" episode of *Star Trek*.

Left: The Lane family, played by Jean Byron, William Schallert, Patty Duke, and Paul O'Keefe.

Opposite top: Cathy and Patty Lane: The way to tell the cousins apart? Cathy always wears her hair curled under (it looks better while doing the minuet), while Patty flips it out à la Laura Petrie (and with the help of some extra-firm AquaNet, that flip can hold a couple of those crazy-making hotdogs she loves).

Opposite bottom: Duke as the first female president of the United States, Julia Mansfield, in the sharply satirical *Hail to the Chief*.

CAST

Patty Duke	Patty Lane/Cathy Lane
William Schallert	Martin Lane/Jed Lane
Jean Byron	Natalie Lane
Paul O'Keefe	Ross Lane
Eddie Applegate	Richard Harrison
Rita McLaughlin	Double for Cathy and Patty
John McGiver	J. R. Castle
Skip Hinnant	Ted
Kitty Sullivan	Sue Ellen

PERFECT STRANGERS

abc | 1986–1993 | 150 episodes

High-strung Larry Appleton gets a knock on his door from his distant cousin, Balki Bartokomous, who turns the American lad's world upside down in a way that Oscar Madison and Felix Unger could never have imagined.

Perfect Strangers was a perfect component of the block programming called TGIF—Thank God It's Friday—dreamed up by ABC executives to create a viable lineup for a night that was notoriously difficult to program. The basic idea was later co-opted by NBC as Must-See Thursdays, featuring a lineup that included *Cheers*, *Friends*, and *Seinfeld*. In each case, new or lower-ranked shows were sandwiched between powerhouse hits to create a roster that could be promoted as an entire evening's entertainment.

The concept had its roots in the crossovers of the Paul Henning rural shows, where Kate Bradley from *Petticoat Junction* or the Clampett clan from *The Beverly Hillbillies* would visit their kinfolk on *Green Acres*. The programming-block concept was also used by NBC on Saturday nights, when they would feature crossovers on three shows (*The Golden Girls*, *Empty Nest*, and *Nurses*) produced by Witt/Thomas/Harris.

The brilliant producers Bob Boyett and Tom Miller saw an even better opportunity in the TGIF programming, and by the fall of 1990 they had created all four shows and were poised to rule Friday nights. Miller and Boyett, who had worked on *Laverne and Shirley*, created in *Perfect Strangers* a show that was a kind of male equivalent to that show, featuring two mismatched roommates who got into all kinds of physical comedy scrapes the way the two Milwaukee bottle cappers had. The show starred Mark Linn-Baker, whose character was the perfect foil for the wild Bronson Pinchot, who had gained attention in the tiny role of Serge in *Beverly Hills Cop*. Adopting a similarly geographically untraceable accent, Pinchot played a distant cousin of Linn-Baker's Everyman, showing up on his doorstep from the mythical land of Mypos, undoubtedly somewhere in the vicinity of the Greek Isles. (The only clues as to its exact location were

Bronson Pinchot and Mark Linn-Baker, as Balki and Cousin Larry, had the Pushme-Pullyou dynamic of *Laverne and Shirley*.

that the island was roughly the shape of a pork chop and its national delicacy was Bibbibabka, which must be prepared extremely carefully, or it will "go blooey.")

Although the show ran eight seasons, the first and last ones were only six episodes each—and the series underwent two distinct "changes of concept." For the first two seasons, the cousins lived above and worked in the Ritz Discount Store, the setting for much of the physical comedy on the show. By the third season, Larry and Balki got jobs at the fictional *Chicago Chronicle*, Larry as a reporter and Balki in the mailroom. (Well, what else could he do? He had been a shepherd on Mypos, and there wasn't much call for one in the Windy City.) This provided Pinchot with the comic weapon of a rolling mail cart, so perfect for slapstick, its use dates back to Aristophanes (those wacky Greeks *loved* mailroom humor).

Perfect Strangers' season finale was broadcast more than a year after the last first-run

Mark Linn-Baker

The wonderful character actor Mark Linn-Baker went to the Yale School of Drama and appeared in Off-Broadway shows with the likes of Meryl Streep before getting his big break opposite Peter O'Toole in the 1982 movie *My Favorite Year*. Following that up with the Broadway musical version of the comic strip *Doonesbury*, he was cast as the high-strung yet lovable Larry Appleton on *Perfect Strangers*, playing opposite Bronson Pinchot for eight successful seasons. Learning what goes on behind the camera during the run of *Perfect Strangers*, Linn-Baker went on to direct numerous episodes of fellow TGIF shows *Hangin' with Mr. Cooper* and *Family Matters*. Returning to Broadway in such shows as *A Funny Thing Happened on the Way to the Forum*; *Laughter on the Twenty-Third Floor*; and *A Year with Frog and Toad*, Linn-Baker's most recent sitcom role was as husband to Melanie Griffith and father to Sara Gilbert (a family unit so bizarre it could only to be found on the WB network) on the short-lived *Twins* (above). Eminently likeable and equally adept as straight man or farceur, Linn-Baker is a natural for the world of the sitcom, an affable funnyman whom viewers gladly welcome into their homes on a weekly basis.

episode had aired. By then, the show had taken another major turn, with Larry and Balki now married to longtime girlfriends Jennifer and Mary Anne, culminating in a series finale concerning a labor-inducing ride in a hot air balloon. (They were grasping at straws, perhaps, but at least they didn't move to Hollywood like Laverne and Shirley.)

It's worth noting that the show had one of the all-time catchiest theme songs, by Jesse Frederick and Bennett Salvay, titled "Nothing's Gonna Stop Me Now" (although many people think of it as "Standing Tall" or "On the Wings of My Dreams," as those are its best remembered lines). It also had a memorable credit sequence showing Balki leaving his family in Mypos and gazing in awe at the Statue of Liberty, while Larry was leaving his family in Wisconsin to conquer the Windy City. Later in the run, the sequence changed to show the mismatched cousins dressed in tuxedos, hurrying to catch a play at the historic Chicago Theatre. The show the perfect strangers were about to see? Neil Simon's *The Odd Couple*, of course.

Mark Linn-Baker does "perturbed" as well as Gale Gordon, while Bronson Pinchot gets a lot of mileage out of "wacky."

CAST

Mark Linn-Baker	Larry Appleton
Bronson Pinchot	Balki Bartokomous
Melanie Wilson	Jennifer Lyons
Rebeca Arthur	Mary Anne Spencer
Ernie Sabella	Donald "Twinkie" Twinkacetti
Lise Cutter	Susan Campbell
Belita Moreno	Lydia Markham
Jo Marie Payton-France	Harriette Winslow

PETTICOAT JUNCTION

 | **1963–1970** | **222 episodes**

Down the track and around the bend, fifteen miles from the middle of nowhere, the struggling Shady Rest has more vacancies than the Bates Motel.

Who'd try to open a hotel outside of Hooterville, anyway? Accessible only by a wheezing old locomotive, featuring a nonworking elevator and a water supply the owner's (albeit fetching) daughters skinny-dip in, the Shady Rest Hotel was hardly a weekend at the Waldorf. But it provided an entertaining backdrop for Paul Henning's rural comedy, *Petticoat Junction*.

The Shady Rest was run by the down-home Kate Bradley, and one of the main pieces of furniture in its none-too-posh lobby was the sedentary Uncle Joe, who moved more than "kinda slow." (In fact, if actor Edgar Buchanan had just picked up his cues, episodes would have run five minutes shorter.) His presence on the front porch may have made the place look more like the Shady Rest Home, but Buchanan was absolutely perfect in the role, another one-of-a-kind character actor brought to us by Paul Henning.

The show had more turnover than the hotel did, with three actresses playing eldest daughter Billie Jo and two playing Bobbie Jo over the show's seven-season run. In addition, two of the show's regulars died: Bea Benaderet, who played Kate, and

The staff of the Shady Rest (left to right), Linda Kaye Henning, Edgar Buchanan, Jeannine Riley, Bea Benaderet, and Pat Woodell. Rufe Davis and Smiley Burnette are standing at the back, having just driven that little train that was rolling down the tracks. And who gets prime position? In this publicity shot Higgins the dog, of course.

Smiley Burnette, who played the engineer of the local locomotive, the Hooterville Cannonball, both passed away during the run, casting a kind of pall that was felt again when three actors (Barbara Colby, Judith Lowry, and Burt Mustin) on the MTM spin-off *Phyllis* died. Talk about an atmosphere unconducive to light and frothy comedy. Benaderet was replaced by June Lockhart, just back to Earth after three years *Lost in Space*, as a city doctor who comes to Hooterville to open her practice. While Lockhart certainly had the maternal presence, she lacked the folksiness of Benaderet, and the show began to wobble on its axis. In fact, while many people think that *Petticoat Junction* was canceled as part of the infamous CBS purge of rural shows, including *Mayberry, RFD*, *Green Acres*, and *The Beverly Hillbillies*, in truth, it had been canceled a year earlier, having never regained a good head of steam (to put it in terms that rid-

Charles Lane

One of the most recognizable character actors in the twentieth century (that may sound like an overstatement, but check his credits … the man was everywhere), Charles Lane had one of his most regular roles on *Petticoat Junction* as the evil Homer Bedloe, the Grinch-like vice president of the C.F. & W. Railroad, forever trying to shut down the Cannonball and put poor Pratt and Smoot out of business. From *I Love Lucy* to *Soap*, Lane appeared on virtually every major sitcom over three decades, on *Bewitched* playing eight different hard-to-please clients of Darrin Stephens. Most comfortable behind a front desk, he was also in over 250 films, beginning in 1931 and including the classic *It's a Wonderful Life*. Lane celebrated his hundredth birthday in 2005, having retired at the ripe old age of ninety.

ers of the Cannonball could understand) after the loss of its beloved Kate.

The first two seasons of the show, shot in black and white, were the subject of long-running rights litigation and were

not included in the syndication package along with the five seasons of color episodes. Indeed, until the first season's release on DVD, many viewers had no recollection of actresses Jeannine Riley and Pat Woodell, who played the two oldest sisters for those seasons. And the color years brought more new faces, including Mike Minor as Steve Elliott, the handsome crop duster who fell from the sky and joined the cast in 1967. Every eligible bachelorette in a fifty-mile radius took turns tending to his injuries. Although Hooterville's town pain-in-the-neck, Selma Plout, tried her darnedest to nab the handsome crop duster for her daughter Henrietta, Minor married (on screen and off) Linda Kaye Henning, who played the youngest Bradley daughter, Betty Jo.

Above: Patron Saint of Character Actors Charles Lane with Danny Thomas and Marjorie Lord on *Make Room for Daddy*.

Left: With all that food and no guests (as usual), it's a miracle that the three svelte Bradley sisters (here, with Gunilla Hutton as Billie Jo and Lori Saunders as Bobby Jo) weren't the size of linebackers.

With the final Billie Jo, Meredith MacRae, in place, the cast of *Petticoat Junction* (now including Frank Cady as Sam Drucker and Mike Minor as Steve the cropduster) sits for a new cast portrait. Look who's front and center again...he must've had one hell of an agent.

While other series have featured such future movie stars as Michael J. Fox, John Travolta, and Sally Field, there was only one actor from *Petticoat Junction* able to make the leap to the big screen—and having four legs undoubtedly made the leap easier. Higgins the dog, usually just called "Dog" on the show, joined the ranks of Asta, Rin Tin Tin, and Lassie in 1974 in the eponymous *Benji* (a film in which poor Edgar Buchanan had to accept a cameo role—after all, he hadn't worked in a while—so it was kind of Higgins to "throw him a bone").

CAST

Bea Benaderet..............Kate Bradley

Edgar Buchanan..........Joe Carson

Linda Kaye Henning...Betty Jo Bradley Elliott

Jeannine Riley.............Billie Jo Bradley (1)

Gunilla Hutton.............Billie Jo Bradley (2)

Meredith MacRae.......Billie Jo Bradley (3)

Pat Woodell...................Bobbie Jo Bradley (1)

Lori Saunders...............Bobbie Jo Bradley (2)

Frank Cady...................Sam Drucker

Smiley Burnette...........Charley Pratt

Rufe Davis....................Floyd Smoot

Mike Minor..................Steve Elliott

June Lockhart.............Dr. Janet Craig

Frank Cady

The only actor to play the same character on three sitcoms at the same time, the kind-faced, Middle American–looking Frank Cady's roots and training were completely at odds with his onscreen image. Born and raised in California, Cady graduated from Stanford University and studied acting in London. After World War II, he arrived in Hollywood and immediately started landing small roles. He made numerous film appearances through the 1940s and '50s as hotel clerks, reporters, and doctors in films such as *The Asphalt Jungle*, *Father of the Bride*, *Rear Window*, and as the long-suffering Mr. Daigle in *The Bad Seed*. While the rise of television meant the end of many movie stars' careers, journeyman character–type Cady thrived, guest-starring on most of the hourlong Westerns as well as bagging a recurring role on *The Adventures of Ozzie and Harriet*. Like the other character actors on Paul Henning's trio of rural sitcoms, Cady was perfectly cast as Sam Drucker, the epitome of the small-town general store owner, on *The Beverly Hillbillies*, *Petticoat Junction*, and *Green Acres*, the only person who could make Oliver Douglas feel the slightest bit sane.

THE PHIL SILVERS SHOW

 | **1955–1959** | **138 episodes**

Sgt. Ernest Bilko, head of the motor pool at Fort Baxter, is always scheming to get something for nothing. His plans often fail, but his heart of gold and quick thinking carry him through.

The lovable rapscallion is a stock character in show business—but is noticeably absent from the world of sitcoms, especially in today's climate of audience polling, mainstreaming, and pandering to Nielsen ratings. That's why Nat Hiken's brilliant, simply conceived character of Sgt. Bilko, especially as personified by Phil Silvers, remains virtually unique in television history.

Silvers made a specialty of fast-talking, loveable cads, a persona he honed in burlesque. In 1955, Silvers had just closed in the successful *Top Banana* when producer/writer Nat Hiken approached him on behalf of CBS programmer Hubbell Robinson to star in a new television series. His friend Jack Benny advised him to stick to the high-class (or at least higher-class) world of the theater and ignore the offers from television. Benny told Silvers that television was a drain, beneath him, and would eat him up, but the Broadway offers didn't come. When Silvers heard Hiken's idea for a comedy set in an army camp, all he could think of were the Universal pictures starring Abbott and Costello: slapstick stupidities with the army as background. Yawn. But when Hiken proposed building the character around Silvers's already existing scoundrel persona, the comedian was intrigued. The motivating force behind Bilko was twofold: his constant scheming and his disdain for authority. And while Bilko was a good guy with the requisite heart of gold, he never missed an opportunity to play the army game to his advantage,

Elizabeth Fraser and Paul Ford listen as Phil Silvers, as Ernie Bilko, tries to talk his way out of another one.

Sgt. Ernie Bilko: "Gladdaseeya!"

East 67th Street. The secret to the success of the show was its momentum. They would film a twenty-five-minute show in less than an hour. No retakes, no stalling, just ready, set, film! Looking at the series now, actors are literally tripping over their lines trying to keep up with the pace. And the sun at the center of the Bilko universe was the indefatigable Phil Silvers.

There were twenty episodes in the can before the show ever got on the air, prompting Silvers's mother to wonder how he could possibly be making good money on a show that she couldn't actually watch. She may have been the only one watching when CBS put it on against the second half of Milton Berle's show on NBC, on Tuesday nights at 8:30. As predicted, the show was creamed by Berle, but when CBS moved it up by a half hour, *Bilko* climbed in the ratings as Berle's numbers fell.

The supporting cast included some of the best character actors to be seen on any sitcom, such as Joe E. Ross, Mickey Freeman, and Paul Ford. One who made a particularly indelible impression was Zippy the chimp, who appeared in what is probably the greatest of all *Bilko* episodes. While Zippy could skate and ride a bike, he wasn't quite as disciplined in acting.

taking in a few suckers along the way. The name "Bilko" itself is a clue to his character.

Hiken named the series *You'll Never Get Rich*, an apt shorthand for Bilko's fate. The show was rehearsed above Lindy's delicatessen on Broadway and filmed in the DuMont studios on

Phil Silvers

A tornado of talent, the impulsive, ingratiating Phil Silvers was a huckster at heart, whose characters were forever grinning, glad-handing, and scheming to get rich quick. Arriving at the tail end of vaudeville, Silvers segued into the down-and-dirty world of burlesque, getting his actor training at the University of Minsky. Honing his talents and developing his persona in comedy sketches performed between stripper acts provided a rough and tumble improvisatory beginning. It proved to be the perfect atmosphere to bring out Silvers's natural energy and drive. Catching Hollywood's eye, he was cast in a series of secondary roles in B pictures. By the mid-1940s, he was firmly established and better movie roles started coming. Silvers also made his mark on Broadway, scoring a hit as conman Harrison Floy in the musical *High-Button Shoes*, going on to star in *Top Banana* and *Do Re Mi*. His greatest legacy

is Bilko, his "gladdaseeya" greeting becoming a buzzword in 1950s America. After the smash success of *The Phil Silvers Show*, he continued to work in films. His next series, *The New Phil Silvers Show*, was a misfire, canceled after only one season, but he was back in guest shots on *Gilligan's Island*, as the no-account Broadway producer Harold Hecuba, and on *The Beverly Hillbillies*, as Shifty Shafer. His last sitcom appearance was on *Happy Days*, opposite his real-life daughter Cathy, who played the outrageous Jenny Piccalo, a character fittingly in line with the Silvers legacy.

Hiken was determined to write a script around the chimp and devised a plot in which the primate is accidentally inducted into the army. The only way to get rid of poor Zippy was to court-marshal him; of course, Bilko acted as the chimp's attorney. The show's tight schedule meant everything would have to go like clockwork—but Zippy was, to say the least, unpredictable. Luckily, Silvers was a master of improvisation. During the trial scene, a prop phone was inadvertently left on the set by a stagehand. When the ever-inquisitive Zippy jumped from his chair and picked up the receiver, Silvers ad-libbed, "I plead for an adjournment. My client is calling for a new attorney!"

That, ladies and gentlemen, is comedy. When a producing team and the cast are secure and sure-footed, and happen to have the ideal vehicle, amazing things can happen. *The Phil Silvers Show*, which became its official name two months after its premiere, was just such a show, blessed with a perfect alignment of every element and beholden to no one but the audience.

CAST

Phil Silvers.............	Master Sergeant Ernie Bilko
Harvey Lembeck ..	Corporal Rocco Barbella
Herbie Faye	Private Sam Fender
Paul Ford.................	Colonel John Hall
Maurice Gosfield ..	Private Duane Doberman
Joe E. Ross	Sergeant Rupert Ritzik
Allan Melvin	Corporal Henshaw
Billy Sands	Private Dino Paparelli
Mickey Freeman ..	Private Zimmerman
Hope Sansberry	Nell Hall
Jimmy Little	Sergeant Grover
Elisabeth Fraser	Sergeant Joan Hogan

Opposite top: Harvey Lembeck, Allan Melvin, Phil Silvers, and Bernard Fein get themselves into a mess hall mess.

Opposite bottom: Silvers with Elena Verdugo, Sandy Descher, and Ronnie Dapo. The three were enlisted to play his widowed sister, niece, and nephew halfway through the first (and only) season of *The New Phil Silvers Show*, in an attempt to jump-start ratings.

Below: Silvers and Maurice Gosfield, ostensibly digging a trench. We're taking bets on who'll end up doing all the work....anyone?

OFF THE SET

THE TELEVISION CARTOON characters Top Cat and Hokey Wolf were based on Bilko, and cast member Maurice Gosfield voiced Benny the Ball on *Top Cat*, an obvious rip-off of Duane Doberman.

FUTURE STARS SUCH as Peggy Cass, Dick Cavett, Dina Merrill, Alan Alda, Dick Van Dyke, Pat Hingle, and Orson Bean all passed through Fort Baxter. George Kennedy was the army's technical advisor to the show. Since he was always around and had that perfect military look, Silvers suggested that Kennedy get a union card and he was given bit roles on the show. He soon built up his credits and appeared in other shows and movies.

ENLISTMENTS IN THE army tripled when the show became a success.

PRIVATE SECRETARY/ THE ANN SOTHERN SHOW

👁 | 1953–1957 | 103 episodes (Private Secretary)
| 1958–1961 | 93 episodes (The Ann Sothern Show)

With the help of fellow secretary Vi Haskins, Susie McNamara is indispensable to her boss, theatrical agent Mr. Sands. Change the setting to a hotel and presto! It's *The Ann Sothern Show*.

Pursed lips, crinkled nose, pencil tapping against her teeth…There you have Ann Sothern's most recognizable traits as she (or, rather, her character, Susie McNamara) thought up ways to save her boss's business or get him out of trouble. Unlike the schemes of Margie and Lucy, Susie's all seemed to work to everyone's benefit and never backfired on her. With the help of her sidekick, the sweet, dim Vi, Susie triumphed over the men who thought they called the shots.

Though "Cagey" Calhoun, Mr. Sands's competition in agenting, was a brash cliché, the rest of the characters seemed very real. This wasn't a case of a calm center surrounded by zanies. In fact, as on many sitcoms of the 1950s, it was the everyday foibles of each and every one of them that provided the humor.

There was desire at the center of the show, but it wasn't Mr. Sands that Susie yearned for—what she wanted was to be recognized as his genuine partner. And make no mistake: though he was the boss, they functioned as partners whether he knew it or not. Mr. Sands was unaware of his shortcomings and usually oblivious to Susie's backstage manipulations on his behalf. Susie's common sense, independence, and take-charge approach made *Private Secretary* one of the earliest proto-feminist sitcoms (or, more accurately, one of the earliest proto-feminist shows of any kind).

The terrific Don Porter as everyone's favorite boss Peter Sands, and Ann Sothern, looking as if she mugged Emmett Kelly for his hat, as private secretary Susie McNamara.

PRIVATE SECRETARY

Ann Sothern	Susan Camille MacNamara
Don Porter	Peter Sands
Ann Tyrrell	Vi Praskins
Jesse White	"Cagey" Calhoun
Joan Banks	Sylvia Platt

THE ANN SOTHERN SHOW

Ann Sothern	Katy O'Connor
Ernest Truex	Jason Macauley
Ann Tyrrell	Olive Smith
Don Porter	James Devery
Louis Nye	Dr. Delbert Gray
Ken Berry	Woody Hamilton
Jesse White	Oscar Pudney

Left: Ann Sothern sports one of her signature black bubble dresses as Katy O'Connor, in the unofficial extension of *Private Secretary*, *The Ann Sothern Show*.

Below: Sothern, on set, on call, and on point.

Ann Sothern perfectly embodied the single working woman who wanted a man but didn't need one to be content and in control.

Strangely, the regular season was broadcast on CBS while the summer reruns aired on NBC. When Ann Sothern lost patience with the producer, Jack Chertok, she stopped production. After an appearance as Susie McNamara on *The Lucy-Desi Comedy Hour*, she began filming the show under the Desilu banner, renaming it *The Ann Sothern Show* and setting it in a hotel. It premiered the very next season on CBS, complete with Ann Tyrrell as her assistant. After a few weeks, along came the new boss of the Barclay House, none other than Don Porter. Jesse White, who had played the quick-talking Cagey Calhoun on *Private Secretary*, soon followed as Oscar Pudney and the foursome was complete. The show went on to run three seasons.

OFF THE SET

PRODUCER DESI ARNAZ offered Ann Sothern one of the two leads in *The Mothers-in-Law*, but NBC rejected her, thinking she was too similar in type to costar Eve Arden. The role was rewritten and cast with the very different Kaye Ballard.

ANN SOTHERN

Sly, sexy Ann Sothern began her career as a Goldwyn Girl in such films as *The Show of Shows* and *Whoopee!* As Harriet Lake, she became a Broadway star in musical comedies. Then it was back to films, notably *Panama Hattie* and *A Letter to Three Wives* as well as the Maisie series (which later became a radio series with Sothern). She was equally successful on television in her two sitcoms, and the role that brought her notoriety (or should that be motoriety?), was the famous flop *My Mother the Car*, for which she provided the voice of the title character. Along with many guest appearances on series through the 1960s and '70s, her final film was *The Whales of August* in 1987, for which she received an Oscar nomination. Over her more than sixty-year career, Sothern exhibited an all-American enthusiasm and intelligence, with a subtle air of vulnerability.

THE REAL McCOYS

 | 1957–1962 | 1962–1963 | **224 episodes**

Like the Clampetts, the McCoys traveled to California from their mountain home back East—but they didn't strike oil, they struck dirt.

The mantra of television is "Nobody knows nuthin'." No matter how they try, no one seems to be able to predict which series will be successful and which will flop. Today, network suits like to rely on focus groups made up of "regular" folk, but *Seinfeld* received abysmal test scores and *Everybody Loves Raymond* and *Friends* didn't do much better. In fact, *Friends* got a "weak" rating and the notes read, "Stated viewing intentions for a series based on this pilot were not encouraging."

When two brothers, Irving and Norman Pincus, approached the networks with their idea of a hick family trying to make it on a dirt farm, they were turned down cold. Even the star they wanted, Walter Brennan, said no. Finally, the Danny Thomas organization backed it and ABC, in last place with nothing to lose, picked it up. And guess what? It became a huge success in cities as well as rural areas.

Cantankerous Grandpa McCoy seemed forever to be in a hurry, limping along as fast as his arthritic legs would carry him (he and *Gunsmoke*'s Chester had the gimpy leg mannerism all tied up), wheezing, "Pepino! Pepino!" between bouts of nosing around in other people's business. Maybe he should have married *December Bride*'s Lily Ruskin. Instead, he had neighbor Flora MacMichael chasing after him.

Grandson Luke, his winsome wife Kate, his sister Hassie, and his younger brother Little Luke (his parents were so happy, they forgot about his brother and named him Luke also), made up the rest of the family—

Walter Brennan—not unlike fellow actors Eve Arden, Phil Silvers, Spring Byington and Wally Cox—spent years in supporting film roles before finding his way to TV sitcoms.

Richard Crenna

It's hard to fathom that skinny, nasal Walter Denton of *Our Miss Brooks* grew up to be Rambo's commander—but that is the arc that Richard Crenna's career took, with a notable stop along the way as the ill-fated husband in *Body Heat*. Crenna's persona was in the vein of James Garner: handsome, low-key, smart, all-American, and all male. He switched easily between comedies and dramas and between television and film. After *Miss Brooks* took him from radio to television, he was featured in the *McCoys* and then *Slattery's People*. His film career really took off with notable parts in *The Sand Pebbles*, *Wait until Dark*, and *Star!* (well, maybe not *Star!*). After making a few European movies of dubious quality, he returned to sitcoms in 1975 in *All's Fair*, opposite Bernadette Peters, and *It Takes Two*, opposite Patty Duke. Then came *Rambo: First Blood* (parts I and II). He ended his notable career with another hit TV show, *Judging Amy*, and died of cancer at age seventy-seven, in 2003.

CAST

Walter Brennan	Grandpa Amos McCoy
Richard Crenna	Luke McCoy
Kathleen Nolan	Kate McCoy
Lydia Reed	"Aunt" Hassie
Michael Winkleman	Little Luke
Tony Martinez	Pepino Garcia
Andy Clyde	George MacMichael
Madge Blake	Flora MacMichael

OFF THE SET

TONY MARTINEZ, WHO played Pepino, was heading a Mambo band when he was discovered and cast by the producers of *The Real McCoys*. He followed up the series by playing the role of Sancho Panza in the musical *Man of La Mancha* over 2,400 times on Broadway and the road.

Grandpa McCoy: "Gol durn it!"

and a genial bunch they were. There were no "very special episodes" or messages in *The Real McCoys*. Watching it was as calming as jest sittin' on the porch and a-rockin'. Until the last season, that is, when Kate died and Hassie and Little Luke simply disappeared off to college and the army, respectively, leaving Grandpa to concentrate on getting Luke hitched again.

Please note that Paul Henning was a writer on the show: he'd go from there directly to creating *The Beverly Hillbillies*, *Petticoat Junction*, and *Green Acres*, three more bucolic sitcoms that can cite Grandpa and the gang as their direct ancestors.

Top: Richard Crenna and Bernadette Peters in the Tracy/Hepburn-like sitcom, *All's Fair*.

Right: Crenna, Kathleen Nolan, and Brennan, jest settin' by the hearth fer a spell.

FLOPS PART II

And now, sitcom aficionados, it's once again time to look back at those "Half-Hour Horrors," those "Midseason Monstrosities," those "Coca Catastrophes."

Above: One of the worst ideas ever for a sitcom: Samantha Eggar and Yul Brynner (reprising his role from Broadway and the film) in *Anna and the King.*

Top right: Peter Kastner masquerades as a fashion model so he can stay in England and pursue the girl of his dreams in the certifiably loopy *The Ugliest Girl in Town.*

Right: Jack Weston and his three kids, Charlie, Enoch, and Candy (also known as the Marquis chimps), in *The Hathaways.*

Above: Nancy Walker, an asset to many television shows as a supporting character, was one of the many Broadway comedians who were too quirky ever to be the center of a show. Witness the 1976 flop, *Blansky's Beauties*.

Top: Perfect for sitcom stardom, the appealing Dean Jones got stuck in the inferior military sitcom *Ensign O'Toole*.

Top right: In today's cut-throat climate it's not unusual for a show to get yanked after a single airing—but the four-episode cancellation of *The Tammy Grimes Show* was shocking in 1966.

Imogene Coca

Pint-sized comedienne Imogene Coca was sparked to perform by her father (an opera conductor) and mother (a magician's assistant), and by thirteen, she was working as an acrobat and tap-dancing ballerina in vaudeville. After some success on the Broadway stage, she became a smash in 1950, starring alongside Sid Caesar on *Your Show of Shows*, which became the mainstay of NBC's Saturday night lineup for four seasons. Working on a live, ninety-minute sketch comedy show turned her into a genius at flying by the seat of her pants, in delicate yet hysterically funny pantomimes and in sketches with Caesar as the bickering marrieds the Hickenloopers. After *Your Show of Shows* went off the air in 1954, Coca's appearances in television series were not met with such acclaim. Her first sitcom, *The Imogene Coca Show*, lasted only one season, and her two vehicles of the 1960s, *Grindl* (above) and *It's About Time*, rank as two of the silliest flops of the decade. Coca saved some of her best work for last, though, including star turns on Broadway (in *On the Twentieth Century*) and in the movies (*National Lampoon's Vacation*).

ROSEANNE

 | **1988–1997** | **222 episodes**

Working-class parents Roseanne and Dan Conner and their three kids battle through life one day at a time with good (if sarcastic) humor as their main weapon.

No take backs! We're tired of television shows deciding that episodes or even whole seasons didn't count. It all started with *Dallas* and that damned "it was all a dream" surprise. OK, it was cheeky. Then, in the most brilliant execution of this kind of cheat, *Newhart* revealed in its finale that the whole series had been a dream. That was inspired and hilarious. Along came *Roseanne* and it turned out that the entire ninth season was fictional. We're getting a little existential here—fiction within fiction. Dan had actually dropped dead at the end of the eighth season and Roseanne was just jerking us around during that whole miserable last year.

Who do you think came up with that brilliant (or misbegotten) final story arc? Roseanne, that's who. She got her way because it was her show. At the time, the tabloids and gossip columns were full of stories of fights between the star and the writers and producers, and about John Goodman's alleged dissatisfaction with the way the series was progressing. Roseanne made the call.

Throughout most of its run, *Roseanne* was one of the funniest, most naturalistic of situation comedies. Roseanne, or was it Roseanne Barr or Roseanne Arnold, er, anyway, she brought her honest and hilarious stand-up persona, a lower-class mother struggling against inflation, her family, and the vicissitudes of life in these United States, to television. The producers wisely let

Right: Roseanne and comic genius Edie McClurg have a moment of bingo-night friction.

Below: Portly-but-Easy Riders John Goodman and Roseanne.

her adapt that character without neatening up the messiness or rounding off the sharp corners. Can you name another show where the two leads weighed more than the entire Brady Bunch, Alice included? And the couple not only had sex, they enjoyed it. Despite the appearance that Roseanne ruled the roost, this was a marriage of equals. Yes, Dan tended to be more easygoing, but his acquiescence was based on trust—and, besides, he could always work out his frustrations on his bike.

Of course there was bickering, but it was of a refreshing kind. Not since Ralph and Alice did such sparring, such silent treatment, such sleeping on the couch (not that the Kramdens owned a couch; Alice had to go home to her mother) achieve such heights of hilarious believability as in the Conner household. The family was gloriously dysfunctional and Roseanne, always smack at the center, didn't take any crap from anyone but kept her sense of humor throughout.

Without any of the "this is good for you" self-

satisfaction of other sitcoms, *Roseanne* dealt with real, everyday subjects like DJ's first erections, Roseanne's boss's homosexuality, her children's flirtation with drugs, the soul-crushing descent into poverty, failures at school and work, masturbation, and more. All serious subjects to be sure, yet Roseanne soldiered on as best as she could, with concern, yes, but with a glint in her eye. It's not too much to say that Roseanne and Dan were role models or at least an inspiration to a lot of struggling Americans. Unlike Margaret and Jim Anderson, Roseanne didn't wash the dishes wearing pearls and Dan wasn't a father who always knew best. In fact, it was often Mother who knew best. *Roseanne* was one of the few series in which a married woman ruled the household. The Conners continually reminded us that not having all the answers was all right, that nobody knows best all the time.

Marcy Carsey and Tom Werner

Marcy Carsey and Tom Werner are among the most successful sitcom producers of the 1990s. They made their mark with *The Cosby Show*, a groundbreaking family comedy and one of the biggest hits of the decade. They then went on to produce its spin-off, *A Different World*. *Grace Under Fire* was their first experience with a temperamental star, Brett Butler, and the experience proved useful when it came to dealing with Roseanne, which the two could only stomach until 1994. Among their other sitcoms are *Cosby*, *Cybill*, *3rd Rock from the Sun*, and *That '70s Show*.

CAST

Roseanne	Roseanne Conner
John Goodman	Dan Conner
Lecy Goranson	Becky Conner Healy (1)
Sarah Chalke	Becky Conner Healy (2)
Sara Gilbert	Darlene Conner
Michael Fishman	D. J. Conner
Laurie Metcalf	Jackie Harris
Natalie West	Crystal Anderson Conner
George Clooney	Booker Brooks
Ron Perkins	Pete Wilkins
Evalina Fernandez	Juanita Herrera
Anne Falkner	Sylvia Foster
Ned Beatty	Ed Conner
Estelle Parsons	Bev Harris
Glenn Quinn	Mark Healy
Johnny Galeki	David Healy
Shelley Winters	Nana Mary
Martin Mull	Leon Carp
Bonnie Sheridan	Bonnie
Sandra Bernhard	Nancy
Michael O'Keefe	Fred

Jackie: Well, we can't all be a happily married couple who love each other and who each weigh five hundred pounds!

And, amidst all of the Sturm und Drang in the Conner household, there were lots of laughs. The humor was balanced with heart, so watching *Roseanne* wasn't just a laugh riot but was warmly reassuring in its own way. The Conners, a typical American family—warts and all—exhibited those basic American qualities of optimism and good nature.

The relationship between Jackie and Roseanne was the most honest and true-to-life sister relationships of any sitcom. Even more than Jan and Marcia Brady. The show was at the top of its game through the fifth season. Then, with many of the top writers fired or driven away, the show began to slide. Pregnant in real life, Roseanne became pregnant on the series and gave birth to a boy. Alarm bells went off in the minds of astute viewers who recognized one of the signs of a show in desperate trouble. By the seventh season, ratings dropped significantly, and the show, which had always been in the top ten, wasn't even in the top twenty.

In the last season, perhaps reflecting the fortunes of the star herself and her alienation from her original base, Roseanne won the lottery and became a millionaire, thus negating the message of the first eight seasons—that one can be happy without money. Imagine if one of Bilko's schemes had actually paid off in a big way. Would he have been any happier? Would the series have survived it?

And it wasn't just the lottery. Roseanne's sister Jackie turned out to be gay, the two Conner girls married each other's boyfriends, and on and on. On second thought, maybe those "take-backs" aren't so bad. It might have been better for loyal *Roseanne* fans if that final season were nothing but a mass hallucination.

Above: Hairnets are Funny, Part 1: Laurie Metcalf and standups-turned-actresses Sandra Bernhard and Roseanne try to keep the diner food follicle-free.

Right: The jaunty, jolly John Goodman.

SANFORD AND SON

NBC | **1972–1976** | **136 episodes**

Comedian Redd Foxx is cranky Fred Sanford, a junk dealer in Watts and a kind of black Archie Bunker (natch, since the show was produced by Norman Lear) who lives with his long-suffering son, Lamont.

edd Foxx was a foul-mouthed, nasty-looking comic when, amazingly, he was chosen to star in *Sanford and Son*, an American version of the Britcom *Steptoe and Son*. If you were familiar with Redd Foxx, one of the most ornery and profane performers in showbiz history, only from his stand-up act, you might find it hard to believe that he could ever cross over to the lily-white world of sitcoms. Yet, *Sanford and Son* was a huge hit among black and white audiences alike.

Let's note that the major networks have always depended on huge ratings, which means that black sitcoms must also entertain white audiences and vice versa. While the fledgling UPN and WB (now the CW network) might at first have been small enough to rely on predominantly black audiences, the big networks have tended to soften their black characters—actually, all of their characters, regardless of race or religion. Yet, when the big three (we're not counting Fox among the majors) have allowed a certified curmudgeon like Archie Bunker or Maude

Redd Foxx as Fred Sanford and Demond Wilson as his "big dummy" son Lamont, in the junky living room of their Watts-district junkyard.

Sanford: I still want to sow some wild oats.
Lamont: At your age, you don't have no wild oats, you got shredded wheat.

Findlay or Roseanne (two rare female cynics) or Fred Sanford to behave outrageously, audiences have mostly been thrilled. (Okay, it didn't work for Jackie Mason, but he annoys everyone, even—especially?—Jews.) There's no disputing that Redd Foxx had to reinvent himself for television. When he removed the four-letter words and sexual content from his stand-up act, there was precious little left: just his persona. As it turned out, that was quite enough to build a series around.

Series are often created for stand-up comics. The thinking is, if they're that funny playing themselves, they will shine in a well-written series. It doesn't always work like that. Some of the greatest TV comics weren't solo performers. Lucille Ball was one of the funniest, if not the funniest, comic on television, but she wasn't a particularly funny person off the set. Her great gift was that she could act funny. Mary Tyler Moore was as winning as they come on her show, but you wouldn't want to hear her tell a string of jokes in a comedy club.

Still, several stand-up performers did star in excellent and successful series. Jerry Seinfeld is their undisputed king. Others include Bob Saget (who also greatly toned down his stand-up schtick), Ellen DeGeneres, Drew Carey, Roseanne, Kevin James, Tim Allen, Paul Reiser, Richard Belzer, and Freddie Prinze. Going back a few years, there were Billy Crystal, Bill Cosby, Bob Newhart, Jimmy Walker, and Robin Williams. If you want to go back even farther, there were the television pioneers Danny Thomas, Jack Benny, and Burns and Allen. More recently, Martin Lawrence, George Lopez, Norm MacDonald, and Bernie Mac have headed up successful sitcoms, though their popularity hasn't always been a reflection of their quality.

Some of the funniest stand-up performers just couldn't make the transition to sitcom success. It wasn't necessarily their fault—but George Carlin, Louie Anderson, Margaret Cho, Buddy Hackett, Louis C. K., Steve Harvey,

Above: Redd Foxx hunches over the stove in the Sanford house which, in 1972, seemed like an antiquated wreck, but thirty years later is a model of retro chic.

Below: Della Reese and Foxx on *The Royal Family*, the show Foxx was shooting when he died with his boots on.

Opposite top: Always ready to quote the Bible (although we're not sure if the phrase "Shut up, you fish-eyed heathen" actually appears anywhere in the Good Book), the fabulous LaWanda Page, as Esther Anderson, never took any lip from anyone, especially Lynn Hamilton as Fred Sanford's girlfriend, Donna Harris.

Opposite bottom: Demond Wilson with Whitman Mayo, who got his own spinoff, *Grady*, from *Sanford and Son*.

Redd Foxx

Blue, blue, blue—but not in the Bobby Vinton sense, Redd Foxx was one of the most foul-mouthed comics on the black theater circuit. Surprisingly, he managed to break out into white entertainment, not an easy task in the early 1950s. He really made it big in the '60s, along with such other black comics as Bill Cosby, Dick Gregory, Godfrey Cambridge, and Richard Pryor. He was made for the part of the cantankerous Sanford on *Sanford and Son*. After various contretemps with the show's writers, producers, and NBC, he decamped to ABC for what was to be a failed variety show. His subsequent television outings also failed, including *The Redd Foxx Show*, in 1986. Foxx did better in films, including the TV movie *Ghost of a Chance*, in which he was paired with Dick Van Dyke, of all people; and *Harlem Nights* in which he supported two of his biggest fans, Eddie Murphy and Richard Pryor. He collapsed on the set while rehearsing his last sitcom, 1991's *The Royal Family*.

286 SITCOMS: THE 101 GREATEST TV COMEDIES OF ALL TIME

Andy Kaufman, Jackie Mason, Don Rickles, Christopher Titus, Phyllis Diller, Whoopi Goldberg, and Nia Vardalos all tried and struck out.

We've all heard of actors leaving shows and being replaced with another performer. The two Darrin Stephenses on *Bewitched* are the most obvious example. But we can only think of two cases where a title character left a series: Valerie Harper left *Valerie* and Redd Foxx, after refusing a salary increase, left *Sanford and Son* in the middle of the 1973–74 season. The writers sent the character to St. Louis for the funeral of a cousin and upgraded the character of his best friend Grady. Then NBC sued Foxx and he returned. He finally left the series for good in 1977, decamping to ABC, who had decided that he would make a great host of…ready?…a variety show!

Sanford and Son didn't die immediately, even with Sanford gone. A new series was proposed, *The Sanford Arms*, starring Demond Wilson. Wilson refused the salary and the show went on without either Sanford or Son. Actor Whitman Mayo, who had played Grady, was rewarded for his effort above and beyond the call of duty with a spin-off called—what else?—*Grady*. It ran one season in 1975. Still, the history of *Sanford and Son* wasn't quite over. In 1980, Redd Foxx decided that he missed playing Sanford (and getting that weekly sitcom salary) and returned in a series cleverly called *Sanford*. The "*and Son*" was notably missing, as Demond Wilson once again refused to return to the character of Lamont. And, after one brief season, that was that for Sanford, his son, Grady, and the residents of the Sanford Arms.

LaWanda Page

"The Bronze Goddess of Fire," as she was billed while performing in black nightclubs, graduated to stand-up comedy at the behest of Redd Foxx, her friend since childhood. Like Foxx, she gained early fame, among black audiences anyway, through a series of comedy albums that featured anything-goes racy material and her own catchphrase, "Watch it, sucka!" Foxx made sure she was cast in his first sitcom, *Sanford and Son*, as his sister-in-law, the Bible-thumping Aunt Esther. Their special rapport added to the chemistry of their two characters, who were always sparring. She was a semiregular on the *Dean Martin Celebrity Roasts* and appeared on several black series, including *Amen* and *Martin*. It's a pity that this excellent character actress was never allowed to cross over to a white series. Her final burst of fame came in a series of music videos for drag queen RuPaul's *Supermodel of the World* album.

OFF THE SET

REDD FOXX'S REAL last name was Sanford. Demond Wilson's real name is Grady Demond Wilson, which is where the writers got the name of the character Grady Wilson.

CLEAVON LITTLE WAS considered for the part of Sanford. He turned it down but suggested Redd Foxx for the part.

CAST

Redd Foxx	Fred Sanford
Demond Wilson	Lamont Sanford
Whitman Mayo	Grady Wilson
LaWanda Page	Aunt Esther
Raymond Allen	Woody Anderson
Don Bexley	Bubba Hoover
Marlene Clark	Janet Lawson
Edward Crawford	Roger Lawson
Lynn Hamilton	Donna Harris
Noam Pitlik	Officer Swanhauser
Howard Platt	Officer "Happy" Hopkins
Beah Richards	Aunt Ethel

SAVED BY THE BELL

NBC | **1989–1994** | **90 episodes**

The endlessly inventive Zack and his high school pals get into and out of trouble before, during, and after class at Bayside High.

Here's the guiltiest of guilty pleasures and the only show in this book that didn't appear on prime time. You woke up on a weekend morning, hit the remote, and up popped Zack and the gang. The show could be dismissed as lightweight crap, but somehow it became the equivalent of easy-listening television, washing over you as you lay there, the pretty young kids, easy jokes, and cheap sets innocuous but inexplicably fascinating.

The show started out as a female *Welcome Back, Kotter* titled *Good Morning, Miss Bliss*, a vehicle for Hayley Mills. It was a typical Disney Channel affair following the experiences of Miss Carrie Bliss, a teacher at JFK Junior High School in Indianapolis. After thirteen episodes, Disney had had enough and the producers, Peter Engel and William F. Phillips, sold the show to NBC under the title *Saved by the Bell*. It was shown twice in prime time before settling into its Saturday morning slot, complete with a mock-rock title tune and a new location, Bayside High School in Pacific Palisades. Somehow, through the magic of television, the characters of Zack, Mr. Belding, Screech, and Lisa (Lisa!) ended up enrolled at Bayside, too.

Wisely, the producers made Mark-Paul Gosselaar's Zack the protagonist. He was the smartest, cutest, most charismatic kid in school and, to top it all off, with a snap of his fingers or a wink at the camera he could stop the action and speak directly to the audience. Also along for the ride were the supposed hot girl, Jessie; the school jock who also knew how to dance and do ballet, Slater; and the girl next door, Kelly. Though it might have taken them longer than real kids, they did grow up on the series, eventually graduating from high school.

As the series progressed, Zack concocted more stupid schemes than Lucy Ricardo. This mini-Ralph Kramden was always looking for a way to make some bucks at the expense of others. Though he constantly got into trouble, he was the smartest kid in school and no matter how badly his schemes backfired—and they always did—he came out on top. Remember when the nerd—make that the annoying nerd—Screech, invented an acne cream and Zack sold gallons of it to the student body? The only

Sam Bobrick

Sam Bobrick, the creator of *Good Morning, Miss Bliss* as well as all of the incarnations of *Saved by the Bell*, got his television start as a writer on *Bewitched* and *Gomer Pyle U.S.M.C.* Bobrick wrote three comedy albums for *Mad Magazine* and had a play on Broadway, *Norman...Is That You?* The play was an immense success—not on Broadway, where it only ran only twelve performances, but in dinner theaters throughout the country. He wrote three more plays, to no avail. So, it was on to the *Saved by the Bell* franchise, which took up the next six years of his life.

Elizabeth Berkley and Mario Lopez in the TV movie *SBTB: Hawaiian Style*, in which Screech, et al., went to Oahu to get lei-ed.

problem was that the cream made the user's skin glow red after a few days. Naturally, all the redskins were a little ticked at Zack—but he convinced them that it was a great way to show school spirit. After all, red was the official school color.

Folks, does that sound any stupider than Lucy with a loving cup stuck on her head? The only difference is brilliance—and that's a word that should never be used in the same sentence with the words *Saved by the Bell*. Still, the show found its audience, eventually evolving into a prime-time comedy called *Saved by the Bell: The College Years*. Zack, Kelly, Slater, and Screech matriculated, but *Saved by the Bell* was better suited to its Saturday morning slot. Adults and the coveted college-age demographic expected more, um, good writing and acting from prime time. It lasted only nineteen lame episodes. The finale was an hourlong prime-time special, *Saved by the Bell: Wedding in Las Vegas*, in which Zack and Kelly finally got married.

Never wanting to let a successful idea die, Peter Engel produced a new Saturday morning show for NBC titled (insert drumroll and cymbal crash here) *Saved by the Bell: The New Class*. Mr. Belding and the now astoundingly annoying Screech were the only ones desperate enough to make the move back to Bayside High.

Bayside's graduates became very successful after college. Tiffani-Amber Thiessen went up Sunset Boulevard to *Beverly Hills 90210*; Mark-Paul Gosselaar found steady work on *NYPD Blue*, *Commander in Chief*, and other shows; Mario Lopez appeared on *Nip/Tuck* and *Dancing with the Stars*; Elizabeth Berkley stretched her acting muscles in the film *Showgirls* (and, despite that, still works); Dustin Diamond has recently been begging for money on the Internet (no kidding); and Lark Voorhies is...around. But they are all still with us on basic cable, still hindering us from leading productive lives.

OFF THE SET

ISODES OF *GOOD MORNING, MISS BLISS* re reedited and, with a wrap-around featuring ck, broadcast as part of *Saved by the Bell*.

SPER VAN DIEN, Scott Wolf, Denise Richards, d Tori Spelling all appeared on the show.

CAST

Mark-Paul Gosselaar	Zack Morris
Tiffani-Amber Thiessen	Kelly Kapowski
Mario Lopez	A. C. Slater
Dustin Diamond	Samuel "Screech" Powers
Lark Voorhies	Lisa Turtle
Elizabeth Berkley	Jessie Spano
Dennis Haskins	Mr. Belding
Leah Rimini	Stacey Carosi
Ernie Sabella	Leon Carosi
Max Battimo	Mikey Gonzalez
Heather Hopper	Nikki Coleman
Joan Ryan	Tina Paladrino

SCRUBS

 NBC | **2001–present** | **139 to date**

Young resident doctor J. D. Dorian, fresh out of medical school and surrounded by offbeat friends and co-workers, deals with the challenges of a big-city hospital and of life itself.

Duct Tape is Funny: Zach Braff in the *Scrubs* episode "My Perspective," in which J.D., with the help of The Janitor, gets to hear what his colleagues *really* think of him. Think of a 2007 version of Tom Sawyer attending his own funeral.

ow many ideas can dance on the head of a sitcom writer? Not since *The Simpsons* have so many concepts, jokes, and references been stuffed into a half hour. It's no surprise that creator Bill Lawrence has stated that he wanted *Scrubs* to rival *The Simpsons* in its density of jokes and multiplicity of guest stars. *Scrubs* is rife with inside jokes, flashbacks, monologues, daydreams, direct address of the audience,

fantasy sequences, what-ifs, and voiceovers. Its endless gimmicks, short scenes, and constant camera movement guarantee that the show is never boring, but *Scrubs* also features some things that are very rare in sitcoms: genuine emotion and a naturalness that borders on reality.

Zach Braff's young doctor sometimes takes on the slack-jawed, wide-eyed look of a dumb deer, but he can also be introspective and, occasionally, on top of his game. Braff has also developed into

SITCOMS: THE 101 GREATEST TV COMEDIES OF ALL TIME

stick mishaps of the wedding. Fast-forward to the sixth season: J.D. is still wondering whether he and Elliot should be together.

A nod, too, is given to the realism of a hospital staffed by whites, blacks, and Hispanics who really don't have a whole lot of time to worry about their racial differences—though they do seem quite obsessed with breasts and booties.

With its intelligence, occasional slapstick interludes, and underlying emotion, *Scrubs* is one of the few current sitcoms to have it all. They've tried a musical episode (when a patient suffered from the delusion that everyone was singing), an episode entirely made up of flashbacks, an episode dealing with the war in Iraq, and even a Very Special two-parter in which a character died. Though never at the top of the ratings, *Scrubs* continues to hold on season after season without suffering from episode fatigue.

a most promising film writer and director with this success, *Garden State*. Other characters are equally well developed. Take the dryly sarcastic Dr. Cox: he lives with his ex-wife and child, and realizes that the spark in their relationship is their constant bickering. They can only get along when they aren't getting along. He won't take any guff from J.D. and is quick with a withering quip—but he's also got morals and a sense of decency.

Most important to the series is J.D.'s relationship with female colleague, Elliot. Referred to in the third season as "Ross and Rachel" (a rare inter-sitcom reference), J.D. and Elliot manage to hook up once each season but never quite make the connection they both want. In season three, J.D., jealous of Elliot's hunky boyfriend Sean, asks her to move in with him. He almost immediately realizes it's a mistake and, after a few days, tells her that he doesn't love her—during the wedding reception of Doctor Turk and Nurse Espinosa. A painful moment between J.D. and Elliot is juxtaposed against the slap-

Below: Today's most talented, quirky leading man, Zach Braff, with the actor who held the title forty years ago, Dick Van Dyke.

CAST

Zach Braff	Dr. John "J.D." Dorian
Donald Faison	Dr. Chris Turk
Sarah Chalke	Dr. Elliot Reid
Ken Jenkins	Dr. Bob Kelso
John C. McGinley	Dr. Perry Cox
Judy Reyes	Nurse Carla Espinosa
Neil Flynn	The Janitor
Aloma Wright	Nurse Laverne Roberts
Robert Maschio	Todd

SEINFELD

  | 1990–1998 | 180 episodes, plus one special

Stand-up comic Jerry Seinfeld, his neighbor Cosmo Kramer, his best friend George Costanza, and his ex-girlfriend Elaine Benes do nothing. Hilariously.

Get a piece of paper and think of your favorite sitcom. Now, write a list of your favorite episodes. It's not as easy as you think. Some series, such as *I Married Joan*, *I Dream of Jeannie*, and *Growing Pains*, were most enjoyable in the moment—it's difficult to remember the details of specific episodes. Then there are the series (even some before the advent of DVDs) where many, many episodes jump to mind. *I Love Lucy*: Yes. *The Lucy Show*: No. *The Dick Van Dyke Show*, *Mary Tyler Moore*: Absolutely. Even *The Simpsons*. Near the top of this short list we'd have to put *Seinfeld*, the sitcom many believe is the greatest of all sitcoms.

The honor is ironic, since *Seinfeld* was the sitcom supposedly about nothing. Yet, after a decade-long run on NBC, Seinfeldians, even casual ones, can rattle off a list of their favorite episodes. Is it the one with the puffy shirt? The accidental poisoning-by-envelope-glue of George's fiancée? The search for the car in the parking garage? Jerry's guilt at his aunt's death? The mansierre? The Chinese restaurant? Shrinkage? Masters of their domain?

Yet in spite of its brilliant, hilarious, trend-setting run, *Seinfeld* bears the curse of the sitcom. As Shakespeare once said, "The evil that men do lives after them" and that's certainly true of *Seinfeld*, both on and off screen, for never was there such a misanthropic group of humans. With seldom anything nice to say about anyone and not once crying over the spilt milk of human kindness, Jerry and his gang found fault with, well, everyone. Some quotes to illustrate the point. Jerry: "I can't

Jerry Seinfeld and Elaine Benes enjoyed the most hilariously complicated (and, in many ways, the most realistic) male-female relationship on television.

Don't misunderstand, *Seinfeld* was undeniably hilarious, sometimes even reaching a level of genius…but compassion can be just as funny. Unfortunately, in the increasingly polarized world of television, a show is either sticky sweet or darkly cynical—which leads to another point. *Seinfeld* has to answer for its role in the development of the sitcom. Without a doubt, the show mined comic gold from the little idiosyncrasies and annoyances of American life, such as imperious maître d's, handi-

go to a bad movie by myself. What, am I gonna make sarcastic remarks to strangers?" George: "I'm much more comfortable criticizing people behind their backs." Elaine: "I couldn't raise a kid? C'mon, I love bossing people around." Sweethearts, one and all.

capped parking, backseat driving, smelly cars, and the rest.

Seinfeld ushered in the era of squeamish comedy. Uncomfortable, embarrassing, hide-your-eyes comedy. Snooping around someone's apartment, getting a masseur to lie to an insurance

Julia Louis-Dreyfus

Queen of misplaced enthusiasm, Julia Louis-Dreyfus has found a home on television, adroitly escaping the *Seinfeld* curse. Her career began when she met her husband, comedian Brad Hall, while both were attending Northwestern University. They joined the troupe on *Saturday Night Live* (the first and only married couple to appear as cast members), and Louis-Dreyfus is the only female former cast member to return as a guest host. After costarring in the failed *Family Ties* spin-off *The Art of Being Nick* in 1986 and as an Elaine Benes-lite character on the short-lived *Day by Day*, she got off the bench and into the big leagues on *Seinfeld*. Her performance, featuring a jaw clenched with urban intensity but also a willingness to be goofy, made her a major television star. A follow-up sitcom, *Watching Ellie* (created by her husband), was almost as big a flop as Jason Alexander's and Michael Richards's post-*Seinfeld* efforts, but that didn't drive her to doing Kentucky Fried Chicken commercials or spewing racist venom at the Laugh Factory. In fact, she regrouped quite nicely and scored a well-deserved hit with *The New Adventures of Old Christine*.

Elaine: Ugh. I hate people.
Jerry: Yeah. They're the worst.

company, shoving old ladies out of the way to escape a fire—the show featured all kinds of activities that were mortifying to watch other people engage in. Given the landscape of television, each sitcom that hoped to follow in *Seinfeld*'s very successful footprints had to ratchet up the unnerving humor, making the audience more and more ill at ease. The apotheosis is the original British sitcom *The Office*—just try to watch more than two episodes in a row on DVD. Or *Seinfeld* co-creator Larry David's *Curb Your Enthusiasm*, on which he constantly places himself in mortifying situations, usually in spite of his good intentions. Then there's Sacha Baron Cohen's *Ali G*, who sets folk up for mammoth embarrassment (admittedly, his targets are idiots, but a pigeon is a pigeon) for our amusement.

All of those shows took their lead (or at least got their license) from *Seinfeld*'s quartet of cranky New Yorkers. Unapologetic and unyielding to the end, Jerry and company got their comeuppance in the last episode, after nearly two hundred episodes of bad behavior, when they were all thrown in jail for eternity. So perhaps *Seinfeld* ended up being about something after all: karmic payback.

One last tip of the hat to the series. We applaud the realistic depiction of the New York apartments of Jerry, Elaine, and Kramer—small, badly painted, multiple locks on the doors—perfect.

Jerry Seinfeld and George Costanza, whose onscreen relationship was based on the real-life friendship of Seinfeld and series co-creator Larry David.

Right top: Estelle Costanza (the hysterical Estelle Harris), gets a hospital visit from son George in one of Seinfeld's most notorious episodes, "The Contest." While she berates George for "treating his body as if it were an amusement park," the sponge bath in the next bed is about to begin.

Right middle: *Seinfeld* employed the best, most offbeat comic writers in Hollywood, including Peter Mehlman, Larry Charles, Carol Leifer, the team of Tom Gammill and Max Pross, and Bruce Eric Kaplan, who wrote the wonderfully bizarre episode in which Kramer reconstructed the set of *The Merv Griffin Show* in his apartment.

Right bottom: Michael Richards and Jerry Stiller show off their invention, the "mansierre." Or the "bro," depending on who you ask.

One simple word can say so much: *Newman*.

CAST

Jerry Seinfeld .... Jerry Seinfeld

Julia Louis-Dreyfus ...... Elaine Benes

Jason Alexander .... George Costanza

Michael Richards .... Cosmo Kramer

Liz Sheridan .... Helen Seinfeld

Barney Martin .... Morty Seinfeld

Len Lesser .... Uncle Leo

Wayne Knight .... Newman

Estelle Harris .... Estelle Costanza

Jerry Stiller .... Frank Costanza

John O'Hurley .... J. Peterman

Phil Morris .... Jackie Chiles

Patrick Warburton .... David Puddy

Bryan Cranston .... Dr. Tim Whatley

Danny Woodburn .... Mickey Abbott

Ian Abercrombie .... Mr. Pitt

THE SIMPSONS

FOX | **1990–present** | **Still going after 18 seasons**

A loving but extremely dysfunctional family lives, works, and gets in and out of trouble in Springfield, State Unknown.

Animated sitcoms: their history began with *The Flintstones*, the first prime-time animated series, but it would be another thirty years before there was another hit animated series. This most intelligent, most satirical, most revolutionary show is also the longest running situation comedy ever—live or animated.

The astounding accomplishments of *The Simpsons* arise from the depth and breadth of its humor, and its connection to a wide audience. The slapstick animated cartoon within an animated cartoon, *Itchy and Scratchy*, appeals to fans of mindless violence; Bart's bad-boy behavior provides wish fulfillment for younger viewers; Homer's doofus quality resonates with adult men; steadfast Marge tugs at the heartstrings of women; Lisa's intellectual frustration rings true for the brainy set; Mr. Burns's corporate greed is a great target for lefties and downtrodden wage slaves. Then there's Waylon Smithers, poster boy for closeted homosexuals; Marge's sisters Patti and Selma representing chain-smoking old maids; barfly Barney embodying hopeless alcoholics, Ned Flanders personifying religious fundamentalists…the list goes on and on.

Which brings us to our next point. Whereas some series, such as *The Honeymooners* and *I Love Lucy*, rested squarely on their four central characters, *The Simpsons* has, seemingly, hundreds. They aren't just occasional drop-ins, either, but full-fledged recurring characters, each perfectly drawn (in both senses of the word). Springfield, Wherever, is a fully populated, if wacked-out, community. And, exploiting the greatest benefit of animation, most of

these distinctive individuals are voiced by the tightest of core acting ensembles ever assembled.

Of course, a profusion of characters does not a successful sitcom make. The writing on the show has been among the best in television history, at least in its first decade on the air. Unlike another Fox show, *Married … with Children*, *The Simpsons* has never been content to rest on the dysfunctionality of the family

Opposite: *The Simpsons* strike one of their trademark weekly sofa tableaux, this time for a special Halloween episode.

Left: *The Simpsons* has commented hilariously on every aspect of American culture, including politics, country music, Broadway musicals, and other animated shows. This *Rear Window* spoof was one of the hundreds of allusions the show has made to classic films.

OFF THE SET

MATT GROENING'S REAL-LIFE parents were Homer and Marge, and his sisters' names were Lisa and Maggie. His mother's maiden name was Wiggum. His sons are named Homer and Abe.

DURING THE OPENING credits, Maggie is accidentally scanned by a bar-code reader in the grocery store. Her price comes up on the register as $847.63, a figure the government once touted as the amount of money required to raise a baby for one month in the United States.

---

unit alone, and it has mostly stayed away from the "very special" heartwarming moments that fueled such shows as *Full House*. *The Simpsons* has parodied everything—modern art (with Jasper Johns as a guest) to television (the satire of *Dallas* was titled "Who Shot Mr. Burns"—it was Maggie, as it turned out); James Bond (Homer gets a job in a perfect town working for an über villain); religion (juvenile authorities take the Simpson kids away from Homer and Marge and put them in the foster care of the Flanders); gun control (Homer becomes addicted to the power of the firearm); the church; homophobia (Homer is afraid that Bart is turning gay); the Internet (whatbadgerseat.com and Homer's blog as Mr. X); and animation itself (Homer takes the family to the Sick, Twisted, and Totally F***ed Up Animation Festival). Many serious subjects have been made palatable—and very funny—due to the writers' fearlessness, wit, and sensitivity.

These large themes, are not all that *The Simpsons* bring to the comedy table. Within each episode, there are dozens of puns, visual jokes, and hit-and-run bits of satire. More goes on in one episode of *The Simpsons* than in an entire season of such shows as *Joey* or the inexplicable hit *Two and a Half Men*. Like *Mad Magazine*,

which doubtlessly inspired much of its humor, *The Simpsons* includes layers and layers of different kinds of humor, as well as numerous running gags beloved by die-hard fans. Even the title sequence is endlessly reinvented: Bart's blackboard writing varies in each episode, Lisa plays a different sax solo, and the family assembles a new couch tableau.

As authors of a book on musical theater, we find it gratifying that the show isn't embarrassed to break out into exuberant song now and then. The musical episodes are simply phenomenal, including one in which Bart and Milhouse, high on pure Squishee syrup, sing "Springfield, Springfield" (a parody of "New York, New York"); a community theater production of *Streetcar!* starring Marge as Blanche DuBois; a musical version of *Planet of the Apes*, featuring the timeless classic "They'll Never Make a Monkey Out of Me"; Mark Hamill, as Luke Skywalker, sing-

Matt Groening

The genius behind *The Simpsons*, Matt Groening came to Los Angeles after graduating from Evergreen State College in Washington State. He was summoned to the offices of producer James L. Brooks to discuss turning his "Life in Hell" comic strip into a series. Fearing loss of the rights to the popular alternative strip, Groening thought up another idea while sitting in Brooks's waiting room, and the result, as you have surely guessed, was *The Simpsons* which premiered as bumpers between sketches on *The Tracey Ullman Show*. Groening took the opportunity to convey his wacky sense of humor as well as his political and societal views to a wide mainstream audience. He was smart enough to hire the brightest young humor writers, many fresh from the *Harvard Lampoon*. Groening's stewardship of the show has ensured its quality and his willingness to stand up to pressures from inside and outside the Fox Television machine has kept the integrity of the show intact.

"Round up the usual suspects": This lineup of possible shooters of the universally loathed Mr. Burns was part of a spot-on satire of *Dallas* and other primetime soap cliffhangers.

Marcia Wallace

With a toothy grin and a devilish twinkle, Marcia Wallace is best remembered as Carol Kester Bondurant (below), the good-spirited receptionist on *The Bob Newhart Show*, but many fans don't realize the breadth of her career. Following appearances on and off Broadway, she arrived in Los Angeles and quickly found small parts on television. After only a year in L.A., and guest shots on *Bewitched* and *The Brady Bunch*, she landed the role on *Bob Newhart*, at the same time adding her wicked sense of humor to the celebrity panel on the game show *Match Game*. After *Newhart* ended, she was seen in one-offs on several series and landed recurring spots on *Alf* and *Full House*. With the animated series *Darkwing Duck*, she began doing voice-overs, eventually working on *Batman* and playing her greatest off-screen role, Edna Krabappel on *The Simpsons*. For that, she won a well-deserved Emmy. Most recently, Wallace appeared on Comedy Central's sitcom *That's My Bush*.

ing "Luke Be a Jedi Tonight"; and "Monorail!"—a razor-sharp parody of *The Music Man*.

Back in the day, radio comics Bob and Ray would often present fake commercials in which the product advertised came as a comic surprise at the end. *The Simpsons'* writers have taken this idea and applied it to plots. Often, the way an episode begins is no clue to how it will end up—in a technique dubbed "plot drift." In one classic episode, Bart and Milhouse go to the Kwik-E-Mart and order a pure syrup Squishee. After the aforementioned musical number, the boys fall into a sugar coma. Bart wakes up embarrassed to find he's joined the Junior Campers, a perverted version of the Cub Scouts, leading to a whitewater rafting trip (with Homer, and the father/son team of Ned and Todd Flanders), which begins as a parody of Hitchcock's *Lifeboat* and winds up a spoof of *Deliverance*. The group is saved when Homer's food-obsessed nose leads them out of the wilderness to a Krusty Burger franchise. The episode ends with scoutmaster Ernest Borgnine sitting around the campfire with the other scouts in a parody of *The Fog*, twenty-three minutes and six changes of plot later.

By the late 1990s, most of the original writers had departed and the quality began to vary wildly. The show became much broader, without the depth of humor that was such an important part of the first decade. Toilet humor (a mainstay of other lame sitcoms) became more prevalent and Homer, in particular, degenerated into sheer stupidity. Still, the show has its supporters and continues to thrive in its nineteenth season.

Despite the slide in quality, hypocrisy doesn't stand a chance on *The Simpsons*, because at its heart is the family. Though Homer's a dope, Marge barely makes ends meet, Bart is a delinquent, and Lisa doesn't get any credit for her brains or talent, they are a loving family and so, in a very real way, reflect our own lives. Therein lies its greatest strength: *The Simpsons* reflects our times and ourselves with unerring accuracy.

CAST

Dan Castellaneta..........Homer Simpson

Julie Kavner ....Marge Simpson

Nancy Cartwright ....Bartholomew Jo-Jo "Bart" Simpson

Yeardley Smith ....Lisa Simpson, Maggie Simpson

Harry Shearer ....Ned Flanders, Mr. Burns, Smithers

Hank Azaria ....Chief Clancy Wiggum, Apu

Marcia Wallace ....Edna Krabappel

SOAP

abc | 1977–1981 | 85 episodes

The Tates and the Campbells, two families so dysfunctional they make the Ewings and the Carringtons look dull in comparison, shock the quiet hamlet of Dunns River with their continuing exhibitions of lust, power, and ventriloquism.

The creation of the talented Susan Harris and her producing partners, Paul Witt and Tony Thomas (son of Danny), *Soap* was a sharply drawn satire of daytime dramas, walking one of the finest lines of tone and taste in sitcom history.

Definitely playing it for laughs, the show was also out to knock down any remaining no-nos in prime time. Suprisingly, seven years after the debut of *All in the Family* and three years after *Maude* hit the airwaves, there were still many subjects that were off limits, especially as part of a central story line. Mike Stivic's brush with infidelity was one thing, but showing marrieds Jessica and Chester Tate jumping in and out of bed with half of Connecticut on a weekly basis was an entirely different matter. And "swinging"

The Tates and the Campbells keep from tearing one another to bits just long enough to pose for this family portrait.

was one of the tamer activities that occupied the days of their lives. Anything went on *Soap*: Homosexuality. Impotence. Interracial marriage. Prostitution. Murder. And then there were the plotlines that expertly skewered daytime television's borderline grasp of reality: alien abduction, demonic possession, and that hoary chestnut, amnesia.

The format followed that of all soap operas: various threads of melodrama and a cliffhanger ending to each episode, complete with narration by *The Price Is Right* announcer Rod Roddy that posed a series of pointed questions to be answered "in the next episode of *Soap*."

A 1977 *Newsweek* article about the approaching fall television season set off a frenzy of negative publicity about the show, particularly when it was incorrectly reported that the pilot featured a seduction scene in a Catholic confessional. Every religious group was nervous about *Soap* before it premiered, in fact, the show was perceived to be such an "equal opportunity offender" that it was condemned by both the National Council of Churches and the National Gay Task Force. Now that's controversy! Picketing, letter-writing campaigns, and vilification by the PTA led several ABC affiliates to refuse to air the show, and advertisers shied away as well, nearly killing *Soap* before it was born. It was saved only by

Katherine Helmond

Sexy character comedienne Katherine Helmond attended the ultraconservative Bob Jones University before heading to New York to be an actress. A late bloomer, she didn't land her breakout role until she was past forty. After costarring with fellow sitcom icon Elizabeth Montgomery in the landmark television movie *The Legend of Lizzie Borden*, among other serious and comic roles, Helmond was catapulted to stardom as the addled Jessica Tate on *Soap*, and was nominated for an Emmy for each of the show's four seasons. After a brilliant performance as Jonathan Pryce's plastic-surgery-addicted mother in the cult film *Brazil*, she found herself in another sitcom hit, as Judith Light's free-spirited mother, Mona, for eight years on *Who's the Boss?* A welcome addition to the cast of any show, she joined the ensemble of *Coach* for its final two seasons, and received her seventh Emmy nomination for her guest-starring role as Patricia Heaton's mother on *Everybody Loves Raymond*.

the passion of ABC chief Fred Silverman. As in most similar cases, the uproar turned out to be much ado about nothing and according to a poll of viewers, after the dreaded pilot aired, 74 percent of its viewers found it inoffensive—and half of those who were offended replied that they would watch the show again.

Through all of the controversy, the only group that didn't complain about the show was the NAACP, not surprising since the only truly sensible character on *Soap* was the Tate's butler Benson, played by the marvelously dry Robert Guillaume. So popular was his character that he was spun off onto his own series and replaced by the equally unflappable Roscoe Lee Browne.

The unusually large cast of regulars was superb. The actors playing the two main married couples came directly from the New York stage: Katherine Helmond as the nymphomaniac space cadet, Jessica; Cathryn Damon, who never got enough credit for her ability to play mock seriousness with such precision and subtlety, as her sister Mary; Robert Mandan as the pompous womanizer, Chester; and

Above: Richard Mulligan with Cathryn Damon (known as "Skipper" to her friends), who started out her career as a dancer on Broadway.

the wild Richard Mulligan, who nearly walked off with the whole show as the buffoonish Burt. There were also hilarious supporting turns by such farceurs as Diana Canova, Ted Wass, Sal Viscuso, Dinah Manoff, and the one who would go on to become the biggest star of the bunch, Billy Crystal, as the sexually confused Jodie.

Shows like *Dallas*, *Dynasty* (which, despite their hourlong form and glossy packaging, became parodies in their own right), and the current hit, *Desperate Housewives*, all owe a debt of gratitude to Susan Harris's arch of an eyebrow and well-deserved ribbing of an institution that had come to take itself far too seriously.

Opposite top: Robert Guillaume and Katherine Helmond let their fingers do the walking.

Opposite bottom: Diana Canova and Sal Viscuso in the storyline that got the Roman Catholic church in a tizzy before they'd even had a chance to see the show's pilot.

Left: Richard Mulligan got his first chance at TV stardom in the series *The Hero*, costarring Mariette Hartley. In it, he played actor Sam Garrett, star of the TV western *Jed Clayton, U.S. Marshal*.

Richard Mulligan

A master at comic befuddlement, Richard Mulligan set out to become a playwright. Switching to acting and appearing in several Broadway plays, he was given an early shot at television stardom alongside Mariette Hartley in the sitcom *The Hero*, but it was canceled after sixteen episodes. He spent the next decade guest-starring on numerous series before getting his star-making role as the dingbat Burt Campbell on *Soap*, winning the first of two Emmys. Appearing in films, including a wonderful performance in Blake Edwards's Hollywood satire *S.O.B.*, Mulligan rebounded from the flop sitcom *Reggie* to star as pediatrician Harry Weston in the seven-season hit *Empty Nest*, reuniting with his former *Soap* bosses Witt/Thomas/Harris. As the 1980 Emmy Awards were derailed by a Screen Actors Guild strike, Mulligan and his onscreen wife, Cathryn Damon, never had a chance to accept their trophies publicly. Always a class act, when Mulligan won his second Emmy, for *Empty Nest*, he dedicated the award to his late friend and costar, Damon.

CHARACTER ACTORS PART II

Allow us to pause once more and pay tribute to some of the versatile actors we've seen again and again (and again) over the last fifty years, the folks whose faces we know in an instant but whose names don't always leap to memory.

Arlene Golonka
Often seen as: shy single girls and ditsy goodtime girls. Best known as: bakery owner Millie Swanson on *Mayberry, RFD*.

Barbara Pepper
Often seen as: innocent bystanders, confused salesladies, and pleasingly plump fellow passengers. Best known as: the slatternly Doris Ziffel on *Green Acres*.

Frank Nelson
Often seen as: overly cheery salesmen and put-upon hotel desk clerks. Best known as: cheesy game show host Freddie Fillmore on *I Love Lucy*.

Edward Winter
Often seen as: lecherous bosses and clueless politicians. Best known as: the ever-paranoid undercover agent, Col. Flagg, on *M*A*S*H*.

J. Pat O'Malley
Often seen as: blarney-filled Irishmen, skeptical judges, and sympathetic barkeeps. Best known as: Mrs. Naugatuck's boyfriend Bert Beasley on *Maude*.

Doris Packer
Often seen as: disapproving mothers-in-law, bewildered dowagers, and snooty society dames. Best known as: super-wealthy Mrs. Chatsworth Osborne Sr. on *The Many Loves of Dobie Gillis*.

Bernard Fox
Often seen as: rigid British generals, befuddled police inspectors, and assorted ninnies. Best known as: Quackish Dr. Bombay on *Bewitched*.

Nita Talbot
Often seen as: sultry yet hilarious seductresses, hip and groovy housewives, and mysterious women with geographically untraceable accents. Best known as: the sexy Russian spy Marya on *Hogan's Heroes*.

Jane Dulo

Often seen as: impossible-to-please customers, sadistic nurses, and loudmouth harpies. Best known as: Agent 99's cantankerous mother on *Get Smart*.

John Fiedler

Often seen as: timid mailmen, henpecked husbands, and bookish professors. Best known as: Bob Hartley's mild-mannered patient, Emil Peterson, on *The Bob Newhart Show*.

Shirley Mitchell

Often seen as: sarcastic nurses, suspicious wives, and condescending country clubbers. Best known as: next-door neighbor Marge Thornton on *Please Don't Eat the Daisies*.

Todd Susman

Often seen as: lovable losers and deadpan clerks. Best known as: the bumbling Officer Shifflett on *Newhart*.

Beverly Sanders

Often seen as: grocery checkers, bowling team members, and loud laughers. Best known as: Rayette, Mary Richards regular waitress on *Mary Tyler Moore*.

Hilary Thompson

Often seen as: young expectant mothers and peace-loving flower children. Best known as: Marge, the football toss booth operator at King's Island that Greg Brady falls for on *The Brady Bunch*.

Bill Quinn

Often seen as: Doctors, doctors, and more doctors. Best known as: Walter Richards, Mary Richards's somewhat distant father on *Mary Tyler Moore*, who was also, you guessed it, a doctor.

Hope Summers

Often seen as: friendly neighbors, kindly teachers and gossipy townsfolk. Best known as: Aunt Bee Taylor's best friend Clara Edwards on *The Andy Griffith Show*.

Reta Shaw

Often seen as: no-nonsense public servants, imposing WACs, and puffed-up socialites. Best known as: the Muirs' starchy housekeeper, Martha Grant, on *The Ghost & Mrs. Muir*.

Harold Gould

Often seen as: kindly doctors, visiting five-star Generals, and lovable fathers. Best known as: Rose Nylund's long-term boyfriend Miles Webber on *The Golden Girls*.

Priscilla Morrill

Often seen as: WASPy mothers, stern nuns, and faithful secretaries. Best known as: Lou Grant's ex-wife Edie on *Mary Tyler Moore*.

Phil Leeds

Often seen as: professional whiners, shifty conmen, and retired borscht-belters. Best known as: Old-as-dirt Uncle Mel on *Everybody Loves Raymond*.

TAXI

Career cabbie Alex Reiger spends the night shift with a group of oddballs, all looking for their big breaks under the ever-watchful eye of their Napoleonic dispatcher, Louie DePalma.

Taxi, one of the best written, most bittersweet sitcoms ever (right down to its lonely, plaintive theme song), was the brainchild of writer/producers James L. Brooks, Stan Daniels, David Davis, and Ed. Weinberger, who left the fold at MTM and created their own production company called the John Charles Walters Company. *Taxi* had many of the hallmarks of the classy, literate shows of their former studio, combined with the New York "street" atmosphere of a *Barney Miller*. The show was a kind of male equivalent to the sitcom *Alice* (although *Taxi*'s writing was clearly superior), dealing with a group of working-class men (plus one woman) under the thumb of a tyrannical, unreasonable boss.

Brooks and Davis had developed the premise while still at MTM, taking inspiration from a magazine article titled "Hip-Shifting for the Night Fleet" by Marc Jacobsen, which appeared

afire. After two seasons in the same programming block as *Three's Company*, ABC moved the show to Wednesday night and the bottom fell out of the ratings. Canceled after its fourth season, a bidding war ensued between HBO and NBC. NBC won and the show was moved to Thursday nights, alongside a brand-new series set in a Boston bar. The shows were clobbered, and while *Cheers* was picked up for a second season, *Taxi* finally ran out of gas for good, a critical hit, but perhaps a little too urban and quirky ever to build a huge audience in the flyover states.

Another reason that *Taxi* was never a blockbuster was that its characters by no means made theirs a "feel-good show," as did the gang at WJM or the beer-swilling throng in *Cheers*. In fact, the only two employees at the Sunshine Cab Company who seemed to be content with their lot in life were garage mechanic Latka Gravas, played by the

Louie: He'll be back…they all come back… the only one who never came back was James Caan…and I'm still waitin'!

in the September 22, 1975, issue of *New York* magazine. Buying the rights to the article back from Grant Tinker (who evidently bore no ill will for the mass defection), the quartet, working with director James Burrows and brothers Glen and Les Charles (the trio who would go on to create *Cheers*), went to work on *Taxi*, the natural bridge between the work-related camaraderie of *Mary Tyler Moore* and later workplace ensemble series such as *Cheers* and *Night Court*.

Winning three Emmys for best comedy series in the course of a relatively brief five-year run, *Taxi* has a reputation as an all-time classic, but the truth is, the show never set the airwaves

insane, insanely talented Andy Kaufman (already in the early stages of the confrontational stand-up humor phase of his career that would ultimately spell professional disaster); and Christopher Lloyd, added to the cast in season two, as Reverend Jim Ignatowski, who had taken enough substances in the 1960s to feel happy enough for three lifetimes. The other members were basically an unfulfilled, unsatisfied group: anchor character Alex Reiger, a cabbie "lifer" who had lost a job and a family to a gambling addiction; Bobby Wheeler, an actor who couldn't catch a break; Tony Banta, a fairly lousy boxer; and Elaine Nardo, a divorcée who was trying to raise her kids while trying to break

into the art world, all the while fending off the grubby advances of dispatcher Louie DePalma. DePalma, unflinchingly depraved as played by Danny DeVito, was the most lovable creep to hit television since Archie Bunker, just as obnoxious and even more irredeemable.

The show's writing was the best of sitcoms of the late 1970s: sharp, insightful, and character-driven, leaving shows like *Three's Company*, *The Jeffersons*, and *Laverne & Shirley*, no matter how mindlessly funny, firmly in its dust. With television in the middle of its craze for either hourlong anthologies (*The Love Boat*, *Fantasy Island*) or prime-time soap operas (*Dallas* and *Dynasty*), by 1981, *Taxi*, along with *Hill Street Blues* and *Lou Grant* (two other urban, work-based series), were among the only literate entertainment to be found. And the cast was perfection: Marilu Henner and Jeff Conaway, who, along with John Travolta and Adrienne Barbeau, were among young sitcom actors tapped from the ranks of the Broadway musical *Grease*; Tony Danza, a New York Italian boxer playing a New York Italian boxer; the transcendent inspiration of Lloyd, Kaufman, DeVito, and Carol Kane (as Latka's even more bizarre wife Simka), and the lovable resignation of Judd Hirsch, with a face that showed every ounce of pain that he had experienced. If only we were blessed with a half hour of its depth of feeling and intelligence today.

Opposite far left: Judd Hirsch, as lonely divorcee John Lacey, tries get a little TLC from Carlene Watkins on *Dear John*.

Opposite right: Christopher Lloyd, as the "organically damaged" Reverend Jim Ignatowski, prepares to deliver one of his famous non sequiturs.

Above: Randall Carver, Tony Danza, Judd Hirsch, Marilu Henner, and Jeff Conaway at the cabbies' local hangout, Mario's.

Judd Hirsch

Perfectly cast as a Jewish Everyman, Judd Hirsch started on the New York stage and broke into television by starring for one season on the police drama *Delvecchio*. Beginning his run on *Taxi* the following year, Hirsch became a television star with his low-key charm, winning two Emmys in the process. After playing roles in the very fine films *Ordinary People* and *Running on Empty*, he returned to television, playing John Lacey, another rather isolated character in the vein of Alex Reiger, the leader of a support group for divorced people on the sitcom *Dear John* for four seasons,

later teaming with fellow sitcom star Bob Newhart on the short-lived *George and Leo*. Returning to the New York theater in such hit plays as *I'm Not Rappaport*, *Conversations with My Father*, and *Art*, Hirsch has also appeared on hourlong dramas, including the FBI mathematician series *NUMB3RS*. Without a doubt, Hirsch's most bizarre role was voicing a character on the animated *Family Guy* who was building a nuclear bomb designed for use by the Keebler Elves against Snap, Crackle, and Pop.

Jim: Yeah, I did some drugs, though probably not as many as you think. How many drugs do you think I did?
Elaine: A lot.
Jim: Wow! Right on the nose!

Tony Danza

Tony Danza has never been known as a chameleon-like actor who disappears in his roles; in fact, Danza basically plays Danza. That's not a criticism, as his appealing, good-natured charm and charisma have served him exceedingly well in Hollywood. Attending college as a wrestler and working as a professional boxer (a 9 and 3 record) before landing the role of Tony Banta on *Taxi*, Danza proved his ability to carry his own show, alongside Judith Light, an eight-year run as Tony Micelli on *Who's the Boss?*

Following up with two unsuccessful shows, *Hudson Street* (as Tony Canetti) and *The Tony Danza Show* (as Tony DiMeo), he began to segue into dramatic roles on Broadway, in *A View From the Bridge* and *The Iceman Cometh* as well as in television, on *The Practice* and for two seasons on *Family Law* (finally appearing as characters not named Tony). After trying a daily talk show, he took over the lead in the musical *The Producers*. Like the tattoo he used to sport on his bicep in *Taxi*, Tony Danza just keeps on truckin'.

Above: Tony Danza and Judith Light on the long-running *Who's the Boss?*

Below: James L Brooks with Marsha Mason and Alex Rocco during rehearsals for the short-lived series *Sibs*.

James L. Brooks

One of the classiest writer/director/producers in Hollywood, James L. Brooks began his career as a news writer for CBS in the 1960s. Getting his first break in episodic television as a story editor on the acclaimed series *Room 222*, he was hired, along with co-writer Allan Burns, by producer Grant Tinker to create a sitcom for Mary Tyler Moore. Drawing upon his roots in

television news, he co-created the WJM newsroom, rising to the head of the class of television's creative geniuses with the inspired specificity of his writing. After launching Mary Tyler Moore's spin-off, *Rhoda*, Brooks went on to create the hit sitcom *Taxi* and the cult classic *The Associates*. After writing, directing, and producing the four-hanky film *Terms of Endearment*, he started his own production company, Gracie Films, going on to produce the brilliant sketch comedy series *The Tracey Ullman Show*, which in turn spawned the animated series *The Simpsons*. Among his other films is the classic *Broadcast News*, which once again mined the humor and drama behind the workings of a TV news show.

OFF THE SET

IN THE CREDIT sequence of *Taxi*, a cab is shown driving across New York City's Queensboro Bridge. It is driven by actor Tony Danza, who was in town to film a sequence for the show. It would be the only scene in the entire series filmed in New York.

COMEDIAN ANDY KAUFMAN completely invented the language that Latka Gravas spoke, teaching it to actress Carol Kane when she appeared as his countrywoman, Simka.

DIRECTOR JAMES BURROWS further developed the sitcom filming technique invented by Desi Arnaz, adding one more camera (bringing the total to four) and revolutionizing the method of shooting sitcoms.

CAST

Judd Hirsch .... Alex Reiger

Danny DeVito .... Louie De Palma

Marilu Henner .... Elaine O'Connor-Nardo

Tony Danza .... Tony Banta

Jeff Conaway .... Bobby Wheeler

Andy Kaufman .... Latka Gravas

Christopher Lloyd ...... Reverend Jim Ignatowski

Carol Kane .... Simka Dahblitz

J. Alan Thomas .... Jeff Bennett

Randall Carver .... John Burns

THAT GIRL

abc | 1966–1971 | 136 episodes

Kooky, adorable Ann Marie packs up her false eyelashes and takes a train to the concrete jungle of Manhattan. In the process of pursuing her dreams of theatrical stardom she falls for Donald Hollinger, a writer for *Newsview* magazine.

She's tinsel on a tree: Marlo Thomas as Ann Marie, dressed like the pole outside Floyd's barbershop and taking Manhattan by storm.

The delightful 1960s hit *That Girl* was directly responsible for sending thousands of young actresses to New York, thinking they, too, could be Ann Marie and have a fantastic wardrobe, meet a handsome man with a good job, and afford a huge one-bedroom apartment—all with no visible means of financial support. But while *That Girl* may have been short on reality, it was most assuredly long on charm. It has stood the test of time well, due to the comic minds of its creators Sam Denoff and Bill Persky, who had written more than thirty episodes of *The Dick Van Dyke Show*.

The main reason one still laughs out loud at *That Girl* is the singular spark of its star, Marlo Thomas. She was the precursor to Mary Tyler Moore in revolutionizing the image of the single woman on television. But while Mary Richards was not only single but a successful career woman to boot, much of the

Marlo Thomas

A member one of the most influential families represented in this book (along with her father, sitcom legend Danny Thomas, and her brother Tony Thomas, producer of such sitcom smashes as *Soap* and *The Golden Girls*), Marlo Thomas was born with an undeniable Hollywood pedigree. Blessed with talent and charisma galore, Thomas had no need to exploit the nepotism factor. Starting with a one-season stint on *The Joey Bishop Show* (right), she was put under contract with Twentieth Century-Fox. After filming an unsold pilot for ABC called *Two's Company*, she was touted as a perfect candidate for television stardom. Thomas decided to form her own company, Daisy Productions. On *That Girl*, she showcased perfectly her effervescent and infectious personality as well as her sharp sense of timing, for nobody could flip from wide-eyed, innocent enthusiasm to comic desperation better (or faster) than manic, "Mod" Marlo Thomas. After *That Girl*'s five-season run, in which she inspired single women to explore their independence, she yearned to make an even greater contribution. Thomas was always passionate about children's education (she had taught school briefly before becoming an actor), and she influenced an entire generation by producing and starring in the wonderful TV special *Free to Be . . . You & Me* in 1974. She began studying "The Method" with Lee Strasberg, while maintaining a presence on television in such

films as *It Happened One Christmas* (a gender-reversed version of *It's a Wonderful Life*), *Consenting Adult*, and a riveting turn as a mentally ill woman in *Nobody's Child*. She took over the reins as spokesperson for St. Jude's Children's Hospital, her father's pet charity, after his death and made a welcome return to comedy as Jennifer Aniston's mother on *Friends*.

comedy on *That Girl* centered on Ann's inability to hold down a job. And in the grand tradition of *Lucy* and other sitcom predecessors, there was physical comedy aplenty: Ann gets her toe stuck in a bowling ball, Ann gets swallowed by a rollaway bed, Ann learns to roller skate for an audition. And while she often came close to hitting the big time, something always thwarted her, whether it was an ear infection that temporarily deafened her and ruined a commercial shoot or getting her finger caught in the kitchen sink on the night of her Broadway debut.

The opening sequence of the show is one of the all-time greats, up there with Rob Petrie tripping over the ottoman and Mary Richards throwing her hat in the air. A cold opening (meaning no theme song, going right into the action) set up the plot of the episode, ending with someone pointing at Thomas and saying "That Girl!" The camera zooms in on her (usually pop-eyed) face, and we smash-cut to a view of railroad tracks as Ann gazes through the train window at the New York skyline. Wearing white gloves and a

sailor hat, Thomas made New York seem as glamorous as Audrey Hepburn had in *Breakfast at Tiffany's*, whether gazing up at the marquees on Broadway, seeing herself dressed as a queen in a window display, or flying a kite in Central Park (with her own likeness on it…just where did she pick that up…Ye Olde Ann Marie Kite Shoppe?). The greatest testimonial to the credit sequence is that it has been spoofed countless times in the intervening forty years, on everything from *The Family Guy* to *Saturday Night Live* (as *That Black Girl*, featuring Danitra Vance).

The secret to *That Girl*'s success was the interplay between Thomas and Ted Bessell, who played Ann's patient-to-a-fault boyfriend Donald Hollinger. He provided a grounding force for Thomas's wackiness that was completely disarming, letting the viewers at home share his weekly forbearance.

Ann: That's what I love about the theater! You know what I mean, Donald? One day you'r nobody, and the next, Ethel Merman is stuffing your cabbage!

Another smart twist was that instead of a stereotypical shrewish mother-in-law character, about which jokes had been done to death since the Year One, it was Ann's father (played by the perfectly sour Lew Parker) who didn't trust Donald farther than he could throw him. Parker had the most untrusting puss on the small screen, and even after they'd been dating for five years, he still called his daughter's boyfriend "Hollinger," never deigning to call him by his first name. One of the show's best episodes involved a double whammy of parental suspicion, when Donald's mother (the fabulous Mabel Albertson, who made a career out of withering condescension) visits and discovers a pair of her son's pants hanging in Ann's closet. When Mr. Marie shows up as well, Ann and Don "have a lot of 'splaining to do."

After five years, Thomas decided to move on, and while ABC wanted Ann to become Mrs. Donald Hollinger, Thomas balked, saying it would be a betrayal of the single women who had watched the show all along to imply that the only happy ending was marriage. The show went off the air with Ann and Don engaged and stuck in an elevator while on the way to a women's liberation meeting.

Finally available on DVD, *That Girl* still seems fresh as a Day-Glo daisy, as producers Persky and Denoff had been acolytes of Carl Reiner on *The Dick Van Dyke Show* and they, like Reiner, wisely avoided topical references, instead creating comedy out of situations (the anxiety of meeting a partner's parents, having a mouse loose in your apartment, or playing a game of Monopoly) that can span decades without ever feeling (wardrobe aside) caught in a time warp.

Opposite left: Ann Marie, working at a newsstand, is about to meet the man of her dreams, Donald Hollinger, in *That Girl*'s pilot.

Above: "Daddy" (Lew Parker) grills Ann about a pair of Donald's trousers he's spotted in her bedroom, in an episode with perhaps the longest title in sitcom history, "Oh Don, Poor Don, Your Pants are Hanging in My Closet and I'm Feeling So Sad" (also known by its abbreviation "ODPDYPAHIMCAIFSS").

Right: Ted Bessell, Scott Kolden, and Jackie the Chimp (as Buttons the chimp) in the series *Me and the Chimp*.

CAST

Marlo Thomas ....Ann Marie

Ted Bessell ....Donald Hollinger

Lew Parker ....Lou Marie

Rosemary DeCamp..Helen Marie

Bonnie Scott..............Judy Bessemer

Dabney Coleman ....Leon Bessemer

Bernie Kopell ....Jerry Bauman

Carolyn Daniels ......Ruthie Bauman (1)

Alice Borden.............Ruthie Bauman (2)

Ruth Buzzi.................Margie "Pete" Peterson

Billy De Wolfe ....Jules Benedict

Mabel Albertson .....Mrs. Hollinger

George Cisar............Mr. Hollinger

Ted Bessell

One of the most underrated light comedians in sitcom history, the ever-congenial Ted Bessell got his big break before taking on the role of Donald Hollinger, the most famous and frustrated television boyfriend of the 1960s. In the same way that his *That Girl* costar, Marlo Thomas, was typecast after the series went off the air, Bessell found it difficult to break the mold of being the good guy, appearing in the flop *Me and the Chimp* in 1972. He helped shake up his image when he played Mary Richards's caddish boyfriend Joe Warner on several episodes of *Mary Tyler Moore*, but lost out on a chance for another hit of *That Girl* proportions when the very promising *Hail to the Chief*, starring fellow 1960s television icon Patty Duke, was prematurely canceled. He began directing, winning multiple Emmy nominations for *The Tracey Ullman Show*. He was doing preproduction on the big screen version of another 1960s classic, *Bewitched* (the movie was finally and woefully made nine years later), when he died suddenly of an aortic aneurysm.

THAT '70S SHOW

FOX | **1998–2006** | **204 episodes**

It's 1976 in the Wisconsin suburbs, and teenaged Eric Forman and his friends undergo the usual rites of passage. As a matter of fact, so do the adults.

A group of adolescents on their way to adulthood could be the description of countless sitcoms, from *Leave It to Beaver* to *The Patty Duke Show* to *Malcolm in the Middle*. What set the successful shows apart from the rest was their writing and casting. But while these sitcoms were rooted in the era in which they were produced, *That '70s Show*, created at the turn of the millennium, cast a nostalgic and gently humorous look at the world of the 1970s. Those who lived through that decade could laugh at its fashions, music, and fads, and even at their own selves of that time. *Happy Days*, the show that created the template for the nostalgic sitcom, did the very same thing for the '50s. Of course, the adventures of Richie, Ralph, and Potsie were hatched in a more innocent television era, without mention of

the drugs and sex that were so much a part of the world of *That '70s Show*, a sitcom well written, produced, and acted and, as the show went along, less about the '70s and more about the rich characters.

The subsequent film success of actors Topher Grace and Ashton Kutcher points to the solid core of talent at the center of the series. Each character in the show was sharply delineated and, amazingly, all were sympathetic. There were no villains; every character had a good heart and, unlike many of the other programs on Fox at the time, there was little, shall we say, off-color humor. If you don't think that's a difficult thing to pull off, we suggest you take a trip to the sitcom graveyard and have a look at all the tortured plots and characters moldering under the headstones. Yes, the '70s setting was a gimmick—but it is to the show's credit that the period aspect was just a backdrop, and it was the characters' lives that provided the focus of the series.

The show started with the usual long development process. Suggested names were *Feelin' All Right*, *Reeling in the Years*, and, in a nod to the rock-and-roll band the Who, *Teenage Wasteland* and *The Kids Are Alright*. Several major plotlines were toyed with: for example, the original plan was that Eric and Hyde would battle for Donna's affections. Luckily, it was decided that only Eric would battle for Donna—with Donna herself.

Once the title was in place, casting was completed (with Chuck "*Walker, Texas Ranger*" Norris originally cast as Red), and relationships set, a pilot was produced that established the era's importance to the plots. The idea was that the kids were finding themselves just as the Vietnam War ended and disco and drugs were entering popular culture. When the show hit the air it didn't exactly wow audiences but Fox renewed it because it was number one in the all-important 18- to 24-year-old age range. Fox confused the faithful by switching its airtimes and broadcasting new episodes in the midst of summer reruns, but gradually, the show gained viewers and became a mainstay of the network. The fact that several of the actors became teen-magazine heartthrobs didn't hurt the show's popularity, and soon they were acknowledged by the general media and, finally, Hollywood producers, directors, and writers.

Pot played a large role in the series but, surprisingly, nary a peep was heard from the moral watchdogs. True, they never actually showed the kids lighting up, but the oft-used gimmick of the camera rotating around a smoke-filled table as the clearly stoned characters free-associated left no doubt as from whence all that smoke was emanating.

Toward the end of its long run, the show experienced the death throes that almost all long-running series endure. The actors began to get a bit long in the tooth for their roles and the writers came up with increasingly weird plots to keep their own interest up. Finally, *That '70s Show* ran out of juice. Hail to producers of shows like *Mary Tyler Moore* who chose to go out on top. There are two tried-and-true desperation moves often employed by sitcoms that have overstayed their welcome: a change of location or the introduction of a new character. In this case, we were introduced to Randy, played by Josh Meyers, who simply confused matters and provided the final nail in the coffin.

But of course old successful shows never die. Following their cancellation, they go on to syndication heaven, followed by eternal life on DVD, including the obligatory "favorite episode" singles and season box sets. That, nature lovers, is the lifespan of the television sitcom, though it is sometimes followed by a brief phoenixlike burst of reunion or spin-off. As with shows like *The Andy Griffith Show*, we can't let the last seasons of *That '70s Show* erase the glory of the majority of its run.

Opposite: On *That '70s Show*, parents Red and Kitty Forman, played by Kurtwood Smith and Debra Jo Rupp, were just as complicated and genuinely flawed as their teenage son Eric, played by the winning Topher Grace.

Above: Ashton Kutcher, Danny Masterson, and Wilmer Valderrama, three blasts from the past.

CAST

Topher Grace	Eric Forman
Mila Kunis	Jackie Burkhardt
Ashton Kutcher	Michael Kelso
Danny Masterson	Steve Hyde
Laura Prepon	Donna Pinciotti
Wilmer Valderrama	Fez
Debra Jo Rupp	Kitty Forman
Kurtwood Smith	Red Forman
Tanya Roberts	Midge Pinciotti
Don Stark	Bob Pinciotti
Lisa Robin Kelly	Laurie Forman #1

Terry and Bonnie Turner

The husband-and-wife team of Terry and Bonnie Turner started their show business careers writing theater revues in Atlanta. After a stint at Turner Broadcasting, in the news division of all places, they cut their writing teeth on *Saturday Night Live*, developing the characters on the "Wayne's World" and "Coneheads" segments, expanding those sketches into one highly successful and one not-so-successful film. They earned their sitcom wings on the homage cum parody film *The Brady Bunch Movie*. Their first sitcom was the highly successful *3rd Rock from the Sun*, which employed the off-kilter humor they had honed on *Saturday Night Live* (and they even brought along their Prymatt Conehead, also known as Jane Curtin). After a short stint writing for *Days Like These*, they found another winning premise with *That '70s Show*. Lightning did not strike again, however, when they developed a spin-off of sorts, *That '80s Show*. Executive producing assignments on *Normal, Ohio* and *Whoopi* were not felicitous, either.

3RD ROCK FROM THE SUN

NBC | 1996–2001 | 139 episodes

A bunch of zany aliens find themselves strangers in a strange land. Their mission? To observe the behavior of Earthlings, and boldly go where no sitcom has gone before.

In the calm after the storm, many episodes of *3rd Rock* ended with the Solomon family gathering on the roof for a recap; in other words, a little extraterrestrial existentialism.

In a sitcom world populated by young, urban thirty-somethings such as Jerry, Elaine, Monica, Chandler, Ellen, Dharma, and Greg, the out-of-this-world cast of *3rd Rock from the Sun* were absolute aliens on the TV dial, not simply because of their otherworldly resemblance to Mork from Ork, Alf, the cat lover from space (mmmm, cat, delicious), or Uncle Martin, with those pesky antennae popping out of his skull. Sticking out like sore thumbs as residents of Rutherford, Ohio, the wonderfully unhinged band of actors on *3rd Rock* didn't fit in with their sitcom brethren, either.

Think about the current crop of television stars. Where are the larger-than-life personalities? There's no Cloris Leachman, Jim Nabors, Eva Gabor, Redd Foxx, Joan Davis, or Sherman Hemsley in today's sitcom world. Carroll O'Connor and Jean Stapleton. Jackie Gleason and Art Carney. Bob Denver and Alan Hale. These were the performers who filled up every inch of the screen, making eccentricity true-to-life, sometimes touching, and always hilarious. And in the way that its writers celebrated the diversity and quirkiness of the cast, *3rd Rock* was a throwback to the great sitcoms of yore.

Casting is key to any sitcom, and *3rd Rock* had two expert farceurs at the helm: John Lithgow, as Mission Commander Dick Solomon, is an Oscar nominated and Tony winning actor, looking like everyone's favorite college professor yet with a streak of true zany bubbling just under the surface; Jane Curtin, as the neurotic, insecure Mary Albright, provided the dry wit and vulnerability that she has brought to television since her days on the original *Saturday Night Live*.

Much of the show's humor came from the naivete of the crew members to the customs, slang, and morality of Earth. Tell Dick Solomon, played by the incomparable John Lithgow, to wait until "the spit hits the fan," and you know exactly what the gentle giant will proceed to do. The contradictory behavior of the members of the mission also made for much of the fun. Dick was the titular head of the mission, yet on Earth he seemed unable to accomplish even the simplest of tasks. Yes, his knowledge of physics and the sciences were far beyond our own (he scoffed at Stephen Hawking's theories), but he became impossibly petulant when not getting his own way. Sally, the statuesque, bombshell security officer played by the Amazonian goofball Kristen Johnston, startlingly fell for the roly-poly slob of a cop Don Leslie Orville, played by Wayne Knight (pulling double duty as a member of the casts of both *3rd Rock* and *Seinfeld*, thereby breaking the first rule of show business: one role to every actor). Harry, the artistic one (in other words, a twit), played by the off-the-wall French Stewart, was a receiving station for messages from their leader the Great Big Head (or GBH for short, who, when he finally appeared in *3rd Rock*'s fourth season, was played by none other

than William Shatner), through a microchip transmitter in his brain. An utter dweeb with squinty eyes and pursed lips (not unlike a male Renee Zellweger), he's inexplicably a babe magnet, with beautiful women hanging on his every inane word. Tommy (played by the terrific young actor Joseph Gordon-Levitt, who has evolved into the Leonardo De Caprio of independent films), who inhabits the body of a teenager, is actually the oldest and wisest member of the group, yet he's particularly puzzled by life following puberty.

The use of mime and slapstick, with roots in classic clown routines, became the show's highlight, as the hapless aliens failed in their misguided attempts to fit in: Lithgow becoming hysterical when he sees snowflakes and thinks they are "brain-sucking parasites" (or, as the sometimes poetic Harry calls them, "Albino Brain Chiggers"); or, most memorably, the entire crew frantically trying to destroy the dreaded substance Jell-O (on their home planet, a dead ringer for a hostile, amorphous carnivore) whenever it appears in all its evil, gelatinous glory.

As the seasons rolled by, the crew, who found themselves teleported into a 1963 Rambler convertible, began to push the envelope fruther and further into a surreal style of humor not seen on television since the heyday of *Green Acres*. Starting with a second-season cliffhanger shot in 3-D, the producers of *3rd Rock* raised the bar higher and higher, making the humor broader and ever more outrageous, turning some viewers off as they headed for over-the-topness but garnering many more fanatical devotees who loved the wackiness and utter absurdity of the show, which was particularly refreshing when compared to "pretty people" shows, such as *Friends* and *Dharma and Greg*. Audiences stayed with the show to the bitter end, a remarkable achievement considering NBC flipped the show around in the schedule no fewer than fifteen times. Light and bouncy, *3rd Rock from the Sun* is like one of those desserts that never demands anything more than pure enjoyment. There's always room for Jell-O...

OFF THE SET

THE SHOW'S PRODUCERS described it as "Carl Sagan meets the Marx Brothers."

BY THE FIFTH season, Joseph Gordon-Levitt left the series and became a recurring character, appearing in roughly half of that seasons episodes.

Left: In the *3rd Rock* episode "Dick and Tuck," Dick (here comparing his cranial mass to Mr. Potato Head) considers plastic surgery. The surgeon he consults? A Dr. Lasker, played by David Hasselhoff, of the perky cheekbones and the perpetually surprised eyes.

Below: Susan Saint James and Jane Curtin get a mark on their permanent records as *Kate & Allie*.

Jane Curtin

Definitely ready for prime time, Jane Curtin's early career was in the theatre and with the improvisational theatre group, The Proposition. That experience led her to *Saturday Night Live*, along with Dan Ackroyd, John Belushi, Gilda Radner, and Chevy Chase. Leaving the grind of late night, she turned to playing a more adult character on her hit series *Kate and Allie,* winning two Emmy Awards and becoming a mainstream television star. After taking some time out to raise her daughter, Curtin put her straight-man skills, honed by her years bouncing off the goofballs on *SNL,* to good use in the role of Dr. Mary Albright on *3rd Rock from the Sun*. Recently back, albeit briefly, on the short-lived *Crumbs*, Curtin seems destined to find another hit series. A true professional, she has eschewed the limelight and concentrated on keeping her home life low key and her professional life on a steady course.

CAST

John Lithgow	Dick Solomon
Kristen Johnston	Sally Solomon
French Stewart	Harry Solomon
Joseph Gordon-Levitt	Tommy Solomon
Jane Curtin	Dr. Mary Albright
Simbi Kahli	Nina
Elmarie Wendel	Mrs. Mamie Dubcek
Wayne Knight	Don Orville
David DeLuise	Bug Pollone
Ian Lithgow	Leon
Danielle Nicolet	Caryn
Chris Hogan	Aubrey Pitman
Jan Hooks	Vicki Dubcek
Shay Astar	August Leffler
Larisa Oleynik	Alissa Strudwick
Ron West	Vincent Strudwick
Ileen Getz	Judith Draper

Left: The hilarious odd couple Curtin and Lithgow, in the episode "Frankie Goes to Rutherford," where, thanks to that impeccable Solomon reasoning, Dick ends up dressing like a Village Person in Training, thinking the local gay bar is a hangout for covert aliens.

Below: Lithgow and Jeffrey Tambor in the 2006 sitcom *Twenty Good Years.*

John Lithgow

Of all the actors in this book, none has exhibited the versatility and brains to pick the best projects as has John Lithgow. No dummy, Lithgow won a Fulbright Scholarship to the London Academy of Music and Dramatic Art. Going to school for acting might seem superfluous for someone who began acting with his father (also a noted performer) at age six, but Lithgow was determined to do it right. His early successes were on the Broadway stage, in plays that showcased his remarkable range. When he played transsexual Roberta Muldoon in *The World According to Garp*, he segued into a career as a top-notch character actor in films, turning in wonderful performances in such films as *Terms of Endearment, Footloose,* and *Twilight Zone: The Movie* (which was hilariously spoofed on an epi-sode of *3rd Rock*). After success on television in such landmark projects as *The Day After* and *The Tuskegee Airmen,* he switched gears again and became the outrageous Dick Solomon on *3rd Rock,* winning three Emmy Awards in the process. Having found a new artistic outlet as a children's book author, Lithgow happily shuttles between the three worlds of stage, movies, and television with his customary panache.

THREE'S COMPANY

 | **1977-1984** | **174 episodes**

Two women take on a male roommate in a Santa Monica apartment. With the disapproving landlord living just downstairs, the only way Jack can cohabit with Janet and Chrissy is to pretend that he's gay.

Chock full of double entendres and sexual innuendo, *Three's Company* was just about as racy as network television got in 1977. Misunderstandings, eavesdropping, and people hiding behind a plethora of swinging and slamming doors made many episodes resemble a twenty-three-minute farce decked out in tube tops and velour track suits.

Based on the hit British sitcom *Man About the House*, the show premiered for a six-episode run in the spring of 1977 and was a ratings smash. Viewers immediately responded to the charms of the show's three stars: the slapstick antics of John Ritter, the warmth and wit of Joyce DeWitt, and the natural assets of Suzanne Somers. Along with Richard Kline as neighbor Larry Dallas, the only other regulars were the landlords the Ropers, played by two seasoned pros: hangdog, curmudgeonly Norman Fell (who, in the second and third seasons, developed a bizarre habit of saying a punch line and then leering directly into the camera lens); and Audra Lindley, a truly gifted character actress stuck in a muumuu and bangle bracelets for her entire three-season run.

The show ranked consistently in the top ten, and when Lindley and Fell left at the end of the third season to star in their spin-off *The Ropers*, the show was lucky enough to nab Don Knotts as the new landlord, Mr. Furley. In canary yellow polyester leisure suits topped off with gold chains and a garish scarf, Ralph Furley, a swinger wannabe, fit right into the show's over-the-top atmosphere. Around the same time, another shift occurred. At the beginning of the series's run, Suzanne Somers had played her character Chrissy Snow as a cross between Gracie Allen and Goldie Hawn. By the third season, however, Chrissy had become less a good-hearted naif and more of a face-screwing, bug-eyed, snorting cartoon straight out of a Chuck Jones production. To Somers, Chrissy Snow was iconic and solely her comic creation. Others were left to observe what they saw as the delusions of a scene-hogging narcissist.

Chrissy, Janet, and Jack, the three sexy singles of *Three's Company*, played by fun-loving farceurs Suzanne Somers, John Ritter, and Joyce DeWitt. At this point Somers was still attempting to create a realistic character, but by the end of the third season, her increasingly cartoonish portrayal of Chrissy made viewers wonder if she was suffering from acute peroxide poisoning.

Yet even bigger trouble lay ahead. Instantly famous, the three stars found themselves on the covers of virtually every magazine but *Popular Mechanics*, and Somers began to believe her own publicity. Demanding an astronomical raise and part ownership of the show, she called in sick until the producers agreed to her terms. With morale in the basement (DeWitt, in particular, felt completely sold out by the producers and Somers), the produc-

John Ritter

John Ritter was born into show business, the son of Western film star and country music legend Tex Ritter. After graduating from the University of Southern California, Ritter started his television career by landing a recurring role as the Reverend Fordwick in *The Waltons*. In one of those fortuitous, once-in-a-lifetime breaks, he became a television superstar in *Three's Company*. His role as Jack Tripper made Ritter the king of physical comedy in the 1970s, equal in inventiveness and specificity (if not in the quality of material he was provided) to pratfall masters Dick Van Dyke and Lucille Ball. After the failure of the *Three's Company* spin-off *Three's a Crowd*, he returned to the weekly format with the half-hour dramedy *Hooperman*, where he began to impress viewers with his dramatic abilities. Starring in more than twenty television movies, and acting as executive producer on the underrated Jamie Lee Curtis/Richard Lewis series *Anything But Love*, his next sitcom, *Hearts Afire*, alongside Markie Post (below), ran from 1992 through 1995. Ritter's motion picture credits include the highly acclaimed *Sling Blade* (perhaps his greatest work as an actor) and a belated Broadway debut in Neil Simon's *The Dinner Party*, costarring fellow 1970s sitcom star Henry Winkler. Tragically, while filming his final series *8 Simple Rules*, in 2003, John fell ill while rehearsing. Rushed to the hospital with a previously undiagnosed aortic dissection, he underwent emergency surgery and died at age fifty-four.

Suzanne Somers with Audra Lindley and Norman Fell as the Ropers. Forever trying to get her husband in the sack, Lindley's Helen Roper was a precursor to the sexually active "women of a certain age" of *The Golden Girls* a decade later. With her expert timing, Lindley made the most of even the hokiest of putdowns, some of which seemed stale when Vivian Vance uttered them to William Frawley twenty-five years earlier.

ers sued Somers and she returned to the show—but as neither of the other two roomies wanted to lay eyes on her, she was relegated to one-minute phone conversations taped on a separate soundstage. With a show now more aptly titled *Two's Company*, newcomer Jenilee Harrison was brought on as Chrissy's cousin Cindy, but the inexperienced Harrison floundered, her only discernible character traits being big teeth, a loud voice, and klutzy behavior. The quality of the show plummeted and the producers knew they had to find a permanent replacement for Somers. Priscilla Barnes, a beautiful and talented actress, came aboard. We can only imagine the pressure she felt: After the misfire with Harrison, the entire future of the series rested on recapturing the early magic of the show. Luckily, Barnes soon hit her stride as a comedienne and helped keep the show afloat for three more seasons.

By 1984, times had definitely changed, and with the rise of smarter ensemble shows like *Cheers*, people were less interested in the antics of the Santa Monica singles. As the eighth season drew to a close, the producers once again dropped a bombshell: The show would be going off the air, with Ritter continuing on as Jack Tripper in a new series completely revolving around him. The new vehicle, *Three's a Crowd*, lasted only a season.

Three's Company endures as nostalgia for all those who were single in the freewheeling late '70s, before Reaganomics, AIDS, and the yuppie invasion of the '80s. Above all, it was a showcase for the hilarious physical-comedy talents of John Ritter, who made comic art out of juggling eggs, trying to tame an uncooperative hammock, or dealing with a cranky landlord while attempting to hide a kitten stuffed inside his shirt. It's easy to see why *Three's Company* was a favorite of the legendary Lucille Ball for, in terms of pure solo slapstick, Jack Tripper's manic antics were the next best thing to Lucy Ricardo riding the subway with a loving cup stuck on her head.

Don Knotts

Don Knotts, the master of comic false bravado, grew up as a fan of radio comedy. After a stint in the army, Knotts ended up in New York, where he worked in the theater, radio, and nightclubs. His first big break came when he joined Tom Poston and Louis Nye in the ensemble of comedians on *The Steve Allen Show*, making a great hit with his "nervous man" in Allen's comic man-on-the-street interviews. Then it was off to California, where he soon joined old friend Andy Griffith, whom Knotts had known since he played a support-ing role to Griffith in the Broadway comedy *No Time for Sergeants*. As Sheriff Andy Taylor's fidgety by-the-book deputy in *The Andy Griffith Show*, Knotts expanded and deepened the persona of the comic scairdy cat into the genuinely original comic cre-ation that was Barney "nip it in the bud" Fife. Knotts became the breakout character on the show, winning an unprecedented five Emmys in six years. An unlikely movie star, Knotts further honed his bug-eyed persona in such classic comedies as *The Incredible Mr. Limpet* and *The Ghost and Mr. Chicken*. Knotts made a welcome return to sitcoms as the hopelessly out-of-date faux lady-killer Ralph Furley on *Three's Company*. Then came semiretirement from onscreen appearances (he became a successful animation actor, as recently as in *Chicken Little* in 2005) with an occasional return to the small screen, for *The Andy Griffith Show* reunion *Return to Mayberry* and as a recurring guest on Griffith's lawyer show, *Matlock*.

CAST

John Ritter	Jack Tripper
Joyce DeWitt	Janet Wood
Suzanne Somers	Chrissy Snow
Priscilla Barnes	Terri Alden
Audra Lindley	Helen Roper
Norman Fell	Stanley Roper
Don Knotts	Ralph Furley
Richard Kline	Larry Dallas
Jenilee Harrison	Cindy Snow
Ann Wedgeworth	Lana Shields
Paul Ainsley	Jim the bartender
William Pierson	Dean Travers
Jordan Charney	Frank Angelino
Gino Conforti	Felipe Gomez

Left: The fast-paced rhythm of *Three's Company* was pumped up to an even greater frenzy with the addition of the jittery Don Knotts as self-annointed stud, Ralph Furley.

OFF THE SET

THE PILOT OF *Three's Company* took place in a triplex apartment complex in North Hollywood called Hacienda Palms, but the ongoing series was set at an apartment house in Santa Monica.

IN THE OPENING credits, the brunette that knocks Jack Tripper off his bike is Suzanne Somers in a wig.

IN THE VERSION of the show's opening that aired beginning in the sixth season, a toddler walks up to Joyce DeWitt as she is feeding a deer. The kid is John Ritter's son Jason, star of the CBS sitcom *The Class*.

AMONG THE ACTORS considered for the role of Jack Tripper was Billy Crystal, soon to be starring on another controversial ABC sitcom, *Soap*.

Expert comedian Richard Kline as upstairs neighbor Larry Dallas, John Ritter, and the gorgeous and talented Priscilla Barnes as fun-loving nurse Teri Alden, the third and final "blonde" of the *Three's Company* roommates.

TOPPER

◉ | **1953–1955** | **78 episodes**

Oh-so-square banker Cosmo Topper is haunted by the ghosts of George and Marion Kerby and their alcoholic Saint Bernard, Neil. Only Topper (and the audience) can see the ghosts, which leads to many merry misadventures and misunderstandings.

It's common knowledge that Hollywood in the 1950s was a hotbed of wild-eyed radicals and pinko commies, with writers among the worst offenders. Although that hero of the ultra-right, Senator Joseph McCarthy, tried to clean up that dirty town, he was stymied by such liberals as newsman Edward R. Murrow. Want proof that McCarthy was absolutely right about the subversive motives of Tinseltown? Just look at the television series *Topper*.

Cosmo Topper and his wife of twenty-five years, Henrietta, find that their new home's previous owners, a couple named Kerby, are still occupying it. The catch is, this pair of squatters are ghosts, a flamboyant couple who had died in an avalanche but didn't have the common decency to stay dead. The Kerbys (played by the glamorous real-life marrieds Anne Jeffreys and Robert Sterling) and their lush of a Saint Bernard, Neil, insist on rocking the Toppers' status quo at every turn. Thanks to these radical spirits, the banker's upstanding American way of life is constantly compromised.

While a bunch of crazy people can be funny by themselves, give a bunch of kooks someone sane to bounce off of and the fun really begins. Take Judd Hirsch at the center of *Taxi*, Eddie Albert as the only voice of reason in *Hooterville*, or Jane Curtin in *3rd Rock from the Sun*. Straight man extraordinaire George Burns, Raymond Bailey's Mr. Drysdale…they all bear the heavy burden of sanity in a world gone cuckoo. Cosmo Topper, as played by the unflappable Leo G. Carroll, handled this chaos better than most. Never losing his temper, he was instead rather resigned to his position, and always had the perfect explanation when the supernatural occurred.

Much of the credit for *Topper*'s bon mots and stiff upper lip goes to series creator and writer George Oppenheimer. A former Broadway playwright and screenwriter, Oppenheimer took the characters invented by novelist Thorne Smith and depicted in three MGM films and made them suitable for the small screen (the Kerbys died in a car crash in the books and movies, but he felt that an avalanche was somehow less threatening and therefore funnier), while, adding his own touches, such as Neil, the spirits-loving canine spirit.

An episode that is fondly remembered is the one in which Henrietta Topper entered a slogan-writing contest for Individual Oats with the immortal "Everyone loves Individual Oats. It's the cereal everyone votes…for." When the ghosts see that she has no chance of winning, they take matters into their own hands by destroying all the other entries. That's about as sophisticated as *Topper* got—but the genial writing and enthusiastic ensemble rose above the sometimes unexceptional plots.

Though it ran only two seasons on CBS, *Topper*'s life span continued long beyond its original production in prime-time reruns on ABC and NBC. Following that came years of syndication on local stations and cable.

Like many series of the 1950s, *Topper*'s reputation has lived on in the memories of baby boomers who haven't seen an episode since they were eight or nine years old. As with many of these programs, the reality sometimes doesn't live up to the memories, but nostalgia and an understanding of their place in television history secure their places among the greatest sitcoms of all time.

CAST

Leo G. Carroll	Cosmo Topper
Anne Jeffreys	Marion Kerby
Robert Sterling	George Kerby
Lee Patrick	Henrietta Topper
Buck	Neil
Kathleen Freeman	Katie
Thurston Hall	Mr. Schuyler

Kathleen Freeman

Kathleen Freeman, the solidly built whirlwind of a character actress, joined her parents' vaudeville act at the age of two and never looked back. Usually playing glowering maids (as in *Topper*), nurses, or saleswomen, she seemed to be propelled into her scenes, bringing energy and drive to whatever role she played. Following graduation from UCLA, she paid her dues in many seasons with numerous theater companies, making her film debut in 1948. She was most recognizable as Lena Lamont's vocal coach, Phoebe Dinsmore, in *Singin' in the Rain*, and as the butt of Jerry Lewis's high-jinks in ten films. Freeman blithely moved back and forth between the big screen and the small, on series such as *The Dick Van Dyke Show*, *I Love Lucy*, and *Hogan's Heroes* (here, as Colonel Klink's lovestruck paramour Gertrude Linkmeyer). She was also heard (but never seen) as Peg Bundy's mother on *Married with Children*. Her last role was in the Broadway musical *The Full Monty*. She kept her lung cancer a secret from the cast, dying only five days after giving her last performance.

WILL & GRACE

 NBC | **1998–2006** | **193 episodes**

Lawyer Will Truman lives with his best friend Grace Adler, an interior designer. They're a perfect match except for one small thing, Will is gay. Will's buddy, the flamboyant, narcissistic Jack, and Grace's over-privileged, undermotivated personal assistant, the equally self-absorbed Karen, complete the comedy quartet.

Why did folks watch *Will & Grace* and make it a favorite for almost a decade? There were several things going for the show: a fine ensemble cast with great chemistry, snappy writing, interesting secondary characters, and well-staged physical comedy. But there were complaints about the series: while .5always useful as a punch line, Will and Jack's homosexuality never seems to have an impact on their daily lives, with Jack becoming increasingly clichéd while Will became more and more sexless; too many movie-star cameos and guest stars; the increasing bitterness between Will and Grace; and the imbalance between the title characters and the second leads (in some episodes the show could have been titled *Jack & Karen*).

Will & Grace has its proponents and detractors, but there is no doubt that it was important in the grand scheme of sitcom history. To be sure, there were gay characters before *Will & Grace*, and, not surprisingly, 1970s sitcom pioneer Norman Lear was among the first to introduce gay themes. On *All in the Family*, Archie Bunker was totally thrown for a loop when one of his drinking buddies turns out to be gay; and later in the series, Archie is disgusted to find that Edith's cousin Liz is a lesbian. On *Maude*, Bea Arthur's character is upset when her husband and their neighbors object to a gay bar opening in the neighborhood. Although sometimes one got the feeling that the Lear series were simply checking off controversial subjects, they were virtually alone in the vast wasteland in even mentioning such unmentionables.

In a 1973 episode of *Sanford and Son*, Lamont accidentally visits a gay bar—accidentally being the operative word. In another liberal-leaning sitcom, *M*A*S*H*, Major Burns gets his panties in a knot when he discovers that Pvt. George Weston, a war hero, is gay. The late '70s sitcom *Soap* featured Billy Crystal as a gay man who wants a sex-change operation, but since nothing on the series was to be taken seriously, it wasn't a surprise that by the end of the show's run, the character changes his mind and turns out to be more palatably bisexual.

The '80s saw the appearance of more and more gay-themed episodes on sitcoms, but still, there wasn't a leading gay character

Right: Eric McCormick with Shelley Morrison as the take-no-prisoners maid, Rosario Salazar.

on television. It almost happened with Tony Randall's *Love, Sidney*, but the network lost its nerve after the pilot and by the time the series hit the air, Sidney's sexuality is hinted at but never mentioned. Things almost changed in 1985, when the pilot for *The Golden Girls* included a gay cook named Coco. Almost.

Finally, television got a real, unambiguously gay character, even though he was animated. It was television's master of unrequited love, Waylon Smithers, who continues to pine for his boss, Mr. Burns, on *The Simpsons*. The love that dared not speak its name didn't have to; it was all too obvious.

Roseanne, never a series to apologize to anyone for anything, cast Martin Mull as Roseanne's business partner Leon, an uptight, obnoxious gay man. Believe it or not, Leon actually marries his partner Scott on the series. *Roseanne* had lots of other gay characters, too, including a friend of Roseanne's played by Sandra Bernhard and, toward the end of the series, Roseanne's mother, played by Estelle Parsons.

By the 1990s, shows like *Mad About You,* in which a secondary character, Debbie, comes out as a lesbian, didn't seem to raise too many hackles with the self-proclaimed arbiters of morality. Perhaps this gave Ellen DeGeneres a false sense that times had changed and that America was ready for her coming-out party. It wasn't to be, especially on ABC, the "family network." The show didn't stand a chance after Ellen came out with the kiss heard 'round the world— and yet, sitcoms were never the same. Almost every series began to have at least one episode with a gay character.

Then came *Will & Grace*. Of course, it was heartily hetero Grace and Karen that made the sitcom palatable to the more conservative viewers (along with the fact that what little action Will and Jack got was very much off-screen). But *Will & Grace's* matter-of-fact gay characters undeniably made a big difference, thanks in large part to the smart writing of creators David Kohan and Max Mutchnick, and the direction by one of the grand masters of the form, James Burrows.

James Burrows

One of the most successful and sought-after directors of modern sitcoms, James Burrows was born into a show business family as son of the Broadway musical author Abe Burrows. In 1974, Burrows was hired by Grant Tinker at MTM to observe other directors. Mentored by veteran director Jay Sandrich, Burrows directed MTM series until 1977, when he teamed up with James L. Brooks on the series *Taxi*, on which he helmed 76 episodes. Due to the especially large set depicting the Sunshine Cab Company, Burrows became one of the first directors to use four cameras, adapting the three-camera system that had been in use since *I Love Lucy*. In 1982, Burrows, along with Glen and Les Charles, formed the Charles-Burrows-Charles Company and created and produced *Cheers*. Since the wildly successful run of *Cheers*, Burrows has continued working as a director of such sitcoms as *Wings*, *Friends*, *NewsRadio*, and every episode of *Will & Grace*.

Karen: She's gone to Mexico for facelifts so many times, I'll bet if you whacked her head with a stick, prizes would fall out.

Above: Just how far we've come: In 1953, sitcoms couldn't even show a man and wife sharing the same bed. By 2003, there were plotlines that put two openly gay men in the sack (but don't be fooled—nothing happened).

Below: Megan Mullally was offered two sitcom roles for the fall of 1998: Karen on *Will & Grace* and Carrie on *The King of Queens*. Mullally came close to accepting the latter role.

CAST

Eric McCormack	...Will Truman
Debra Messing	........Grace Adler
Sean Hayes	.................Jack McFarland
Megan Mullally	......Karen Walker
Shelley Morrison	....Rosario Salazar
Woody Harrelson	.....Nathan
Bobby Cannavale	....Vince D'Angelo
Debbie Reynolds	.....Bobbi Adler
Corey Parker	.............Josh
Gregory Hines	..........Ben Doucette
Blythe Danner	...........Marilyn Truman
Sidney Pollack	..........George Truman
Harry Connick Jr.	.....Leo Markus

OFF THE SET

ALEXIS ARQUETTE LOST the part of Jack to Sean Hayes at the final auditions.

NICOLLETTE SHERIDAN LOST the part of Grace to Debra Messing at the final auditions.

ORIGINALLY, MAX MUTCHNICK and David Kohan pitched a straightforward couples comedy in which a gay man and his straight female roommate were supporting characters. NBC liked the supporting characters better.

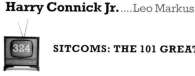

WINGS

NBC | **1990–1997** | **172 episodes**

At a small airport on tiny Nantucket Island, minuscule Sandpiper Airlines is run by the Hackett brothers—the sturdy, straitlaced Joe and the carefree, irresponsible Brian.

An underrated, often highly amusing sitcom, *Wings* was unfairly dismissed by many critics as *Cheers* lite relocated to an airport setting. To be sure, there were some similarities, as the show was created by David Angell, Peter Casey, and David Lee, all of whom had worked on *Cheers* and later went

on to create *Frasier*. It didn't help matters that *Wings* came on directly after *Cheers* and, as the show took place just a stone's throw from Boston, the characters from the long-running hit occasionally wandered into *Wings*'s hangar.

But *Wings* was not just a rip-off. In some ways the show was ahead of its time, presaging the hit *Friends* in its exploration

Flour is Funny: Tim Daly and Crystal Bernard treat each other like pieces of meat.

Helen: I got suckered into making the stupid welcoming speech at the reunion tonight.
Fay: Oh, come on, it can't be that bad. Let me hear your opening line.
Helen: That was it.

of the romantic entanglements of its main characters. With three attractive and likeable actors in the leads, *Wings* centered on the constantly evolving dynamic between brothers Joe and Brian Hackett and their childhood friend Helen Chappel. Prior to the start of the series, Helen had been an obese "ugly duckling" as a child (not unlike Monica, Courtney Cox's character on *Friends*) and had emerged as a swan; Brian had run off with Joe's fiancée the day before his wedding (not unlike another *Friends* back story, in which Ross's wife left him for a woman). With the later addition of characters played by Farrah Forke (who both Hackett brothers tried to woo) and Amy Yasbeck (as Helen's sister, with whom Brian ended up having a torrid affair), the incestuous interplay among friends on *Wings* was a distinct precursor to the ins and outs of Ross, Chandler, Phoebe, Joey, Monica, and Rachel.

The on-again, off-again relationship of Joe and Helen (who had carried a torch for the hunky Joe since she was ten years old) and the yin-yang of brothers Joe and Brian, as played by the extremely appealing trio of Timothy Daly, Steven Weber, and Crystal Bernard, gave the show an undeniable sexual undercurrent. Joe and Brian are constantly trying to save Sandpiper Air (with its fleet of one) from bankruptcy, while Helen, an aspiring classical cellist, is stuck running the lunch counter at the airport. These characters seemingly struck a chord with many 1990s thirty-somethings who were experiencing a similarly unfulfilling hand-to-mouth existence.

The supporting cast could not have been better: Rebecca Schull played ticket agent Fay Evelyn Schlob Dumbly DeVay Cochran (a widow three times, and all of her husbands had been named George); David Schramm was the unctuous windbag Roy Biggins, owner of Nantucket's rival airline; and Thomas Haden Church played the lunkhead mechanic Lowell Mather, who ultimately enters the Witness Relocation Program after the sixth season (when Church left the show to star in the Fox series *Ned & Stacey*). These three gifted comedians could turn dialogue into bits of comic gold, so completely unapologetic were they about their skewed view of the world. And special mention must be made of the phenomenal talents of Valerie Mahaffey. Nobody does "comic stalker" better than Mahaffey (she did it again recently on *Desperate Housewives*), and in a few guest appearances as Sandy Cooper, obsessed with Joe since high school, she created one of the most hilariously scary characters in recent memory.

Wings had an undeniably successful run, but the true testament to its quality is its lasting appeal. It continues to be a hit in syndication, while some of its contemporaries (*Murphy Brown* comes to mind) have not worn well with the passage of time. In retrospect, with all the comparisons to *Cheers*, *Wings* owes more to *Taxi* than to any other show, particularly in its group scenes in the terminal. (The more time the show spent away from the airport, the less unusual it became.) Daly, Weber, and Bernard were very much like Judd Hirsch, Marilu Henner, and Jeff Conaway on *Taxi*, all frustrated by the hand

Tony Shalhoub

A contemporary television star who actually looks like a real person, Tony Shalhoub was raised in Wisconsin and attended the Yale School of Drama. Working for four seasons at the American Repertory Theatre before making his Broadway debut in the female version of *The Odd Couple*, starring Rita Moreno and Sally Struthers, he was nominated for a Tony Award for his role opposite fellow sitcom cabdriver Judd Hirsch in *Conversations with My Father*. Married to actress Brooke Adams, whom Shalhoub met during the play *The Heidi Chronicles*, he moved to Los Angeles, and in his first audition after the move west landed the role of Italian cabdriver Antonio Scarpacci on *Wings*, starting out as a recurring character but soon joining the show full time. After six years on the show, Shalhoub appeared in such films as *The Big Night*, which he also produced. He now stars as the OCD-afflicted detective Adrian Monk on the critically acclaimed and award-winning *Monk*.

life had dealt them and hoping for greener pastures. The batty and vague Schull and Church lived in the same alternate reality inhabited by the more eccentric members of the Sunshine Cab Company, including Carol Kane and Christopher Lloyd; and obvious parallels can be drawn between Schramm's Roy Biggins and Danny DeVito's Louie DePalma, a pair of utterly irredeemable louses…er…lice. Heck, *Wings* even had its own foreign-born goof-ball (Nantucket's version of Andy Kaufman's Latka Gravas), wonderfully played by Tony Shalhoub. Shalhoub's character's job? Cabdriver.

Left: Rebecca Schull, David Schramm, and Tony Shalhoub, three of the most appealing character actors of the 1990s.

Opposite: A germaphobic detective? You bet, and hilarious, too, as played by Tony Shalhoub on *Monk*.

Above: Thomas Haden Church as the obtuse mechanic, Lowell Mather and Steven Weber as the perpetually boyish ne'er-do-well, Brian Hackett.

OFF THE SET

THE SHOW'S THEME music is an abbreviated version of the Rondo from Franz Schubert's Piano Sonata in A Major.

CAST

Timothy Daly	Joe Hackett
Steven Weber	Brian Hackett
Crystal Bernard	Helen Chappel Hackett
Thomas Haden Church	Lowell Mather
David Schramm	Roy Biggins
Rebecca Schull	Fay Cochran
Tony Shalhoub	Antonio Scarpacci
Farrah Forke	Alex Lambert
Amy Yasbeck	Casey Davenport
Brian Haley	Budd Bronsky
Laura Innes	Bunny Mather
Mark Harelik	Lewis Blanchard

WKRP IN CINCINNATI

1978–1982 | 90 episodes

Radio-programming director Andy Travis gets "tired of packing and unpacking, town to town, up and down the dial" and comes to Cincinnati to save station WKRP, with its staff of lovable oddballs, by changing the format from easy listening to rock-and-roll.

Dealing with the staff of misfits at a struggling radio station, *WKRP in Cincinnati* is an example of art imitating life. While onscreen the station *WKRP* was in constant danger of closing, the off-screen *WKRP* was another of those great shows that networks almost allowed to die a quiet death. Produced by MTM Studios and created by Hugh Wilson, it was similar to *Mary Tyler Moore* and *The Bob Newhart Show* in that its humor was largely character driven, as opposed to the slapstick antics of *WKRP*'s contemporaries *Three's Company* and *Mork & Mindy*. In spite of great reviews for its pilot, it was dealt a deadly time slot and its ratings were anything but stellar. CBS put the show on hiatus after only eight airings and most assumed it would never return.

Miraculously, it was the buzz around a single episode that convinced CBS of the show's potential. Titled "Turkeys Away," it was a classic example of that moment when all the elements of a sitcom (writing, directing, and acting) come together in twenty-four minutes of inspired comic alchemy. In this terrifically funny, bizarre half-hour, the inept station manager, Arthur Carlson (Gordon Jump), tries a Thanksgiving publicity stunt that ends up in a tragedy of Hindenburg-like proportions (for the city of Cincinnati at least). It involves releasing (okay, tossing) turkeys out of a helicopter.

The CBS powers brought the show back in January of 1979 in a much better time slot with a sure-fire lead-in, the long-running smash *M*A*S*H* .

The staff of *WKRP*, clockwise from left: Richard Sanders, Gary Sandy, Frank Bonner, Loni Anderson, Gordon Jump, Tim Reid, Howard Hesseman, and Jan Smithers.

The show's eight regular characters were well balanced in its storylines, making it one of the truest ensemble shows ever. As on the other MTM shows, there was a straight man (the station's new program director Andy Travis, played by Gary Sandy wearing the tightest jeans on prime time) surrounded by a group of eccentrics, including the ineffectual station manager, Jump's Arthur "Big Guy" Carlson; news director Les Nessman (Richard Sanders), a Wally Cox clone who taped the floor of the newsroom to indicate the imaginary walls of an office and makes people knock on an invisible door to gain entry; two deejays, the "organically damaged" Dr. Johnny Fever (Howard Hesseman), and the smooth and funky Venus Flytrap (Tim Reid); the sexy receptionist Jennifer Marlowe (Loni Anderson), the highest-paid employee at the station and the rare smart blonde in sitcoms; the tacky sales manager Herb Tarlek (Frank Bonner); and the wholesome journalism student Bailey Quarters (Jan Smithers). In addition to the regular staff, there was the constant fear of a visit from Carlson's mother (played by the positively predatory, smoky-voiced Carol Bruce), who owns the station and drops in to menace her employees, just for kicks.

Tim Reid

After humble beginnings in Norfolk, Virginia, and a stint at DuPont Industries, the multitalented Tim Reid left the world of big business for the world of show business, teaming up with former insurance salesman Tom Dreesen to form a stand-up act called "Tim and Tom." After the act broke up, he worked as a comedy writer and performer, doing his solo act on the 1970s variety shows of Richard Pryor and singers Marilyn McCoo and Billy Davis Jr. After his big break—the role of Venus on *WKRP*—Reid played a recurring role on the hourlong *Simon & Simon* before creating (along with *WKRP*'s Hugh Wilson) and starring in the short-lived cult hit *Frank's Place* in 1987. Playing opposite his wife, Daphne Maxwell-Reid (they had met when she guest starred on *WKRP*), the classy, witty show set in a New Orleans restaurant was yanked from the schedule far too soon, despite critical acclaim. After recurring roles on *Sister, Sister* and *That '70s Show*, Reid and wife Daphne started their own production company and studio, New Millennium, in his home state of Virginia. The dedicated couple has set out to create TV and movie projects focusing on social issues and promoting racial awareness.

Just as the show was building steam and a broad fan base, it was moved out of its prime-time slot and shuffled around the schedule, as CBS hoped its newfound success could help out one of its other nights. A network can turn away from a particular show just as quickly as it embraces it, and *WKRP* was abruptly canceled at the end of its fourth season. Ironically, its final episode ranked number seven of all shows that week.

Achieving cult status in syndication, *WKRP* is currently missing-in-action on the air. As it was one of the only shows to use the era's top rock-and-roll music as a plot point, the licensing of the music, which at the time did not include provisions for the then-unknown frontier of DVDs, has proved so prohibitively expensive that the show was finally released with its songs replaced by generic music.

Richard Sanders and Frank Bonner as Les Nessman and Herb Tarlek, two of television's greatest fashion victims.

Arthur Carlson: As God is my witness, I thought turkeys could fly.

OFF THE SET

THE BUMBLING NEWS director, Les Nessman, wears a bandage on some part of his body in practically every episode. The idea originated when actor Richard Sanders hit his head prior to the taping of the first episode and was forced to wear a bandage on the air; he decided to make it Les's trademark.

***WKRP* CREATOR HUGH** Wilson had previously worked for an advertising agency in Atlanta, mining his experiences there for story ideas. One of the firm's clients, radio station WQXI, had tried a publicity stunt that ended disastrously when ducks were placed on a hot plate to make them look as if they were dancing.

CAST

Gary Sandy	Andy Travis
Gordon Jump	Arthur Carlson
Howard Hesseman	Dr. Johnny Fever
Loni Anderson	Jennifer Marlowe
Richard Sanders	Les Nessman
Frank Bonner	Herb Tarlek
Tim Reid	Venus Flytrap
Jan Smithers	Bailey Quarters

Joe E. Ross, Imogene Coca, Mary Grace, and Pat Cardi, a modern Stone Age family, enjoying the scenery of Wilshire Boulevard in the wacky *It's About Time*.

INDEX

Bold indicates illustration.

ʃething old, something older: Guest granny Jeanette Nolan, with Eve Arden and Kaye Ballard, those ʃbering Mothers-In-Law.

Hurry, hurry, hurry, take the 'A' train: Valerie Harper in one of the funniest "on location" shoots in sitcom history, the wedding of Joe and Rhoda.

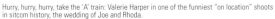

Richard Lewis (realizing he coulda had a V-8) and Jamie Lee Curtis in the very funny *Anything But Love*.

Freddie Prinze and Jack Albertson in *Chico and the Man*, whose run was cut short by the tragic suicide of Prinze.

PHOTO CREDITS

F Troop's Melody Patterson and Forrest Tucker tool around the Warner Brothers lot in a motorized surrey with the fringe on top.